THE
NATIONAL PASTORALS
OF THE
AMERICAN HIERARCHY

THE

NATIONAL PASTORALS

OF THE

AMERICAN HIERARCHY

(1792 - 1919)

With a Foreword, Notes, and Index

BY

REV. PETER GUILDAY, Ph. D.

Author of "The English Catholic Refugees on the Continent,"
"The Three Hours' Agony of Our Lord Jesus Christ,"
"The Life and Times of John Carroll,
Archbishop of Baltimore," etc.

———

NATIONAL CATHOLIC WELFARE COUNCIL
1312 MASSACHUSETTS AVENUE
WASHINGTON, D. C.
1923

Nibil Obstat

JOHN J. BURKE, C.S.P.
Censor Deputatus

Imprimatur:

✠ MICHAEL J. CURLEY, D.D.
Archbishop of Baltimore

Washington, May 6th, 1923

DEDICATED

to

THE MOST REVEREND MICHAEL JOSEPH CURLEY, D.D.

ARCHBISHOP OF BALTIMORE.

FOREWORD

THE thirteen Pastorals which form the contents of this volume are the official messages issued to the clergy and the faithful of the United States by the Hierarchy of the Catholic Church. Twelve of these Pastorals were issued as the result of a conciliar assembly of the American bishops. It is not an essential factor in the proceedings of a provincial or national council to issue a Pastoral Letter, or Charge, at the close of its sessions, but the custom has been preserved in the American Church since the First National Synod of Baltimore, held in 1791. The tradition was not forgotten in 1919, when a general meeting of the bishops was held in Washington. This meeting was not a council in the canonical meaning of the term, but the assembled prelates decided to issue a Pastoral Letter on the great religious and social problems of the day.

Once, under Bishop Carroll in 1792; seven times from 1829 to 1849, under the metropolitan jurisdiction of the See of Baltimore; and three times under the Archbishops of that See as Apostolic Delegates of the Holy See for their plenary sessions—eleven times in all, the Catholic Church of the United States has assembled its leaders in solemn convocation for the purpose of legislating on Church discipline. On each of these occasions, beginning with John Carroll in 1792, and ending with the late Cardinal Gibbons in 1884, the American Hierarchy has made known in a Pastoral Letter the result of its deliberations and decrees regarding the problems which then demanded the attention of our prelates. The twelve Pastorals issued by these eleven conciliar assemblies (two Pastorals were issued by the Council of 1829), together with what is undoubtedly the most momentous of all the messages from the American Hierarchy, namely, the reconstruction Pastoral issued by the general meeting of the bishops at the close of the

World War, in 1919, are in a certain sense the living constitution of the Church in this country. While each of them
emphasizes in a special way the moral and spiritual needs
of its own period, all of them urge upon the American people, regardless of creed or party, the practice of the very
virtues the importance of which is now so keenly realized
by those who have at heart the welfare of the nation.

Two reasons prompted the publication of these solemn
messages from the spiritual leaders of the Church in the
United States. The first of these is that there does not exist
a complete set of these National Pastorals of the American
Hierarchy. Printed copies of some of the provincial Pastorals were found in the library of the Archbishop's House,
in Baltimore, but the Pastorals of 1729 and of 1829, were
found only in the *Catholic Miscellany,* of Charleston, S. C.,
from which they were taken. That of the Second Provincial
Council of Baltimore (1833) is taken from the Catholic
Weekly Register, of New York City, for that year. The
Pastorals of 1866, 1884, and 1919 were originally published
with sectional captions, and in order to keep the volume
uniform, the editor has added sectional headings to the
other Pastorals. Apart from the desire to preserve these
noble documents to posterity, by bringing them together
for the first time, a second and more important reason
actuated their publication. They contain not only the
history of the Catholic faith in this country from the establishment of the Hierarchy down to the present time, but
they offer a prudent and sagacious commentary upon the
events of the past and upon the influences which have at
various epochs affected the Catholic life of our beloved
country. Scarcely a single problem which exists today in
the Church of the United States has escaped the attention
of the assembled prelates, and in many of these serious
reflections upon the critical situations that arose in the past,
the present-day reader will find direction and guidance for
problems that, while apparently new, are already solved in
these Pastorals of the American Hierarchy. The purpose
of the index at the end of the volume has been to reveal
not only the striking identity of most of these problems
past and present, but to enable the reader to ascertain with

facility the advice as well as the direction given by the bishops of these Councils to their particular time and environment.

Ecclesiastical councils are of four kinds: œcumenical or general; plenary or national; provincial; and diocesan. Though the word *Council* and *Synod* are synonymous, the term synod is usually applied to the diocesan assembly. A general or œcumenical council of the universal Church is convened for extraordinary occasions, the Pope alone having the right to summon such an assembly. Twenty œcumenical councils have been held during the past twenty centuries. Only in one of these did American prelates participate, namely, in the Vatican Council of 1869-70. With the death of Cardinal Gibbons (March 24, 1921), the last of the American bishops and, indeed, the last of all the bishops who were there present, passed away. Plenary councils are described by the Fathers of the Second Plenary Council of Balitmore (1866) as those which represent "several ecclesiastical provinces—ordinarily under one civil Government, and therefore sometimes called National." A National Council is assembled by the express direction of the Sovereign Pontiff, who appoints an Apostolic Delegate to preside over the assembly in his name. Three National or Plenary Councils of the American Church were held in Baltimore, in 1852, 1866, and 1884. A further delimination of the Council is that called Provincial, that is, an assembly composed of the archbishop and the suffragan bishops of a province. Seven Provincial Councils were held in Baltimore between the years 1829 and 1849. These seven assemblies are justly considered by American canonists as national in scope and in authority, since the Archbishop of Baltimore was the sole metropolitan in the United States up to 1846, and was conceded quasi-primatial honors by the other prelates. The seventh Provincial Council (1849) postulated the Holy See for this extraordinary privilege, but the Sacred Congregation de Propaganda Fide (which then governed the Church of the United States) postponed granting a primacy of honor to the See of Baltimore.

The meeting of the American Hierarchy at the Catholic University of America, Washington, D. C., in September,

1919, was the first assembly in which all the bishops of the
United States participated since the Third Plenary Council
of Baltimore (1884). "Thirty-five years have elapsed," we
read in the Pastoral they issued on September 26, 1919,
"since the Fathers of the Third Plenary Council of Baltimore addressed their Pastoral Letter to the faithful of their
charge. In it they expressed their deliberate thought upon
the state of religion at the time, upon its needs and its
abundant resources. Surveying the growth of the Church
during a century, they saw with thankfulness the evident
design of God in behalf of our country; and turning to the
future, they beheld the promise of a still more fruitful
development. With wise enactment and admonition they
imparted new vigor to our Catholic life. With a foresight
which we can now appreciate, they prepared the Church in
America to meet, on the solid ground of faith and discipline,
the changing conditions of our earthly existence. . . .
Following the example of our predecessors, and like them
trusting in the guidance of the Holy Spirit, we lately took
counsel together for the welfare of the Church and of our
country. The whole Hierarchy of the United States assembled in Washington to consider the problems, the needs
and the possibilities for good which invite us to new undertakings. In the record of the last three decades, we
found much to console and inspire us. We also knew well
that you with whom and for whom we have labored, would
rejoice in considering how abundantly God has blessed our
endeavors. And we therefore determined, for His glory
and for your comfort, to point out the significant phases
in our progress, and to set forth the truths which contain
the solution of the world's great problems."

The Pastoral of 1919 reaches out into realms that were
not trodden by the prelates of former days; it has been
justly praised by Catholics and non-Catholics of this and
other lands; and it must always be reckoned among the
greatest documents of the reconstruction crisis which followed the World War.

With these documents in their possession, the clergy
and the faithful have a key to the history of the Catholic
Church in this country. They are, as it were, mirrors re-

flecting the inner life of the Church during the hundred and
thirty years which has passed since the establishment of
the Catholic Hierarchy here.

The volume is dedicated to Archbishop Curley, the tenth
in the line of succession from Archbishop Carroll, and now
feliciter regnans over the venerable See of Baltimore which
has been recognized from the beginning as the spiritual
center of the Catholic Church in the United States.

PETER GUILDAY.

Catholic University of America
November 4, 1922.

CONTENTS

THE NATIONAL PASTORALS

OF THE

AMERICAN HIERARCHY

(1792-1919)

CHAPTER I

BISHOP CARROLL'S PASTORAL LETTER (MAY 28, 1792)

THE Pastoral Letter of Bishop Carroll is the first document of this nature in the history of this Church in the United States. It was begun shortly after the close of the first National Synod of Baltimore (Nov. 7-10, 1791), and was published on May 28, 1792. Shea tells us that it was spread by the newspapers of the day, was widely read and genuinely admired. Copies of the printed document are exceedingly scarce, and it is reprinted here from the *Catholic Miscellany* of 1829.[1] Bishop England gives as his reason for publishing the Pastoral the fact that very few copies existed at that time.

Among the many disadvantages the Catholics of that day labored under, Dr. Carroll chose for the particular instruction of his people the necessity of a Christian education for the young. To fill this need and to provide for their religious education, the College of Georgetown, founded in 1789, was specially recommended to Catholic parents. There was no longer any excuse for Catholic parents who could not afford to send their sons across the ocean to be educated in the Catholic colleges of Belgium and France, to deprive their children of Catholic instruction. The other topics discussed in this pastoral are: vocations to the priesthood and the founding of St. Mary's Sulpician Seminary, Baltimore; the maintenance of the clergy; the financial support of the Church in the diocese; attendance at Sunday Mass; prayers for the dead; and devotion to the Mother of God, the Patroness of the diocese. Dr. Carroll's signature at the end of the Pastoral caused an attack by

[1] Vol. IX., pp. 297-299.

"Liberal" in one of the newspapers of the day, and Bishop Carroll published a reply on November 21, 1792, in which he said: "The subject of the contention is so trifling in itself, and it affords so much room for ridicule, that if 'Liberal' takes up his pen again he must appear with something more material to engage the further attention of John, Bishop of Baltimore."

THE PASTORAL LETTER OF 1792

John, by Divine permission and with the approbation of the Holy See, Bishop of Baltimore: To my dearly beloved Brethren, the members of the Catholic Church in this Diocess, Health and Blessing, Grace to you and peace from God our Father, and from the Lord Jesus Christ.

THE great extent of my diocese and the necessity of ordering many things concerning its government at the beginning of my episcopacy, have not yet permitted me, my dear brethren, to enjoy the consolation, for which I most earnestly pray, of seeing you all, and of leaving with you, according to the nature of my duty, some words of exhortation, by which you may be strengthened in faith, and encouraged in the exercises of a Christian life. Esteeming myself as a debtor to all, and knowing the rigorous account which I must render for your souls, to the Shepherd of Shepherds, our Lord and Saviour Jesus Christ, I shall have cause to tremble, while I leave anything undone, by which religion and true piety may be promoted, and the means of salvation multiplied for you.

In compliance with the obligation, resulting from the relation in which I stand to you, my endeavours have been turned towards obtaining and applying, for the preservation and extension of faith and for the sanctification of souls, means calculated to produce lasting effects, not only on the present, but on future generations. I thought that Almighty God would make the ministers of His sanctuary, and myself particularly, accountable to Him, if we did not avail ourselves of the liberty enjoyed under our equitable government and just laws, to attempt establishments, in which you, dear brethren, may find permanent resources, suited to your greatest exigencies.

Knowing, therefore, that the principles instilled in the course of a Christian education, are generally preserved through life, and that *a young man according to his way, even when he is old, he will not depart from it,*[2] I have considered the virtuous and Christian instruction of youth as a principal object of pastoral solicitude. Now who can contribute so much to lighten this burthen, which weighs so heavy on the shoulders of the pastors of souls and who can have so great an interest and special duty in the forming of youthful minds to habits of virtue and religion, as their parents themselves? Especially while their children retain their native docility, and their hearts are uncorrupted by vice. How many motives of reason and religion require, that parents should be unwearied in their endeavours, to inspire in them the love and fear of God; docility and submission to His doctrines, and a careful attention to fulfil His commandments? Fathers—bring up your children *in the discipline and correction of the Lord.*[3] If all, to whom God has given sons and daughters, were assiduous in the discharge of this important obligation, a foundation would be laid for, and great progress made in, the work of establishing a prevailing purity of manners. The same habits of obedience to the will of God; the same principles of a reverential love and fear of Him; and of continual respect for His Holy Name; the same practices of morning and evening prayer; and of the frequentation of the sacraments; the same dread of cursing and swearing; of fraud and duplicity; of lewdness and drunkenness; the same respectful and dutiful behaviour to their fathers and mothers; in a word, the remembrance and influence of the parental counsels and examples received in their youth, would continue with them during life. And if ever the frailty of nature, or worldly seduction, should cause them to offend God, they would be brought back again to His service and to true repentance by the efficacy of the religious instruction received in their early age. Wherefore, fathers and mothers, be mindful of the words of the Apostles, and bring up your

> The Advantages of a Christian Education.

2 Prov. xxii. 6.   3 Ephes. vi. 4.

children in the discipline and correction of the Lord. In doing this, you not only render an acceptable service to God, and acquit yourselves of a most important duty, but you labour for the preservation and increase of true religion, for the benefit of our common country, whose welfare depends on the morals of its citizens, and for your own happiness here as well as hereafter; since you may be assured of finding, in those sons and daughters whom you shall train up to virtue and piety, by your instructions and examples, support and consolation in sickness and old age. They will remember with gratitude, and repay with religious duty, your solicitude for them in their infancy and youth.

These being the advantages of a religious education, I was solicitous for the attainment of a blessing so desirable to that precious portion of my flock, the growing generation. A school has been instituted at George-Town, which will continue to be under the superintendence and government of some of my reverend brethren, that is, of men devoted by principle and profession to instruct all, who resort to them, in useful learning, and those of our own religion, in its principles and duties. I earnestly wish, dear brethren, that as many of you, as are able, would send your sons to this school of letters and virtue. I know and lament, that the expense will be too great for many families, and that their children must be deprived of the immediate benefit of this institution; but, indirectly, they will receive it; at least, it may be reasonably expected, that some after being educated at George-Town, and having returned into their own neighbourhood, will become, in their turn, the instructors of the youths who cannot be sent from home; and, by pursuing the same system of uniting much attention to religion with a solicitude for other improvements, the general result will be a great increase of piety, the necessary consequence of a careful instruction in the principles of faith, and Christian morality.

The school, dear brethren, if aided by your benevolence, and favoured with your confidence, will be the foundation of an additional advantage to true religion in this our country. Many amongst us you have experienced in-

Georgetown College. [margin note]

convenience and disadvantage from the want of spiritual
assistance in your greatest necessities, in sickness, in
troubles of conscience, and counsels and
offices of the ministers of religion. It is   **Necessity of**
notorious to you all, that the present clergy-   **Vocations to the**
men are insufficient for the exigencies of   **Priesthood.**
the faithful; and that they will be more
and more so, as the population of our country increases so
rapidly; unless, by the providence of our good and merciful God, a constant supply of zealous and able pastors can
be formed amongst ourselves; that is, of men accustomed to
our climate, and acquainted with the tempers, manners,
and government of the people, to whom they are to dispense the ministry of salvation. Now, may we not reasonably hope, that one of the effects of a virtuous course of
education will be the preparing of the minds of some,
whom providence may select, to receive and cherish a call
from God to an ecclesiastical state?

Should such be the designs of infinite mercy on this
portion of His flock, all of us, dear brethren, will have new
cause to return God thanks for having con-
ducted to our assistance a number of   **The Sulpician**
learned and exemplary clergymen, de-   **Fathers.**
voted by choice, and formed by experience
to the important function of training young Ecclesiastics
to all the duties of the ministry. This essential service is
already begun by these my respectable brethren. An ecclesiastical seminary, under their immediate direction, and
episcopal superintendence, has entered on the important
function of raising pastors for your future consolation and
improvement; and I cannot forbear recommending their
undertaking to your patronage, and what a benefit will they
confer on this and future generations, who shall contribute
to endow it with some portion of those goods, which themselves have received from a benevolent providence, and
for the use of which they must account to Him, from whom
they received them? What a consolation will it be to them
in this life, and a source of happiness in the next, if, through
their benefactions, the seminary be enabled not only to
support its directors and professors, but likewise some

young men, candidates for holy orders, whose virtues and
abilities may be far superior to their worldly fortunes? By
endowments, such as I now recommend, great services have
been rendered to religion and morality. If donations for
objects of piety have ever been excessive, as some have
pretended, the particular one now recommended to your
charity, and the temper of our times and laws, leave no
cause to apprehend the renewal of such an abuse.

Other objects, besides those already mentioned, claim
our common solicitude. It will be of little use to prepare
ministers for the work of the ministry, if
Maintenance of afterwards they cannot be employed, for
the Clergy. want of necessary maintenance, in the
laborious discharge of pastoral functions.
Whilst the offices of our religion were performed only in
two of the United States, and even in them, the number
of Catholics was much less than at present, fewer labourers
were wanted; and there were funds sufficient for their sub-
sistance, independent of any contributions from the justice
or the charity of the respective congregations. But our
holy faith being now spread through other States, and the
number of Catholics being much increased in those, where
it existed before, it is become absolutely necessary to recur
to the means of supporting public worship and instruction,
which are prescribed not only by natural equity, but likewise by the positive ordinances of divine wisdom, both in
the Jewish and gospel dispensations. *Know you not*, says
St. Paul,[4] *that they who work in the holy place . . . and
they that serve the altar, partake with the altar? So also
the Lord ordained that they who preach the gospel, should
live by the Gospel.*

In obedience to this divine ordinance, primitive Christians, when they went to the celebration of the sacred offices
of religion, presented their offerings on the altar of the
Lord, signifying by this act, that they were not intended so
much for their pastors, as consecrated to God Himself. And,
indeed, the Church regarded them in this light; and decreed in her canons, that the religious oblations of the
faithful should be employed, first, for the maintenance of

4 1 Cor. ix. 13, 14.

the ministers of the sanctuary; which being provided for, the remainder should be applied towards the relief of the poor, and the building and repairing of churches and places of worship, necessary for public convenience, and the decent ordering of divine service.

God has made it our duty to join in the solemn rites of sacrifice and prayer, and in receiving the sacraments instituted for our benefit and the improvement of our souls in piety and grace. The **The Support** administration of these requires men set **of the Church.** apart for and consecrated to so sacred a function; men not assuming of themselves, but receiving their authority from God, through His church, and their succession from the Apostles, through the Bishops, by whom they are ordained. Now it is evident, that since these are acts of religion, He requires likewise, that all should use the necessary means for acquitting themselves of that obligation; and consequently, that each one bear his proportion of common and necessary expense for the support of public worship. This duty has been insisted on so little amongst us, as long as the assistance of the faithful was unnecessary for the maintenance of their pastors, that many will often do without pastors; of course they become remiss in their religious duties, and finally regardless of them. Their offspring, uninstructed and ignorant of the principles of faith, are led astray by false doctrines, and seduced by corrupt examples. Hence, likewise, churches for the celebration of divine service, and the great Eucharistic sacrifice of the law of grace, are not built at all, or are suffered to fall into decay.

They are without chalices, without the decent and necessary furniture of the altars, without vestments suited to the different services of the Church, in a word, without those sacred utensils, which its ordinances require, and which contribute to impress the mind with a becoming sense of the majesty of religion, and conciliate respect for its august ceremonies. Hence, finally, results the great evil, and the source of many disorders, that, by failing to make provision for the necessary support of pastors, and the maintenance of public worship, you fail likewise of fulfilling the obligation of being present at Mass on every Sunday and holiday; you lose the opportunity of receiving necessary and salutary instruction; and, finally, an habitual disregard for the sanctification of the Lord's day, and for the exercise of prayer and religion becomes prevalent.

In this matter, I recommend earnestly to you, my dear brethren, not to be too indulgent to yourselves, in forming principles, which indeed may satisfy an erroneous conscience, and suit your attachment to your case, and your worldly interest; but cannot afford you a reasonable assurance of having fulfilled your necessary and essential duty to Almighty God. Every inconvenience is not sufficient to exempt you from the obligation from attending at Mass on Sundays and other days prescribed by the Church. The obstacle must be grievous and weighty, amounting almost to an impossibility, moral or physical. Has such an obstacle or inconvenience existed with respect to all those, who hear Mass, perhaps not more than once a month, or seldomer? Are there not congregations, where now divine service is performed only once a month, which are fully competent to the expense of keeping a clergyman to reside amidst them, and to administer to them continually in all holy things? To offer every day for them, and in the presence of some at least of them the great sacrifice of the law of grace? To teach, to admonish and reprove them? To instruct their children and servants in the doctrines and exercises of religion? And thus to make lighter the burthen, which rests on parents and heads of families? To watch perpetually over the morals of all, and prevent the contagion of error or evil example? To be ready, and have at hand, to administer to all, in times of sickness, the spiritual succours committed to his dispensation? I cannot, dear brethren, enumerate the advantages, which will result from so desirable a situation, as that of having constantly amongst you, your pastor and spiritual guide; and I exhort you with great earnestness to use much industry, and with thankfulness to Almighty God, for the temporal blessings received from His hand, generously to devote a part of them to the obtaining a benefit, from which such important

Attendance at Sunday Mass.

consequences will be derived. The sacrifice of property, which you make, for a purpose so useful and religious, is a kind of restitution to Him, Who first gave it to you; and, besides being an act of the virtue of religion, because it is suggested by the desire of encouraging and supporting divine worship, it is moreover an act of exalted charity towards the poor and ignorant, who will be enabled to obtain essential instruction and relief in all their spiritual necessities, through the means and contributions of the rich and middle classes of life; and these will thus become partakers in the merit and rewards promised in these words of the prophet Daniel, that *they that instruct many to justice,* [shall shine]*as stars for all eternity.*[5]

I will venture to add, that even with respect to this world, you will find it to be no loss to concur towards the regular support of the ministry, and services of religion. Habits of temperance and frugality are generally the effects of evangelical instruction. The lessons and duty of industry are frequently inculcated by virtuous and careful pastors. Your children and servants will be admonished perpetually to shun idleness, dishonesty, dissipations, and that train of expense which always follows them. These, by their effect on domestic economy, will make abundant compensation for the charges in support of religion. Besides, you have a divine promise, that God will use a more special providence for your subsistence, when you make it your first care, to fulfil His holy law: *Seek . . . . . first the kingdom of God, and His justice, and all these things shall be added unto you.*[6]

Amongst all obstructions to the due celebration of divine service, and the regular attendance on the sacred functions of religion, this backwardness of the faithful to contribute for its support is one of the greatest, as was generally agreed and represented by my venerable brethren, the clergy of the Diocess, in a synod held some months ago. When I convoked them, I formed some statutes of general concern, which will be communicated to you, and amongst them are the following, relative to the matter, of which I have just now treated, and enforcing the same observations:

[5] Chap. xii. 3.　　　　　　　　[6] Matt. vi. 33.

Statutes of the Diocesan Synod, held at Baltimore, from the 7th to the 10th day of November, 1791.

Statute V. That the Holy Eucharistic Sacrifice may be celebrated with all reverence and becoming respect, and that the faithful may be excited more and more to a lively devotion towards this singular pledge of divine mercy, it is decreed, that the congregations be reminded frequently, how disrespectful it is, that anything used for the Holy Sacrifice should be of the meanest materials, or not kept cleanly and entire, and that suitable vessels and utensils for the altar, as chalices, ciboriums, and cruets; decent vestments and linen for the ministry of the altar, wax candles and wine fit for Mass be not provided. Let the Christian people be told, with how minute attention God Himself was pleased to ordain everything relating to His service in the Jewish law and temple. How much more care therefore should Christians use, for the decency of divine worship, since they possess, not the shadow of future blessings, as the Jews, but the substance and reality of them! Let them be admonished likewise of the offerings made by primitive Christians at the time of Mass; and let them know that such must be very regardless of the honour of God, as refuse or neglect to contribute for those things, without which the functions of religion seem to lose their dignity and authority; and the devotion and veneration for the Blessed Eucharist is greatly diminished.

VI. It is decreed, therefore, that in every congregation, two or three persons of approved virtue and respectability be chosen by the congregation, or appointed by the pastor, to be Church-wardens or guardians; and that the persons so appointed, on Sundays and other festivals, after the reading of the 1st gospel at Mass, or after the sermon, shall collect the offerings of the faithful.

VII. The offerings, according to the practice of the church, are to be divided into three parts; so that one be applied to the maintenance of the pastor; another to the relief of the poor; and a third to the procuring of all things requisite for divine worship, and for building and repairing the church. But if provision be made otherwise for the maintenance of the pastor and the poor, all offerings are to be appropriated to the fabric of the church, or to furnishing it with proper utensils and ornaments for the more dignified celebration of divine worship.

VIII. The offerings made by the faithful, to render God propitious to themselves or others, through the efficacy of the Holy Sacrifice of Mass, should be accepted by the ministers of the altar in such manner, as to afford no room for suspicions of avarice or simony; let them be contented, therefore, with such an acknowledgment of their services as cannot be burthensome to the bestowers of it; nor yet so insignificant, as to render the priestly ministry despicable in the opinion of inconsiderate men.

XXIII. The number of Catholics having increased, and being dispersed through the different States, and at great distances from each other, it is become necessary to have likewise a greater number of spiritual labourers; but these cannot be brought from foreign countries or maintained, unless the faithful concur towards bearing that expense, as they are bound by the law of God, and according to the testimony of St. Paul, who says, *if we have sown unto you spiritual things, is it a great matter if we reap your carnal things?*[7] The faithful therefore are to be reminded often of this duty, with which, if they neglect to comply, they will omit, through their own fault, hearing Mass on Sundays and festivals, and receiving the Sacraments at those seasons, in which they need them most, the seasons of sickness, of Easter; and when through the prevalence of sinful passions, or long habits of vice a speedy reconciliation with God becomes indispensably necessary. Wherefore, as long as they refuse to contribute for the ministry of salvation, according to the measure of worldly fortune given to them by a beneficent God, and thus violate the divine and ecclesiastical laws, they are to know that they are in a state of sin, unworthy of obtaining forgiveness in the tribunal of confession; and that they will be answerable to God, not only for their own non-compliance with duties so sacred, but likewise for the ignorance and vices of the poor people, who remain destitute of Christian instruction on account of the sordid avarice of those, who are more favoured with the gifts of fortune. To begin then, in this Diocess, that which is practised in other Christian countries, the preceding regulations were formed, relative to the oblations of the faithful; and others will be added hereafter."

I trust, that you, my dear brethren, will consider these statutes with the same candour and in the same spirit in which they were formed. It was not in the spirit of avarice, but of real solicitude for the preservation of faith, and for your increase in godliness and heavenly knowledge. They were suggested by the desire of seeing you assisted, with the same means of salvation, as your Catholic brethren in all other countries; and with the hope, that you would use

7 1 Cor. ix. 11.

the same endeavours as they to appropriate to yourselves
the blessings of a regular instruction, and uninterrupted
ministration of divine worship. To accomplish this salutary purpose more effectually, and render more certain
the subsistence of the ministers of religion, they are directed
to require at marriages, burials and funeral services, a certain very moderate compensation, to which they, whom God
has blessed with abundance, may add according to their
benevolence; and which my reverend brethren are hereby
charged not to require from those, to whom, on account of
their great poverty, any compensation would be burthensome.

On this occasion, I cannot forbear mentioning an abuse,
or rather a prevalent neglect and indifference with respect
to your departed parents and relations.
Prayers for   When death has removed them from your
the Dead.   sight, you seem to forget that doctrine of
your divine religion which ought to call
forth all your tenderness: I mean the doctrine, that *it is
a holy and wholesome thought to pray for the dead, that
they may be loosed from sins.*[8] How different is your
behaviour, when such events happen, from that of your
Catholic brethren all over the world? Their sensibility is
not confined to the unprofitable tears and lamentations of
a few days, their faith follows their deceased friends into
the mansions of another life, and enkindles all their charity.
They procure prayers and sacrifices to be offered to God for
the repose of their souls. The exercises of charity to the
poor, and all the works of mercy and religion are employed
for their relief, as long as there remains a reasonable
ground to fear, that they may want it. Thus St. Augustine
testified his sensibility, after the death of his holy mother
Monica; thus, as Tertullian, St. Cyprian, and other primitive
fathers teach us, children expressed their duty and veneration for their parents; and surviving Christian spouses for
them, to whom they had been united by the ties and duties
of a virtuous marriage.

When it pleases God to call your friends out of this
world, do you, my dear brethren, give such proofs of your

8 2 Mac. xii. 46.

affection for them? You attend them to the grave; you shed over it a few tears; and there is the term of your care and solicitude. If a charitable priest offer up to the throne of mercy, for their sake, the blood of the lamb of God, who takes away the sins of the world, he does it, generally unsolicited and unthanked by you. You make no sacrifices of interest or enjoyments to charity and religion, that the deceased may find speedy mercy, and an anticipated enjoyment of everlasting bliss. I earnestly beseech you, to deserve no longer this reproach on your charity and sensibility. Follow your departed brethren into the regions of eternity, with your prayers, and all the assistance, which is suggested by the principles of faith and piety. Let the great sacrifice of propitiation be offered for all, who die in the unity of the Catholic Church, and in due submission to her wholesome precepts. Where it is possible, let a funeral service be performed: and I recommend it strongly to the pastors of all congregations, and to the faithful themselves, to promote the forming of pious associations, whose special object shall be, to bestow on the dead, and especially on those who die poor and friendless, the best offices of religion, that is, to procure for them a decent interment, accompanied with the prayers and sacred rites ordained by the church.

In this, my address to you, my dear brethren, I have been chiefly solicitous to recommend to your attention those things which will be of general advantage to the preservation and increase **Devotion to the** of true religion. I have no doubt, but that **Mother of God.** your immediate pastors will give you caution frequently against the prevailing and most dangerous vices; and will instruct you, how to walk in the observance of all Christian duties. I shall only add this my earnest request, that to the exercise of the sublimest virtues, faith, hope and charity, you will join a fervent and well regulated devotion to the Holy Mother of our Lord and Saviour Jesus Christ; that you will place great confidence in Her intercession; and have recourse to Her in all your necessities. Having chosen Her the special patroness of this Diocess, you are placed, of course, under Her powerful protection; and it becomes your duty to be careful to deserve its continuance by a zealous imitation of Her virtues, and reliance on Her motherly superintendence.

The Sunday immediately following the feast of Her glorious assumption into heaven; or the feast itself, whenever it happens to fall on a Sunday, is to be cele-
The Pastoral brated as a principal solemnity of this Dio-
Feast of the cess; on which we are to unite with one
Diocese. heart, and in one earnest supplication to the father of all mercies, and the giver of every good gift, through the intercession of the Blessed Virgin, that He may be graciously pleased to preserve, increase, and diffuse a sincere and well-grounded attachment to the principles of our holy religion; to advert from us the seduction of error and pestilential infidelity; to awake and renew in us the spirit of solid piety, and of watchfulness over our unruly passions; to animate us to the fulfilling of all the commandments; to pour down on our country blessings spiritual and temporal; and to receive our grateful and humble thanks for the innumerable favours, which we continually receive from a bountiful providence.

That these acts of religion may be more acceptable, by being offered with purified hearts, I earnestly exhort and recommend to all, who shall join in the celebration of this great festival, to expiate their offences by sincere compunction in the sacrament of penance, and to enrich their souls by those abundant graces, which are annexed to a worthy participation of Christ's body and blood. I have solicited, for your sake, my dear brethren, from the Holy See, special spiritual favours, for this solemnity; and have no doubt, but the fatherly solicitude, which his holiness, the vicar of Jesus Christ, has always shown hitherto for your improvement in every Christian virtue, will induce him to grant the favours requested; of which in due time you shall receive proper notice.

What may not be hoped, if to other means of salvation, such as are always to be found in the salutary institutions of the Church, you will add, every year, this likewise, that is now suggested? If you recur to God, the fountain of mercy and grace, through the intercession of the Queen of

Angels? If you honour Her greatest festival with peculiar and fervent exercises of piety, and with a determined will of making the precepts of the gospel the rule of your lives? The Church bears Her this honourable testimony, that it is often owing to Her patronage, that nations preserve or recover the integrity of Christian faith and morality. Let this be exemplified in our own country. *Walk worthy of the vocation in which you are called.*[9] Give no cause of its being said of any one of you: *thou, that makest the boast of the law, by transgression of the law dishonourest God.*[10] On the contrary, endeavour continually, *that you may declare His virtues, who has called you out of the darkness into His marvellous light;*[11] that they, among whom is your conversation—considering you by your good works, may give glory to God in the day of visitation. *For this cause I bow my knees to the Father of our Lord Jesus Christ, ... that He would grant you according to the riches of His glory . . . . . that Christ may dwell by faith in your hearts; that being rooted and founded in charity, you may be able . . . . . to know also the charity of Christ, which surpasseth knowledge, that you may be filled unto all the fulness of God. Now to Him, who is able to do all things more abundantly than we desire or understand . . . . to Him be glory in the church, and in Christ Jesus unto all generations, world without end. Amen.*

✝JOHN, *Bishop of Baltimore.*

Baltimore, May 28, 1792.

Bishop Carroll had already experienced considerable trouble with the trustees of the Catholic congregations in Philadelphia and Baltimore, when this Pastoral was written. During the next five years the evils of trusteeism increased, and in 1797, he wrote a *Pastoral Letter to the Congregation of Trinity Church, in Philadelphia,* in which he dealt with this issue between unruly priests and laity and espiscopal authority. The Pastoral of 1797 is a scarce document today. It is not included in this collection, however, since it is confined to one locality, albeit the message was to the Church at large in the diocese then coterminous with the Republic. None realized so keenly

---

9 Eph. iv. 1.　　　　10 Rom. ii. 23.　　　　11 1 Peter ii. 9.

as Carroll the increasing difficulty of ruling this great territory. At his request the Holy See, in 1808, divided the United States into five dioceses—Baltimore, which became an archdiocese, Boston, New York, Philadelphia, and Bardstown. The bishops appointed to the new Sees were consecrated at Baltimore between October 28 and November 4, 1810. These prelates remained for several weeks in consultation with Archbishop Carroll, and before separating for their respective dioceses, they drew up an Agreement for the unification of Catholic discipline in the United States. This Agreement forms, with the Synodal Acts of 1791, the earliest code of canon law in the American Church. The result of their deliberations was published in a Pastoral, dated November 15, 1810. This document is not included in this collection, because it is mainly a restatement of the decrees of 1791. The Bishops of Philadelphia, Boston and Bardstown whose names, with those of Carroll and Neale, are appended to the document, state that "they reserved to a future occasion a general review of the ecclesiastical discipline now observed throughout the different dioceses, and the reducing of it everywhere to as strict conformity with that of the universal Church, as our peculiar situation, circumstances and general benefit of the faithful will allow."

A generation was to pass before this promise was fulfilled. Between 1810 and the convocation of the First Provincial Council of Baltimore in 1829, there is one ecclesiastical document which is so exceptional in its contents that it approaches national importance—Archbishop Maréchal's *Pastoral Letter to the Roman Catholics of Norfolk, Virginia,* dated September 28, 1819. This document is likewise very scarce today, but since it deals with a particular situation, it is not included in this collection.

CHAPTER II

The Pastoral Letter to the Laity (1829)

IT would take us too far from the main purpose of this volume
to discuss the reasons for the long delay (1810-1829) before
Archbishop Whitfield convoked the First Provincial Council
of Baltimore. The consultations of the five bishops at Baltimore in November, 1810, were concluded with the decision to
hold a National Council two years later. Bishop Cheverus of
Boston objected so strongly to the meeting that Archbishop
Carroll reluctantly agreed to postpone it. The future Cardinal-
Archbishop of Bordeaux did not see why the bishops should take
the long and, at the time, rather arduous journey to Batimore
to settle questions which, as he wrote, "the professors at the
Seminary could just as easily decide." Two years later, when
Bishop Egan, of Philadelphia, died (July 22, 1814), the war
was on, and the last illness of Archbishop Carroll prevented
any assembly of the prelates. It would seem from even a cur-
sory reading of the unpublished sources for the next decade
that Archbishop Maréchal saw no necessity of convoking a
national assembly of the bishops. No member of the American
hierarchy of that period was more impressed with the need of
such a council than John England, Bishop of Charleston (1820-
1842). By every means in his power he strove to prove to his
colleagues in the episcopacy the need of creating a uniform
system of discipline in the American Church. The Holy See
was likewise so minded, but it was not until after Maréchal's
death (June 28, 1828), that the first Provincial Council was
called. In December of that year, Archbishop Whitfield convoked the Council to meet in Baltimore during the following
October. On the last day of September, 1829, the seven prelates who composed the Council met at the Archbishop's house,
and the sessions lasted from that date until October the eigh-
teenth. Among the causes which required the attention of the
Fathers were: the disorganized state of affairs in some of the
dioceses, where episcopal authority was then being set at
naught by troublesome clerics and laymen; the grave problem
of foreign interference in nominations to vacant sees in the

United States; the importance of a more direct and authentic communication of the Church affairs here with the Holy See; the erection of new dioceses which would be in conformity with the geographical and political divisions of the country; and the redress of the grievances which had multipied as the result of the lack of a uniform Church discipline. The great changes which had taken place in the Church here between 1791 and 1829 are eloquently sketched in the letter sent by the Fathers of the Council to Pope Pius VIII, on October 24, 1829: "Not two centuries have elapsed since, in a remote and obscure corner of Maryland, a little band of Catholics, guided by a few missionaries, exiles from their native land, flying from the cruel persecution inflicted on them for adhering to the faith of their forefathers, laid the foundation of this American Church. It is scarcely forty years since this body of the faithful in the United States of America was found sufficient to demand, in the opinion of the sovereign pontiff, the erection of the first episcopal see of Baltimore. Not twenty years have rolled by since a decree of the holy pontiff, Pius VII, exalted the church of Baltimore to the dignity and rights of a metropolitan; and, like a joyful mother of children, she has beheld in recently erected suffragan dioceses, quickened by a heaven-bestowed fruitfulness, an offspring in new churches which she has borne to Christ. We see so many blessings bestowed by God on these rising churches, such increase given to this vineyard, that those who planted and those who watered, and those who harvested and tread the overflowing wine-press, are compelled to confess and admire wholly the finger of God. The number of the faithful increases daily; churches not unworthy of divine worship are everywhere erected; the Word of God is preached everywhere, and not without fruit; the hatred and prejudice spread against the church and faithful vanish; holy religion, once despised and held in contempt, receives honour from her very enemies; the priests of Christ are venerated even by those without; the truth and divinity of our faith is proclaimed and vindicated from the calumny of heresy and unbelief, not only in churches and from pulpits, but from the press in widely scattered periodicals and books. Six ecclesiastical seminaries, the hope of our churches, have already been established, and are governed in holy discipline by pious and learned priests; nine colleges under ecclesiastical control have been erected in different States to train boys and young men in piety, arts, and higher branches of science; three of these have been chartered as universities by the legislatures; thirty-three monasteries and houses of religious women of different orders and congregations—Ursulines, Visitandines, Carmelites, Sacred Heart, Sisters of Charity, Loretto, etc.—are everywhere established in our dioceses, whence emanate not only the observance of the evangelical counsels and the exercise of all other virtues, but the good order of Christ in the pious training of innumerable girls; houses of religious of the Order of Preachers and the Society of Jesus, of secular priests of the Congregation of the Mission and of St. Sulpice, from which, as centres, priests are sent out to missions; many schools where the poor of both sexes are taught gratuitously; hospitals carried on by religious women, who daily give signs of heroic charity, to the great benefit of souls and of religion. These, Most Holy Father, are the signal benefits which God has bestowed upon us in a few years."

The decrees of the First Provincial Council were thirty-eight in number, and the salient features of the legislation passed by the Fathers concerned the reorganization of clerical discipline, the abolition of trusteeism, in the discussion of which Roger Taney, afterwards Chief Justice of the Supreme Court of the United States, took an important part, and the necessity of founding a Catholic parochial school system.

Two Pastoral Letters were issued by the First Provincial Council of 1829: one to the laity, and another to the clergy, of the United States. The Pastoral to the laity was written by Bishop England, and was printed in English and French. No copy of the English version was found and the following reprint is taken from the *Catholic Miscellany* of 1829.[1]

THE PASTORAL LETTER TO THE LAITY

(First Provincial Council of Baltimore)

The Archbishops and other prelates in Provincial Council at Baltimore to their children in Christ, the Laity of the Roman Catholic Church in the United States of America Health and blessing: Grace to you, and peace from God our Father, and Lord Jesus Christ, in the unity of the Holy Ghost.

ASSEMBLED to consult for the welfare of that portion of the Church entrusted to our care, we have, after mature deliberation with several learned and pious priests, made

[1] Vol. IX, pp. 145-148.

ordinances, which to us seemed necessary for the regulation of the clergy, the administration of the Sacraments and other Ecclesiastical concerns. These we have transmitted for examination to the See at Rome, in order that we might not in any way swerve from that unity which has been established by the great Pastor of our souls, who collected his faithful children into one flock, under one shepherd. But we cannot separate without addressing you in the sincerity of affection.

When we look around us and behold how, within a few years, our churches have multiplied and our numbers increased, we feel deeply grateful to Him

The Growth of the Church. who, being able "from the very stones to rise up children of Abraham," has allured them to the paths of salvation. From the East and the West strangers have come to sit down at our table, and our hearts have rejoiced at this return of the children to that parent from whom they had been too long estranged. The far greater number of those who have thus been clasped in the warm embrace of tender and gratified affection, have edified us by their virtue; several have thus made a suitable return for the talent entrusted to their care. It has added to our satisfaction to have observed that, owing to our admirable civil and political institutions, those results of conscientious conviction have produced scarcely any temporal inconvenience; that they have seldom snapped or ever strained the bonds of Charity. Rejoice with us, therefore, and give thanks to the Lord who has vouchsafed this gladness to our hearts.

The vast tide of emigration which has rolled across the Atlantic during the half century just elapsed, together with the natural growth of a prosperous people under free institutions, with an ample territory and varied soil, in almost every climate, has swelled our population to an extraordinary extent, and our flock has necessarily participated in the increase. Large acquisitions of territory which has been occupied by Catholic nations, were made to the south and the west, and thousands have thus become incorporated with our ecclesiastical body.

When our first See was erected our venerable predecessor found himself at the head of a sparse and extended population, with a very insufficient number of assistants in the ministry. The zeal of those good men was ardent, their virtues were conspicuous, and their labours were oppressive. Combining the energy, the poverty and the self-denial of the Apostles, they sometimes were spread abroad in the wilderness, bearing the bread of life, as well as to the remote pioneer of civilization, as to that child of the forest, who yet adhered to the lessons of his first missionary; sometimes in the cities, in the towns and villages, they were found endeavouring to organize and to perpetuate the congregations which had been previously formed, to educate the youth, to direct the adult, to counsel the doubtful, to confirm the wavering, to console the afflicted, to sustain the firm, and despising the evanescent enjoyments or follies of the world, they were found with tender and absorbing interest, in the regions of pestilence, by the side of their dying children, cheering the soul which nature taught to shudder at the portal of death, even though it led to the vestibule of Heaven. Admirable men! What an example for their successors? "In the sight of the unwise they seemed to die, and their departure was taken for misery, and their going away from us, utter destruction: but they are in peace." In their day also the sword of the persecutor had been unsheathed, and even when, by the energy of the nation it was stricken from his hand, their name continued to be as a word of reproach, and they had much obloquy to endure. "In the sight of men they suffered torments, but now their hope is full of immortality: afflicted in a few things," we trust, "they are well rewarded; because God tried them and found them worthy of Himself."

If therefore, in the vast regions we inhabit, we have to deplore the defection of millions from the faith of their fathers, which is also yours and ours, let it not be imagined that the memory of those good men is lessened in our esteem: they exerted their powers to the utmost, but they were too few for the extent of the field; and far removed from their ministry or influence, thousands of those who vainly sought their aid in conveying to them those "waters that spring

Losses.

up to eternal life," wearied and disappointed, "dug cisterns for themselves," or had recourse to those which men had dug, and their children, and their childrens' children now forget the rock from which their progenitors have been separated.

The convulsions of Europe, however disastrous to itself, have not been without advantage to us. When the extermi-

Gains.

nating infidel went forth like to him who sat upon the pale horse of the Apocalypse, Hell followed in his train, and because of the power that was given to him to kill with the sword, with famine, and the plague, many were slain for the word of God, and the testimony which they held, whilst their brethren who were saved for a little time, were scattered to the four winds of Heaven through various regions of the earth. Whilst they bowed in humble resignation to the wise, but mysterious dispensations of Providence, they felt that though in all things they suffered tribulation, they were not distressed; though straightened they were not destitute; though suffering persecution, they were not forsaken; though cast down, they did not perish; but always bearing about in their bodies the dying of Jesus, the life of Jesus was also made manifest in their bodies. By their example rather than by their words, by their utility rather than by their worldly exhibition, numbers of them in our States, as elsewhere, preached not themselves, but Jesus Christ our Lord, and exhibited themselves your servants through Jesus, for God, who commanded the light to shine out of darkness, hath shined in their hearts to give the light of the knowledge of the glory of God unto you. Thus was our ministry upheld and extended; thus were our seminaries of education founded and improved; and thus were raised up among us several of our most useful priests and promising aspirants. As our congregations have in a great measure been hitherto an emigrant population, so has our ministry been to a considerable extent composed of adopted citizens. But the children of the former, and the successors of the latter have for some time past assumed more of our native character, and must necessarily become chiefly, if not altogether national, henceforth.

During the whole period of our pastoral charge we have
felt the utmost want of a sufficient ministry: from every
quarter our children call to us for the bread
of life, and we have not a sufficient number   The Need of
of those to whom we could entrust its   Priests.
breaking; already the fields are white for
the harvest, and we have not a proper supply of labourers,
the vintage has ripened, and its clusters are decaying. It
is absolutely necessary that by your exertions, we should
take the proper steps for remedying this deficiency. Though
we have been frequently aided by excellent clergymen from
abroad, we cannot expect that other countries will continue
their generosity in permitting the most meritorious subjects
to withdraw from their own service to our advantage; nor
are the situations which we could offer them, so secure or
so advantageous as such men might find at home. Neither
would you desire, nor are we disposed any longer to permit, that priests who have been elsewhere held in disrepute,
shall be received into our churches, to create schisms, to encourage strife, to perpetuate abuses, and to disseminate
scandal; to degrade that which is holy, and to bring upon a
religion that has emanated from God, that obloquy which
belongs only to the vices that have been found in the individual man. Beloved children, we have endured much affliction on this score, having been forced by our necessities
to dispense with much of that scrutiny and caution which
our canons have enjoined. With you it rests to support us;
by furnishing the means for educating proper candidates
under our own inspection, that we may secure the benefits
of religion to you and to your descendants.

We feel gratitude to our benefactors, and take some
reproach to our province, in stating to you the fact, that
almost each of us has received, for this purpose, considerable aid from a benevolent society in France, whilst our
own flocks have as yet done so little for so important a
purpose. Permit us to arouse you to exertion on this head.
How shall your remote and destitute fellow-Catholics be
attended? How shall the increasing wants of our increasing people be met, if you do not powerfully aid us in the
creation and maintenance of our seminaries? Call to mind

what you have so generously done for your brethren of the
Faith in Ireland; we ask whether you could not make
similar exertions for yourselves and your own descendants?

From this topic we naturally pass to that of the education of your children. How important, how interesting, how
'awful, how responsible a charge! "Suffer
little children to come unto me, and forbid
them not" says the amiable Jesus, "for of
such is the kingdom of Heaven." Yes! the
characteristic of the child, as St. John Chrysostom well observes, is the characteristic of the saint. Genuine simplicity without guile, uncalculating ardent devotion to the loving parent, preferring an humble mother in her homely
garb, to a queen in her variegated decoration; exercising
an irresistible power over the parental heart by the bewitch-
ing confidence of helplessness itself. Those children, the
dear pledges of your elevated and sanctified affection, deserve and demand your utmost solicitude. For them you
brave danger, on their account you endure toil; you weep
over their afflictions, you rejoice at their gratification, you
look forward to their prosperity, you anticipate their gratitude, your souls are knit to theirs, your happiness is cen-
tred in their good conduct; and you cherish the enlightening
hope that when you and they shall have passed through this
vale of tears, you will be reunited in the kingdom of a common father. How would your hearts be torn with grief did
you foresee, that through eternity those objects of all your
best feelings should be cast into outward darkness, where
there is weeping and gnashing of teeth! May God in His
infinite mercy preserve you and them from the just antici-
pation of any such result! But, dearly beloved, this is too
frequently the necessary consequence of a neglected or an
improper education. God has made you the guardians of
those children to lead them to His service upon earth, that
they might become saints in Heaven. "What will it avail
them to gain the whole world if they lose their souls?" Or
could it console you in the progress of eternity to recollect
that you had for a time beheld them elevated to power, applauded by fame, entrusted with command, swaying nations, dispensing wealth and honours; but misled by vice

*Christian
Education.*

and now tortured in disgrace; and, thus to be tortured for eternity? If you would avert this dreadful calamity, attend to the education of your child; teaching him first to seek the kingdom of God and His justice, and having food and raiment to be therewith content. Teach him to be industrious, to be frugal, to be humble and fully resigned to the will of that God who feeds the birds of the air, clothes the lily of the field; and who so loved the children of men that when they were His enemies they were reconciled to him by the death of His Son, that being reconciled they might be saved from eternal death by His life being justified now by His blood.

Alas! beloved children, how many are there, who, yielding to the pride of life, and ashamed of Him who was not ashamed for our sakes to die upon an ignominious cross, "being made the reproach of men and the outcast of the people," how many such wretched parents have trained up their children to be themselves the victims of passions in time, and of that death from which there is no resurrection in eternity!

How frequently have their brightest hopes faded away into a settled gloom? How often has the foot which they elevated, spurned them? How often whilst the children of revelry occupied the hall of mirth, has the drink of the wretched parent been mingled with his tears, and whilst his ungrateful offspring, regardless of his admonition, rose in the careless triumph of enjoyment, have his gray hairs been brought with sorrow to the grave? Believe us; it is only by the religious education of your children that you can so train them up, as to ensure that, by their filial piety and their steady virtue, they may be to you the staff of your old age, the source of your consolation, and reward in a better world. Begin with them in their earliest childhood, whilst the mind is yet pure and docile, and their baptismal innocence uncontaminated; let their unfolding perceptions be imbued with the mild and lovely tints of religious truth and pure devotion; allure them to the service of their creator who delights in the homage of innocence; and give to their reason, as it becomes developed, that substantial nutriment which it requires, and which our holy religion so abundantly affords; shew your children by your conduct, that you believe what you inculcate; natural affection disposes them to imitate your example, you should, therefore, be awfully impressed by that solemn admonition of the Saviour: "Woe to him that shall scandalize one of these little ones that believe in me, it were better for him that a millstone were tied round his neck, and that he were drowned in the depths of the sea." In placing them at school, seek for those teachers who will cultivate the seed which you have sown; for of what avail will it be, that you have done so much, if the germs which begin to put forth, shall now be stifled or eradicated; and should tares be sown where you had prepared the soil? Again, and again, would we impress upon your minds the extreme importance of this great duty, and your responsibility to the God of truth, in its regard. How well would it be, if your means and opportunities permitted, were you at this period to commit your children to the care of those whom we have for their special fitness, placed over our seminaries and our female religious institutions? It would be at once the best mode of discharging your obligations to your children, and of aiding us in promoting the great object which we have already endeavoured to impress upon your minds. Remember also, that not only affection, but, duty requires of you to be vigilant in securing the spiritual concerns of your offspring, during the period of their preparation for business or for professions; that this security can, in general, be far better attained under the parent's roof; or if it be necessary to entrust the sacred deposit of your child's soul to another, it ought to be one of tried virtue, and surrounded by favourable circumstances. Should your family be thus educated, you may naturally expect that they will freely allow your just influence in that most important of all temporal concerns, the selection of a wife or husband; and it becomes you, whilst you pay a proper respect to the affections of those most deeply interested, to be careful that you have more regard to those things which belong to eternity, than to those of a mere transient nature. What we have written might appear importunate. But remember we watch over you in order to render unto God an account of your souls; therefore, it is that we write these things to you, to admonish you as our dearest children, "to confirm your hearts without blame, in holiness, before God and our father," because you are our joy and our crown, and therefore, we labour, whether absent or present, for your advantage, in the word of truth, in the power of God; through honour and dishonour, through infamy and good name, our mouth is open to you, our heart is enlarged; great is our confidence in you, we are consoled by your joy, we are saddened by your sorrow, we write, not as commanding, but as entreating our children in whom we confide.

Amongst the various misfortunes to which we have been exposed, one of the greatest is misrepresentation of the tenets, the principles and the practices of our church. This is not the place to account for the origin and continuance of this evil; we merely remind you of the melancholy fact. Good men,—men, otherwise well informed, deeply versed in science, in history, in politics; men who have improved their education by their travels abroad as well as they who have merely acquired the very rudiments of knowledge at home; the virtuous women who influence that society which they decorate, and yielding to the benevolence of their hearts desire to extend useful knowledge; the public press, the very bench of public justice, have been all influenced by extraordinary efforts directed against us; so that from the very highest place in our land to all its remotest borders, we are exhibited as what we are not, and charged with maintaining what we detest. Repetition has given to those statements a semblance of evidence; and groundless assertions remaining almost uncontradicted, wear the appearance of admitted and irrefragable truth. It is true, that during some years past, an effort has been made to uphold a periodical publication in the south, which has refuted some of those allegations; but we say with regret that it has been permitted to languish for want of ordinary support, and must, we are informed, be discontinued, unless it receives your more extended patronage. Other publications for similar objects have lately been established in Boston and Hartford. We would advise you to encourage well-conducted works of this description. If you look around and see how many such are maintained, for their own purposes, by our separated brethren, it will indeed be a matter of reproach should we not uphold at least a few of our own.

But not only are the misrepresentations of which we complain, propagated so as to affect the mature; but with zeal worthy of a better cause, and which some persons have exhibited in contrast with our seeming apathy, the mind of the very infant is predisposed against us by the recitals of the nursery; and the school-boy can scarcely find a book in which some one or more of our institutions or practices is not exhibited far otherwise than it really is, and greatly to our disadvantage: the entire system of education is thus tinged throughout its whole course; and history itself has been distorted to our serious injury. We have during a long time been oppressed by this evil, and from a variety of causes, have found it almost impossible to apply any remedy; but we have deemed it expedient now to make some effort towards a beginning. We have therefore associated ourselves and some others, whom we deem well qualified for that object, to encourage the publication of elementary books free from any of those false colourings, and in which whilst our own feelings are protected, those of our fellow-citizens of other religious denominations shall be respected. We should desire also to see other histories corrected, as that of England has been by the judicious and erudite Doctor Lingard; that our standard books should be carefully and faithfully printed under proper supervision, and even that temperate and useful explanatory essays to exhibit and vindicate truth, should be written without harsh or unkind expressions, and published, so that our brethren might have better opportunities of knowing us as we really are, and not imagine us to be what in bad times, unprincipled and interested men have exhibited as our picture.

One of the most precious legacies bequeathed to us by the Apostles and Evangelists is the sacred volume of the Holy Scriptures, which, having been written under divine inspiration, is profitable for the pastor, who is a man of

God, to teach, to reprove, to correct, to instruct unto justice;
for much of the revelation of God is contained therein; it
is also profitable when used with due care,
and an humble and docile spirit, for the   Holy
edification and instruction of the faithful;   Scripture.
but it must not be had recourse to, for
the purpose of raising "vain questions and strifes of
words from which arise envies, contentions, blasphemies,
evil suspicions, conflicts of men corrupted in mind
and who are destitute of the truth, esteeming gain to be
piety;" neither should it be approached with arrogant self-
sufficiency, for it contains "some things hard to be understood, which the unlearned and unstable wrest to their
own perdition. You therefore knowing these things before, beware lest being led away by error of the unwise
you fall from your own steadfastness." When in the moments of leisure and reflection you take up the sacred book,
be impressed with the conviction that you then converse
with God himself; commence therefore by prayer, to obtain
that it may be to you a lamp to guide your feet in safety
through the shades of this valley of death. We cannot give
to you a better rule than that of the holy council of Trent,
where it informs us "that the divine writings are to be
understood in that sense, which our holy mother the church,
to which alone it belongs to judge of the true sense
and interpretation of the scriptures, has always held and
does hold; and that we should never take and interpret
them otherwise than according to the unanimous consent
of the fathers." And dearly beloved children, the word
of God being unalterable truth, cannot vary its meaning
with the fluctuating opinions of men. The heavens and
the earth may pass away, but the word of God remains the
same, "Jesus Christ yesterday, to-day, and forever the
same." The Apostles, who were the first fathers, received
the explanations of his doctrines from the lips of the Saviour
himself, and they were still more confirmed in their minds
by that Spirit of Truth, the Paraclete whom the Father sent
in his name to lead them unto all truth and to teach them
all things, and to bring to their minds whatsoever he said
to them. From the lips of those witnesses, the fathers of

the next age received what they transmitted to their successors, and thus thro' a series of ages, has this cloud of holy witnesses gone before us, to guide us to the true land of promise, by their blazing glory in the night of doubt and error, and as a pillar of truth in the day of steady faith. Neither the improvement of science nor the progress of the arts can make false, that which Christ revealed as true; nor make that truth, which he declared to be error. The perfection of faith is to be found in the unchangeableness of doctrine, and the meaning of his word is that which was proclaimed by his Apostles. Thus, new and arbitrary interpretations of the sacred volume would be, not the declaration of the doctrine of redemption, but would be the substitution of human opinion for the testimony of God.

Deeming it therefore to be their most sacred duty, the Bishops of the Church have scrupulously preserved unchanged through the innovations of time and the alterations of ages, the testimony of Faith, and as a most precious portion thereof, the written word of God. Equally anxious to fulfil our important trust, we too desire to guard you against mistake and error. We therefore earnestly caution you against the indiscriminate use of unauthorised versions, for unfortunately many of those which are placed within your reach are extremely erroneous and defective. The Doway translation from the vulgate of the Old Testament, together with the Remish translation of the New Testament, are our best English versions; but as some printers have undertaken in these States, by their own authority, without our sanction, to print and publish editions which have not been submitted to our examination, we cannot hold ourselves responsible for the correctness of such copies. We trust that henceforth it will be otherwise. We would also desire to correct that irregularity by which prayer books and other works of devotion and instruction are produced from the press, in several instances, without authority or correction: some of the books thus published are rather occasions of scandal than of edification. We would entreat of you not to encourage such proceedings.

We would also draw your attention to another subject, upon which we have too often felt much pain, but thanks be to our Lord, the evil has greatly diminished. Beloved children in Christ, you are   Unity Among aware that the constitution of our church   Catholics. was formed by our blessed Saviour, and that although we are commissioned to legislate to a certain extent in its concerns, we have no power to alter that constitution. By it the mode of our government is unchangeably fixed, and the great founder of our hierarchy, Christ himself, according to his promise, built his church upon Peter, as the basis upon which it was to remain secure, not only against the winds and floods, but against the efforts of the gates of hell. And some indeed he gave in this unit of faith and government to be "Apostles, and some prophets, and other some evangelists, and other some pastors and doctors· for the perfecting of the saints, for the work of the ministry, for the edifying of the body of Christ." "And now as the body is one, but hath many members, though they may be many, yet are only one body." So it is in the church of Christ. "If the foot should say, because I am not the hand, I am not of the body: is it not therefore of the body? And if the ear should say, because I am not the eye, I am not of the body; is it, therefore, not of the body? If the whole body were hearing, where would be the smelling? But now God hath set the members, every one of them, in the body as it hath pleased him," "and the eye cannot say to the hand: I need not thy help, nor again the head to the feet, I have no need of you. Yea, much more those that seem to be the more feeble members of the body, are more necessary;" but God hath tempered the body together, giving the more abundant honour to that which wanted it, that there might be no schism in the body, but that the members might be mutually careful one for another, and if one member suffer anything, all the members suffer with it; or if one member glory, all the members rejoice with it. Now you are the body of Christ and members of member. To us, unworthy as we are, the same Apostle who thus describes the knitting together of our members into compact unity, addresses himself, warning that

we "take heed to ourselves and to all the flock over
which the Holy Ghost hath placed us Bishops to
govern the church of God, which he hath purchased
with his blood." And indeed we may truly say with the
Apostle, that "we think God hath set us forth as the last"
amongst you, because "we are made a spectacle to the
world, to angels and to men," we are assimilated to him
in many things, though we follow only at a distance in his
footsteps, "we write not these things to shame you, but to
admonish you as our dearest children." Let no man take
us to be foolish if we imitate even in this, the great model,
after whom we would gladly copy. "Seeing that many
glory according to the flesh, we will glory also. Are we
not found for your sakes in journeys often, in perils of
rivers, in perils in the city, in perils in the wilderness, in
perils in the sea, in labour and painfulness, in watching
often, in hunger and thirst, in many fastings, in cold and
heat? Besides all those things that are without; our daily
instances, the solicitude for all the churches; who is weak
and we are not weak, who is scandalized and we do not
burn? And in all this what can be our object?—We have
not sought the stations which we fill, but with a full knowledge of their difficulties, not relying upon our own sufficiency, but upon the grace of God and your co-operation,
we boldly say before the God who will judge us, that it
was for your sake and for that of your children, we have
taken the yoke upon us. We ask not your riches; for ourselves they would be useless, having food and raiment we
are satisfied; we have no families to provide for, we have
no relatives to enrich; to your service we have devoted ourselves, solemnly pledging our souls to God for your advantage; for you we would willingly spend and be spent. What
we could save from your contributions, what we could obtain in foreign nations by entreaty, what charity has entrusted to our own disposal; all this we have expended for
the establishment of religion amongst you. For the truth
of our assertions we appeal to yourselves.—Are we then
unworthy of your confidence? Has our conduct been domination? Before God we are conscious of many faults, and
we confess and lament our imperfections; but as regards

you, we have kept back nothing that was profitable to you, but have preached it to you, and taught you publickly, and from house to house, testifying penance towards God and faith in our Lord Jesus Christ, wherefore we take you witness to-day, that we are free from the blood of all; for we have not been wanting to declare to you all the counsel of God.

Yet there have been found amongst you, men who, not fully acquainted with the principles of our church government, either presumed to reform it upon the model of those who have separated from   Trusteeism. us, or claimed imaginary rights from the misapprehension of facts and laws with which they were badly, if at all acquainted; they have sometimes been abetted by ignorant or unprincipled priests; and disastrous schisms have thereby occasionally arisen. We have shed bitter tears when we beheld those usurping and frequently immoral delinquents, standing in the holy places, and profaning the services of the living God; we have deplored the delusion of their adherents. But we trust those evil days have passed away, and forever. Still we feel it to be our duty to declare to you, that in no part of the Catholic Church does the right of instituting or dismissing a clergyman to or from any benefice or mission, with or without the care of souls, exist in any one, save the ordinary prelate of the diocese or district in which such benefice or mission is found. We, of course, consider our holy father the Pope, as the ordinary prelate of the whole church, yet it is not usual for him to interfere, save on very extraordinary occasions; this right never has been conceded by the church to any other body, nor could it be conceded, consistently with our faith and discipline.—We further declare to you, that no right of presentation or patronage to any one of our churches or missions, has ever existed or does now exist canonically, in these United States, and, moreover, even if it were desirable to create such right, which we are far from believing; it would be altogether impossible, canonically to do so, from the manner in which the church-property in these states is vested; and that even did we desire to create such right, it would not be in our power, after what we have learned from eminent lawyers in various states, to point out any mode in which it could be canonically created; the nature of our state constitutions and the dispositions of our state legislatures regarding church-property, being so perfectly at variance with the principles upon which such property must be secured, before such right could be created. It is our duty, as it is our disposition, so to exercise that power which resides in us, of making or changing the appointments of your pastors, as to meet not only your wants but your wishes, so far as our conscientious convictions and the just desires and expectations of meritorious priests will permit, and we trust and that in the discharge of this most important and most delicate duty, we shall always meet with your support; as our only object can be your spiritual welfare, for the attainment of which we are, at the risk of our eternal salvation, to lay aside all prejudice and partiality respecting those whom we appoint.

Beloved children, we exhort you to "be zealous for the better gifts, and we yet show to you a more excellent way." If you had the appointment to all the churches, and yet had not the benefit of the sacramental institutions, it would profit you nothing.—"Except you eat the flesh of the son of man and drink his blood, you cannot have life in you." The great object of religion is the creation and the perpetuation of this life; this is "the vocation in which you are called." Alas! How often have our spirits been depressed, and our hearts smitten whilst we walked amidst the dry bones that lay scattered on the plain, entrusted to our care? Once they were covered with sinews and flesh, and animated with the spirit of God; those bodies were the tabernacles of the Holy Ghost; delighted angels hovered round, to enter into holy converse with the kindred souls which dwelt within; the elastic air was fragrant with the breathings of prayer; the soft eye of pious gratitude reflected in its effulgence the complacency of Heaven; it was like to another Eden where God vouchsafed to become familiar with the children of dust; it was well for us to be there; how we desired to build tabernacles and to make it our abode! But alas, the serpent came, sin was entertained, death triumphed, and the silence of desolation and the ruins of mortality are spread around.

O! that our voice could effect in you, the change which that of the Prophet was destined to produce upon the house of Israel. "Say not our bones are dried up, and our hope is lost, and we are cut off," for the Lord God who first breathed into Adam a living soul, has commanded us to proclaim to those slain by sin, that they may live again. We entreat you, therefore, that deserting the ways of iniquity, you "be now converted to the pastor and bishop of your souls," "who, when we all were as sheep going astray," "his own self bore our sins in his body upon the tree, that we being dead to sin, might live to justice; by whose stripes we are healed." You acknowledge the power of the tribunal which he has himself established when he "breathed upon his disciples, and said to them, receive ye the Holy Ghost, whose sins you shall forgive, they are forgiven them; and whose you shall retain they are retained." Have recourse thereto. Our Holy Father Pope Pius VIII. the successor of St. Peter, the head of the Catholic Church, unites his supplication to ours, beseeching you to have pity upon your own souls, and offers you the benefits of a plenary indulgence in the form of a jubilee, to excite and encourage you to advance. If then, this day, through our ministry, you hear the voice of the Lord, harden not your hearts, lest having filled up the measure of your iniquities, he should swear in his wrath; and the time of mercy be no more. We are edified by the piety of thousands who regularly partake of the sacred gifts; we entreat you who have been hitherto remiss, to fill up the measure of our consolation by uniting yourselves to them.

Be constant at the Holy Sacrifice of the Mass with becoming dispositions of heart, for "God is a spirit" and seeks true adorers "in spirit and in truth." Be frequent at the other public offices of the church, carefully observe the command- **Attendance at Mass.** ments of God; and steadily obey the precepts of that spouse of Christ, "the pillar and the ground of truth," of which he declares himself, "he that will not hear the church, let him be to you as a heathen and a publican;"

"let no man deceive you with vain words, for because of
these things cometh the anger of God upon the children
of unbelief. Be ye not, therefore, partakers with them."
You know "that no fornicator nor unclean, nor covetous
persons which is a serving of idols, hath any inheritance in
the kingdom of Christ and of God." "Have no fellowship
with the unfruitful works of darkness, but rather reprove
them." "Be not drunk with wine wherein is luxury, but be
ye filled with the Holy Ghost." You cannot be partakers of
the sacraments of the church whilst you condemn her authority or disregard her precepts. The laws of fasting and
abstinence are part of the earliest, the most necessary, and
most wholesome discipline of the church, yet there are
many, and we write it with affliction of soul, who profess
to be of our body, and who disregard those sacred ordinances, making themselves slaves to gluttony rather than
servants of God, who prefer the gratification of their appetite to the practice of religion, "enemies of the Cross of
Christ, whose end is destruction, whose God is their belly,
and whose glory is their shame, who mind earthly things."
—Others, through a discreditable pusillanimity, blush to be
consistent in observing the usages of a church to which
they are known to belong; they violate its ordinances to
escape the sneer of the unbeliever, who cannot himself avoid
despising the weakness which dreads the smile of a man,
rather than the displeasure of God. We entreat of you to be
more consistent in your practice with your profession.

Whilst we caution you against that demoralizing and un-
reasonable semblance of liberality now so prevalent, which
confounds truth and error, by asserting
that all religions are alike, as if contradictory propositions could be at the same time
true; we exhort you to charity and affection
towards your citizens of every denomination. To God and
not to you, nor to us, do they stand or fall; to him and not
to us is reserved the judgment of individuals. We know it
to be clearly declared by the inspiration of heaven, as it is
also manifest from the plain evidence of reason, that there
cannot be now upon this earth, two true churches. We
know that we have preserved the deposit of the faith, which

False
Liberalism.

we ought to adorn by our virtue, and whilst we testify those facts to you we exhort you to imitate the glorious and creditable example of those good men who first sowed the mustard seed of our faith in this part of our continent.—They were so fully convinced of those great truths which we now proclaim, that they suffered joyfully every description of persecution rather than swerve from that one holy Catholic and Apostolic Church to which you and they and we belong. Yet neither the principles of that faith, nor the affliction which they endured, created any unkind feeling in their benevolent hearts; and though even at this side of the Atlantic, upon their arrival, they found persecution everywhere armed with the implements of torture, inflicting pain and death under the pretext of piety, they ventured to introduce a milder, a better, a more Christian like principle; that of genuine religious liberty, which though it declares that truth is single, that religious indifference is criminal in the eye of God, and that religious error wilfully entertained is destructive to the soul; yet also proclaims that the Saviour has not commanded his gospel to be disseminated by violence, and therefore they enacted, that within their borders, all other Christians should securely repose in the enjoyment of all their civil and political rights, though they were in religious error. If our brethren of other denominations have, since that period, adopted the principle, and now cherish it, they will not be displeased at our gratification that it emanated from the body to which we belong, and at our inculcating upon you, to preserve the same spirit that those good men manifested not only in our civil and political, but also in your social relations with your separated brethren.

"Therefore stand fast, and hold the traditions which you have learned, whether by word or by epistle." "Pray for us, that the word of God may run, and may be glorified even as among you: for we have confidence in the Lord concerning you that the things which we command, you will do: and the Lord direct your hearts in the charity of God and the patience of Christ." "For the rest, beloved children, whatsoever things are true, whatsoever things are modest, whatsoever things are just, whatsoever holy, whatsoever amiable, whatsoever of good repute, if there be any virtue, if any praise of discipline, think on these things."— "The things which you have both learned and received· and heard and seen, these do ye, and the God of peace be with you." "And the peace of God, which surpasseth all understanding, keep your hearts and minds in Christ Jesus."

Given in Council, at Baltimore, this 17th day of October, in the year of our Lord, 1829.

✝JAMES, *Archbishop of Baltimore.*

✝BENEDICT JOSEPH, *Bishop of Bardstown.*

✝JOHN, *Bishop of Charleston and V. G. of East Florida.*

✝EDWARD, *Bishop of Cincinnati.*

✝JOSEPH, *Bishop of St. Louis and Adminr. of New Orleans.*

✝BENEDICT JOSEPH, *Bishop of Boston.*

✝WILLIAM MATTHEWS, *V. A. and Administrator of Philadelphia.*

EDWARD DAMPHOUX, D.D., *Secretary.*

CHAPTER III

THE PASTORAL LETTER TO THE CLERGY (1829)

THERE is no gainsaying the fact that in the decrees of the Council of 1829 the clergy of the Province of Baltimore were especially considered. To quote the significant words of one commentator, "things were generally in a loose state, many unworthy priests who had been sent out of Europe taking up their abode in various places, either without authorization of the spiritual rulers or else on false pretenses, and thus creating scandal among the community at large. There were few native priests; most of them came from foreign parts; and in this another drawback lay." [1]

The Pastoral Letter to the Clergy was written by Bishop John England, after a special committee of bishops had selected the topics which were to be discussed in this important document. At the opening of the Council (October 4, 1829), the hierarchy of the United States consisted of the metropolitan of Baltimore, with six suffragan Bishops; outside the Baltimore Province were three bishoprics subject directly to Rome—New Orleans, St. Louis, and the Vicariate of Alabama-Florida. The First Provincial Council of Baltimore was the most imposing of all ecclesiastical assemblies in the American Church up to that time. It marks the beginning of a better knowledge of the entire Church of the country on the part of the prelates, and it gave to Catholicism in the Republic a dignity in the eyes of non-Catholics which up to that period it had not enjoyed.

THE PASTORAL LETTER TO THE CLERGY

(First Provincial Council of Baltimore)

The Archbishop of Baltimore, and the other prelates of the United States of America, in Council assembled, to their very reverend and reverend co-operators and Brethren in Christ, the Clergy of the Roman Catholic Church in the same States: Health and Blessing. Grace be to you, and peace from God our Father and the Lord Jesus Christ, in the unity of the Holy Ghost.

[1] McELRONE, "The Councils of Baltimore," in the *Memorial Volume of the Third Plenary Council of Baltimore*, p. 33. Baltimore, 1885.

DEARLY BELOVED,

Following the ancient usage of the Church, after beseeching the aid of the Father of Lights, we have considered those things which appeared to us necessary to be regulated in the present state of our discipline. Whilst performing this sacred duty, we have endeavoured, under the hope of being guided by "him who chiefly loves equity, not to be disturbers of justice;" and have taken counsel, so that we might not be misled by ignorance, or drawn aside by favour; nor has any temptation to do wrong been cast in our way. Our Conferences have been in charity and kindness, with that mutual reverence which the sacred institutions of the Son of God demand; especially for those whom, because of his goodness, not of their deserts, he vouchsafes to elevate to the station of successors of the apostles, whom "the Holy Ghost hath placed Bishops to govern the Church of God, which he hath acquired with his blood." We have transmitted to our Holy Father the decrees and regulations that we have thus formed, so that being made perfect by the authority of Peter, they may be to ourselves and to you, beloved brethren, the correct rules of orderly demeanour, which, we trust, you will cheerfully unite with us in observing. We have addressed in the spirit of affection the laity entrusted to our charge: allow us in the solicitude of those tender attachments to express our feelings and wishes to you, the co-operators in our ministry, the ambassadors of Christ, the dispensers of the mysteries of God. We most urgently entreat you not only to continue to walk as you have hitherto done, but to make even greater exertions, so that you may, through the merits of Christ our Redeemer, not only procure your own salvation but that of many others whose souls are entrusted to your care, and for whom you must render an account before angels and men at the tribunal of that Judge, in whose presence even they by whom he was surrounded have been found imperfect.

"You are the light of the world," the lustre of your example must irradiate its obscurity, and alas! how many are they who sit "in darkness and in the shadow of death." He by whom you have been sent, came to enlighten the world, and communicating to his apostles his strength, his power

and his charity in tongues of fire, through their successors
the sacred flame has alighted upon your head in ordination:
to you therefore he specially addresses
himself, that your light may so shine before   **The Clergy**
men that they may see your good works,   **the Light**
and glorify your father who is in Heaven.   **of the World.**
How glorious is your vocation! How ele-
vated your dignity! How important your duties! How
awful your responsibility!

The world tends to corruption, "you are the salt" by
which it must be preserved from putrescence; but if you
"lose your savour" wherewith shall it be preserved? Its
loss is a natural consequence; and if you become worthless
you are doomed to be "cast out and trodden under foot."
It is not said, if you become corrupt, but if you lose your
savour. You are aware, beloved brethren, that the faults
which are trivial in the layman are crimes in the priest:
and that, as your place is higher, so are the virtues which
a God of justice demands from you of a far superior grade
to those required from a layman. It is then, brethren, our
duty and yours to aim at being "the light of the world,"
and "the salt of the earth." "Be you perfect as your
Heavenly Father is perfect."

We need scarcely remind you, reverend brethren, that
your perfection will be found in being fully animated by
the spirit of your holy state. For all men,
because of our weakness and corruption,   **Sacerdotal**
prayer is essential that "through grace we   **Perfection.**
might obtain seasonable aid;" but for us
it is more especially necessary. We are called upon to be
pure and holy in the midst of profanity and vice; the
apostle admonishes us, that evil communication corrupts
good morals, and the examples which are so fearfully exhibited in the sacred records shew us but too plainly, the
piety of David, the wisdom of Solomon and the strength of
Samson, yielding to the influence of sin. How many similar instances might we not easily adduce to confirm more
fully in our minds the conviction of that admirable charge,
"let him that standeth beware lest he fall?" We cannot depart from this pestilential region in which the duty that we

owe to God detains us, but upon the mountain of prayer
we may occasionally breathe a purer atmosphere; there we
may expose the wounds of our heart to the loving physician
of our souls; there we may be renewed in spirit, and invigorated when we shall have been healed; thence we may
bring down to others the means of their spiritual health
and everlasting salvation.

How often, beloved brethren, have we not been disheartened at the little progress which we make in bringing
souls to God? "All night we have laboured and we have
taken nothing." Talent was not wanting, information had
enriched the mind, truth was on our side, circumstances
appeared favourable, and yet we have been unsuccessful;
our people were obdurate, and our prospects were un-
promising. The mystery admits of easy solution. It is
ours to plant, it is ours to water, but it belongs to God to
give the increase: our reliance was too much upon our own
sufficiency: too little upon his power! Have we not often
beheld him select weak humility to confound strong pride?
"that no flesh should glory in his sight." Ask of him earnestly in prayer and you shall receive, and then when you
give to him the glory, your joy will be complete. Or, if for a
time he should withhold the expected fruit, he will console
you when he will speak to your heart and teach you perfect
resignation to his will.

Alas! how often has it happened that he whom the world
admired and applauded, upon whose lips men hung with
delight, and whose deeds were exhibited
as the great results of combined wisdom
and energy and zeal, was lost in these external occupations, became estranged from
converse with his God, was filled with the vanity that is too
often the sad result of human praise, and continuing from
habit, and with imperfect motives, what he had begun in
the spirit of true love for his Redeemer, lost all relish for
interior piety, and became mere sounding brass! Brethren,
it is only by the spirit of prayer you can be preserved from
this worst calamity. It is only by prayer that you can obtain light from above, to discern between leprosy and leprosy, in that tribunal where you are made the judges of

**The Spirit
of Prayer.**

souls, and commissioned to restore, by your authoritative
sentence, the lonely one which had been separated from
the holy fellowship of the children of God, to the communion of the just and the participation of the Body of
Christ. True repentance comes from God alone, and too
often is there a deceitful semblance which misleads not only
the inattentive observer, but even the sinner himself, and
the judge who has not, by intimate conversation with the
father of spirits, learned to discriminate the characteristics
of a penitent made worthy of his affection. How dreadful
if the habit results from the ignorance of that priest
who is not a man of prayer! dearly beloved, be instant in
prayer, that you may avoid the cause of your own ruin
and that of those for whom the precious blood of the Redeemer has been so copiously shed. Too often have the
great and salutary maxims of Christian morality given way
to a destructive expediency, which attempts to reconcile the
spirit of the gospel to the bad practices of the world: too
often has human respect been insensibly submitted to by
him, who as the herald of heaven, ought to stand to his post
with the firmness of an archangel. The self-love which we
cherish, has dreaded the reproach of our conscience should
we require others to be more perfect than we felt we were
ourselves; and thus because of the neglect of prayer, the
mounds which had been erected to avert the progress of immorality were permitted to decay, and virtue was swept
from those gardens in which it had been so successfully cultivated. In vain did the eye seek refreshment, and the
fragrance which once delighted us was no more. If the
priest be a man of prayer, when he mixes with his flock
he will bring amongst them the maxims, the spirit, and the
blessing of that God with whom he converses; but, if he be
negligent in the discharge of this great duty, his disappointed
people will undervalue his calling, he will perceive their
want of attention, and he will study their habits and amusements, that, by joining in them, he may become acceptable
to them. He is no longer the messenger of heaven; his profession is an inconsistency, and the interests of religion suffer, even from his very advocacy itself.

If you desire then to be useful to your people, you must

endeavour to unite in yourselves the qualities of Moses and Josue. When the Amalecite approaches, you must lift your hands in prayer upon the mountain ere you go down into the plain to combat. You are mediators between God and his people; when his wrath is enkindled, you must, like Aaron, instantly seize upon the censer and rush between the living and the dead, that, your prayers ascending with a sweet odour, from the warm affection of your burning hearts, he may be appeased because of the merits of his son, whose representatives you are. It is true that, because of your other avocations, you cannot devote large portions of your time continually to this most important of your obligations. But in reciting the Psalms and other portions of scripture, which the church requires of you daily to read in your office, you can be filled with the spirit which they contain; and besides your morning and evening devotions, you can retire at intervals during the day, for a few moments, to converse with God, and keep yourselves always in his presence, sending forth your ejaculations as you call to mind your own weakness and his perfections, your solemn obligations and his justice and mercy.

Brethren, no man can make progress in virtue without strict examination of his conscience, and intimate conversation with heaven. The carnal man is con-

Meditation.   versant with external objects, the spiritual man studies his own interior, and as it were carries his soul in his hands, always subject to his inspection. It was said to the Levites of old, "be you cleansed who carry the vessels of the Lord." You bear about with you more than the vessels. "Blessed are the clean of heart for they shall see God," was the declaration of the Saviour. It is your duty to see God, and to converse with him for the advantage of his people; it is your duty, when forgetful of his law they proclaim a festival for passion and excite his anger, to cast yourselves at his feet upon the mountain, to avert his wrath even before you descend to reprove them for their criminality. Your hearts must be clean that your prayer may be efficacious. Unfortunately, you dwell in the midst of contamination, you should, therefore, be perpetually vigilant, that by the tear of penance and

the blood of the Lamb, you may immediately wash away
the soil to which you are occasionally liable; you are well
aware that whilst it remains it penetrates, and stains more
deeply; hence it is of the utmost importance to have it instantly discovered and rapidly removed. Watch, therefore,
that you enter not into temptation, and devote at least some
portion of your morning to that most necessary duty of
meditation. You will thus sanctify yourselves and those entrusted to your charge. You have been trained up in this
way, but, beloved brethren, you will excuse us if we express
our apprehension that some amongst you have been insensibly drawn by worldly habits into a fatal neglect.

You are the instructors of your people; if their eye be
darkened, how shall they see? "If the blind lead the blind,
they shall both fall into the pit and perish
together;" and how many dangerous prec-   **Reading the**
ipices lie along the narrow way that leads   **Scriptures.**
to Heaven! If you walk carefully in the
footsteps of the saints who have preceded you, your journey
will be in security; if you attend to the instructions of the
spouse of Christ you cannot mistake your path; you should
therefore seek daily to extend your knowledge, that you
may improve your people: the field which lies before you
is immense, the wealth of ages is spread upon its surface,
and it is moreover enriched with the treasures of Heaven.
The sacred volume of the Scriptures should be to you as
the rolled book was to Ezechiel; you should eat it before
you go to speak to the children of Israel. When you approach to partake thereof, it will be to you sweet as honey
in your mouth; you shall be filled; from the fulness of your
heart your words will proceed, your discourses will not be
in the expressions of human wisdom but in the power of
God; and the word which is thus sent forth, will not return
without fruit. To those who are negligent or arrogant, on
this head, the same book is like to the flying volume of
Zacharias; it is a curse that goeth forth over the face of the
earth for judgment and destruction. Seek then in this
sacred place to learn what, from the days of the Apostles,
our Holy Mother the Church has held and preserved as genuine interpretation of those passages which so many of the

learned and unlearned and unstable wrest to their own perdition. Be intimately conversant therewith; for the lips of
the priest should keep knowledge; the people seek the law
at his mouth, "because he is the Angel of the Lord of hosts."
Wo to them who because of their ignorance would cause
persons to stumble at the law; they make void the covenant;
not only are they contemptible and base before the people,
but they have a dreadful account to render at the bar of
divine justice.

Brethren, we entreat of you, not to be taken in the delusive snare which has entangled several, who, leaving the
law and the gospel, have wasted their time
Preaching.   and destroyed their usefulness by indulg-
ing in the study of vain and frivolous
ephemeral productions, under the pretext of acquiring a
pleasing style. The truths of religion should be delivered
in becoming language, but it is a sad mistake to leave the
substance in order to acquire the appearance: and we fear
that in general this disposition evinces rather a dissipation
of mind than a zeal for improvement: we should hope that
it never springs from the unholy ambition of exhibiting the
individual for human applause rather than of preaching
the doctrines of a crucified Redeemer.

We would not be understood as disposed to restrain our
brethren from the pursuit of useful human science, which
might be so often turned to the advantage of religion, as the
blending of various rays gives the purest light; but we would
impress upon their minds the superior excellence of that
which God has taught over that which man acquires: thus
whilst we urge a decided preference we are far from insisting upon an exclusive occupation. It becomes our character
always to read for information, never for amusement.

They who sometimes complain of the want of leisure for
study, are frequently found at a loss for employment; they
are not unusually found spending hours
Study.   together in unprofitable conversations, and
even sometimes engaged in mere worldly
concerns. It is true that there are not many amongst us,
beloved brethren, against whom such a charge can be made
with propriety; but it would greatly console us if not one

could be discovered who so far forgot the dignity of his place and the extent of his obligation. No large stock of books is requisite; a very few will answer; but those few should be in perpetual use. The doctrines of faith, the great principles of morality, the history of the Church, the admonitions of the holy Bible, a few volumes which would aid in your own spiritual improvement, by example and reflection, this would suffice, and this every one could procure. An intimate acquaintance with the meaning of our instructive ceremonials, and the force of our admirable liturgy, would be at once deep lessons of admonition to the priest, and of sublime and beautiful and impressive instruction to the people, who are too often left to behold without edification that which was constructed to convey to the mind of the flock, the doctrines, the history, and the efficacy of religion, as well as the dispositions which should animate them at our public offices. We entreat you, brethren, to give heed to those important concerns.

When we entered upon our holy state, we renounced the prospects of worldly gain and the claim to worldly enjoyment; we took the Lord for our inheritance, and looked for our reward in a bet- **The Priesthood.**
ter world; we undertook to protect with
inviolable fidelity the interests of religion, when the mystic keys under which the deposit was kept were placed in our hands. When we were privileged to stand in an elevated place in the Church, to instruct the faithful, the solemn monition was given to us that our exaltation was for example, not for domination; it was expected that after we had by divine aid expelled the enemy of God from our own souls, we should succeed in dispossessing others by the influences of our conduct and the efficacy of prayer; when we were told to let our light so shine before men that they may see our good works and glorify our Father who is in Heaven; we were admonished to walk as children of light, and informed that the fruit of light is in all goodness and justice and truth. At a more solemn moment of our devotion, when the sacred vessels were placed in our hands, we were charged to have the altar of the living God decorated with the purity of virtue, so that the beholders might

be enamoured with the beauty of the house of the Lord. Raised to the levitical rank and becoming incorporated with that lovely tribe of which the heroic Stephen was the precious ornament, it was committed to us to bear and watch the tabernacle in the holy attire of virtue, proclaiming the precepts of the Gospel whilst we ourselves were models of their observance, so that by the exhibition of our spiritual cleanliness, splendour, purity and charity, we might be fitted to occupy the station of the active vanguard of the sacred host, and the joyous multitude should be excited to declare, that blessed are the feet of those announcing the Gospel of good things. On a more awful day, we pledged ourselves to have profound respect for our own station, and whilst we were authorised to shew forth the death of the Lord until his second coming, we undertook to mortify ourselves, that being made like to Christ in death, we may be raised with him to a more perfect life and assimilated in permanent glory. To attain this we promised that our doctrine should be a spiritual medicine for the people of God, the sweet odour of our life the delight of the Church of Christ, and that we would, by the grace of the Holy Ghost, by word and deed build up with an holy people the living temple of the eternal God. Thus, brethren, are you segregated from the laity, and made to appear within the sanctuary robed in that ancient and mysterious vesture which testifies the origin of our Church, the facts which we commemorate, and the many virtues of which you should be the bright examples. Surely, you need not our exhortation, when the wisdom of our institutions thus inculcates upon your memory the bonds which you have given, and the absolute claim which God and his people have so firmly established against you, for a virtuous life and conduct not only without reproach but above suspicion.

You are the ministers of the sacraments whose efficacy, it is true, is derived not from your virtue, but from the power of God, the merits of the Saviour, **Ministry of the** the institution of Christ, the influence of **Sacraments.** the Holy Ghost and the dispositions of those who receive them. But you are well aware that those dispositions are more or less excited as

your conduct is more or less beneficially influential. **Does
not your zeal, beloved brethren, urge you powerfully to
increase the blessings of your people?** Alas! how has it
sometimes happened that they who hesitated between duty
and temptation, have been determined to neglect, by the
tepidity, by the worldly spirit, by the mere want of conformity between his appearance and his station in the pastor.
We do not here allude to absolute scandal, nor to gross
neglect, nor even a disposition to vice or irregularity, nor
yet to such a dereliction of duty as would deserve our official
reprimand. We merely advert to the want of that influence
which is naturally created by the presence of a man whose
correct demeanour proclaims that he is a priest of God.
When you look around you, beloved brethren, you will
agree with us and with all those who have narrowly in-
spected our concerns in all places and ages, that the example of a pious and zealous clergyman though of limited
attainments is a richer treasure to the Church, than talents
and learning and eloquence united. When Samuel reviewed
the children of Isai, the voice of the Lord declared, "look
not on his countenance, nor on the height of his stature, because I have rejected him, nor do I judge according to the
look of man, for man seeth those things that appear, but
the Lord beholdeth the heart."[1] It is some humble one
whom the mighty overlook, but who is fiilled with the
spirit of his state, that God frequently chooses to go forth
against the blasphemer before whom the stoutest warriors
have quailed, though unprovided with sword or spear or
shield, yet to triumph in the name of the Lord of hosts.

We live in the midst of a world that scrutinizes our conduct with habitual jealousy; the most perfect amongst us
are liable to have their very best actions
misconstrued, their sayings misinterpreted,   **Clerical
their motives unappreciated, and their im-   Life.**
perfections magnified and blazoned forth
to public observation. It is natural that this should be the
case, because since we are established as censors of the conduct of others, human nature urges upon them the inquiry
into our own demeanour; and that self-love whose dominion

1 1 Kings xvi. 7.

we all feel, is gratified at the discovery of what appears
to palliate the aberration of the observer. Thus they who
are most virtuous in the ministry can with difficulty escape
the remarks of the uncharitable, and the general disposition of mankind is to proclaim our faults with unsparing
assiduity. What a lesson of caution to us! What an additional motive to excite us to such vigilance, that not only
shall we have nothing of serious reproach against ourselves,
but we shall afford no semblance of ground for others to
suspect us! You must yourselves be aware of a temptation
on this head to which we are all liable. It is natural when
we are conscious of our integrity, to assert our freedom,
and to feel indisposed to yield to unnecessary restraint,
because others choose to be hypercritically censorious.
Some too will allege that a change of conduct where no
crime has been committed, would rather argue that the suspicions were well founded, than that it was a prudent concession for the public good. Generally speaking, we should
on such occasions recollect that declaration of the apostle,
"wherefore if meat scandalize my brother, I will never
eat flesh, lest I should scandalize my brother."[2]

We are led from this topick to another that fills us with
painful recollections. The Saviour declared wo to the
world because of scandals, and also foretold that, owing to the imperfection of our

Scandals.

nature and the evil propensities of the human race, scandals must come; but he denounced his wrath
against those by whose fault these evils would arise. We
trust, and are disposed to believe, reverend brethren, that
few if any of you are likely to incur this malediction; yet
we cannot forget that it was chiefly through the misconduct
of clergymen that several occasions of lamentable schism
were given in our province. How has the progress of religion been impeded! How have strife and tumult profaned
the sanctuary of the God of peace! How have we been exposed to the unpleasant observations of our fellow citizens!
How have our most sacred rights been thoughtlessly and
criminally invaded! How has the venerable spouse of the
Saviour of the world been ridiculed and insulted! How

[2] 1 Cor. viii. 13.

many criminal souls have been precluded from a return to
mercy! How many of the wavering have been thrown back
in despair! How many have been driven from the sacraments! How many of the faithful and firm have been oppressed with anguish and shame! In other days and in
other nations the crimes of the clergy have caused the degradation of the Church, the contempt of the institutions of
religion, sanctioned the vices of the laity, been the sources
of schism, and the origin of heresy. If we look over the
dark catalogue from the time of Nicholas the deacon to our
own, what a frightful accumulation is presented to the eye?
We would invite you to weep with us over this abomination!
But what would tears avail? Let us rather call upon you to
aid us in guarding our infant churches against such dreadful calamities for the time to come; and though you should
feel that we ought to be convinced, as we are, of the purity
of your intentions, the correctness of your demeanour, and
your zeal for the glory of God, yet you will acknowledge
that it is with such a clergy, and under such circumstances,
the discipline can be most easily established, that will preserve and improve those dispositions and render their effects more generally beneficial. It is from men of such
dispositions we can with great confidence require the cheerful adoption of those wholesome restraints of ecclesiastical
laws, which are more required to prevent future evils than
to remedy any that exist. It must, however, be confessed
that owing to a variety of circumstances not hitherto under
our control, our organization has not been so perfect, nor
our observances so exact, as we could desire; but with your
zealous co-operation we now expect to make considerable
progress towards a more orderly and efficient state of being.

As to your intercourse with the world; we would suggest
that you always remember that you are the ambassadors
of Christ. Let the dignity of your vocation
be made manifest in your conversation, in   **Ambassadors**
your attire, and in the becoming gravity of   **of Christ.**
your conduct. Your flocks may find suffi-
cient relaxation and amusement in their intercourse with
each other: from you they expect instruction for the service
of God, not suggestions as to the regulation of their own

temporal concerns with which you should scrupulously avoid any entanglement; from you they seek useful and attractive lessons leading to virtue, not the idle and frivolous amusements or conversations of the day, which are too often calculated to wound reputation, to disseminate scandal, to create jealousies, and to destroy that confidence, without which you cannot learn the state of that conscience which you are charged to direct; from you they derive consolation in their afflictions, and when they are disgusted with the bitterness of time, you should point out the manner in which they may attain the sweets of eternity. But, whilst you treat them with kindness and affection, you will recollect the bounds within which this affection should be contained; and be watchful that your kindness be not liable to misconstruction. In general, if you apply yourselves to attain the perfection of your state, you will be seldom abroad, and very little in society, save with those amongst whom the Saviour was generally found as a benefactor, the poor, the afflicted and the sick. We know that we need not urge upon you the solemn and indispensable obligation of the most devoted attention to your dear children, when they are about to be summoned before the tribunal, at which you must one day yourselves be arraigned, and when sloth on your part might be the cause of eternal ruin to a soul which needs all your assiduity to prepare it for the benefits to which it is entitled by the death of Christ.

Many things that may appear trivial, are to you important. The very fashion of your dress is, in the eye of the world, calculated to elevate or to depress your character, and to extend or restrict your usefulness. In almost every organised public association, such a subject is matter of regulation; the soldier who loves his profession is laudably exact in its regard; and however philosophism might speculate, every practical officer will feel that the character of the individual is generally ascertained from his appearance. You are the officers of the militia of Christ. You bear his commission. Is it possible that there can be found one amongst you who would feel disposed to conceal the dignity with which he is invested? Such a renegade would be unworthy of his place. Can he presume to seek precedence in the church who is disguised in the world? Is he ashamed of that station to which he sought, with so much earnestness, to be raised? He should be forthwith discharged to make room for one more worthy of the honour. The canons of the church equally censure the thoughtless folly or censurable vanity which is made ridiculous by its efforts to be fashionable, and the unbecoming slovenliness which degrades the dignity of the order, by the meanness of the individual; the simple cleanliness of the attire should evince the plain innocence of the wearer, and his conformity to the regulations of the church should manifest the esteem in which he holds its authority.

In the discharge of your ritual offices, especially in offering the holy sacrifice of the Mass, and the administration of the sacraments, we would intreat you always to be impressed with the recollec- **The Liturgy of** tion that you are continuing the ministry **the Church.** of reconciliation instituted and established by the Son of God himself. When you first engaged in the awful and important charge, your sentiments were of the most elevated and pious description; you felt that you were employed in the palace of the monarch of the universe; that you stood at the gate of heaven; and trembling like the patriarch upon the mountain when he consecrated his pillar, you were aware of the presence of your God. His sanctity is not diminished, but your familiarity is increased. You should be extremely careful lest this intimacy degenerate into disrespect: cherish those feelings of devotion in which you originally indulged, and as you advance in life, recollect that your example ought to be more edifying for those who look to you as their model. When you observe the exactness which God himself required from the Aaronitic priesthood in the most minute ceremonials, you must feel, that though the forms are not the essence of religion, they are useful means for its attainment and its preservation. He who smote Nadab and Abiu before the altar, permits now to live, several upon whom his lasting indignation will inflict eternal death for their disregard of the ceremonials of his church. If you have zeal for the Lord, you will love the beauty of his house, and you will be led by your

piety to enter fully into those dispositions which your holy
vestments signify, to appreciate the sublime lessons which
our rights inculcate; and your sense of charity of justice
and of responsibility will procure for your flocks that frequent explanation, without which what is presented to the
eye can seldom fully enlighten the understanding or impress the heart.

We are placed, beloved and reverend brethren, as his
substitutes on earth, by that good shepherd who laid down
his life for his sheep; he instructs us in that
parable where he exhibits the true pastor
as leaving, for the moment, those who were
obedient to his voice, that he might with
zealous anxiety, seek for that which strayed in the desert,
not to injure, not to drive, not to exhibit his anger, for he
was meek and humble, but to caress and to bring it back
upon his shoulders, and in serenity to rejoice that what had
been lost was recovered. Such too was the conduct of our
great predecessors in the ministry, the Apostles of Christ
and their successors, who bore his name before kings and
rulers and the nations of the earth: they reproved vice, but
they mildly gained upon the sinner, and powerfully drew
him to the society of the elect. Alas! brethren, how afflict-
ing would be the spectacle should we behold one of our fel-
low-labourers negligent and careless, whilst the ravagers
of the fold make incursions on every side, and bear away
thousands to destruction? Such an one might allege that
he had done all that his duty required; that he perceived
farther exertion was useless. This is not the language of a
good shepherd of souls: he considers himself to be a useless
servant after he has done not merely what a prescribed
rule would indicate as the lowest point where he ceases to
be censurable before a human tribunal, but when he has
spent himself in the service of God, and in the salvation of
those for whom he is accountable. When we contemplate
the energy of Peter, the labours of Paul, the zeal of the
sons of Zebedee, the unceasing efforts of their associates
and followers, and contrast them with our own inefficiency,
how are we humbled and put to silence! These were men
of whom the world was not worthy: its accumulated wealth

*Priestly
Zeal.*

and power had been no adequate recompence for their toils, their sacrifices and their success: they sought a more lasting inheritance, a more splendid reward; their virtuous ambition has been gratified; they have sent myriads to bliss, and God found them worthy of himself. They were slain on earth; they are crowned in Heaven. Surely brethren, it is not for the perishable things of this world that you labour. You are intent upon fulfilling the duties of your high calling, in accordance with the institutions of him who sent forth our great forerunners, telling them to go without scrip or bread or money; and yet they were so aided by him, whose hand feeds all his creatures, that they wanted nothing. Brethren, we have no cause to suspect you of avarice which is the root of evil; but blame us not, if we still exhort you, that in the performance of your duties you seek rather the souls of your people than their contributions. And we remind those who are by far the greater number of our associates, those who feel the difficulties of very limited means, that they are thus assimilated to our Redeemer himself, to him who lived in poverty, declaring that the birds of the air had nests, and the foxes had dens, but he had not a place wherein to lay his head; they may also feel another consolation, for they can declare, as he did, that through them the gospel is preached to the poor. In their ministry, there is little room for an unholy ambition, little excitement to vanity, little danger of human respect: they are not tempted to destroy the spirit of the gospel in the effort to conciliate the rich and the powerful by basely reconciling to its letter that very conduct which it has written to condemn. Their station is obscure in the eye of the world, but in the sight of angels it is most honourable; they walk in the valleys of life, there is less danger of their stumbling over those precipices with which the more elevated paths abound; their way is more plain and more secure, and theirs is the road through which the great majority of those who now reign in Heaven have unostentatiously proceeded to their happy abode.

It will occasionally happen, beloved brethren, that temptations of another kind will prove dangerous. When we find, notwithstanding all our efforts, that no progress is made, wearied, disheartened and disgusted, we seek to change the station of our labours. We despair at our ability to stem the torrent of vice. Were our dependence upon ourselves we might well despair,—but our sufficiency is from God, in whose hands are the hearts of men; and it is not given to us to know the day nor the hour which the Father has fixed for the conversion of his children. It is our duty to plant and to water, it is his prerogative to bestow the increase—let us be assiduous in the performance of that which is ours, and leave the rest to his disposal. Did the men who converted nations succeed at once? Had they upon every similar disappointment abandoned their charge, would those nations have been Christian to-day? In general, they who sowed did not reap, but others entered into the field where they had laboured, and gathered the fruit; but this fruit could not have been produced had not he who first persevered upon a stubborn soil subdued it to cultivation. How often was it necessary that its sterility should be enriched with not only the sweat but the very blood of faithful husbandmen? You have not yet been called upon to endure unto blood.—Perhaps in the order of Providence the fruit is withheld for a time and given to another for your advantage: lest you glory as if the increase was from you and not from God. It would be a melancholy result if, whilst you opened the gates of glory to others, you should yourselves be cast forth in disgrace. Labour to remove this obstacle, in the manner that is described by the great Apostle of nations, who feared lest whilst he preached to others he should become a reprobate himself. Brethren, we have never seen a people obdurate where their pastor was truly pious; where he did not mistake a repulsive pride for superior virtue of his own; where he did not imagine that human passion was a zeal for God's honour; but in those places where zeal was regulated by discretion and charity, where the pastor was patient, vigilant, laborious, and affectionate to his people, he won their favour; he gained upon their obduracy; he secured their confidence, and was successful in bringing them to God.

Even to those who oppose you whilst you firmly adhere to those principles which it would be criminal to abandon,

be meek, be charitable, be courteous, be kind; not returning
evil for evil, not using scurrility which would be equally degrading to your characters as men and as christians, and
altogether unbecoming the ministers of God.　When they
misrepresent, correct in the calmness of conscious truth:
if they speak evil, bear it in imitation of him who did not
reprove when he was ill spoken of.　Preserve always in
yourselves the disposition to "love your enemies, to do
good to them who hate you, and to pray for them that
persecute and calumniate you, that you may be children of
your Father who is in Heaven, who makes his sun to rise
upon the good and the bad, and rains upon the just and
the unjust."　Ask your Father to forgive them, because
owing to unfortunate circumstances several of them, we are
convinced, know not what they do.　Have charity for all
men, it is the bond of peace, and one of the characteristics
of the children of God.

Of one other duty, brethren, we would affectionately but
earnestly remind you.—The solicitude for the instruction of
youth.　Continue your efforts in this most
useful and indispensable line of duty. 　　Instructing
Thus will you render comparatively light 　　the Young.
and incalculably more beneficial, the labours of yourselves and of your successors.　If the great
truths of religion be not deeply inculcated upon the youthful mind, your discourses will be scarcely intelligible to
those who will have been left untaught; they know not the
facts to which you allude; they do not appreciate the principles from which you reason; they do not feel the obligations which you enforce; your assertions appear to be unfounded, and they grow weary of hearing what they cannot
understand: you beat the air and spend yourself without
advantage.　Unless you watch over them when they are first
exposed to temptation, they will be robbed of their innocence, they will lose their horror for vice, they will be famil-
iarised with crime, and when their habits are thus formed in
early life, what prospect can you have of successfully en-
grafting virtue upon this stock of evil which has been deeply
rooted in a soil of sin?　What a task do you leave for your
successors!　What an account have you to render to the

Great Father of those children entrusted to your care! Beloved, we rejoice to behold you assiduous in the instruction of youth. O! it is a godlike, though to a man a laborious occupation; it is indeed redeeming a world, or rather, it is creating a new earth as the preparation for a new Heaven. How we do rejoice and bless God at beholding the venerable institutions of our Church springing up to your aid! Do, we entreat of you, encourage and cherish those pious souls that so meritoriously devote themselves to the instruction of children in the way of the God of truth.

Doing these things, beloved and reverend brethren, you will add to our joy; you will find in your own souls that peace which the world cannot give; you Conclusion. will save your people, you will procure honour for the Church of God. Walk steadily in that way which we have endeavoured to point out; and you cannot fail to arrive at that paradise in which the just expect you. But if you become distracted by the allurements of those who would decoy you; if you lose sight of the track in which you have been placed; if you be occupied with other cares and become regardless of the admonitions that have been so frequently repeated; if, instead of pressing forward with energy to that crown of glory which is only to be attained at the termination of your course, you seek some resting place where you may indulge yourself with worldly gratifications, your labours will have been useless, your progress unavailing, the shades of evening will descend before you expect them, night will close around you, and you will grope about, in all probability, to destruction.

May God avert so dreadful a calamity from us and from those whom we love with sincere affection. "Dearly beloved, we trust better things of you, and nearer to salvation; though thus we speak. For God is not unjust, that he should forget your work and the love which you have shown in his name, you who have ministered, and do minister to the saints. And we desire that every one of you should show forth the same carefulness to the accomplishing of hope unto the end: that you become not slothful, but followers of them who through faith and patience shall inherit the promises."³ Thus shall you "come to mount Sion and to the city of the living God, the heavenly Jerusalem, and the company of many thousands of angels, and to the church of the first born who are written in the heavens, and to God the judge of all, and to the spirits of the just made perfect, and to Jesus the mediator of the new testament," ⁴ through whom we have received grace, and from whom we expect the glory of redemption, being sprinkled and sanctified with his blood.

"The grace of our Lord Jesus Christ be with your spirit, brethren. Amen."

Given in council at Baltimore this 17th day of October, in the year of our Lord, 1829.

✝JAMES, *Archbishop of Baltimore.*

✝BENEDICT JOSEPH, *Bishop of Bardstown.*

✝JOHN, *Bishop of Charleston and V. G. of East Florida.*

✝EDWARD, *Bishop of Cincinnati.*

✝JOSEPH, *Bishop of St. Louis and Administrator of New Orleans.*

✝BENEDICT JOSEPH, *Bishop of Boston.*

WILLIAM MATTHEWS, *V. A. and Administrator of Philadelphia.*

EDWARD DAMPHOUX, D.D., *Secretary.*

3 Heb. vi. 9, 10, 11, 12.   4 Heb. xii. 22.

CHAPTER IV

THE PASTORAL LETTER OF 1833

THAT continual legislation for the Church in this country
was necessary owing to the many rapid changes which
occurred during these years, is evident from the number of
Provincial Councils held from 1829 to 1849. The first seven
Provincial Councils of Baltimore were practically, though
not formally, National Councils of the Church in the United
States. The *Acta et Decreta* of these seven Provincial Councils will be found in the collection: *Concilia Provincialia
Baltimori habita ab anno 1829 usque ad annum 1849* (Baltimore, 1853). The Council of 1829 decided that within three
years the hierarchy should meet to report upon the progress
made in unifying Church discipline in the United States. While
its public decisions are silent regarding the method of filling
vacant Sees in the American Church, there is considerable con-
temporary evidence to show that this grave problem which disturbed the peace of the Church from the days of Carroll, occupied the minds of the prelates during its private sessions. It
is not surprising, therefore, that the question was seriously
discussed when the Second Provincial Council met at Baltimore
in 1833. Under the presidency of Archbishop Whitfield, nine
bishops, whose names are signed to the pastoral of 1833, were
assembled on October 20, 1833, and deliberated for a week on
Church problems. The prelates were not unmindful of all that
the Church in the United States owed to the generosity of the
priests and people of Ireland, France, Germany and Austria;
but it was felt at the time that the days of a quasi-paternalism
of a foreign kind were passed, and that the American Church
had grown to maturity. In the third decree enacted by the
Second Council a more definite delimitation of the American
dioceses was suggested to Propaganda, and a fixed method of
selecting bishops for vacant American Sees was outlined. The
Holy See readily agreed to these important modifications.
Other decrees of the Council recommended the Jesuit missions
among the Indians of the Far West, the erection of diocesan
seminaries, and the creation of a more efficient Catholic pa-

rochial school system. A committee was also appointed to inquire into the textbooks then in use in the American schools, which contained erroneous views on matters of Catholic faith and discipline.

The Pastoral Letter of 1833 is a mirror in which we can easily read the status of Catholic life at the time. The bishops deplored especially the want of priests and the lack of sufficient churches for the rapidly increasing body of the faithful. They exhorted all who could not hear Mass on Sundays and holydays to meet together for prayer and catechetical instruction. They appealed in particular to their flocks not to lose courage in the face of the vicious attacks upon the faith which unfortunately were prevalent at the time. Catholic Emancipation in the British Isles had evoked much hostile comment in England and in the United States, and a steadily increasing current of anti-Catholic feeling, as Shea has written, "was gaining ground steadily and becoming, though no one seemed to comprehend the fact, a menace to the peace and harmony of the country." The Fathers of the Council foresaw the danger and embodied in their Pastoral a stirring appeal to the faithful to be patient and courageous in the crisis. The following reprint is taken from the *New York Weekly Register* of 1833.[1]

THE PASTORAL LETTER OF 1833

(*Second Provincial Council of Baltimore*)

Reverend Brethren of the Clergy and beloved of the Laity:
Grace be to you and peace, from God our Father, and
from the Lord Jesus Christ.

DESIROUS of fulfilling our duty in your regard, by consulting how provision might be made for the wants of our infant churches, how discipline might be promoted, and how faith might be secured, we have, under the sanction of ancient and Apostolic usage, and in accordance with the spirit of the canons, assembled to deliberate. In the performance of this duty we sought the divine aid, through the promise of Him who declared that where two or three were assembled in His name, He would be in the midst of them; and Who encouraged us moreover by the assurance, that He

1 Vol. I., pp. 130-131, 162-163, 177-178.

would not leave in orphanage those who, however unworthy they might be, had been commissioned to be ambassadors to testify to His doctrine, ministers to dispense His sacraments, and bishops placed by the Holy Ghost in the weighty charge of governing that Church which had been purchased by the blood of an incarnate God.

We have submitted to the See of Peter, the centre of the Catholic unity, that Church, to which, because of its superior presidency, every other of those spread through the world should have recourse, the results of our deliberations; that if conformable to the faith and general discipline of the Church, those portions upon which we are competent to legislate might receive their perfection by the acquiescence of the Holy Father; and that he might, at our request, be induced to interpose the authority of the Apostolic See for the performance of what is beyond our office to effect. But we cannot separate, without addressing to you, our glory and our joy, some words of admonition as the token of our affection, the evidence of our solicitude, and the fulfilment of our duty.

Beloved brethren, "what will it profit a man to gain the whole world, if he lose his own soul?"—When the eye is closed by death, the riches of the world are valueless as the dust of its surface; its enjoyments cease to gratify, its honours are but empty names, the object of its children's ambition have disappeared like so many floating bubbles which enchanted the eye, but perished in the grasp; the simpleton and the beggar walk over the graves of the philosopher and the monarch. "What then doth pride profit us, or what advantage doth the boasting of riches bring?" We pass along like the bird swiftly going through the air which closes upon his track; and in vain you seek for the path in which he moved. Our journey is to the portal of the tomb; beyond which there opens the expansion of eternity. "There the just shall live for evermore: and their reward is with the Lord, and the care of them with the Most High." "It shall go well" then "with him that feareth the Lord; and in the days of his end shall he be blessed."— Even upon this earth "the fear of the Lord is honour and

The Meaning of Life.

glory and gladness, and a crown of joy. The fear of the Lord shall delight the heart, and shall give joy and gladness and length of days."

They who are wise, then, seek by the affectionate fear of the Lord to serve him upon earth, that they may attain his enjoyment in Heaven. To save our souls, through the merits of our Blessed Redeemer, should be our great object. In this we are all deeply interested; it is indeed the only thing necessary, for again, beloved brethren, we ask, "What will it profit a man to gain the whole world, if he lose his own soul?" In our several stations this should be our common effort, as it is our common concern. And it is the special obligation of your bishops, as you know, entreating and comforting you (as a father doeth his children) to testify to every one of you that you should walk worthy of God who hath called you to his kingdom and glory, that thus they may contribute to feed the flock of God which is amongst them, taking care thereof, not by constraint, but willingly according to God: neither for the sake of filthy lucre, but voluntarily: neither as domineering over the clergy, but as being made a pattern of the flock from the heart. And this, indeed, we daily entreat of God to enable us to perform, and we beseech you that by your prayers at the throne of grace, you would make intercession in our behalf.

You are aware that as in the first Adam we all fell, so in the second Adam (Jesus Christ) we must be redeemed; and that this bountiful Saviour so copiously poured forth his favours, as that where sin abounded, grace abounded more. Hence, though by prevarication of our first father our understanding was darkened, so that various impediments arose to render the discovery of the truth difficult; our will was weakened by a serious diminution of its energy, and our affections greatly inclined to evil, so that a sort of predisposition thereto exists within us, and the power of the tempter was greatly enlarged; still when the Orient, foretold by the prophet whose tongue was loosed, beamed upon those who sat in darkness and in the shadow of death, the minds of the multitude were enlightened by the splendour of faith; their will received a mighty accession of

energy, and, cheered by invigorating warmth, their affections began to glow with the ardour of heavenly love; not
only did virtue and wisdom now appear to them arrayed in
the beauty of heaven, but the hearts of the beholders were
attracted towards them by the purest emotions of admiration
and attachment. The head of the serpent had also been
crushed by the seed of that woman, for whose heel he had
lain in wait, and a bright stream of celestial light marked
through the dark and immense chaos which intervened
between the heaven and the earth, that way which had been
opened by him who having ransomed us by his blood, rose
from his tomb like a giant refreshed by sleep, and arraying
himself in that splendour which was his before the morning
of creation, led the first saints from their detention below,
to their seats of glory above.

It is unnecessary for us to remind you that it is only by
the merits of your Saviour, through the mercy of your God,
this heavenly bliss can be attained. His
grace is not a natural aid, which merely
increases the energies that were yours by
reason of your creation: neither have you
any natural claim or inherent right thereto; nor when he
bestows his favours are we left without the power of resistance and rejection. If he spreads the light of faith around
the understanding; yet, alas! how many are there who close
the eye and will not be illuminated! They are wedded to
peculiar and favorite opinions, they are attached to friends
they love the honours, and the applause, and the pleasures
of the world; they are too proud to avow that they have
been misled or that they have been mistaken. The day is
clear, and the objects are plainly set in their view, but they
either will not behold them, or they only seek for imperfections, and thus, though there is no want of evidence, there
is no disposition to believe. In this case the illustration
which the Almighty gives, is by an influence above the force
of nature; the resistance is from the depravity of the human
heart, consequent to the fall of our first parents. The influence of God is perceived in the suggestions that urge the will
to determine upon embracing the truth, but the freedom of
man is evinced by the resistance which prevents that de-

**Supernatural
Grace.**

termination. The affections are drawn by the influence of
the Creator towards what he has plainly exhibited; but the
creature, too frequently, after struggles of no small trial,
preserves the attachments which impede its progress. The
supernatural influence of heaven is sufficient to lead us
unto justification; if the being upon whom it is exerted
would correspond therewith, this aid bestowed by reason
of the merits of Jesus Christ is accordingly great; yet, though
bountifully given, it does not overwhelm or destroy the
freedom of the agent. It is the free gift of heaven bestowed
gratuitously upon us, and therefore it is grace. Without
it we can do nothing meritorious of heaven, for the Saviour
declared, "As the branch cannot bear fruit of itself unless
it abide in the vine; so neither can you unless you abide in
me."[2]

Beware, then, my beloved brethren, that you receive not
the grace of God in vain. We exhort you not only to correspond faithfully with that which is thus
every day bestowed, and upon every one;   **Prayer and**
but that you would moreover, use your best   **Supplication.**
exertions to induce your Merciful Father
to pour it forth more abundantly upon you. And for this
purpose we indicate those means which the Saviour has
pointed out or instituted as the most efficacious. Prayer is
one of the most obvious, as it is the most useful. Be you
therefore instant in prayer. Be not weary of supplication.
Recollect how, whilst Moses lifted up his hands upon the
mountain to intreat the God of his fathers, Israel prevailed
against Amelec upon the plain; but if the intercessor through
weariness permitted his arm to fall, then immediately the
ranks of his people were broken, and the enemy became
victorious. "Elias was a man passable unto us: and with
prayer he prayed it might not rain upon the earth; and it
rained not for three years and six months. And he prayed
again: and the heavens gave rain, and the earth yielded
her fruit."—The Saviour, exhorting us to pray, assured us,
"Whatsoever you shall ask in my name, that will I do."
But we too frequently seem to forget that God is a spirit
who seeketh true adorers that shall worship him in spirit

2 John xv. 4.

and in truth. The mere motion of the lips is not prayer; the mere repetition of the form is useless, unless the sentiments expressed by the mouth be also entertained by the soul. The best figure of acceptable prayer is presented to us in the ancient divine institution of the incense burned morning and evening to accompany the oblation of the lamb. If our hearts be purified from sin, and like the imperishable wood of which the altar was built, they be free from corruption; if they be enriched with virtue as that altar was covered with gold; if they have burning within them the fire of divine love; then will our prayers ascend to heaven like the smoke of the incense consumed in that fire; angels will present our aspirations morning and evening, together with the offering of that lamb that was slain for our iniquities, and by whose death we were healed! and the benedictions of heaven will descend upon us in return. From his mercy-seat the Lord himself will show us the brightness of his approbation; his truth shall compass us with a shield; our assailants shall fall at the right hand and the left; no evil shall come to us, nor shall the scourge approach our dwelling.

Instruction regarding the duties we owe to God, and the necessity of working out our salvation, is all important. Various means of information present themselves to you. For our brethren in the ministry, the continual study of the Holy Bible is absolutely of obligation; we need not, we are convinced, remind them of the repeated injunctions of the sacred canons, of the frequent admonitions of the eminent saints and sages, the glorious men of erudition, the zealous prelates, and so many others of every degree in the Church of God, who have so earnestly inculcated the necessity of this study which St. Paul so highly commended in Timothy. The people seek the law from the lips of the priest, and how shall he communicate that with which he has not been intimately conversant? The meaning of this sacred volume has been too frequently perverted; for in it are "some things hard to be understood, which the unlearned and unstable wrest to their own perdition." We know not that it is the word of God, except by the testimony

The Sacred Scriptures.

of that cloud of holy witnesses which the Saviour vouchsafed to established as our guide through this desert over
which we journey towards our permanent abode. Together
with the book they gave to us the testimony of its meaning; and this explanation no man has power to change.
The doctrines of faith are the testimony of heaven, and that
testimony is unchangeable. "Jesus Christ is yesterday, today, and for ever the same;" these doctrines cannot vary
with the mutations of fashion, the progress of science, the
modifications of government, or the caprices of age. "God
is not as a man that he should lie, nor as the son of man
that he should be changed." The progress of science and the
improvements arising from human experience, are evidences at once, of the imperfection and of the powers of the
mind which remedies former defects by subsequent information. The testimony of God is the communication of a
being infinitely perfect, unsusceptible of improvement, in-
capable of change: from eternity he has seen all things
through all their gradations of existence, and his resolution
stands, unchanging, and is available for eternity; all things
else may vary, but his declarations are unalterably perfect;
hence the Apostle of the Corinthians reminds them that the
preaching of himself and of Silvanus and Timothy was not
"It is and it is not, but it is," for revealed truth could not be
contradictory, but must be consistent. Upon the same principles he informs the Galatians, "though we, or an angel
from heaven, preach a gospel to you besides that we have
preached to you, let him be anathema," because truth is essentially irreformable, and the declarations of God are essentially true. Thus the recorded testimony of those ancient
and venerable witnesses, who in every nation and every age,
proclaimed in the name of the Catholic Church, and with
its approbation, the interpretation of the Holy Bible,
whether they were assembled in their councils or dispersed over the surface of the Christian world, is an harmonious collection of pure light, which sheds upon the inspired page the mild lustre which renders it pleasing to the
eye, grateful to the understanding, and consoling to the
heart. By thus learning the true sense and meaning of the
divine writings, Reverend and learned brethren, you will

"keep that committed to your truth, avoiding the profane novelties of words, and oppositions of knowledge falsely so called;" you will "shun profane and vain speeches; for they grow much towards impiety;" you will be easily distinguished from those who are "always learning and never attaining to the knowledge of truth;" you will "continue in the things you have learned, and which have been committed to you;" you will "hold the form of sound words," which you have heard from *us and from our predecessors* in the faith, and in the love of Christ Jesus.

To you, our brethren of the laity, we would recommend frequent perusal of the same books of instruction according to your opportunities, capacities, and dispositions, always, however, in the spirit of humble, docile desire of being led by the spirit of truth into the way of piety, avoiding "vain talk, not desiring to be teachers of the law," when too often you might become like others described by the Apostle, "understanding neither the things they say, nor whereof they affirm." "Not contending in words, for it is to no profit, but to the subversion of the hearers." Be constant at preaching and the other instruction in your churches; sustain, as far as your means will permit, those publications, whether periodical or otherwise, which are calculated to explain our doctrines, to protect our feelings, and to increase our devotion. We rejoice to find that their number is rapidly increasing, and we trust to your zeal, your piety and your liberality, to encourage their publishers by your patronage, and to profit yourselves by their perusal.

Beloved and reverend brethren, our co-operators in the work of ministry, we would, in the sincerity of our affection, address to you, in particular, those words of the Apostle to Timothy: "Meditate upon these things; be wholly in these things; that your proficiency may be made manifest to all. Attend to yourselves, and to doctrines; be earnest in them, for in doing this you shall save both yourselves and those who hear you." There is not a topic upon which we would more willingly dwell, nor a duty

Spiritual Reading.

Exhortation to the Clergy.

which we would more earnestly urge upon your solemn
and deliberate consideration, than that of meditation upon
the great truths which are developed in the books to which
we have called your attention.—Perhaps we might without
rashness assert that your own salvation and that of the people committed to your charge, depend altogether upon the
mode in which this great duty is performed by yourselves.
—This is the mountain to which the Lord invites you to holy
conference; here, within a cloud, which the eye of the multitude cannot penetrate, he converses with you familiarly as
one friend is wont to speak with another. Removed from the
distractions of the world, elevated above its concerns, though
your feet still rest upon the earth, your mind already soars
into the heavens; you review your imperfections with ease,
at leisure; you discover the sources and the occasions of
your faults; you become acquainted with their appropriate
remedies, or you take the necessary precautions against
relapse; you become conscious of your weakness and inefficiency; you learn humility when you behold yourselves;
you are brought to a reliance upon your God, whose mercy
is equal to his might: you are sustained by his power, you
are purified by his goodness, you receive from his hand the
lessons by which your people are to profit, and you descend
amongst them radiant with the splendour of that virtue
which, derived from him, now shines from you. Do not,
beloved brethren, we entreat you, do not permit any seeming necessity to urge you to lay aside this holy practice to
which you have been trained up in the days of your preparation for orders, and in which it was expected you would
continue to make progress as you advanced in life. We believe that half an hour or an hour devoted to this exercise
in the morning, will cause you to enter with a proper spirit
upon the performance of the other duties of the day; it is
not only of its own nature calculated greatly to enable you
to go through them with more zeal and accuracy, but it is
well adapted to bring down the special blessings of heaven
upon everything you undertake. The worst dissipation of
time follows its neglect; a rigid adherence to its discharge
is your most profitable economy. Bear with us, then, beloved, if we seem over earnest in exhorting, in persuading,

in compelling to this most salutary, most necessary, most profitable regularity in your daily meditations. Be you in this made the pattern of your flocks, and not only will they be led to imitate your example, but you will yourselves reap the most abundant fruit in their improvement in the science of the Saints, and in the practice of virtue. No other exertion of yours, how excellent soever, can compensate for its neglect. Permit us to repeat the words of the Apostle: "Be earnest, for in this you shall save both yourselves and those who hear you."

The Sacraments, beloved brethren, have been instituted by the Saviour as the ordinary channels through which he might convey his grace to our souls. In them he has chosen the foolish things of the world that he may confound the wise: and the weak things of the world hath God chosen, that he may confound the strong: and the mean things of the world and the things that are contemptible, hath God chosen, and the things that are not, that he might destroy the things that are; "that no flesh should glory in his sight." To the simplest elements used with reference to his institution and with reliance upon his power, and the proper dispositions, he has attached effects that surpass the power of the world to produce, so that "he that glorieth may glory in the Lord."

The Grace of the Sacraments.

Many persons who will not view the Christian institutions as they really exist, imagine that the effects expected from the sacraments are those which the laws of nature would indicate. And therefore they ask: What natural connection exists between the use of water and of oil, and the remission of sins? We answer,—None whatever. The effect is not the result of any natural fitness, but the divine agency in accordance with the divine institution. When Naaman the Syrian was told by the prophet Eliseus to wash seven times in the Jordan for the cleansing of his leprosy, he was angry, and said, "I thought he would have come out to me, and standing would have invoked the name of the Lord his God, and touched with his hand the place of the leprosy, and healed me. Are not the Abana and the Pharphar rivers of Damascus better than the waters of Israel,

that I may wash in them and be made clean?" Yet, when
he did wash in the Jordan, he was healed, not because of
any natural qualities of the waters, but by the special will
of the Lord, who can cleanse without any means or by occasion any which he might choose to select. So, when the
Saviour gave sight to the man who was blind, in the way related by St. John in chapter IX., the effect was not produced
by any natural quality of the clay or the spittle or the wash-
ing: nor of their union, but by the special will of him who
formed the eye, and poured light upon it, and fitted the
soul to receive the corresponding sensation. Thus it is with
the Sacraments. They have no natural efficacy, though they
are the ordinary means instituted by the Saviour to produce in us supernatural effects. Water is poured on the
body; it is God who cleanses the soul. But as neither
Naaman nor the blind man would have been restored without having recourse to the means prescribed, so we cannot
expect the extensive graces attached to the Sacraments, unless we receive them. "Unless you eat the flesh of the Son
of Man and drink his blood, you shall not have life in you."
And in order to prove ourselves worthy for approaching
this holy Sacrament, we would have recourse to that other
established by our blessed Lord to take away iniquity,
lest it should be our ruin. When breathing upon his
Apostles, he said to them, "Receive ye the Holy Ghost:
whose sins you shall forgive, they are forgiven them; and
whose you shall retain, they are retained." The solemn precept of the church, empowered by Jesus Christ to enact
laws of discipline, which, though passed on earth, yet have
their sanction in heaven, binds you to receive both these
sacraments at or about the time of Easter; the bond is bound
upon your conscience, and though you may not be pun-
ished upon earth for its disregard, yet the transgressor shall
not escape the vengeance of the eternal God.

But, beloved brethren, our object is not to terrify by
threats those whom we would induce by persuasion and
entreaty to perform those duties which are so essential
to their welfare. We refer you to the affecting invitation
of your Redeemer: "Come to me all you that labour and
are heavily laden, and you will find rest to your souls."

From how much torture of soul, from what excruciating anguish, from how many errors of conscience, would some of our brethren be relieved, how much true peace, such as the world cannot give, such as the children of the world can never experience, would they find, if after having washed away the stains of iniquity in their penitential tears mingled with the blood of the lamb, they should, clothed in their whitened garments, accept the invitation and be seated at the great festival of the Son of God!

Thanks be to our heavenly Father: our hearts have been greatly consoled by the increasing multitude that since our last Council has on every side exhibited itself to us, pressing forward to this life-giving food. We have indeed been made joyful by the vast increase; still we have to lament the absence of numbers. Oh, that they would reduce their principles to practice! That they would feel the importance of providing for eternity! That they would follow the plain and explicit declarations of the incarnate Son of God, rather than hazard every thing upon the miserable sophistry of the deceitful world! Brethren, we openly announce to you that there is no other name under heaven in which you can be saved but by our Lord Jesus. And there is no salvation in his name but by means of his institutions, and these are principally the sacraments which he has established. We beseech, we conjure you not to continue the criminality of this neglect.

Frequent Communion.

In viewing the members of our flocks who are spread abroad over the surface of this country, and the comparatively small number of our clergy, we have been often forced to deplore the destitution of spiritual aid under which multitudes labour. God is our witness, that so far as we had the means we have endeavoured to supply the wants of our beloved children. We have not been sparing of ourselves, nor have our brethren in the priesthood been spared. Of this you, brethren, are also witnesses! but notwithstanding those efforts, the Catholic has been too frequently removed far from the voice of his pastor, far from the altar of his redeeming victim, far from the bread

The Need of Priests.

of angels, far from the other sacraments and institutions of religion. The emigrant who comes to our shores for the purpose of turning his industry to more profitable account than he could do in regions long and thickly inhabited, has wandered through our forests, our fields, our towns, and even some of our cities, in amazement at not being able to find a church in which he could worship according to the rites of his ancestors; he has left our republic in the bitterness of disappointment; or he has not unfrequently become indifferent. Others have with firm faith preserved the sacred deposit, and transmitted it to their children, looking forward with hope to that day, when they would be again cheered by the ancient sounds of a liturgy derived from the Apostolic ages, and known through all the nations of the earth; when they would behold that ceremonial to which they had been accustomed from their infancy, and which, though it seems strange and unmeaning to the uninstructed, yet is a symbolic observance, by which the wisdom of the knowledge of God, and the history of merciful redemption are proclaimed intelligibly to all tribes and tongues and nations. We exhort those good persons to continue faithful. Let them fortify their faith, by reading those explanations and compilations which are calculated to strengthen themselves and to enable them to instruct their children; let them be earnest and regular in the great duty of prayer, especially on the Lord's day, the holy days and days of devotion; on these occasions, we advise them to assemble together if there be two or more families, and uniting in spirit with the priest who offers the holy sacrifice in their vicinity, or with the bishop of the Diocese, let them at the usual hour of worship, unless some other be more convenient, recite their form of prayers for the Mass, read some approved books of instruction, or some Catholic sermon; have their children catechised; preserve and increase a spirit of charity and affection for each other; mutually encourage each other to perseverance, and consult occasionally how they might be able to procure a visit from some priest for the necessary purposes of religion. Let them cautiously abstain from vice; for it has sometimes unfortunately happened that, despairing of that ministry upon which they placed their reliance, they became reckless and criminal. We assure them that though unfortunately thus placed beyond the reach of our ministerial aid, they are dear to our hearts; they are not forgotten in our suffrages; we are solicitous for their welfare, and we entreat and desire those priests who may by any exertion be able to afford them the benefit of their ministry, to regard as one of their first obligations, the duty of visiting and sustaining them when at all compatible with those other functions to which they are specially devoted.

The education of the rising generation is, beloved brethren, a subject of the first importance; and we have accordingly, at all times, used our best efforts Catholic   to provide, as far as our means would per-
Education.   mit, not only ecclesiastical seminaries to insure a succession in our priesthood and its extension; but we have moreover sought to create colleges and schools in which your children, whether male or female, might have the best opportunities of literature and science, united to a strict protection of their morals and the best safeguards of their faith. You are aware that the success and the permanence of such institutions rest almost exclusively with you. It will be our most gratifying duty to see that their superiors and professors are worthy of the high trust reposed in them; but it is only by your patronage and zealous co-operation that their existence can be secured, their prosperity and usefulness be increased, and' your children's children be made to bless the memory, and to pray for the souls of those who originated and upheld such establishments.

Neither you nor we should exercise an undue influence over the minds of your children in regard to their embracing the ecclesiastical state. We desire to Vocations to   see no persons enter into it except those the Priesthood.   whom God has called, and whom by his special graces he enables to fulfil in an useful and edifying manner its serious obligations. We would not urge it upon the consideration of youth; but we think it equally improper to dissuade them from offering themselves as candidates to the ministry. This is not, it is true, amongst us a road to worldly honours, to preferments, to enjoyments, or to fame; but it is the glorious part of a co-operation with the Saviour of the world in the salvation of souls. It is an occupation in which men labour to bring to their fellow beings peace on earth, happiness in heaven. The head of the monarch moulders beneath his crown, and the diadem itself will blend into the common ruin of all earthly things; the laurel will fade upon the conqueror's brow, his arm will be resolved into dust, and rust will consume that sword upon which the lustre of victory shone: the fame of the statesman will terminate at least with time; the benefactions of the humane confer only a temporary and transient relief: but the faithful minister of God, after having spread consolation upon earth, will in the eternal abode be delighted at beholding those upon whom he was instrumental in conferring the joys of immortality. Do not urge your sons towards the sanctuary: but, beware how you interpose between them and its vestibules the impediments which worldly ambition and paternal authority furnish. We cannot be always, we should not be, when we can avoid it, dependent upon other nations for our ministry. We desire to see your children prepared to occupy our places. We call upon you to aid us in this effort. Some foreign churches, whose people have emigrated hither, have liberally assisted us to supply their brethren with the opportunities of religion: they deserve our gratitude and our prayers. France and Austria have the strongest claims upon us in this respect. Where they have been so zealous, you should emulate their holy ardour. Aid us in your respective Dioceses to raise up and perpetuate an efficient body of clergy sufficient for the wants of our churches.

You need not, brethren, that we should inform you of that which the Apostle has taught, and our own experience confirms, that there exists in us a warfare between the flesh and the spirit, and the Fasting and justification of the law is fulfilled in those Abstinence. who walk not according to the flesh, but according to the spirit: for if we live according to the flesh, we shall die the eternal death; but if by the spirit we mortify the deeds of the flesh, we shall live for ever. Hence,

they who are Christ's, have crucified their flesh with their
vices and concupiscences, by subjecting the appetites to restraint, and, accustoming themselves to refrain occasionally from those indulgences which, though lawful in themselves, yet might, without impropriety, be omitted. The
first Christians, by a holy austerity, reduced the body to
obedience, and removed the opportunity of many temptations. By such practices of fasting and of abstinence, they
likewise united their works of penance to the oblation of
the Saviour, that they might fill up in their own flesh those
things which are wanting of the sufferings of Christ; not
that anything was deficient for perfection of his atonement
as to its sufficiency and even abundance, but that something
was required for its application to themselves individually.
In the earliest days this great principle became the subject
of disciplinary regulation, and though they called no food
unclean, knowing that the ancient legal distinction of the
Hebrew people had been abrogated by the same divine
authority by which it had been established; yet even in the
Apostolic council a prohibition was enacted by the authority which Christ left to the legislative assembly of his
church, that there should be an abstinence from blood and
from things strangled. This discipline was also abrogated by
the same authority, and other abstinence substituted. And
though there be no essential difference, in a religious point
of view, between one day and another, so as to require, of
necessity, an abstinence from any particular food on any
special day; yet, in the enactment of her laws, the church
was empowered so to regulate her discipline as to specify
not only the abstinence, but the time when it should be observed, and to modify both the time and the manner of that
observance according to the variation of climate, of productions, and other circumstances. The sanction of this
legislative power is found spread through the gospels, and
is evinced in various other parts of the sacred writings;
it was always recognised by the body of the faithful, who
knew that what this tribunal bound on earth, was bound
in heaven, and that what was loosed on earth, was loosed
in heaven. And they always considered any of their
brethren who would not hear the church on this, as well as

on other subjects placed under her jurisdiction, in that
light in which they were exhibited by the divine Founder
himself, as heathens and publicans; that is, as persons who,
in reality, had practically separated themselves from the
benefits of his institutions.

You are aware, that, in a large portion of this province,
the discipline required abstinence from flesh meat on Fri-
days of the year, on the greater number of the Saturdays,
and on some other days. The power of dispensing with
the observance of the laws regarding general discipline,
when he shall see sufficient cause therefor, is, by the divine
constitution of our church, vested in the Supreme Pontiff.
And we, brethren, viewing the peculiar circumstances under
which our congregations are placed, have applied to him to
obtain for you a dispensation for flesh meat on those Saturdays on which the prohibition existed, with the exception of
those on which there was an obligation also of fasting from
one meal. We also prayed that the obligation of abstinence
on the festival of St. Mark the Evangelist, which has sub-
sisted for centuries, and on the Rogation days, should cease.
And we have to announce to you, that our request has been,
in a great measure, complied with. The obligation of observing abstinence on the festival of St. Mark, and on the
Rogation days, has been altogether abrogated, except when
the festival of St. Mark occurs on Friday: and a dispensation has been granted, for the space of ten years, from the
obligation of abstaining from flesh meat on those Saturdays
which are not days of obligation to fast upon one meal;
such are the Saturdays in Lent, on Quarter-tenses, or when
any vigil, that is a fast-day, occurs on Saturday.

We trust, beloved brethren, that as this relaxation of
discipline has been deemed necessary by our peculiar circumstances, you will endeavour, by more frequent prayer,
by more copious alms to your destitute brethren, and by
more exalted virtue, and other acts of mortification, to obtain from Heaven grace to subdue your passions, and to
present yourselves holy and acceptable through Jesus
Christ. Be not assimilated to those of whom the Apostle
so often told the Philippians, and told them weeping, that
they "are enemies to the cross of Christ; whose end is de-

struction; whose God is their belly; whose glory is their shame; who mind earthly things." Be your conversation in heaven.

We notice, with regret, a spirit exhibited by some of the conductors of the press, engaged in the interests of those

Attacks Upon the Church.

brethren separated from our communion, which has, within a few years become more unkind and unjust in our regard. Not only do they assail us and our institutions in a style of vituperation and offence, misrepresent our tenets, vilify our practices, repeat the hundred times refuted calumnies of days of angry and bitter contention in other lands, but they have even denounced you and us as enemies to the liberties of the republic, and have openly proclaimed the fancied necessity of not only obstructing our progress, but of using their best efforts to extirpate our religion: and for this purpose they have collected large sums of money. It is neither our principle nor our practice to render evil for evil, nor railing for railing: and we exhort you rather to the contrary, to render blessing, for unto this are you called, that you, by inheritance, may obtain a blessing. Recollect the assurance of the Saviour— "Blessed are you, when men shall revile you, and persecute you, and shall say all manner of evil against you falsely for my sake; rejoice and be exceeding glad: because your reward is very great in heaven: for so they persecuted the prophets that were before you." We are too well known to our fellow-citizens to render it now necessary that we should exhibit the utter want of any ground upon which such charges could rest. We, therefore, advise you to heed them not: but to continue, whilst you serve your God with fidelity, to discharge, honestly, faithfully, and with affectionate attachment, your duties to the government under which you live, so that we may, in common with our fellow-citizens, sustain that edifice of rational liberty in which we find such excellent protection.

And now, brethren, we exhort you, we beseech you, not to be led away by the delusions of this transitory world, to the neglect of your immortal souls. Be solicitous for your eternal concerns: lay up for yourself treasures in heaven, where neither the rust nor the moth can consume, and where no thieves can dig through and steal. O! that you would be wise, and would understand, and would provide for your last end. What peace   Conclusion. would you enjoy in time! What delight would encompass you for eternity! Be you, therefore, perfect as your Heavenly Father is perfect. "And may God supply all your wants according to his riches in Christ Jesus," "that you may walk worthy of him, in all things pleasing; being fruitful in every good work, and increasing in the knowledge of God; strengthened with all might according to the power of his glory, in all patience and long-suffering with joy, giving thanks to God the Father, who hath made us worthy to be partakers of the lot of the saints in light; who hath delivered us from the power of darkness, and hath translated us into the kingdom of his beloved Son: in whom we have redemption through his blood, the remission of sins."

Given in Council at Baltimore on this 27th day of October, in the year of our Lord, 1833.

✝JAMES, *Archbishop of Baltimore.*

✝JOHN BAPTIST, *Bishop of Mauricastro, Coadjutor of Bardstown.*

✝JOHN, *Bishop of Charleston.*

✝JOSEPH, *Bishop of St. Louis.*

✝BENEDICT J., *Bishop of Boston.*

✝JOHN, *Bishop of New York.*

✝MICHAEL, *Bishop of Mobile.*

✝FRANCIS PATRICK, *Bishop of Arath, Coadjutor and Administrator of Philadelphia.*

✝FREDERICK, *Bishop of Detroit.*

✝JOHN, *Bishop of Cincinnati.*

CHAPTER V

THE PASTORAL LETTER OF 1837

THE four years which intervened between the Second and Third Provincial Councils of Baltimore (1833-1837) witnessed an alarming growth of anti-Catholic bitterness. The burning of the Ursuline Convent at Charlestown on the night of August 11, 1834, and the publication of several books calculated to arouse bigotry, the vilest of which were *Six Months in a Convent*, by Rebecca Reed (New York, 1835), and the *Awful Disclosures*, by Maria Monk (New York, 1836), are some of the unhappy factors of the period. The Catholic clergy and laity were looking with anguished eyes to their leaders for guidance in the miasma of fanaticism which had arisen from the soil of free America. It was to be expected that the prelates assembled in the Third Provincial Council of Baltimore (April 16-23, 1837) would issue a message to their flocks on the grave question that faced the Catholic Church in the United States, and that they were not disappointed is evident from the masterly Pastoral which follows.

THE PASTORAL LETTER OF 1837

(*Third Provincial Council of Baltimore*)

Reverend Brethren of the Clergy, and beloved of the Laity:
Peace be to you, and faith with charity from God the Father and the Lord Jesus Christ, with the consolations of the Holy Ghost.

ASSEMBLED to consult for the welfare of that portion of the church entrusted to our care, we cannot separate for the purpose of renewing our labours amongst you, without yielding to an impulse that we feel of addressing to you our joint exhortation.—We are daily more and more consoled in witnessing the progress of religion amongst you, though this joy is mingled with affliction at

finding how much remains to be done, more than we are yet
able to perform; as also at beholding the various obstacles
which the enemy of souls creates, for the purpose of retard-
ing the work of the Lord, amongst us.

Amongst these obstacles we are painfully constrained
to notice the misrepresentation and persecution to which
you and we have been exposed since our
last council. We advert to this topic with   Persecution of
deep regret: but any effort on our part to   the Church.
conceal from the world this melancholy
fact, to which its perpetrators have given such blazing notoriety would be equally useless, as the attempt to disguise
those feelings with which we are affected, and which we
may, by God's aid, in a great degree restrain, but which it is
not in our power utterly to destroy.

We are filled with regret because no sacrifices or exertions that we could make would be sufficient to prevent
the baleful consequences which must necessarily flow from
the conduct of our gainsayers, and which we see it has already extensively and unhappily produced in our republic. The affection of fellow-citizens is destroyed, the offices of charity are neglected, the kindly intercourse of
neighbours has been interrupted, suspicion, jealousy and
hatred have succeeded to confidence, mutual respect and
affection; the demon of discord has usurped that station
where the angel of peace abode: and that day has gone by,
when every American citizen could truly say, that whatever may be the religious opinion which he entertained,
or whatever the form of worship which he followed, he enjoyed in full freedom the opportunity of securing for himself what he vindicated for others, the communion with his
God in that way which his conviction or his taste might
prefer. It has even been loudly proclaimed that our religion
should not enjoy toleration in fact, whilst, in theory, the
constitutions of our several states, proclaim to the world,
that as Catholics, we have the same rights respecting religion that are fully and peaceably enjoyed by our fellow-
citizens of every other denomination, by whatever style they
may be described whether Christian, Hebrew, or Unbeliever; and whilst the constitution of our federal Govern-

ment in addition declares, that "Congress shall make no law respecting the establishment of religion, or prohibiting the free exercise thereof." Yes, beloved brethren: our religious rights are secured to us by those same instruments which secure to our fellow-citizens and to ourselves, all those other valuable possessions which have been acquired for them and for us, by the lives, by the fortunes, and by the sacred honour of that devoted assembly who though widely differing in religion, yet were in love of country, a band of brothers. And he who would rashly pluck our franchise from the frame of the constitution would loosen the entire mass and facilitate the confusion and abstraction of the remainder. Whatever may be the dispositions or efforts of those whose misconduct we bewail, they cannot despoil us without insuring the general ruin. Our regret does not however arise from any apprehension of civil disfranchisement of ourselves, but we lament that a bad spirit has been evoked, and that its pestilential blasts have contaminated our atmosphere, that the peace of society is endangered, the domestic circle is disturbed, and that charity has departed from amongst us.

But when we look abroad and observe the nations in which the name of America was symbolic of brotherhood, and where the contemplation of our peace and of our prosperity induced statesmen to seek their cause, and when the conviction had been nearly produced, that these blessings were the result of our wise abstinence from persecution for the sake of creed; when the admiration and the respect which had taken possession of men's minds, were leading them to imitate our policy! How are matters changed?— Gratified at the exhibition of our weakness they exult in our shame and they predict our confusion and our fall. They avow indeed that, blinded by prejudice and infuriated by the spirit of party which was miscalled religious zeal, other men in other days, made upon our predecessors in the faith, assaults similar to those now made upon us; and that, when under its influence having with the gall of bitterness indited upon their statute books laws of acrimony, of plunder and of affliction, they strove by new misrepresentations to palliate their unjustifiable proceedings, and by the aid of falsehood they sought to give to persecution the appearance of self-protection. Time, investigation and reflection have however proved to the children the injustice of their fathers and caused them to purge away from their records, not only in this country but in England, the foul enactments and to bear honourable testimony to the innocence of those who had been oppressed: yet it is at such a moment as this, when Britain, blushing at her former folly and injustice and imitating what America had done fifty years before, abandons her false position and takes an honourable rank amongst the nations, that it is sought to drive our states from the lofty station which they had hitherto held, to that place of degradation from which she has just removed: and we are filled with regret at the humiliation to which a land that we love is exposed, when they who once admired it, point thereto, asking with amazement: how it can be possible for men of reading and of sagacity to be duped at this side of the Atlantic by charges refuted in Europe more than a century since; abandoned even by the party which originally invented them, disbelieved by every one who has the most moderate pretensions to information; charges to advance which even in an exceedingly modified shape, requires at present, the most desperate effort of the boldest and most interested partizans of a body now making its mightiest struggle for existence. The people of other nations are astonished at beholding those charges renewed here, in language far more vulgar and obscene than ever disgraced their worst exhibition in Europe. We avow that we witness this with shame and with regret, and the pain which we feel is caused not by any apprehension that the falsehood could be ultimately received as truth, amongst a people, who however they may be led astray for a moment, will always return to examine maturely that in which they are interested, but we are mortified, that because of this unseemly effort, the American name may be exposed to reproach when it had been hitherto respected.

We regret this spirit of misrepresentation upon other accounts; though we foresee that it will ultimately produce effects beneficial to ourselves. The love of truth exists amongst our fellow-citizens, and it becomes a more fervid attachment when the effect of misrepresentation has been discovered: yet until that discovery is made, many who are disposed to enter upon inquiry hesitate, and even those who are convinced have some reluctance. and vacillation. Misrepresentation spreads a thick mist around the vestibule of truth; it there exhibits appalling though shadowy forms to terrify those who would approach. And we regret to add from our positive knowledge that it is not by phantoms only that the approach is guarded; for though the laws of the land do not arm the persecutor with the sword, yet have the contrivances and exertions of individuals and of associations, in many instances, supplied this deficiency by their own acts of persecution.

Yet brethren in the midst of those trials we have received much comfort from the God of all consolation. This very misrepresentation of our tenets, of our principles and of our practices exhibits the best proof that the doctrine which we believe and teach cannot be successfully assailed by fair argument nor our principles rendered odious by honest exposition. It is therefore that forms of belief which we reject as absurd are imputed to us, so that our assailants by refuting them may obtain the semblance of a victory over us: it is for that reason that practices which we abhor are charged upon us, so that covered with a mantle of iniquity which we detest, we may be held up to the execration of a people desirous of paying its just tribute to virtue: and since our own conduct as citizens was not liable to reproach, it was deemed requisite to libel the governments of Europe which profess our faith, and to feign imaginary conspiracies in order to excite amongst our fellow-citizens the prejudice of the thoughtless and the fears of the patriotic. Even men who assumed the garb of religion and who affected extraordinary zeal and extravagant piety set forth to the public as solemn truths, statements whose falsehood they could have easily detected, and of which it is scarcely possible to imagine them ignorant. If they who, through prejudice, persuaded themselves that they would do a service to God and to society by our extermination, and who most laboriously sought to accomplish this purpose,

had convincing proof of our being involved in error or engaged in crime, they would have unhestitatingly produced
it; and this proof, when manifested, would have made its
due impression upon the public mind. Our assailants
wanted neither the will nor the ability, and we are consoled at the evidence which their failure must ultimately
give to the world, of the truth of our doctrines and the correctness of our principles.

We are indeed comparatively few amongst the millions
of our fellow-citizens; the greater portion of our flocks are
in the humble, laborious, but useful occupations of life:
we do not aspire to power, we do not calculate by what
process we should be able, at some future day, to control
the councils of the republic, neither do we combine to raise
the members of our society to places of trust, of honor, or of
profit: we seek not to make friends for our church by exhibiting the ability of our party to reward and to sustain its
benefactors; but, relying upon the protection of our God,
we endeavour to live in peace with our brethren whilst we
are occupied in our several appropriate duties. And we
have been consoled by the manifestation of his fatherly
care; especially when our assailants opened their mouth
and would seem ready to destroy us: the number of our
friends has increased, the good and the wise and the reflecting crowded around us for our defence: though they
dissented from our creed, in many instances they have
generously vindicated our rights: and the advantages that
we have gained from the sympathy and the affection of one
portion of our fellow-citizens, has more than compensated
for what we have endured from the hatred of the other.
Nor will this be the term of those beneficial results. Such
events cannot occur in the midst of a people free, educated
and desirous of information, without creating enquiry.
Calm and unprejudiced investigation is all that we believe
to be necessary, with that grace which Heaven is always
ready to bestow, for attaining the discovery of truth. Many
have already been roused to enquiry; several misconceptions have been destroyed, various early and long standing
prejudices have been laid aside, numberless mistakes have
been corrected, a spirit of examination is abroad; we have

rejoiced at its excitement, because we have felt its beneficial effects, and we anticipate still happier consequences
from its continuation, its activity and its increase. Thus,
always, beloved brethren, our kind and providential father,
blends some consolations with his chastisements.

And this view leads us to the consideration of our
duty under the circumstances in which we are placed.

Patience in Tribulation. "Take up your yoke," said our Blessed
Lord, "and learn of me because I am meek
and humble of heart, and you shall find
rest to your souls."[1] "Shall not my soul be subject to God?
for from him is my salvation:"[2] Asks the royal prophet,
and he answers, "Be thou O my soul subject to God, for
from him is my patience."[3] And when in another place
he prays "Deliver me, O my God out of the hand of the
sinner and of the unjust,"[4] he exhibits his own duty;
"for thou art my patience, O Lord: my hope, O Lord,
from my youth."[5] It is by the injustice of others, that
the Lord proves and makes perfect those whom he brings
to his service; and therefore the wise man exhorts us:
"Incline thine ear and receive the words of understanding, and make not haste in the time of clouds. Wait on
God with patience: join thyself to God and endure, that
thy life may be increased in the latter end. Take all that
shall be brought upon thee: and in thy sorrow endure,
and in thy humiliation, keep patience. For gold and silver
are tried in the fire, but acceptable men in the furnace of
humiliation."[6] The merciful father whom we serve, requires from us this proof of our attachment, and he so orders everything in his providence as to produce lasting
benefit for those who, resigned to his dispensation, observe
his injunction. Hence, the apostle Peter tells us to be "merciful, modest, humble, not rendering evil for evil, nor railing for railing, but contrariwise, blessing, for unto this we
are called that we may inherit a blessing."[7] And in answer
to an objection natural to most men, he adds, "And who is
he that can hurt you if you be zealous of good? But if also
you suffer any thing for justice sake; blessed are you, and

1 Matt. xi. 29.   2 Ps. lxi. 1.   3 Ps. lxi. 6.   4 Ps. lxx. 4.
    5 Ps. lxx. 5.   6 Eccli. ii. 2, 3, 4, 5.   7 Pet. iii. 8, 9.

be not afraid of their fear, and be not troubled, but sanctify the Lord Christ in your hearts, . . . that whereas they speak evil of you, they may be ashamed who falsely accuse your good conversation in Christ. For it is better, doing well (if such be the will of God,) to suffer, than doing ill, because Christ also died once for our sins, the just for the unjust."[8] Upon the same principle St. Paul writes to the Thessalonians, "See that none render evil for evil to any man: but ever follow that which is good towards each other, and towards all men."[9] These injunctions are in conformity with that of our blessed Lord, "Love your enemies, do good to them that hate you: and pray for them that persecute and calumniate you, that you may be children of your Father who is in heaven, who maketh his sun to rise upon the good and the bad, and raineth upon the just and the unjust."[10] The best refutation which we can oppose to the slanders with which we are assailed will be the exhibition of the christian virtues in our conduct. Let your lives be the answer to those that vituperate us. "Be you then perfect as your heavenly Father is perfect;"[11] and "Let your light shine before men, that they may see your good works and glorify your Father who is in heaven."[12] Thus will you insure blessings for yourselves, and, perhaps, convert your opponents.—This, beloved brethren, is the vengeance of christianity.

It may not however be amiss for us here to record some instances of the misrepresentation and persecution which have called forth these remarks.—We shall select but two out of many—The first is **The Outrage** the destruction of the Ursuline Convent on **of Charlestown.** Mount Benedict, near Boston, on the night of the 11th of August, 1834. The ruins of this establishment yet blacken the vicinity of Bunkers's Hill, and cast a dark shade upon the soil of Massachusetts. You need not our recital of the dastardly assault, the extensive robbery, the deliberate arson, the wanton insolence, the cold cruelty and the horrid sacrilege of that awful night.

We shall quote the words of one of the few members of

8 Pet. iii. 13, 14, 15, 16, 17, 18.   9 Thess. v. 15.   10 Matt. v. 44, 45.
11 Matt. v. 4.   12 Matt. v. 16.

the legislature of that State, who exhibited themselves an honorable exception to the body in which they were found. This gentleman told them upon their floor. "You may go from Maine to the Gulph of Mexico, and you cannot find an act similar to this—the destruction of an institution for instruction, inhabited by females, mostly children; religion was trampled upon; the Bible was destroyed; the tomb was broken open; the ashes of the dead were insulted; the females were driven from their beds at midnight, half naked; whilst the mob was exulting, shouting, dancing and triumphing amongst the warm ashes of the ruin which they had made, amidst a community, the most enlightened in the United States; ten thousand persons were looking on, and not one arm was raised to protect these females and their property. If, sir, the stain of blood is not upon the land, the stain of cruelty is there."

It was planned in the vicinity, and executed within view of the capital of the New England States; a city which aspired to the character of liberality, and had an ambition to be ranked amongst the seats of literature, of science, and of taste. The most unfounded calumnies had been previously circulated, in order to furnish a pretext to achieve what had been plotted, but even this pretext had been removed, for the local magistracy had examined into the alleged grounds, and declared themselves fully convinced of their falsehood.

In this case therefore there was a blending of misrepresentation and of persecution of the worst description.— Would to God that we could rest here! But of what use would it be for us to endeavour to hide that which has astonished distant nations, and which a thousand public journals have spread in such a variety of languages, before the eyes of the civilized world?

The declaration of a most respectable committee appointed at a public meeting of the citizens of Boston, to investigate the case, after the destruction had been perpetrated; having refuted the calumnies and described the outrage, add the following expressions of their sentiments:

"The fact that the dwelling of inoffensive females and children, guiltless of wrong to the persons, property or reputation of others, and reposing in fancied security, under the protection of the law, has been thus assaulted by a riotous mob, and ransacked, plundered and burnt to the ground and its terrified inmates, in the dead hour of the night driven from their beds into the fields; and that this should be done within the limits of one of the most populous towns in the commonwealth, and in the midst of an assembled multitude of spectators; that the perpetrators should have been engaged for *seven* hours or more in the work of destruction, with hardly an effort to prevent or arrest them; that many of them should afterwards be so far sheltered by public sympathy or opinion, as to render the ordinary means of detection ineffectual; and that the sufferers are entitled to no legal redress from the public, for this outrage against their persons and destruction of their property, is an event of fearful import, as well as of the profoundest shame and humiliation."

And this declaration was followed by solemn and repeated judicial enquiries and trials, in the process of which, however, full license was afforded to insult the feelings and the religion of that community whose property was destroyed and some of whose members died soon after the hardships which they suffered on the occasion; whilst miscreants who boasted of their activity and who were identified by most respectable witnesses, as being leaders in the transaction, were not only judicially absolved, but were rewarded by the spontaneous contributions of that public which thronged round the court of justice, to rejoice with them upon their deliverance. For our own part, we had no desire for their punishment; but we feel the justice of an opinion, that has been frequently expressed, that it would have been infinitely more creditable to the State of Massachusetts, if they had never been brought to trial.

It is equally notorious that notwithstanding every effort to obstruct the expression of what it could not deny, viz. the innocence of our religion and the guilt of the aggressors, the legislature of that State was fully convinced of the falsehood of the pretences and the atrocity of the outrage, and it declared that the convent was destroyed by a *lawless* and *ferocious* mob; and declared that it "felt itself bound in support of the constitution, and in *vindication* of the honor of the commonwealth to declare its deliberate and indignant condemnation of such an atrocious infraction of the laws." And yet we must avow that upon reading the list of the enormous majority which decided against affording any redress or compensation, we lament to find that it contains names which we did not expect to see upon it. And if the continuation of the same conduct be evidence of the existence of the same disposition, our opinion respecting that State and its legislature must continue unchanged.

In a committee of the legislature, appointed to consider the petition, for compensation, presented by the sufferers,

Catholic Allegiance.

a majority reported that though the injured persons could not claim indemnity for their losses from the government as a matter of right, yet, to enforce respect for religious freedom, and the security of life, liberty, property, " as also to do what yet may be done, to soften the reproach which rests upon the character of the state, by reason of the aforesaid outrage," a gratuity should be given.—A minority of the committee reported against granting this relief; sustaining its recommendation, amongst other grounds, upon the following:—viz. *"That Catholics acknowledging, as they do, the supremacy of a foreign potentate or power, could not claim under our government the protection as citizens of the commonwealth, but were entitled only to our countenance and aid so far as the rites of national hospitality might serve to dictate."*

We scarcely need observe to you, that this passage opens with what is notoriously untrue, viz., *"That we acknowledge the supremacy of a foreign potentate or power,"* in that sense which can interfere with our duty as citizens. We owe no religious allegiance to any State in this Union, nor to its general government. No one of them claims any supremacy or dominion over us in our spiritual or ecclesiastical concerns: nor does it claim any such right or power over any of our fellow citizens, of what soever religion they may be: and if such a claim was made, neither would our fellow citizens, nor would we submit thereto. They and we, by our constitutional principles, are free to give this ecclesiastical supremacy to whom we please, or to refuse it to every one, if we so think proper: but, they and we owe civil and political allegiance to the several States in which we reside, and also, to our general government. When, therefore, using our undoubted right, we acknowledge the spiritual and ecclesiastical supremacy of the chief bishop of our universal church, the Pope or bishop of Rome, we do not thereby forfeit our claim to the civil and political protection of the commonwealth; for, we do not detract from the allegiance to which the temporal governments are plainly entitled, and which we cheerfully give; nor do we acknowledge any civil or political supremacy, or power over us in any foreign potentate or power, though that potentate might be the chief pastor of our church.

Moreover, it is a notorious fact, that upon preparing to be admitted to citizenship, every Catholic emigrant distinctly renounces upon oath, all allegiance in civil and political concerns to any foreign prince, power, state, or potentate.

The passage also contains another manifest falsehood and absurdity, viz., that Catholics cannot claim protection under our government as citizens.—Now, it is notorious that they who are born in the country are citizens by the fact of their birth, and respecting Catholic emigrants, the government fully aware of their spiritual and ecclesiastical relations to the head of their church, has deliberately admitted them to become citizens; and therefore it is manifestly absurd to assert, that citizens can not, under our government, claim protection in that character in which they have been admitted by the government itself.

This attempt to proclaim the members of our church actually deprived of their rights of citizenship, was adding new and more extensive and more odious persecution to the atrocity of the cruel sacrilege for which they refused redress, and although the majority of the legislature repudiated this outrageous and absurd passage; yet, by an overwhelming vote, they acceded to the sentiments of its compilers, in withholding compensation and to the present day, the Catholics of the diocess of Boston are left without redress, notwithstanding the valueless declaration of the legislature, "in vindication of the commonwealth, of its deliberate and indignant condemnation of such an atrocious violation of the laws."

The other instance which we would specify is one which though exceedingly to be lamented, is not of a novel char-
acter. It is the development in this country
Anti-Catholic   of a spirit which has during ages fre-
Books.   quently manifested itself in other regions.
It has been exhibited in New York princi-
pally in the patronage afforded by the religious teachers of highly respectable bodies of our fellow citizens, to degraded beings of the most profligate class, who calumniated the most pure and useful institutions. Did not the history of other places exhibit to us similar revolting instances, we should indeed question the possibility of what we have witnessed. Men reputed to have understanding and considered to be of good character, vouching to the world for the correctness of charges of the most atrocious nature, made against the most respectable clergymen and religious communities, whose members have during more than a century, by their personal virtue, by their public charities and by their self devotion, won the esteem and applause not only of the members of their own church but of those who were opposed thereto; charges which, if true, involved the condemnation of the city which tolerated the existence of the criminals against whom those charges were made; charges, which necessarily implicated the public authorities of Canada and the whole British government, as abettors of the grossest crimes; charges whose falsehood was exposed by American Protestants, the impossibility of whose truth was attested by Canadian Protestants, and whose imputation was indignantly rejected by both. Yet has the world witnessed those charges again brought forward with unblushing front, by obscure imposters of the most vile description, whose notorious profligacy has been testified by the voice of the city which they polluted and slandered; beings in whom it was hard to say whether vice, or recklessness, or insanity predominated; and those charges sustained, perhaps suggested, and pertinaciously adhered to after the demonstration of their absurdity, by men whose station supposes intelligence and integrity.

In making the effort to persuade ourselves that men of this class were imposed upon and continued to be the dupes of such wretched beings, what a picture of human weakness do we contemplate? Yet assenting to this supposition, we may, perhaps, be able to account for the general exertions made by the pulpit and the press, to exhibit us as what we are not, and to excite against us unmerited hostility and persecution. We should, moreover, in this extraordinary supposition, cease to be astonished at the credulity and delusion of many of our fellow citizens, and we could imagine some cause for that want of charity in our regard, whose prevalence we witness and deplore.

Yet, whatever allowances we may feel disposed to make in favor of those who persecute and calumniate us and who speak all manner of evil falsely concerning us, we must point out two exceedingly bad consequences of this misrepresentation. The first is the extensive corruption of morality; the other is the encouragement of unbelief.

Nothing is more surely calculated for the destruction of that purity which is the soul of virtue, than the perusal of lascivious tales; and never did the most unprincipled author compile any work more foul in this respect, than the productions of our assailants, and never was there exhibited a more voracious appetite for mischievous aliment than that which they have unfortunately excited. With what avidity have not the numerous and heavy editions of those immodest fictions been taken up, disseminated through the country, purchased and introduced in the name of religion amongst the aged and the young of both sexes, in every state and territory of our Union? "The father waketh for the daughter when no man knoweth, 'says the wise man, in the book of inspiration,' and the care for her taketh away his sleep . . . in her virginity, lest she should be corrupted, and having a husband, lest she should misbehave herself."[13] And yet he places these obscene libels in her hands as books of religious instruction! "Hedge in thine ears with thorns; hear not a wicked tongue,"[14] was one of his admonitions. "On a daughter that turneth not away herself, set a strict watch: lest finding an opportunity

---

[13] Eccli. xlii. 9, 10.   [14] Eccli. xxviii. 2, 8.

she abuse herself: take heed of the impudence of her eyes and wonder not if she slight thee."[15] Here we perceive the consequence of allowing the imagination to be contaminated by familiarity with dangerous reading. And we are persuaded that the cause of pure morality and the security of domestic happiness have seldom been more grievously injured, than by the contrivers and the abettors of those indecent falsehoods, which in the name of religion are promulgated against our institutions. Affecting the guardianship of virtue, they undermine its foundations.

The effort for our destruction is a charge against five-sixths of the christian world. It is not a charge made exclusively upon those of our church, who in the various parts of the globe form a body of fully two-thirds of the whole number that profess the religion of the Saviour; but it is an accusation against all those who, though separated from our communion, believe in those doctrines and adhere to those practices which the compilers of those libels proclaim to be antichristian; and when their numbers are added to ours, the aggregate is at least the amount that we have stated. What an encouragement is it then, to the opponents of Christianity when our revilers proclaim that five-sixths of the christian world are immoral hypocrites or the dupes of such monsters of iniquity? Yet such is the accusation seriously made! We have then, since the production of those charges, and we believe, encouraged by their promulgation, beheld organized bands of unbelievers, systematically arrayed, occupying the ground thus yielded to them by those who affect such zeal for Christianity; we have seen them celebrating with anticipated but indeed premature triumph the destruction of the christian name. How will our accusers dislodge them from their position, when they exultingly proclaim that the principles and practice of five-sixths of the christian world during three centuries; and of entire Christendom, during the preceding ages, have been grossly corrupt, necessarily demoralizing, and in direct opposition to what they call the spirit of christianity?

We shall dwell no longer upon this painful subject. We have before us the admonition of the Saviour, "if the world

15 Eccli. xxvi. 13, 14.

hate you, know ye that it hated me before you. If you had
been of the world, the world would love its own: but because you are not of the world, but I have
chosen you out of the world, therefore the   **Christ and**
world hateth you. Remember my word   **the World.**
that I said to you: the servant is not greater
than his master, if they have persecuted me they will also
persecute you; if they have kept my word they will keep
yours also. But these things will they do to you for my
name's sake, because they know not him who sent me."[16]
"These things I have spoken to you that in me you may have
peace. In the world you shall have distress: but have confidence, I have overcome the world."[17] We claim protection from the laws of our country; we have the sympathy
of a large portion of our fellow-citizens; our trials will
have an end, and like our divine Saviour we too shall overcome the world; but our victory is to be achieved not by the
arm of the flesh but by the sword of the spirit and the might
of the Lord of Hosts. "In our patience we must possess
our souls."[18] Our forefathers in the faith, the immediate
disciples of the Saviour, the apostles themselves, were vili-
fied, misrepresented and suffered patiently for sake of
him who for their sake was made willingly a victim upon
the cross. The apostle of nations says "we are fools for
Christ's sake, . . . even unto this hour we both hunger
and thirst, and are naked, and we are buffetted, and have
no fixed abode, and we labour working with our own hands:
we are reviled and we bless, we are persecuted and we suffer it, we are blasphemed and we entreat; we are made as the
refuse of this world, the offscouring of all even until now."[19]
In his second epistle to his beloved Timothy, he assures him
that "all that will live godly in Christ Jesus shall suffer persecution."[20] Whence the prince of the apostles, Peter, admonishes his flock: "Let none of you suffer as a murderer,
or a thief, or a railer, or a coveter of other men's things:
but if as a christian, let him not be ashamed, but let him

16 John xv. 18, 19, 20, 21.   17 John xvii. 33.   18 Luke xxi. 19,
19 1 Cor. iv. 10, 11, 12, 13.   20 1 Tim. iii. 12.

glorify God in this name,"[21] and therefore we read of this apostle and his associate, in the Acts: that when they were scourged "they indeed went from the presence of the council rejoicing that they were accounted worthy to suffer reproach for the name of Jesus."[22] Thus in every age, from that period to the present, we find that in some region or other does the Lord call upon some of his followers to endure mockery and reproof and even death for his sake, but every where we find that not only is the blood of the martyr the enrichment of the soil of christianity, but the imitation of the meekness of the Saviour by the professor of his law, is the edification of the world and the triumph of religion. Let the models here proposed be then examples for our imitation. Let the maxims here inculcated be the rules of our conduct, and we shall walk worthy of the vocation in which we are called, and of the saints with whom we are, by our doctrine, associated.

Far be it from us, beloved brethren, even were it in our power, to seek the injury of those persons by whom we are assailed. They who belong not to the household of the faith are daily called from the east and from the west, to be seated at the tables from which not only were they estranged but to which they had declared hostility. How many such glorious conversions have we not witnessed? And has it not been so from the beginning? "Saul as yet breathing out threatenings and slaughter against the disciples of the Lord, went to the high priest, and asked of him letters to Damascus to the synagogues that if he found any men or women of this way he might bring them to Jerusalem."[23] Yet the Lord declared to Ananias "this man is to me a vessel of election to carry my name before kings and gentiles and the children of Israel, for I will shew him how great things he must suffer for my name's sake." [24] And how nobly did he fulfil his glorious commission? Yet when "the witnesses laid down their garments at the feet of a young man whose name was Saul and who was consenting to the death of Stephen"[25] whilst they stoned him; did not this Saul stand forth as the prominent persecutor

21 1 Peter iv. 15, 16.   22 Acts v. 41.   23 Acts ix. 1, 2.
24 Acts ix. 15, 16.   25 Acts vii. 57.

of our holy religion? How was God glorified and the church aided by his conversion? How noble, how becoming was the demeanor of the first martyr of the church, when imitating the example of his master, whilst he was overwhelmed by the missiles of his foes, he besought his Saviour, saying, "O Lord, lay not this sin to their charge?"[26] And the prayer of Stephen gave a Paul to christianity. Beloved brethren, his conduct is the exhibition of our duty.

We now, brethren, address you with affectionate interest upon another topic. We are gratified by the spiritual progress of numbers, but deeply affected by the negligence of too many who, however sound may be their faith, yet do not reduce their principles to practice. We are aware of the many difficulties which exist, because of the fewness of the clergy, the remoteness of churches, the sparseness of the flocks, and a variety of other causes. Yet, brethren, we are constrained to say, that there exists much room for some reproof because of negligence even where those obstacles are not found. Attend, we entreat you, to the admonition of St. James: "Be ye doers of the word and not hearers only, deceiving your own selves. For if a man be a hearer of the word and not a doer he shall be compared to a man beholding his own countenance in a glass. For he beheld himself and went his way, and presently forgot what manner of man he was. But he that hath looked into the perfect law of liberty, and hath continued therein, not becoming a forgetful hearer but a doer of the work; this man shall be blessed indeed."[27] And again, "For even as the body without the spirit is dead, so also faith without works is dead."[28] We have noticed with regret that even where belief of doctrine was in full vigour, the duties of religion were not always regularly fulfilled, but yielding to the tempter or corrupted by evil communication; even they who professed the word of truth rejected wisdom and discipline, and wearied themselves in the way of iniquity and destruction. And whilst we are consoled and edified by the visible increase of piety with which our regions have been blessed, we would call earnestly upon

Religious Duties of the Catholic.

[26] Acts vii. 59.   [27] James 1. 22, 23, 24, 25.   [28] James ii. 26.

those who as yet seem insensible.   We would lay before them
the assurance of the Lord by this prophet: "But if the wicked
do penance for all his sins which he hath committed, and
keep all my commandments, and do judgment and justice
living, he shall live and he shall not die.   I will not remember all the iniquities that he hath done: in his justice which he
hath wrought he shall live. Is it my will that a sinner should
die, saith the Lord God, and not that he should be converted from his ways and live?"[29]   Well may we address
such of you as have been unwise, in this tender strain of
invitation used by the Lord himself: "Be converted and
do penance for all your iniquities and iniquity shall not
be your ruin.   Cast away from you all your transgressions,
by which you have transgressed, and make to yourselves
a new heart and a new spirit, and why will you die, O house
of Israel? For I desire not the death of him that dieth,
saith the Lord God; return ye and live."[30]   To those who
feel that they have "wearied themselves in the way of
iniquity and destruction and have walked through hard
ways, but the way of the Lord they have not known."[31] The
Saviour especially addresses those affectionate words:
"Come to me all you that labour and are heavy burdened,
and I will refresh you."[32]

We should all exert ourselves to establish the dominion
of religion in our souls.   The end thereof is, by serving God
in the manner that he desires, to eradicate vice and purify
ourselves from sin.   Born children of wrath, dead in our
offences and sins, we can be raised up and quickened only
through the exceeding charity wherewith he loves us and
gives us the abundant riches of his grace in his bounty
towards us in Christ Jesus.

Religion is not satisfied with the mere rooting out of vice,
there must be efforts to do positive good.   It is therefore
that the Lord says, by the prophet Isaias, "Wash yourselves,
be clean, take away the evil of your devices from my eyes:
cease to do perversely: learn to do well,"[33] and to the same
effect the apostle St. Peter tells him that will love life and
see good days, "Let him decline from evil, and do good, let

---

[29] Ezec. xviii. 21, 22, 23.   [30] Ezec. xviii. 30, 31, 32.   [31] Wisd. v. 7.
[32] Matt. xi. 28.   [33] Isaias i. 16, 17.

him seek after peace and pursue it. Because the eyes of the
Lord are upon the just, and his ears unto their prayers: but
the countenance of the Lord is upon them that do evil
things."[34] Upon the same principle it is declared by Eze-
kiel,[35] that besides doing penance for all his sins which he
hath committed, the wicked man should "Keep all good
commandments and do judgment and justice," if he would
obtain life and again,[36] "and when the wicked turneth himself from his wickedness which he hath wrought, and doeth
judgment and justice: he shall save his soul alive." The
beloved disciple St. John, assures us,[37] that "he that doth
the will of God abideth forever;" and again,[38] "Know ye
that every one also, who doth justice is born of God;"[39]
"Little children, let no man deceive you. He that doth justice is just, even as God is just:" farther,[40] "And whatsoever
we shall ask we shall receive of him: because we keep his
commandments, and do those things which are pleasing in
his sight."[41] For this is the charity of God, that we keep his
commandments.

The religious man then not only refrains from evil but
he does good; he not only offends no man, but endeavours,
as far as he is able, to do service to every one: he not only
purifies himself and his dwelling from the filth of iniquity,
but he enriches his abode and decorates his soul with ornaments of virtue. In his relation to society, he endeavours to
do unto others as he would be done by, not only is he strictly
just, but he is kind, merciful, compassionate, and charitable. To the state he is loyal, faithful, obedient and attached, using those rights which he possesses, not for the
purpose of party, nor for the private emolument of himself
or of his friends, but for the general welfare and advantage;
discharging the duties of any office in which he may be
placed, not capriciously, nor negligently, nor influenced by
prejudice, or by partiality; but honestly without fear or
favour, or affection, for the welfare of the people, the credit
of the state and the approbation of his God. To his neighbours he is attentive, conciliating, respectful and useful: for
his family industrious, affectionate and devoted, he feels

---

[34] 1 Pet. iii. 11, 12.   [35] xviii. 21.   [36] xviii. 28.   [37] 1 John ii. 16.
[38] 1 John ii. 29.   [39] 1 John iii. 7.   [40] 1 John iii. 22.   [41] 1 John v. 3.

the responsibility under which he is placed of guarding their health, of providing for their wants, of promoting their interest, of securing their prosperity, of watching over their education, of superintending their discipline, of cultivating their minds, of regulating their morals, of winning their hearts to the love of virtue, and of leading them by his example in the path to heaven.   These, beloved brethren, are the important objects to which your earliest and most assiduous care should be devoted.   And doing these things, you shall through the merits of your blessed Saviour obtain that glorious inheritance which he has purchased for you at the price of his blood, and the attainment of which is the chief object of religion.

But to secure this desirable end, we must use the proper means: and first, beloved brethren, we would remind you, that "our confidence must be through Christ towards God,"[42] for "we are not sufficient to think any thing of ourselves, as of ourselves; but, our sufficiency is from God."[43] Who hath delivered us from the powers of darkness and hath translated us into the kingdom of the son of his love; in whom we have redemption through his blood for the remission of sins. . . . [44] "and through him to reconcile all things unto himself, making peace through the blood of his cross, both as to things in earth, and things in heaven." It is therefore that we can have "peace with God through our Lord Jesus Christ."[45]   "For if when we were enemies, we were reconciled to God by the death of his son: much more being reconciled, shall we be saved by his life and not only so, but we also glory in God through our Lord Jesus Christ, by whom we have received reconciliation."[46]   For it is impossible, that with the blood of oxen and goats, sins should be taken away, wherefore, when he cometh into the world he saith, "sacrifice and oblation thou wouldst not: but, a body thou hast fitted to me: holocausts for sin did not please thee: then, said I, behold I come, in the head of the book it is written of me, that I should do thy will O God . . . . In the which will we are sanctified by the oblation of the body of Jesus Christ once."[47]   But how once at the

42 2 Cor. iii. 5.   43 Coloss, i. 13, 14.   44 i. 20.
45 Rom. v. 10, 11.   46 Heb. x. 4, 5, 6, 7, 10.   47 Heb. x. 10.

end of ages he hath appeared for the destruction of sin by the sacrifice of himself. Therefore did the apostle St. Peter testify.[48] "This is the stone which was rejected by you the builders: which is become the head of the corner: neither is there salvation in any other. For there is no other name under heaven given to man whereby we must be saved." Thus it is through the redemption by our Lord Jesus Christ, that we must have access to God for the remission of sins, and the grace to advance in virtue.

And this must be done by the belief of those doctrines which he has revealed, for the apostle assures us that "without faith it is impossible to please God: for he that cometh to God must believe that he is, and that he is a rewarder to them that seek him."[49] This was but publishing what the Saviour himself had declared, in that beautiful prayer which he addressed to his Father at the termination of the discourse which he made to his disciples when, about to be taken from them, his affection was exhibited in extraordinary tenderness of expressions."[50] "Now this is eternal life, that they may know thee the only and true God, and Jesus Christ whom thou hast sent." And to this end he besought,[51] "Sanctify them in truth: thy word is truth."[52] "And not for them only do I pray, but for them also who through their word shall believe in me:[53] that they may all be one as thou, Father in me, and I in thee: that they may also be one in us." St. Paul exhibits to us the manner in which this apostolic testimony is given, as the foundation of faith, so that persons may be brought through the word of those apostles to believe in Christ.[54] "For whosoever shall call upon the name of the Lord shall be saved. How then shall they call upon him in whom they have not believed? Or how shall they believe him of whom they have not heard, and how shall they hear without a preacher? And how shall they preach unless they be sent? As it is written. How beautiful are the feet of them that preach the gospel of peace, of them that bring the tidings of good things! But all do not obey the gospel. For Isaias saith: "Lord who hath believed our report? Faith then cometh by hearing,

---

48 Acts iv. 11, 12.   49 Heb. xi. 6.   50 John xvii. 3.   51 v. 17.
52 20.   53 21.   54 Rom. x. 13, 14, 15, 16, 17.

and hearing by the word of Christ." And we find it re-corded in the Acts,[55] that Christ declared to those apostles, "You shall receive the power of the Holy Ghost coming upon you, and you shall be witnesses unto me in Jerusa-lem, and in all Judea and Samaria, and even to the utter-most parts of the earth." St. Matthew informs us of what things they were to testify,[56] "And Jesus coming, spoke to them, saying, all power is given to me in heaven and in earth. Going therefore teach ye all nations, baptizing them in the name of the Father, and of the Son, and of the Holy Ghost, teaching them to observe all things whatsoever I commanded you: and behold, I am with you all days to the end of the world." But as they were a very limited number, they could not teach all nations, by their mere personal ex-ertions; and since they were mortal, they could not continue teaching all days to the end of the world. To effect what he directed, therefore, he communicated to them the power of extending to others that authority which was contained in their own commission; as he came forth, sent by his Father, not merely to instruct by his personal teaching, but to con-stitute other witnesses, with authority to testify by their teaching what he had said and done; wherefore St. John informs us,[57] "The disciples therefore were glad when they saw the Lord, He therefore said to them again, peace be to you, as the Father sent me, so I also send you." In the same gospel we are instructed by himself of the manner in which the Father sent him.[58] "For I have not spoken of myself, but the Father who sent me, he gave me commandment what I should say, and what I should speak, and I know that his commandment is life everlasting. The things therefore that I speak, even as the Father said unto me do I speak." Thus we find the apostles fulfilling his views by immediately as-sociating several well instructed members of the faithful into their commission, ordaining them to be their co-oper-ators for the purpose of spreading abroad the good tidings into every nation, and of perpetuating the testimony to the end of the world. Thus St. Paul directs Timothy,[59] "The things which thou hast heard of me by many witnesses, the

55 Acts, i. 8.   56 xxviii. 18, 19, 20.   57 xx. 20, 21.
            58 xii. 49, 50.   59 2 Tim. ii. 2.

same command to faithful men who may be fit to teach others also." And to Titus he writes,[60] "For this cause I left thee in Crete that thou shouldst set in order the things that are wanting and shouldst ordain priests in every city." And this had been so extensively accomplished in the days of the apostles, that St. Paul proclaims,[61] "But I say, have they not heard? Yes verily, their sound hath gone forth into all the earth, and their words unto the ends of the world." And therefore it was only required to continue in the same manner, and upon the same principle to perpetuate the teaching body, by securing in the same manner the continuation of its members; and this has been evidently done, even to this day, by preserving the succession of the bishops of the church in communion with the successor of that apostle, to whom the Saviour declared,[62] "behold Satan hath desired to have you, that he may sift you as wheat; but I have prayed for thee that thy faith fail not: and thou being once converted, confirm thy brethren." Their commission is not of human origin, nor by men's authority, but derived from heaven by virtue of the institution of Christ, sustained by the power of that Holy Ghost, which descended visibly upon the first prelates of the church, on the day of Pentecost,[63] wherefore St. Paul addresses their associates, in the following words,[64] "Take heed to yourselves, and to the whole flock, wherein the Holy Ghost hath placed you bishops to rule the church of God, which he hath purchased with his own blood." Thus were they to be "accounted as the ministers of Christ;"[65] testifying his doctrines, not speaking of themselves, but as He who sent them gave them commandment, what they should say, and what they should speak, whilst according to his own promise, he would continue with them all days to the end of the world, so that his church should be what the apostle describes it,[66] "The house of God, the church of the living God, the pillar and the ground of truth." To this fold was he to bring all his sheep,[67] so that they should by its testimony, "Hear his voice and there should be one fold and one shepherd;" as was foretold by many of the prophets, but espe-

---

60 i. 5.   61 Rom. x. 18.   62 Luke xxii. 31,   63 Acts ii. 4.
64 Acts xx. 28.   65 1 Cor. iv. 1,   66 1 Tim. iii. 15.   67 John x. 16,

cially by Ezechiel:[68] "And my servant David shall be king over them, and they shall have one shepherd: they shall walk in my judgments and shall keep my commandments. . . . And I will make a covenant of peace with them, it shall be an everlasting covenant with them: and I will establish them and multiply them, and will set my sanctuary in the midst of them forever, and my tabernacle shall be with them: and I will be their God, and they shall be my people."[69] "And I will set up one shepherd over them, and he shall feed them, even my servant David, he shall feed them, and he shall be their shepherd and I the Lord will be their God, and my servant David the prince in the midst of them: I the Lord have spoken it."

Thus beloved brethren, do we receive by the testimony of this "cloud of witnesses," an indication of the path in which we should follow after the ark of our safety, "it is a holy way,"[70] "it shall be unto you a straight way, so that fools shall not err therein," for by this testimony we are assured of what God has revealed; his word is to us the foundation and the measure of our faith, as it is the code which also regulates our morality; we believe what he declares, we should also obey his commands. He has established the society of his church upon the principles of a well ordered community, making it the witness of his revelation, so that secured in "the unity of faith"[71] and of the knowledge of the Son of God, . . . we be no more children tossed to and fro and carried about with every wind of doctrine, by the wickedness of men, by cunning craftiness by which they lie in wait to deceive." Entreating then, we exhort you to continue steadily attached to this firm anchor of our hope, and submit your necks to the sweet yoke of Christ by regulating your conduct unrestrictedly by the great maxims of the gospel, as your code of morality.

But, beloved brethren, you are aware that it is by the institutions of the Saviour you must be made partakers of the fruits of his redemption. Your obedience to his law must be perfect. You cannot expect salvation upon any other terms than those which he has established. You must

---

68 Ezech. xxxviii. 24, &c.   69 Ezech. xxxiv. 23, 24.   70 Isaias xxxv. 8.
71 Ephes. iv. 13, 14.

be enriched to growth and beauty in the heavenly garden, not by your natural powers, but by being engrafted upon Christ and drawing the sustenance of heavenly aid, in his grace, from his institutions. Neither by your own natural power are you able without the influence of that grace, to believe or to hope, or to have useful sorrow for sin, or to love or to serve God as you ought, so as to obtain heaven. You are, as the apostle St. Paul expresses it, "Cut out of the wild olive tree, which is natural to thee; and, contrary to nature, wert grafted into the good olive tree," [72] so that drawing from Christ, the root of holiness, you may be purified from sin and bloom in virtue and bring forth fruit to eternal life. This the Saviour himself explains to us, when he informs us that he is the door by which the sheep enter into the fold;" [73] and more at length when he says, "I am the true vine; and my father is the husbandman. Every branch in me that beareth not fruit he will take away: and every one that beareth fruit he will purge it that it may bring forth more fruit. . . . Abide in me, and I in you. As the branch cannot bear fruit of itself unless it abide in the vine, so neither can you unless you abide in me. I am the vine, you the branches, he that abideth in me and I in him, the same beareth much fruit: for without me you can do nothing. If any one abide not in me, he shall be cast forth as a branch and shall wither and they shall gather him up, and cast him into the fire, and he burneth."[74]

Now it is by the means of his sacraments that he has provided in the ordinary communication of this grace for the various modes of our regeneration and sanctification. "Amen, amen, I say to thee, unless a man be born again of water and the Holy Ghost he cannot enter the kingdom of God."[75] "Now when the apostles who were in Jerusalem, had heard that Samaria had received the word of God, they sent unto them Peter and John: who, when they were come, prayed for them, that they might receive the Holy Ghost. For he was not as yet come upon any of them: but they were only baptised in the name of the Lord Jesus. Then they laid their hands upon them and they received the Holy Ghost."[76] In the gospel of St. John we read, "Then Jesus

[72] Rom. xi. 24.   [73] John x.   [74] John xv.   [75] John iii. v.   [76] Acts 14, 15, 16, 17,

said to them: Amen, amen, I say unto you, except you eat of the flesh of the son of man, and drink his blood you shall not have life in you."[77]   As also his other statement, "When he had said this he breathed on them and he said to them: Receive ye the Holy Ghost, whose sins ye shall forgive they are forgiven to them: and whose sins you shall retain they are retained."[78]   The apostle St. James also exhibits to us another source of grace when he writes, "Is any man sick amongst you, let him bring in the priests of the church, and let them pray over him anointing him with oil in the name of the Lord.   And the prayer of faith shall save the sick man: and the Lord will raise him up, and if he be in sins they shall be forgiven him."[79]   In the Acts of the apostles we read, "These they set before the apostles: and they praying imposed hands upon them."[80]   One of the effects of this rite is expressed in another place: "Then they exhorting and praying, and imposing their hands upon them, sent them away, so they being sent by the Holy Ghost went to Seleucia;"[81] but more clearly exhibited by St. Paul, "Neglect not that grace that is in thee, which was given thee by prophecy with imposition of the hands of the priesthood;"[82] and again, "For which cause I admonish thee that thou stir up the grace of God which is in thee, by the imposition of my hands."[83]   Concerning matrimony we read in the Gospel of St. Matthew, "What therefore God hath joined together, let no man put asunder;"[84] and St. Paul informs us, "For this cause shall a man leave his father and mother, and shall cleave to his wife, and they shall be two in one flesh.   This is a great sacrament: but I speak in Christ and in the church."[85]

How many sources of grace are thus opened to us for the several circumstances in which we may be placed? Again therefore, beloved; entreating, we exhort you not to despise the mercy of our God; not to reject the bounties of Christ, not to neglect the means of salvation thus placed within your reach.   Not only for your own sakes, but for the sake of your children, of your families, of the whole church of Christ are you, especially the heads of those families, bound

---

[77] John vi. 54.   [78] John xx. 22, 23.   [79] James v. 14, 15.   [80] Acts vi. 6.
[81] Acts xiii. 3.   [82] 1 Tim. iv. 14.   [83] 2 Tim. i. 6.   [84] Matt. xix. 6
[85] Ephes. v. 31, 32.

to have recourse to such of those divine institutions as are befitting your circumstances.

Your example is powerful for good or for evil. You desire to train up your children in the way in which they should walk; of what value will your advice be in contradiction to your example? "He that shall scandalize one of these little ones that believe in me, it were better for him that a mill stone should be hanged about his neck, and that he should be drowned in the depth of the sea. Wo to the world because of scandals! For it must needs be that scandals come: but nevertheless, wo to that man by whom the scandal cometh. And if thy hand or thy foot scandalize thee, cut it off and cast it from thee. It is better for thee to go into life maimed or lame, than having two hands or two feet, to be cast into everlasting fire."[86] And in another place, we find a corresponding declaration of the Saviour, "He therefore, that shall break one of these least commandments, and shall so teach men, shall be called the least in the kingdom of heaven. But he that shall do and teach, shall be called great in the kingdom of heaven."[87] We would therefore earnestly and solemnly impress upon our brethren, to walk worthy of the vocation in which they are called and by their example, to draw others to the practice of those great duties which on earth give a peace of which children of the world have scarcely an idea, and which procures for us in heaven a joy and a glory, the like of which no earthly eye has seen, no description of which has penetrated mortal ear, nor to conceive which is the mind of man capable in its present state, and the contemplation of which bore the rapt apostle into such ecstatic enjoyment. [88]

These things we have written to you, beloved brethren, respecting your first and greatest obligations, but there are others upon which we find it proper to express to you our views. They regard your exertions to provide for the external wants of religion and to establish those means by **Support of the Church.**
which instruction will be more generally diffused, the ministry more widely extended, the spiritual wants of great numbers better attended to, and even the temporal conso-

[86] Matt. xviii. 6, 7, 8,   [87] Matt. v. 19,   [88] 2 Cor. xii.

lations of our afflicted fellow creatures, whether members of our church or estranged therefrom, better secured.

We should first call your attention to the erection and the decoration of churches and their proper furniture. From the very origin of christianity it was an object of great interest to your predecessors in the faith: it is essential for the decency of public worship, and nothing tends more to unite and to preserve in the bonds of affection, as well as the purity of faith, the Catholics who reside in any vicinage: it is moreover exceedingly useful for the purpose of preserving the faith of the children and affording to the well disposed enquirer an opportunity of learning our doctrines and correcting misapprehensions.

But in the creation of those edifices we would remark, that it has frequently occurred, that through a sad mistake
Trusteeism.   respecting the nature of our church government, and the influence caused by the example of religious societies, whose principles are in direct contradiction to those which have come down to us from the days of the apostles, some of the managers have usurped powers to which they had no title, which are incompatible with our discipline and in some instances even with our faith. And when we were constrained in the discharge of our duty to oppose their pretensions, they complained that we interfered with their rights: and they sought by the law of the land, in contradiction to the spirit of those constitutions which guarantee our religious freedom, to subject our ecclesiastical administration to their supervision, and to withhold the funds created for the support of religion from their destined object, unless their irregular demands were acceded to. The results in some instances have been extremely disgraceful and disastrous; but we thank God, that at present the spirit of which we complain has nearly disappeared. We think it right however to apprise you, that viewing before God, and singly with an eye to the welfare of religion, this case, we have felt it to be our duty at all hazards, to preserve that faith, for whose defence you and we are bound if required to imitate the devotion of the glorious martys; and also to prefer officiating, as many of our predecessors have done, in the open air, in private

houses, or in humble sheds, for those who are faithful to their principles and attached to their religion, rather than to enter the most gorgeous temples and accept of the most abundant stipends as the price of that freedom of ecclesiastical administration which it is our obligation to preserve, and the dimunition of which would be most injurious to religion. Nor do we think it irrelevant in this place to observe, that it has almost uniformly occurred that the persons who thus affected zeal for religion and attachment to liberty, by perpetuating those usurpations, were notorious for their total neglect of religious practices and were found most ready to abuse any power they were able to obtain. We therefore admonish you of the necessity of being properly informed of the due mode of conforming to the principles of your own church before you undertake to erect buildings for her worship. There is nothing in either the spirit of the constitutions or in the laws of our republic which is incompatible with the perfect freedom of our ecclesiastical institutions; no country affords better means for their security and protection by legal provisions; but the power which our states properly allow to each religious denomination to manage its own ecclesiastical concerns may be easily abused, as it has been in many instances, by persons who were members of bodies to whose spirit they were opposed. We exhort you then, in acting for the church, to consult with the recognized authorities of that church; let there be a full and perfect accordance between you and them, this will produce co-operation, success, charity, affection and peace, and will moreover secure to you the blessings of religion. We would also remark upon the necessity of providing for every church that furniture for the altar and the sacristy which will give to the divine offices, especially to the holy sacrifice of the Mass, that external dignity which becomes the service of the Most High. When God vouchsafed to prescribe special decorations for his tabernacle, in the desert, the people of Israel were invited to make their offerings, and their zeal and devotion urged their generosity to such a point that "The workmen being constrained to come, said to Moses: the people offereth more than is necessary. Moses therefore commanded proclamation to be made by the crier's voice: Let neither man or woman offer any more for the sanctuary."[89] We need not remind you of the special benedictions which the Lord continues to bestow upon those who, animated with the due sentiments of religion, contribute with cheerful hearts to promote the great work of his service upon this earth.

"Let the priests that rule well, be esteemed worthy of double honour, especially they who labor in word and doctrine,"[90] was the admonition of St. Paul to his disciple Timothy who at that period, according to the primitive usages, had the entire apportionment and distribution of the means contributed for the purposes of religion: and in his first epistle to the Corinthians, the apostle asks, "Who serveth as a soldier at any time, at his own charges? who planteth a vineyard and eateth not of the fruit thereof? who feedeth a flock, and eateth not of the milk of the flock? speak I these things according to man? or doth not the law also say these things? For it is written in the law of Moses, Thou shalt not muzzle the mouth of the ox that treadeth out the corn. Doth God take care of oxen? or doth he say this indeed for our sakes, for these things are written for our sakes, that he that plougheth should plough in hope: and he that thresheth in hope to receive fruit. If we have sown to you spiritual things, is it a great matter if we reap your carnal things." [91] . . . "Know ye not that they who work in the holy place eat the things that are of the holy place; and they that serve the altar partake with the altar? So also the Lord ordained that they who preach the gospel should live by the gospel."[92]

We have placed this passage under your view, not so much for the purpose of insinuating against you any want of disposition to perform the duty which it inculcates, as of bringing to your consideration a subject which has been heretofore overlooked. We are ready to testify, that in many instances you exert yourselves in a manner very creditable to yourselves and beneficial to religion, in

Support of the Clergy.

---

[89] Exod. xxxvi. 4, 5, 6.   [90] 1 Tim. v. 17.   [91] 1 Cor. ix. 7, 8, 9, 10, 11.
[92] 1 Cor. ix. 13, 14.

contributing to the support of your pastors; and we also are gratified at knowing that, as a body, our clergy are well deserving of what they thus receive. Indeed, we know of no other portion of the church in any region of the world, where in one sense, the words of the Apostle "who planteth a vineyard and eateth not of the fruit thereof," would be so properly applicable as in the United States. For besides that almost all our churches have been built chiefly by the laborious exertions of the clergyman; their whole income is produced by his services; and if he ceases to officiate, the revenue would be small indeed! Nothing can then be more just than that the provision for the clergy should be the principal object of its application: as St. Paul declares to Timothy, "the husbandman that laboureth must first partake of the fruits."[93]

In those countries where parochial or other benefices exist, the incumbent, when worn out by labour or age, or incapacitated by sickness or accident, is not cast aside; he still enjoys his right to the place, and continues in possession of the income; and it is fit that it should be so: for to use the expressions of the Apostle, who, when he admonishes Timothy to "labour as a good soldier of Jesus Christ,"[94] tells him also, that "no man being a soldier to God entangleth him with secular businesses, that he may please him to whom he hath engaged himself;" the clergy are prohibited by the canons of the church from being engaged in traffic, that they may be wholly occupied in their ministerial duties. The emolument which they receive is comparatively moderate, sometimes wretchedly small; they are liable to applications from the distressd, and to demands for the purposes of religion, sufficient to deprive them of the power, even if they had the will, of laying up for themselves a provision for age or infirmity, and the canonical regulations, in such contingencies, provide for their support out of the funds of the benefice, and for the discharge of the duty by giving an assistant, to maintain whom both the incumbent and they who are served contribute. Our circumstances render the creation of such benefices at the present moment extremely inexpedient, even if the canoni-

93 2 Tim. ii. 6.   94 2 Tim. ii. 3, 4.

cal grounds for their creation existed: and instances have occurred where meritorious priests, after a faithful discharge of duty, have been neglected and left in great destitution; and few missions are known, in which the income of a clergyman is smaller than on these of the United States. We would appeal to your own feelings of justice to say whether this was as it ought to be. Cases may however arise, in which the clergyman would be in need of aid which he deserves, without having a sufficient claim upon any special church to entitle him to require that it should support him. To provide for cases of this description, and others of a similar character, we have recommended, that in each Diocess, the clergy themselves should create a fund applicable to such purposes, under the superintendence of the Bishop; and we should hope you will also feel that this object merits your aid.

For ourselves, we feel that we have always received, as we have endeavored to merit, your support: but we would suggest that as the duties of the bishop regard the welfare of the whole Diocess, and as he is principally occupied in its general concerns, it would be fitting that all the churches and congregations should aid in creating a fund, not merely sufficient for his individual support; but also adequate to afford him the services of one or more clergymen, according to the extent and duties and means of the Diocess, to aid him in efficiently labouring to the advantage of the entire Diocess, for the promotion of religion and the spiritual welfare of his whole flock.

To provide for a succession of the clergy, is also a general concern of the churches and congregations, which, however well they may be served at the **The Need** moment, cannot insure themselves against **of Priests.** the casualties which produce a vacancy: and if no measures be taken to educate and to form, by proper discipline, a body of clergy to supply those vacancies as they occur, what must be the consequence? Many of our most flourishing churches have had to undergo long destitution, to struggle through great difficulties, to witness many scandals and to suffer heavy losses, because of the want of a clergy sufficiently numerous and properly

qualified for our missions. Many catholics who came
hither from other nations, as well as several of our own
citizens who have removed to the interior, were condemned
to wander in spiritual desolation, until becoming estranged
from their religion they were indifferent to its concerns or
its practices; and they and thousands of their children have
been themselves lost to the church. It is an obligation of
pressing importance, therefore, for every one to contribute
according to his means, to supply this deficiency. The
ecclesiastical state, especially in our church, is not a profession, to prepare his child for which a parent will make
an extraordinary sacrifice, in the expectation that the future income will justify the present outlay; and the education necessary for a priest is one not to be acquired without considerable time, and no small expense. The body
which is to be served has been accustomed to undertake
that expense in many parts of Europe, by the creation of
Seminaries sustained by the public funds of the nation;
and when these could not be obtained, the object was effected by the contributions of the faithful or the donations
or legacies of the wealthy or pious. In these United States,
our fellow-citizens of various religious denominations, have
numerous, large and well endowed theological schools, to
which their yearly contributions are very considerable.
Hitherto you have done little or nothing to aid our seminaries. Many of us have received for this purpose, moderate aid from the piety of our fellow catholics in France,
in Austria, and in one or two instances from Ireland. The
Holy See has also generously admitted some of our youths
into the Urban College of the Propaganda at Rome, where
they gratuitously receive their education and have their
wants supplied. We strenuously exhort you to do your
duty, by contributing to raise up a national clergy; exert
ourselves to provide that your own sons should minister
at your altars. In your several Dioceses you can co-operate, each of you with his proper prelate, for this most important object.

We have on former occasions addressed to you our advice and exhortation respecting the use and the abuse of
the public press, as respects our religion. It is a powerful

engine for good or for evil: and in those states it has been,
and still is, extensively used against us, both openly and
covertly. We do not dwell upon the gross
Catholic   untruths, the false charges, the notorious
Books.   perversions, the ribald abuse which are
continually spread before the eyes of mil-
lions of our fellow-citizens against you and us, and our religion, by what is called the periodical religious press: we
need not exhibit to you the pages of several public journals
to show the adverse spirit of a large portion of political
editors to truth and justice, where we are concerned. Not
only are the public libraries and the literary institutions
formed upon the same principle, and tracts and pamphlets
which exhale the poison of virulent misrepresentation and
obloquy, widely disseminated, but the very school-books for
even the youngest learners are infected; so that from the
most tender childhood to the decrepitude of age, the great
portion of the reading public may be taught to detest and
to despise what they are led to believe is our religion.

Within a few years however, some publishers have put
forth a number of books containing a correct exposition of
our doctrines and the defence of our tenets; though we regret that in some instances, either acting from their own
views or having consulted with persons not sufficiently
qualified to advise them, they have occasionally exhibited a
want of judgment in their selection: We find that amongst
you the spirit of encouraging their efforts has been daily
becoming more strong, and we trust, that they will themselves feel it to be their duty, as it will be their interest
henceforward to consult in the proper manner, with the
ordinary ecclesiastical superior, before they undertake such
publications.

We feel disposed also to exhort you to sustain with
better efforts those journals, which though not officially
sanctioned by us, still are most useful to
The Catholic   explain our tenets, to defend our rights
Press.   and to vindicate our conduct. We regret
to learn that in several instances those
conducted under the eye of the ordinary ecclesiastical authority are continued only at a pecuniary sacrifice to their

proprietors, and by the zealous and gratuitous exertions
of their editors. We would impress upon you the necessity of exertion on your parts, to have them better sustained and their circulation extended as widely as possible.

We have formed ourselves into a Society for the production and dissemination of books useful to the cause of
truth and of virtue, leaving to each prelate its adaptation
to the peculiar circumstances of his own Diocess, but com-
mitting for the present the administration of its general
affairs chiefly to the Archbishop, who as soon as his leisure
will permit, will proceed to execute what he has undertaken. Our object is, as far as practicable, to apply some
remedy to those evils which we lament, and we trust that
your love of truth and your zeal for virtue will lead you
to co-operate with us, to the best of your power, for this
most necessary purpose.

We would also beloved brethren, renew the entreaty
which we have made to you on other occasions, to unite
your efforts to ours for upholding those
institutions which we have created for the
education of your children. It is our most
earnest wish to make them as perfect as
possible, in their fitness for the communi-

Education of the Young.

cation and improvement of science, as well as for the
cultivation of pure solid and enlightened piety. And if we
occasionally experience some difficulty and do not advance
as rapidly as the wishes of our friends, or their too sanguine hopes would look for, some allowance must be made
for the difficulties by which we are surrounded and the
opposition which we experience. Yet, these notwithstanding, we are persuaded, that amongst those under our superintendence, are to be found, some of the most scientific and
literary houses of education which our nation possesses;
some establishments for the instruction of youth, male and
female, in which there are successfully taught those speculative and practical lessons which inform the understanding,
regulate the imagination, cultivate the taste, ameliorate
the heart, improve the disposition, impress the importance
and obligation of fulfilling every social, civic, domestic
and religious duty, and teach the best mode of their per-

formance. And we trust, that by a continuation of that patronage which they have received, we shall be enabled to behold them take deep root in our soul, flourish in beauty and vigour, and furnish an abundant supply of useful citizens and christians, fitted for conferring blessings upon that country which protects them and that religion which they profess.

We would especially commend to your fostering care those pious and meritorious sisterhoods, which in addition to the culture of the youthful mind, gather up the little orphan whom Heaven has deprived of its mother's care, who attend the couch of sickness to moisten the burning lip, to assuage the anguish of pain, to whisper consolation to the raving spirit and to point to the true source of the sinner's hope, when in the dimness of his eye he begins to be sensible of the darkness of the grave. These are the women, who generously devoting themselves to the whole cause of godlike charity, are found in good and in evil report; in the school, in the hospital, in the prison, in the hovel of poverty, in the maniac's cell, in the midst of pestilence, surrounded by the bodies of the dying and the corpses of the dead; discharging the duties of their holy zeal, alike to the professor of their faith and to its opponent, and tending with the same assiduity the wretched calumniator of their creed, their virtue and their sex, as they would their most generous defender.

To you, our venerable co-operators in the ministry, priests of Christ Jesus, we say in particular. "Continue you in those things which you have learned and which have been committed to you: knowing of whom you have learned. And because from your infancy, you have known the holy scriptures, which can instruct you to salvation, by the faith which is in Christ Jesus. All scripture inspired by God, is profitable to teach, to reprove, to correct, to instruct unto justice, that the man of God may be perfect, furnished unto every good work."[95] "Flee youthful desires, and pursue justice, faith, charity and peace, with them that call upon

The Sisterhoods.

Exhortation to the Clergy.

[95] 2 Tim. iii. 14, 15, 16, 17.

the Lord out of a pure heart. And avoid foolish and unlearned questions, knowing that they beget strifes. But
the servant of the Lord must not wrangle, but be mild towards all men, apt to teach, patient, with modesty, admon-
ishing them that resist the truth: if peradventure God may
give them repentance to know the truth, and they may recover themselves from the snares of the devil, by whom
they are held captive at his will."[96] "Hold the form of sound
words which you have heard of us in faith, and in the love
which is in Christ Jesus. Keep the good thing committed to
your trust by the Holy Ghost that dwelleth in us."[97] "But
according to him that hath called you, who is holy, be you
also in all manner of conversation holy: because it is writ-
ton, *you shall be holy, for I am holy.*"[98] "Be prudent therefore, and watch in prayers. But before all things have a
constant, mutual charity among yourselves; for charity
covereth a multitude of sins. Using hospitality one towards
another without murmuring. As every man hath received
grace, ministering the same to one another: as good stewards
of the manifold grace of God."[99] "And you, employing all
care, minister in your faith, virtue: and in virtue, knowledge: and in knowledge abstinence: and in abstinence, patience: and in patience, godliness: and in godliness, love of
brotherhood: and in love of brotherhood, charity. For if
these things be with you and abound, they will make you to
be neither empty nor unfruitful in the knowledge of our
Lord Jesus Christ. For he that hath not these things with
him, is blind and groping, having forgotten that he was
purged from his old sins. Wherefore, brethren, labour the
more, that by good works, you may make sure your calling
and election. For doing these things you will not sin at any
time."[100] "Feed the flock of God which is among you, taking care of it, not by constraint, but willingly according to
God: not for filthy lucre's sake, but voluntarily: . . . being
made a pattern of the flock from the heart. And when the
prince of pastors shall appear you shall receive a never-fad-
ing crown of glory."[101] "Be you an example of the faithful in
word, in conversation, in charity, in faith, in chastity. . . .

[96] 2 Tim. ii. 22, 23, 24, 25. 26.   [97] 2 Tim. i. 13, 14.   [98] 1 Pet. i. 15, 16.
[99] 1 Pet. iv. 7, 8, 9, 10.   [100] 2 Pet. i. 5, 6, 7, 8, 9, 10.   [101] 1 Pet. v. 2, 3, 4.

Attend unto reading, to exhortation and to doctrine. Neglect not the grace that is in you, which was given to you by prophecy, with the imposition of the hands of the priesthood. Meditate upon these things, be wholly in these things; that your profiting may be manifested to all. Take heed to yourselves and to doctrine: be earnest in them. For in doing this you shall both save yourselves and them that hear you."[102] "We charge you before God and the Lord Jesus Christ, who shall judge the living and the dead, by his coming and his kingdom: Preach the word: be instant in season, out of season: reprove, entreat, rebuke in all patience and doctrine. . . . Be vigilant, labour in all things, do the work of evangelists, fulfil the ministry, be sober."[103] "Charge the rich of this world not to be high-minded, nor to trust in the uncertainty of riches, but in the living God (who giveth us abundantly all things to enjoy). To do good, to be rich in good works, to give easily, to communicate to others, to lay up in store for themselves a good foundation against the time to come, that they may lay hold on the true life."[104] "Whosoever are servants under the yoke, let them count their masters worthy of all honour; lest the name of the Lord and his doctrine be blasphemed. But they that have believing masters, let them not despise them, because they are brethren, but serve them the rather, because they are faithful and beloved, who are partakers of the benefit. These things teach and exhort."[105] "And now we commend you to God and to the word of his grace, who is able to build up and to give an inheritance among all the sanctified."[106]

Beloved brethren of the clergy and laity, "God is not unjust that he should forget your work and the love which you have shewn in his name, you who have ministered and do minister to the saints;

Conclusion.   and we desire that every one of you shew forth the same carefulness to the accomplishing of hope unto the end: that you become not slothful, but followers of them, who through faith and patience shall inherit the promises."[107] "Wherefore we pray always for you: that our God would make you

102 1 Tim. iv. 12, 13, 14, 15, 16.   103 2 Tim. iv. 1, 2, 5.
104 1 Tim. vi. 17, 18, 19.   105 1 Tim. vi. 1, 2.
106 Acts xx. 32.   107 Heb. vi. 10, 11, 12.

worthy of his vocation, and fulfil all good pleasure of his goodness, and the work of faith and power, that the name of our Lord Jesus may be glorified in you and you in him, according to the grace of our God and of the Lord Jesus Christ."[108]—"But we ought to give thanks to God always for you, brethren, beloved of God, for that God hath chosen you first fruits unto salvation, in sanctification of the spirit and faith of the truth: whereunto he hath called you by our gospel unto the purchasing of the glory of our Lord Jesus Christ. Therefore, brethren, stand fast; and hold to the traditions which you have learned, whether by word or by our epistle. Now our Lord Jesus Christ himself, and God and our Father who hath loved us, and had given us everlasting consolation and good hope in grace, exhort your hearts and confirm you in every good work and word."[109]

"For the rest, brethren, pray for us, that the word of God may run and may be glorified, even as among you: and that we may be delivered from importunate and evil men: for all men have not faith. But God is faithful, who will strengthen and keep you from evil. And we have confidence concerning you in the Lord that the things which we command, you both do and will do. And the Lord direct your hearts in the charity of God, and the patience of Christ." [110]

"The grace of our Lord Jesus Christ, be with you all. Amen."

Given in Council, at Baltimore, this 22d day of April, in the year of our Lord, 1837.

✠Samuel, *Archbishop of Baltimore.*

✠John, *Bishop of Charleston.*

✠Joseph, *Bishop of St. Louis.*

✠Benedict Jos., *Bishop of Boston.*

✠Francis Patrick, *Bishop of Arath, Coadjutor of Philadelphia.*

✠John Baptist, *Bishop of Cincinnati.*

✠Guy Ignatius, *Bishop of Bolina, Coadjutor of Bardstown.*

✠Simon Gabriel, *Bishop of Vincennes.*

✠William, *Bishop of Orio., Coad. of Charleston.*

✠Anthony, *Bishop of New Orleans.*

---

[108] 2 Thessal. i. 11, 12.   [109] 2 Thessal. ii. 12, 13, 14, 15, 16.
[110] 2 Thessal. iii. 1, 2, 3, 4, 5. 18.

CHAPTER VI

THE PASTORAL LETTER OF 1840

WHEN the Fourth Provincial Council was assembled at Baltimore on May 16, 1840, under the presidency of Archbishop Eccleston, the number of Sees in the United States had increased to fifteen; the dioceses of Dubuque, Nashville, and Natchez having been erected by Pope Gregory XVI. on July 28, 1837. Among the prelates who attended the sessions of the Council was Monseigneur Charles-Auguste, Comte de Forbin-Janson, Bishop of Nancy and Primate of Lorraine. The principal decrees enacted by the Council were those concerning the ceremonies for mixed marriages, the formation of temperance societies in all parishes, the safe-guarding the faith of the children who attended the public schools, the condemnation of certain secret societies, and clerical discipline. The Fathers of the Council sent a letter of consolation to the hierarchy of Poland, and a letter of thanksgiving to the Leopoldine Association of Vienna for its generous support of the Catholic Church in this country. Open persecution of the Church here had abated to a large extent in 1840, but the Pastoral Letter records the continuance of attacks upon the faith from the non-sectarian press and from non-Catholic pulpits.

THE PASTORAL LETTER OF 1840

(Fourth Provincial Council of Baltimore)

Beloved Brethren: Peace be to you, and grace from God the Father, through our Lord Jesus Christ, with the consolation of the Holy Ghost.

AGAIN has it been granted us to unite for the purpose of consulting how we may best discharge the weighty obligations of our Apostleship in your regard. We have, after having besought aid through your prayers, united with our own supplications to the Author of wisdom, endeavored to set in order those things which the imperfections of our nature cause occasionally to become confused. We have examined by what means within our power, the great cause of pure and undefiled religion may be promoted, and before departing for our several Dioceses, we desire to impart to you our advice and exhortation.

And first, permit us to congratulate you on the progress that has been made by the aid of the Most High in our ecclesiastical provinces. You behold, since we last addressed you, the two new Episcopal Institutions of Dubuque and Nashville happily erected, and usefully filled; the number of our clergy has also considerably increased, though not yet adequately to our demands. Our seminaries are enlarged: aided by the generosity of our flocks and of our benefactors, they are becoming daily better fitted for the education of our candidates for the priesthood. The religious houses, especially of females, have been multiplied. These are retreats wherein justly many indulge their desire of frequent attendance upon the Lord, in which the youthful mind is trained to industry, to science and to virtue—in which the orphan is cherished, protected, and fitted to occupy an useful and an honorable place in society. Since that period also the zeal and the charity of many congregations have been manifested in the erection and in the embellishment of several churches. Piety has diffused its influence widely through our flocks; the Sacraments have been more generally respected and received; the spirit of cordial attachment between the pastors and their congregations has been still strengthened by their mutual confidence and zealous co-operation for the advancement of religion, and as a natural consequence, their efforts have been crowned with much success.

Progress of the Faith.

Though we have not to complain of such acts of barbarity and sacrilegious destruction as it afflicted us to place on record in our last address to you, still we have to lament that the State of Massachusetts, which has neither protected the property of its Catholic citizens nor vindicated the majesty of its own laws, has not as yet manifested any disposition to retrieve its character by compensating for the injury, and thus doing such a tardy act of

Massachusetts.

strict justice. What a contrast is to be found between the conduct of the authorities of this city and those of one that claimed a place of pre-eminence amongst the most polished and the most liberal of our republics! We should be happy to discover in its deeds of compensation some evidence of that good feeling and generous spirit which would restore it to the position that it formerly held, which would soothe the affliction of the sufferers, and would blot from the minds of those who were insulted all recollection of that foul deed which stains the escutcheon of an old state; of one that beholds side by side, the cradle of our liberties, the first field of honour of our federation, and the spot which blackens her own fame. We cannot but indulge the hope that it may yet be given to us to moisten with the tear of joy a blur whose existence we deplore, and which we should rejoice to see thus washed away.

It is also matter of consolation to us, that not only has there been no augmentation of those bad efforts which were previously made by religious teachers high in the estimation of some of our fellow-citizens of other denominations to sully the reputation of our church, to bring suspicion upon our best institutions, and to insinuate against our clergy crimes the most inconsistent with their obligations and the religion to which we adhere. We relied upon the good sense, the calm spirit of investigation, the intelligence and the honour of our fellow-citizens—nor have we been disappointed. The miserable libels have had their day; their compilers and the unfortunate and degraded instruments of their guilt, if not already fallen to their proper level, are fast sinking in the estimation of those whom they sought to delude. For ourselves, we may well feel satisfied with that judgment which is rather admitted than published even by those who, through want of information, would think they do a service to God by impeding our efforts.

We must, however, deplore not only the guilt of the fabricators, but amongst the consequences of their misconduct, one to which it is now impossible to apply a remedy; the contamination of the minds of the delicate and the young, in those numerous families into which either an unchecked

spirit of bad curiosity or miscalculating and reckless hatred
to our religion, had introduced the polluting romances: another is, that from the mass of these inventions which have
been so extensively scattered abroad, several copies must
descend to future generations: it will then probably happen, as it has happened in our own day, that either folly or
malice will reproduce as the record of facts whose truth is
incontrovertible, that slander which is now despised. The
bulk of the obloquy with which we are assailed, as the
history of earlier times or of distant occurrences, has no
better foundation than these. Our church has always had
libelling opponents.

It is true that still the pulpit and the press are indus-
triously used for our defamation, but it does not appear
to us that at the present moment, they are
conducted with the same violence nor upon   **The Enemies**
the same system of preconcerted action for   **of the Church.**
our destruction. Would to God, that our
brethren, in place of directing the powers of their mind,
their energy and their resources in hostility to us, would
seek to learn what God has revealed to us by the Patriarchs
and Prophets, and last of all, by his beloved Son, our Lord
Jesus Christ, "in whom we have redemption through his
blood, the remission of sins!"[1] Would to God that we could
behold them united with us "adoring the Father in spirit
and in truth!"[2] Then would we "all speak the same thing,
and there be no schisms amongst us: and we be perfect in
the same mind and in the same judgment."[3]   Beloved
brethren, we entreat you to pray without ceasing for the
copious effusion of this grace, "till we all meet in unity of
faith, and of the knowledge of the Son of God, unto a perfect man, unto the measure of the age of the fulness of
Christ: that we may not now be children, tossed to and fro,
and carried about with every wind of doctrine, in the
wickedness of men, in craftiness by which they lie in wait
to deceive: but performing the truth in charity, we may in
all things grow up in him who is the head, Christ."[4] "Being
of one mind one to another: not high-minded but condescending to the humble. Be not wise in your own conceits:

1 Col. i. 14.   2 John iv. 23.   3 1 Cor. i. 10.   4 Eph. iv. 13, 14, 15.

render to no man evil for evil; provide things good not only in the sight of God, but also in the sight of all men. Revenge not yourselves, dearly beloved, but give place to wrath; for it is written: Revenge is mine, I will repay, saith the Lord. But if thy enemy be hungry, give him to eat: if he thirst, give him to drink: for doing this, thou shalt heap coals of fire on his head. Be not overcome by evil, but overcome evil by good."[5] We are aware, beloved brethren, that continued misrepresentation, the repetition of refuted calumnies, unkind efforts to create hostile feelings against us in the public mind, and bitter vituperation with expressions of censure and contempt, are calculated to excite our passions and to urge us to the indulgence of a kindred spirit; but we intreat you, once again, to give heed to the admonition of the apostle and of the sublime motive by which he enforces it:—"Let no evil speech proceed from your mouth, but that which is good to the edification of faith: that it may afford grace to the hearers. And grieve not the holy spirit of God, whereby you are sealed unto the day of redemption. Let all bitterness and anger, and indignation and clamour, and blasphemy be taken away from you, with all malice; and be kind to one another, merciful, forgiving one another, even as God hath forgiven you in Christ."[6] "Love your enemies, do good to them that hate you: and pray for them that persecute and calumniate you." [7]

There are few subjects dearer to us than the proper education of your children, on this mainly depends their true respectability in this world, also the consolation of your own declining years, the prosperity of religion, the honor of God on earth, and your eternal salvation and that of your descendants. It is therefore that we have always deemed it to be one of our most pressing obligations to use our best and earliest efforts in providing establishments where they may be carefully educated by competent persons in all that is necessary for their prosperity in this life, whilst they were taught by admonition and example to walk in that path which leads to heaven. In general we have found our flocks disposed to profit by the opportunities thus

Catholic Education.

[5] Rom. xii. 16, 17, 18, 19, 20, 21.   [6] Eph. iv. 29, 30, 31, 32.   [7] Matt. v. 44.

afforded, but not always so ready to aid in defraying the
expenses which should necessarily be incurred in having
them secured and made permanent. In many instances also,
they who belong not to the household of faith have discovered
the advantages which accompanied the system of education
in our schools and colleges; they have often been more industrious to profit by them than have you, for whom they
were principally intended. We would then admonish you,
in a spirit of affectionate interest for your own and your
children's welfare, that we have in many instances observed
two serious mistakes upon this head. The first that of
parents, who altogether deprived their offspring of that education to which they were entitled, upon the plea that thereby they would be better served by placing in their hands at
their entrance upon a life of industry, the money which had
been saved by the restriction of their education. The second that of a mistaken and thriftless economy, which led
them to keep their children, especially females, at an inferior school of less cost, until they had nearly gone through
those years allotted to education, and then sent them for a
comparatively short time to an establishment in which they
should have been placed years before.

The great evil in both cases is the danger to which they
are exposed, of having their faith undermined, the imperfect instruction which they receive, if they get any, upon
the most important subject of religion, the nearly total
abandonment of their religious practices and their exposure
in their tender youth to the fatal influence of that false
shame which generally arises from the mockery or the su-
perciliousness of those who undervalue their creed. Beloved brethren we address you not in the language of speculation or of abstract reasoning; our words are the faint effort to convey to you the deep impression which long and
melancholy experience has made upon our minds; for we
have witnessed the blastings of our hopes in the ravages
which have thus been made.

Intimately connected with the topic of education is one
upon which there exists much misconception in the minds
of our separated brethren; and we have sometimes observed
even amongst our own flocks not a little confusion of ideas

upon the subject: we therefore desire to place it distinctly
before you. The Saviour of the world commissioned his
apostles to teach "all nations" of the earth,
during "all days, even to the consummation of the world," promising that he would
be "always with them;" [8] and that the
Holy Ghost "would teach them all things and bring to their
minds all that (the Saviour) taught." [9] This promise was
fulfilled on the day of Pentecost, [10] and they were thereby
constituted a tribunal competent and commissioned to testify the revelation of God to the whole human race, to the
consummation of the world. [11] This tribunal was extended
and perpetuated in consequence of the authorised association to their body by the Apostles, of others whom they
found duly qualified, [12] whom they fitted by ordination to

Holy
Scripture.

[8] Matt. xxvii. 19, 20.   [9] John xiv. 26.   [10] Acts ii. 4.

[11] 18. And I say to thee: Thou art Peter, (Rock) and upon this rock I will
build my church; and the gates of hell shall not prevail against it. 19. And to
thee will I give the keys of the kingdom of heaven: and whatsoever thou shalt
bind upon earth, it shall be bound also in heaven; and whatsoever thou shalt
loose upon earth, it shall be loosed also in heaven.—*Matthew* xvi.

19. Go ye, therefore, and teach all nations; baptizing them in the name of the
Father and of the Son and of the Holy Ghost: 20. Teaching them to observe
all things whatsoever I commanded you; and behold, I am with you all days,
even to the consummation of the world.—*Matthew* xxviii.

15. And he said to them: Go ye into the whole world and preach the Gospel to
every creature.—*Mark* xvi.

46. And he said to them: Thus it is written, and thus it behoved Christ to
suffer, and to rise again the third day: 47. And that penance and remission of
sins should be preached in his name among all nations, beginning at Jerusalem,
48. And you are witnesses of these things. 49. And I send the promise of my
Father upon you: but stay you in the city till you be endued with power from
on high.—*Luke* xxiv.

16. And I will ask the Father and he shall give you another Paraclete, that
he may abide with you forever: 17. The Spirit of truth whom the world cannot
receive; because it seeth him not, nor knoweth him: but you shall know him,
because he shall abide with you and be in you. . . . 26. But the Paraclete,
the Holy Ghost whom the Father will send in my name, he will teach you all
things, and bring all things to your mind, whatsoever I shall have said to you.—
John xiv.

13. But when he, the Spirit of truth shall come, he will teach you all truth.—
John xvi.

8. But you shall receive the power of the Holy Ghost coming upon you, and
you shall be witnesses unto me in Jerusalem, and in all Judea, and Samaria,
and even to the uttermost part of the earth.—*Acts* i.

[12] 21. Wherefore of these men who have been with us all the time that the
Lord Jesus came in and went out among us, 22. Beginning from the baptism of
John until the day when he was taken up from us, one of these must be made
a witness with us of his resurrection. . . . 25. To take the place of this ministry and apostleship, from which Judas hath by transgression fallen. 26. And

perform the duty,[13] and to whom they gave the necessary commission by sending them into the field when thus prepared and commissioned.[14] It is manifest that the Church thus constituted, formed one visible body under one visible head,[15] and that it had the full authority of requiring

they gave them lots, and the lot fell upon Matthias, and he was numbered with the eleven apostles.—*Acts* i.

2. And the things which thou hast heard from me before many witnesses, the same commend to faithful men who shall be fit to teach others also.—*2 Timothy* ii.

5. For this cause I left thee in Crete, that thou shouldst set in order the things that are wanting, and shouldest ordain priests in every city, as I appointed thee.—*Titus* i.

13 6. These they placed in the presence of the apostles: and they praying, imposed hands upon them.—*Acts* vi.

2. And as they were ministering to the Lord and fasting, the Holy Ghost said to them: Separate me Saul and Barnabas for the work to which I have taken them. 3. Then they fasting and praying, and imposing hands upon them, sent them away. 4. So they being sent by the Holy Ghost, went to Seleucia, &c.—*Acts* xiii.

22. And when they had ordained for them priests in every church, and had prayed with fasting, they commended them to the Lord, in whom they believed.—*Acts* xiv.

14. Neglect not the grace which is in thee, which was given thee by prophecy (prayer) and the imposition of the hands of the priesthood.—*1 Timothy* iv.

6. For which cause I admonish thee that thou stir up the grace of God which is in thee, by the imposition of my hands.—*2 Timothy* i.

14 1. And after these things the Lord appointed also other seventy-two, and he sent them two and two before his face, into every city and place whither he himself was to come.—*Luke* x.

21. And he said to them again: Peace be to you, as the Father hath sent me, I also send you. 22. When he had said this, he breathed on them: and he said to them: Receive ye the Holy Ghost, 23. Whose sins you shall forgive, they are forgiven them: and whose you shall retain, they are retained.—*John* xx.

See note 13, *Acts* xiii. 2, 3, 4.

14. How shall they call on him in whom they have not believed? Or how shall they believe him of whom they have not heard? And how shall they hear without a preacher? 15. And how can they preach unless they be sent? . . . 17. Faith, then cometh by hearing: and hearing by the word of Christ.—*Romans* x.

15 See note 11. *Matthew* xvi. 18, 19.

31. And the Lord said: Simon, Simon, behold Satan hath desired to have you, that he may sift you as wheat: 32. But I have prayed for thee that thy faith fail not: and thou being once converted, confirm thy brethren.—*Luke* xxii.

16. And other sheep I have that are not of this fold: them also I must bring: and they shall hear my voice: and these shall be made one fold and one shepherd.—*John* x.

11. Holy Father keep them in thy name whom thou hast given me, that they may be one as we also. . . . . . 17. Sanctify them in truth. 18. As thou hast sent me into this world, I also have sent them into the world. 19. And for them also do I sanctify myself; that they also may be sanctified in truth. 20. And not for them only do I pray, but for those who through their word, shall believe in me, 21. That they all may be one, as thou Father in me, and I in thee, that they may be one as we also are one.—*John* xvii.

15. When, therefore, they had dined, Jesus saith to Simon Peter: Simon, *son of John*, lovest thou me more than these? He saith to him: Yea, Lord, thou knowest that I love thee. He saith to him: Feed my lambs. 16. He saith to him again:

from each of its members or portions, not forming an evident majority of the whole body, that respect and obedience which the principle of unity required, and which the Saviour commanded.[16]   It is plain, that as the commission

Simon, *son* of John, lovest thou me? He saith to him, Yea, Lord, thou knowest that I love thee. He saith to him: Feed my lambs. 17. He saith to him the third time: Simon, *son* of John, lovest thou me? Peter was grieved, because he said to him the third time, Lovest thou me? And he said to him: Lord thou knowest all things: thou knowest that I love thee. He said to him: Feed my sheep.—*John* xxi.

For as one body we have many members, but all the members have not the same office; 5. So we, being many, are one body in Christ, and each one members, one of another.—*Romans* xii.

17. For we being many are one bread, one body, all who partake of one bread.—*1 Corinthians* x.

12. For as the body is one, and hath many members, and all the members of the body, whereas they are many, are yet one body; so also is Christ. 13. For in one spirit were we all baptized into one body, whether Jews or Gentiles, whether bond or free: . . . . 20. But now there are many members indeed, yet one body. . . . . 25. That there might be no schism in the body, but the members might be mutually careful one for another. 26. And if one member suffer anything, all the members suffer with it: or if one member glory, all the members rejoice with it. 27. Now you are the body of Christ and members of member.—*Ibid.* xii.

26. For you are all children of God by faith in Christ Jesus. 27. For as many of you as have been baptized have put on Christ. 28. There is neither Jew nor Greek, there is neither bond nor free; there is neither male nor female. For you are all one in Christ Jesus.—*Galatians* iii.

19. Now, therefore, you are no more strangers and foreigners, but you are fellow-citizens with the saints, and the domestics of God, 20. Built upon the foundation of the apostles and prophets. Jesus Christ himself being the chief corner stone: 21. In whom all the building framed together, groweth into a holy temple in the Lord: 22. In whom you also are built together into a habitation of God in the Spirit.—*Ephesians* ii.

3. Careful to keep the unity of the Spirit in the bond of peace. 4. One body and one Spirit, as you are called in one hope of your vocation. 5. One Lord, one faith, one baptism, 6. One God and father of all, who is above all, and through all and in us all. . . . 12. Unto the edification of the body of Christ. 13. Till we all meet in the unity of faith, and of the knowledge of the Son of God, unto a perfect man, unto the measure of the age of the fulness of Christ. 14. That we may not now be children, tossed to and fro and carried about by every wind of doctrine, in the wickedness of men, in craftiness, by which they lie in wait to deceive. 15. But performing the truth in charity, we may in all things grow up in him who is the head, Christ.—*Ibid.* iv.

27. Only let your conversation be worthy of the Gospel of Christ: that whether I come and see you, or be absent, I may hear of you, that you stand fast in one spirit, with one mind, laboring together for the faith of the Gospel.—*Philippians* i.

15. And let the peace of Christ rejoice in your hearts, wherein also, you are called in one body: and be ye thankful.—*Colossians* iii.

16 17. And if he will not hear them, tell the church; and if he will not hear the church, let him be to thee as the heathen and the publican.—*Matthew* xviii.

16. He that heareth you, heareth me: and he that despiseth you, despiseth me, and he that despiseth me, despiseth him that sent me.—*Luke* x.

21. And he said to them again: Peace be to you, as the Father hath sent me, I also send you.—*John* xx.

11. And some indeed he gave to be apostles, and some prophets, and others evangelists, and others pastors and teachers, 12. For the perfection of the saints,

was lodged with the whole body united to its head, no minority, however, respectable, especially when opposed to the majority and separated from the head, could lawfully claim to act under that commission; nor could any individual or voluntary association reasonably arrogate to itself the power of performing the functions of that commissioned tribunal, or denounce it as apostate. Such a position might seem plausible if they who take it could produce unquestionable evidence, that the word of Christ had been vainly given for the authority and the perpetuity of the general body, and that its commission had been superseded. Even this would not, however, suffice to place themselves in authority, because it would be still farther necessary to produce with unquestionable evidence, a new commission; for upon every principle of common sense as well as of religion, the Apostle testifies. "Neither doth any man take the honor to himself, but he that is called by God as Aaron was."[17] In a case of this description conjectures, surmises, probabilities, analogies or opinions do not form evidence. The destruction of one commission, and the substitution of another in so important a crisis, should have the same character as that which Jesus Christ furnished in his own person, when superseding the commission of the Sanhedrim, as the prophesies shewed must be the case, he substituted that of the Christian Church. "If I had not done among them the works that no other man hath done, they would not have sin: but now they have both seen and hated both me and my Father."[18]

Nothing is more plain to the ordinary observer, than that from the days of the Saviour to the present, no such evidence has been adduced. And indeed its non-existence is so manifest, that although innumerable separatists have

for the work of the ministry unto the edification of the body of Christ.—*Ephesians* iv.

7. Remember your prelates who have spoken to you the word of God, considering well the end of their conversation, imitate their faith. 17. Obey your prelates and be subject to them, for they watch, as being to render an account of your souls, that they may do this with joy and not with grief, for this is not expedient for you.—*Hebrews* xiii.

6. We are of God. He that knoweth God, heareth us. He that is not of God, heareth us not: by this we know the spirit of truth and the spirit of error.— *John* iv.

17 Heb. v. 4.   18 John xv. 24.

gone out from the great body which adhered to the regularly commissioned and regularly perpetuated tribunal, not
one of them pretends to adduce even its semblance; but
each seeks to justify its own secession by alleging its own
opinion, that the original tribunal has erred, yet they do
not agree in specifying the alleged error, nor does any one
of them pretend to an exemption from liability to error
itself: and thus they concur in sustaining the principle, that
no one can be certain of knowing at this day, with precision
and accuracy, the doctrine of Christ upon every particular
subject of revealed religion; though they say that we may
have a general knowledge of what he taught. Thus you will
observe, upon their principle, that since each individual
and each congregation and aggregation, and even the whole
Church may err upon each separate subject, it inevitably
follows that no person or Church can say with certainty,
that upon any given point there is not error, and therefore
it is clearly impossible in their supposition, to point out at
present any one doctrine of the Saviour with absolute certainty. This necessarily involves the destruction of revealed
religion; for no one is bound to believe as the word of God
any statement of man, without evidence that it has been revealed by God; which evidence can never be given upon the
grounds which they furnish.

Now rejecting this supposition and its consequences,
we look upon it as evident that when Jesus Christ, by his
works, established his own authority, he next established
the tribunal of the Church as a credible witness of his teaching, not only for all nations but for all ages; we also behold
the notorious fact of its continuance; we therefore possess
this day the authorised witness given to us by the Saviour.
This witness which St. Paul describes as "the Church of the
living God, the pillar and ground of the truth,"[19] gives to us,
amongst other teachings of God, the sacred volume of the
Holy Scriptures, the value of which we can learn only by
her testimony. But as St. Peter tells of this valuable record
"Holy men of God spake inspired by the Holy Ghost,"[20]
and he immediately adds, "But there were also false prophets among the people, even as there shall be lying teach-

[19] Tim. iii. 15.

[20] 2 Peter i. 21.

ers among you, who shall bring in sects of perdition, and
deny the Lord who bought them, bringing upon themselves
swift destruction."[21] The mode of separating the genuine
inspired writing from the production of the false prophet,
was not by the private authority of one or more individuals,
but it was the prerogative, as it was one of the most important duties of the authorised tribunal of the Church. It is
also manifest that when at a subsequent period, the valuable legacy was ascertained and furnished by her testimony, it had a distinct, precise and well known meaning,
perfectly in accordance with the doctrines committed by the
Saviour to the guardianship of the Church, and one of the
most necessary obligations and functions of the apostolic
body in all succeeding ages, was to testify and to preserve
unchanged, that meaning so as to guard against the evil
which St. Peter subsequently describes, "Our most dear
brother Paul, according to the wisdom given to him hath
written to you, as also in all his epistles, speaking in them
of these things: in which there are some things hard to be
understood, which the unlearned and unstable wrest,
as also the other Scriptures, to their own perdition. You,
therefore, brethren, knowing these things before, beware;
lest, being led away by the error of the unwise, you fall
from your own steadfastness."[22]

You perceive then, beloved brethren, that we receive the
Holy Scriptures upon the testimony of the Church, that it
is by her guardianship and her authority, we are assured
of their genuineness, their integrity, their purity from corruption, their inspiration, and their original and correct
meaning. We therefore profess that we receive the Holy
Scriptures in that sense which our holy mother, the Church,
to which it belongs to judge of their true sense and meaning,
has always held and now holds: neither will we ever take
and interpret them except according to the unanimous
sense of the fathers.

But it is not only by additions or multilations, or alterations, that the original text may cease to be of value; the
sacred books may be corrupted by incorrect translations,
and it is therefore necessary, that a responsible and author-

21 ii. 1.   22 iii. 15, 16, 17.

ised member of the tribunal of the Church, should in her
name, vouch for the correctness of the translation, otherwise it is considered of no authority; it may or it may not be
correct, but it is not regarded as the word of God, because
it does not appear sustained by the proper evidence. All
books purporting to be the Holy Bible, or any portion thereof, which are published without this testimony, are not regarded by us as the word of God, not that we examine into
their correctness or corruption, but upon the plain principle
of the total absence of the requisite evidence from the
proper tribunal and its proper officer. Thus without pro-
nouncing upon the merits of any translation set forth by
the Churches or Societies separated from our communion,
we do not receive them as the word of God, precisely upon
the ground of total want of the requisite evidence.

And as it frequently happens that persons who reject the
authority of the Church, undertake to expound upon their
own private views and judgment the sacred volume, or what
they assume to be the word of God, it is clear that whether
the interpretation given by them be correct or incorrect,
they who sustain or encourage them, do thereby sustain two
false principles: first, that it is not criminal to despise the
Church, to oppose her authority, and having rejected it, to
usurp her commission; the second, that the interpretation
of the sacred books, is the right of each individual, and
not that of the authorised tribunal which the Saviour established to teach all nations, during all days to the
consummation of the world.

In our country it is assumed by the larger portion of our
fellow-citizens that versions of the Bible, not sustained by
that evidence which we require, are the word of God; and
moreover, that all individuals and all churches are liable
to error in declaring its meaning, and they admit, as the
mode by which we shall learn what God has taught, the
opinions, conjectures and judgment of each individual, for
himself—all of which upon the ground that we have set forth
is subversive of the purity of doctrine and the unity of faith;
and the admission of which would be a dereliction of our
duty. It is moreover generally prevalent that in public
schools, some one of those versions should be read by the

children as the word of God, and frequently that the teacher
who is an unauthorised individual, should give his own opinions as its proper interpretation, and that the child should
be habituated practically to the principle, that it is the right
of each individual to use his own private judgment, and not
the public testimony of the Church as the standard of interpretation; whence you will at once perceive, the total opposition of the principle on which such schools are conducted, to the unchangeable doctrines and discipline of
our Church.

We are desirous that all under our charge should be as
well acquainted with the doctrine found in the Holy Scriptures as with any other portion of the word of God, we also
highly approve of their being familiar with the edifying histories and admirable moral instruction which abound therein,
in, we therefore recommend that the authorised version
be found in the houses of the faithful, and that portions of
it be frequently read with the veneration which it so well
deserves, and meditated upon for the purpose of becoming
better acquainted with the providential ways of the Lord,
for the amendment of life, for the edification of the well
disposed and for the encouragement of virtue. We desire
that at an early period, children should be instructed in
the Sacred History, that they may be made acquainted with
the nature and value of the divine volume, that they be
gradually brought to its perusal with docile hearts, and
that in place of allowing them an indiscriminate use of
that which is difficult and liable to gross misconstruction,
together with what is simple and edifying, they be judi-
ciously led by proper selections, under discreet and pious
guides, to the right use of this rich treasure. Moreover, we
are disposed to doubt seriously whether the introduction
of this sacred volume as an ordinary class book into
schools, is beneficial to religion. It is thereby exposed to
that irreverend familiarity, which is calculated to produce
more contempt than veneration; it is placed side by side
with mere human productions, with the fables of mythol-
ogy and the speculations of a vain philosophy: it is thus
too often made the subject of a vulgar jest, it sinks to the
level of task-books, and shares the aversion and the remarks

which are generally bestowed upon them by children. If
the authorised version be used in a school, it should be
under circumstances very different from those which are
usually found in the public institutions of our States, and
this shows the necessity of your better exertions to establish and uphold seminaries and schools, fitted according
to our own principles, and for the education of the children
who are daily rising up, and numbers of whom are lost for
want of such institutions.

There is another evil of which we have still to complain.
We can scarcely point out a book in general use in the ordinary schools, or even in higher seminaries,
wherein covert and insidious efforts are
not made to misrepresent our principles,
to distort our tenets, to vilify our practices
and to bring contempt upon our Church and its members.
The system of which this is a part has been of long standing,
and is not peculiar to the United States. It is no easy matter
thus to preserve the faith of your children in the midst of
so many difficulties. It is not then because of any unkind
feeling to our fellow-citizens, it is not through any reluctance on our part, to contribute whatever little we can to
the prosperity of what are called the common institutions
of the country, that we are always better pleased to have
a separate system of education for the children of our communion, but because we have found by a painful experience, that in any common effort it was always expected
that our distinctive principles of religious belief and practice should be yielded to the demands of those who thought
proper to charge us with error; and because we saw with
great pain the differences which an attempt to combine
and to conciliate principles, which we have never been
able to reconcile, has produced in a distant Church which
has always been found faithful. We are happy to perceive
the existence of a spirit to sustain the efforts recently made
to supply our schools, and our families with some books,
which whilst they remove the discolourings of fiction, and
vindicate the truth of history, will rescue from unmerited
censure a portion of our illustrious dead, without doing violence to the feelings of even our opponents. We are

**Non-Catholic
Text-Books.**

anxious that truth and charity should have dominion in every place, but especially in our schools. We should be gratified to behold the books of earlier instruction also prepared upon the same principle, and we strenuously recommend to you to encourage and to sustain those who, being properly qualified, may undertake the task.

It is but a few years since the schools which the female religious orders and congregations so usefully superintend, were extensively spread abroad through our Union; already you have gathered rich fruits from the exertions of those virtuous and laborious sisters. The peculiar blessing of heaven appears to rest upon their work, calumny has failed in her vile efforts to taint their fair fame: popular frenzy has been excited by every bad art to effect their ruin, but with one notorious exception, it has been restrained and rebuked, and now we may feel confident, under the blessing of heaven, that in a short period, under your auspices our female children will have secured to them, whether they be blessed with the goods of this world or tried by poverty, the mighty boon of as perfect a system of education as need be admired; nor shall we be subject to the partizan spirit of political leaders, nor dependent upon the unsteady and contested votes of legislative halls for its continuance.

The Sisterhoods.

Respecting our colleges and schools for males, though much has been effected, yet much remains to be done by their multiplication, and we exhort you for the sake of your children, your country and your religion, to come to our aid for the purpose of making the effort thus to provide for the literary, moral and religious education of one sex as well as of the other. We have exposed to you the danger of their position, we confide in your charity and in your zeal.

Catholic Higher Education.

We have heretofore called your attention to the necessity and the obligation of providing for the succession of the ministry as well as for its extension, by erecting and by supporting seminaries for the education of those who aspire to serve at the altar, and to break the bread of life to you and to your descendants. You cannot but be sensible of its abiding importance. We rejoice to find that since our last council much has been done to secure **Vocations to** this object,—America must gradually be-**the Priesthood.** come independent of foreign churches for the perpetuation of her priesthood. At present the tide of immigration is too copious to prevent our dispensing with the aid of an immigrant clergy. The people and the priest are derived from the same source; but gradually we must find our resources within ourselves, and we should make timely preparation. We exhort you then to continue your efforts, and to enkindle your zeal to co-operate with us for this most necessary object.

Neither be you forgetful of the aged and the infirm, who have labored in the vineyard and been exposed to bear the fatigue and the heat of the day. In each Diocess it is fit that there should be a fund for their support and solace, but as yet little has been done to create it or to augment it when created.

There is a subject upon which we have more reason to address you of late than heretofore; not only because of the serious consequences which it has pro-**Christian** duced in Europe, but because of the evils **Marriage.** which it has caused amongst ourselves. We address you upon it freely as our duty requires. There is no state of society which needs a more affectionate bond of union than that of marriage: St. Paul in his epistle to the Ephesians, says, "Husbands love your wives, as Christ also loved the Church, and delivered himself up for it, . . . For this cause shall a man leave father and mother; and shall adhere to his wife: and they shall be two in one flesh,"[23] and to shew the dignity to which it was raised he immediately adds, "This is a great sacrament: but I speak in Christ and in the Church."[24] This was developing what the Saviour stated, as we find in the gospel of St. Matthew, and of which he said "What therefore God hath joined together, let not man put asunder."[25] Hence a valid marriage is indissoluble as the Saviour declared;[26] it is

---

[23] v. 25, &c.   [24] v. 32.   [25] xix. 5, 6.

[26] 8, He saith to them; Moses, because of the hardness of your hearts, per-

therefore of the utmost consequence that they who enter into that holy state, should take all due precaution for their peace on earth, the continuance of their affection, its security and increase, and for having a reasonable hope that they and their children should serve God in spirit and in truth whilst in this world, and should be brought to the enjoyment of his glory in a better.

It is hard to imagine a more painful state of mind than that of a person firmly convinced of the truths of religion, bound to one whose persuasions are different, and beholding beloved children either   **Mixed** lost to the truth or in continual danger of   **Marriages.** perversion. Nor does the mind confine itself to the view of the first generation, it spreads forward over times yet to arise, and multitudes that are successively to make their appearance, and the parent feels accountable for the negligence which spreads amongst them the principle of unbelief. Very many instances of bitter repentance, unavailing as respects the progeny, have come under our observation, and have filled us with sorrow deepened by our sharing in that bitter grief which corroded the heart of one who under the influence of ill regulated attachment flung over the field of future life, the seeds productive for long years of unassuaged affliction. It was to guard against this evil and the consequent loss of so many souls that St.

mitted you to put away your wives: but from the beginning it was not so. 9. And I say unto you whosoever shall put away his wife, except it be for fornication, and shall marry another, committeth adultery: and he who marrieth her that is put away committeth adultery.—*Matthew* xix.

11. And he said to them: Whosoever shall put away his wife and marry another, committeth adultery against her. 12. And if the wife shall put away her husband, and be married to another she committeth adultery.—*Mark* x.

18. Every one that putteth away his wife and marrieth another, committeth adultery; and he that marrieth her that is put away from her husband, committeth adultery.—*Luke* xvi.

2. For a woman that hath a husband, while her husband liveth, is bound to the law: but if her husband be dead, she is loosed from the law of her husband. 3. Wherefore, whilst her husband liveth she shall be called an adulteress if she be with another man: but if her husband be dead, she is free from the law of her husband: so that she is not an adulteress, if she be with another man.—*Romans* vii.

10. But to them that are married, not I, but the Lord commandeth, that the wife depart not from the husband. 11. And if she depart that she remain unmarried, or be reconciled to her husband. And let not the husband put away his wife. . . . 39. A woman is bound by the law, as long as her husband liveth: but if her husband die, she is at liberty: let her marry whom she will, only in the Lord (*in the communion of the Church*).—*Corinthians* vii.

Paul warned the Corinthians "Bear not the yoke with
unbelievers." [27]   He had previously admonished them
that if upon the Christian religion being embraced by one
party, the unbelieving husband or wife would consent to
dwell peaceably with the believer and not prevent the children from being cleansed and made holy through Christ,
the believer was bound by virtue of the previous contract to
remain. But that if the unbeliever would not allow this to
be done in peace, and would depart, then the believing party
was not under bondage, and the marriage which was not
made in the Christian Church, and under the Christian law,
did not produce the Christian obligation.[28]   Here the parties had been united previously to the conversion of the believer, and the case was very different from that to which
he refers in the prohibition in which allusion has been
made above. The principle was explained by the Lord himself, very distinctly at an early period. It is the danger of
perversion.[29]   Neither should any one calculate upon his
self-sufficiency. What an exemplification have we in Solomon![30]

27 2 Cor. vi. 14.

28 12. If any brother have a wife that believeth not, and she consent to dwell
with him, let him not put her away. 13. And if any woman have a husband that
believeth not and he consent to dwell with her; let her not put away her husband. 14. For the unbelieving husband is sanctified by the believing wife; and
the unbelieving wife is sanctified by the believing husband: otherwise your children should be unclean; but now they are holy. 15. But if the unbeliever depart, let him depart. For a brother and sister is not under bondage in such *cases.*
—*1 Corinthians* vii.

29 16. Neither shalt thou take of their daughters a wife for thy son, lest
after they themselves have committed fornication they make thy sons also to
commit fornication with their gods.—*Exodus* xxxiv.
3. Neither shalt thou make marriages with them. Thou shalt not give thy
daughter to his son, nor take his daughter for thy son. 4. For she will turn
away thy son from following me, that he may rather serve strange gods: and
the wrath of the Lord will be kindled, and will quickly destroy thee.—*Deuter-
onomy* vii.

30 1. And King Solomon loved many strange women, besides the daughters
of Pharaoh, and women of Moab, and of Ammon, and of Edom, and of Sidon,
and of the Hethites: 2. Of all the nations concerning which the Lord said to
the children of Israel: You shall not go into them, neither shall any of them
come into yours; for they will most certainly turn away your hearts to follow
their gods. . . . 4. And when he was now old, his heart was turned away by
women to follow strange gods. . . . 5. Solomon worshipped Astarthe, the
goddess of the Sidonians, and Moloch the idol of the Ammonites. . . . 7. Solomon built a temple for Chamos, the idol of the Moab, on the hill that is over
against Jerusalem. . . 8. And he did in this manner for all his wives that
were strangers, who burned incense and offered sacrifice to their gods. 9. And
the Lord was angry with Solomon. . . . . 11. And the Lord therefore said to

From the earliest period of the Christian dispensation, we find the code of discipline invariably opposed to those marriages of members of the Church with persons estranged from her communion; and if occasionally, in a few instances, she unwillingly tolerated the departure, it was only under very peculiar circumstances, and the nuptials were not to receive the blessing of the Church, though the Clergyman was permitted to attend as a witness of the contract. Age succeeding age, we find this discipline continually enforced. Nor was the presence of the Priest permitted, now as a witness, unless upon the previous solemn pledge of both parties, who desired to contract, that all the offspring of the marriage should be baptized and educated in the faith of the Church. We have to lament that this wholesome discipline has been not every where in our province rigidly observed; and we have taken those steps that prudent counsel and our duty suggested, to cause the ancient salutary regulations in this regard, to be brought into full operation. We trust no Priest will be found negligent in the discharge of his duty; and that our effort to preserve unimpaired the doctrine and discipline of our province will meet with the cordial support of our faithful people.

Need we draw your attention to the perfidious conduct of the king of Prussia and his councillors in this regard? After having received in addition to his former domains a large portion of territory **Persecution** inhabited by Catholics, upon pledging his **in Prussia.** royal word that his new subjects should enjoy all their ancient rights and liberties, especially those appertaining to religion; after having entered into several solemn treaties upon the subject of these religious rights, with the holy See, and some of them specially on the discipline of marriage; he sought under the pretext of political regulations to subvert those liberties and to destroy these rights; he introduced hordes of Protestant office holders into the Catholic provinces, and in violation of all his engagements sought by means of their intermarriage with the Catholic

Solomon: because thou hast done this, and hast not kept my covenant, and my precepts which I have commanded thee, I will divide and rend thy kingdom; and will give it to thy servant.—*3 Kings* xi. (Prot. version, 1 Kings.)

females, to spread the new religion through the land, by enacting that whatever might be the stipulation of the parents, all the children should be educated in the Protestant religion. And he cast into prison or sent into banishment the glorious prelates who refused to become the minions of his will. We have found the sentiments of our clergy and of our people in their regard in unison with our own, and we have in their name and in ours sent letters of condolence and affection to the persecuted Archbishops of Cologne, and of Gnesen and Posnen, and also one to our holy father, who has approved of their conduct, and complained of the injustice of which they are victims. Whilst then beloved brethren your sentiments and ours are thus expressed to those glorious confessors of the faith, let us prove by your own conduct that we are animated by a similar spirit to that which they have displayed.

At all times the Church has censured such of her children as became members of societies, bound by solemn obligations to secrecy, by whatever name they may be called, or whatever object they may profess to attain. Experience has taught that some of them having an appearance of inculcating morality, were calculated, if not intended, to subvert the great principles of revealed religion, by sapping the foundations of that faith, without which, as St. Paul says, it is impossible to please God.[31] They acted upon the maxim that moral honesty without regard to difference of belief, was sufficient to render man perfect, and that whatever form of religion he followed, whatever religious doctrine he admitted or rejected, he was equally a true and faithful servant, provided he reduced to practice the precept of fraternal love, and led a moral life according to the principles recognized by the society. You will observe, beloved brethren, that this is a manifest departure from the declaration of the Apostle, from that of the Saviour, requiring that persons should believe his doctrine as promulgated by his Apostle.[32] It is in direct opposition to the

Secret Societies.

31 Heb. xi. 6.

32 16. He that believeth and is baptized, shall be saved: but he that believeth not shall be consumed.—*Mark* xvi.

first principles of our Church, viz. "That man is bound to worship God in that special manner, which is directed by himself and not according to the speculation, or the caprice, or the fashion of the world." Man is bound to believe God when he vouchsafes to reveal his will or his knowledge. In plain opposition to the undoubted principles here laid down, it is proclaimed that all moral members of these Societies, are equally true servants of the great Master of the Universe—Christians of every denomination, Jews, Mahometans, Pagans and Infidels are all associated upon the principle adduced, and thus under the pretext of an expansive liberality, every species of error is admitted to associate with truth, and he who would attempt to introduce amongst the brethren, any distinction upon the ground of religious truth or religious error, would violate the order of the brotherhood. Without entering then into the detail of any of the numerous objections upon other grounds to the principles and the practices of secret Societies, our duty compels us to repeat, that upon this single ground, they who adhere to such Societies, by whatever name they may be recognized, are inadmissible to the Sacraments, and excluded from all the benefits of the Church, until they shall have completely severed the connexion.

It is not our intention to confine the above remarks exclusively to any one Society, they extend to all that are accustomed to have secret proceedings, mysterious symbols, private tokens of recognition and oaths or other pledges of like solemnity, assuming to bind them to secrecy, especially not to divulge a communication to be subsequently made, and upon whose nature they can pass no reasonable judgment when they undertake the obligation.

Amongst those Societies we learn with deep regret, that upon our public works where large masses of the labouring population are kept together, there exist associations of a most demoralizing and dangerous character.

As far as we can discover, the pretext is their own protection, but the practice is monopoly, blasphemy, insubordi-

47. And the Lord added daily to their society, such as should be saved.—*Acts* ii.

12. Nor is there salvation in any other. For there is no other name under heaven even to men, whereby we must be saved.—*Acts* iv.

nation, drunkenness, idleness, riot and the terror of the vicinity. This abundantly explains the rapid demoralization of a class that was originally virtuous, industrious, laborious, useful and peaceable. When once the custom of forming secret Societies is established in any part of a community, it rapidly pervades the entire, and demoralization is the necessary consequence. We earnestly conjure you, then, beloved brethren, to have no part in this pernicious practice, and to use your best efforts to guard others against the delusion that these associations are compatible with good order and religion.

And here, beloved brethren, whilst we disclaim all right to interfere with your judgment in the political affairs of our common country, and are far from entertaining the wish to control you in the constitutional exercises of your freedom— we cannot in justice to ourselves, refrain from addressing to you a few observations equally demanded by the love that we bear to our civil and political institutions, and the obligations of morality. You cannot but be aware that our own views and sentiments, respecting the political parties which divide our national counsels, are as little in harmony as are your own, or those of any other religious body in our land. You cannot, therefore, attribute our monition to any political bias, nor entertain the suspicion that it is meant to produce any political effect. Our object is exclusively the respectability of our land, the stability of our constitution, the perpetuation of our liberties, and the preservation of pure and undefiled religion.

The periods which precede our great elections are usually marked by extraordinary excitement. Associations are formed, committees are appointed, clubs are organised, party spirit is excited, the tongue and the pen are embittered by virulence, truth is disregarded, and more melancholy and more censurable still! freemen of every religious denomination, electors upon the proper exercise of whose judgment we receive statesmen who may save our republic from ruin, or who may degrade them in the eyes of the world, and may destroy our peace and our liberty; voters

The Sacred Obligation of the Ballot.

upon whose virtues and prudence our dearest rights depend,
are brutalized by pampering their meanest passions, are by
vile bribery debased to the lowest grade of infamy and recklessness; and thus what was meant to be a blessing is turned
into a curse. Beloved brethren, flee this contamination,
keep aloof from these crimes—reflect that you are accountable not only to society but to God, for the honest independent and fearless exercise of your own franchise, that it is
a trust confided to you not for your private gain but for
the public good, and that if yielding to any undue influence you act either through favor, affection, or the motives
of dishonest gain against your own deliberate view of what
will promote your country's good, you have violated your
trust, you have betrayed your conscience, and you are a
renegade to your country. Do then, we entreat of you, avoid
the contaminating influence of political strife, keep yourselves aloof from the pestilential atmosphere in which
honor, virtue, patriotism and religion perish; and be assured that our republic never can be respected abroad, nor
sustained at home, save by an uncompromising adherence
to honor, to virtue, to patriotism and to religion. How often
have we had to weep over the havoc of morals, and the
wreck of religion which political excitement has produced.

One word more upon a subject analogous to this. The
divine wisdom assures us [33] that "where pride is, there also
shall be reproach: but where humility is,
there also is wisdom. The simplicity of   The Danger
the just shall guide them: and the deceit-   of Riches.
fulness of the wicked shall destroy them.
Riches shall not profit in the day of revenge. . . . He
that trusteth in riches shall fall: but the just shall spring
up as a green leaf," and again [34] "a covetous man shall not
be satisfied with money, and he that loveth riches shall reap
no fruit from them." And the Saviour warned us,[35] "Take
heed and beware of covetousness: for a man's life doth not
consist in the abundance of things which he possesseth."
The pervading temptations of our land are the pride of
luxury, the speculations of avarice, the love of riches, the
inordinate desire of gain; by these, millions are riveted to

[33] Prov. xi.   [34] Ecc. v.   [35] Luke xii. 15.

this world and become forgetful of God, for wherever our treasure is there also will our hearts be.[36] Be you not then carried away thus, but content with the moderate acquisitions of honest industry, do unto all men as you would they should do unto you, "lay up for yourselves treasures in heaven: where neither the rust nor the moth doth consume, and where thieves do not dig through and steal."

Our attention has been repeatedly given to the subject of intemperance; this vice has spread wide desolation through many lands, it has blighted the **Intemperance.** worldly prospects of several who promised to decorate society by their talents, their acquirements and virtues, it has caused the tear of silent bitterness to consume the strength and to exhaust the happiness of many a family, whilst it has degraded the image of God in man, and filled the world with scandal.[37] It has always been one of the great objects of the Church, to establish the wholesome discipline of temperance amongst her children. Several of her cherished religious orders, have voluntarily renounced the use of wines and ardent spirits, except in cases of the last extremity. Her most learned doctors, her holiest prelates, her devoted missionaries, many who bore high rule over millions, whilst with David they praised the Lord in the midst of splendid courts, were amongst the brightest models of temperance, and even

---

36 Matt. vi. 21.

37 1. Wine is a luxurious thing, and drunkenness riotous: whosoever is delighted therewith, shall not be wise.—*Proverbs* xx.

31. Lamuel! give not wine to kings: because there is no secret where drunkenness reigneth. 32. And lest they drink and forget judgments, and pervert the cause of the children of the poor.—*Ibid.* xxxi.

30. Challength not them that love wine: for wine hath destroyed very many. 31. Fire trieth hard iron: so wine drunk to excess shall rebuke the hearts of the proud. . . . 38. Wine drunken with excess raiseth quarrels and wrath, and many ruins. 39. Wine drunken with excess is bitterness of the soul. 40. The heat of drunkenness is the stumbling block of the fool, lessening strength and causing wounds.—*Ecclesiasticus* xxxi.

11. Wo to you that rise up early in the morning to follow drunkenness, and to drink till the evening to be inflamed with wine. . . . 14. Therefore hath hell enlarged her soul, and opened her mouth without any bounds, &c. . . . 22. Wo to you that are mighty to drink wine, and stout men at drunkenness.—*Isaias* v.

7. But these also have been ignorant through wine, and through drunkenness have erred: the priest and the prophet have been ignorant through drunkenness: they have not known him that seeth, they have been ignorant of judgment. 8. For all tables were full of vomit and filth, so that there was no more any place.—*Ibid.* xxviii.

of austerity; severe to themselves they were more indulgent to others. They were aware of the distinction which our blessed Saviour established between the precepts of the gospel, and its counsels of perfection.[38] And whilst they aspired to follow the latter as a rule for their own conduct, they exhibited the former as the obligation of the Christian. Unlike to those who bound heavy and insupportable burden's upon men's shoulders, without applying a finger of their own to move them,[39] they undertook to carry the yoke, and to bear the weight, and to allure others by their example, declaring that they experienced the truth of our Saviour's assurance, that his yoke was sweet, and his burden light.[40]

Endeavouring to imitate their prudence, if we do not emulate their austerity, we neither feel ourselves warranted to require, nor called upon to recommend to all our flocks, a total abstinence from a beverage which the sacred Scriptures do not prohibit, and of which the most holy persons have occasionally partaken.[41] We however, do commend the resolution of those persons who, to guard the more effectually against temptation, and to endeavour by their

[38] 16. And behold one came and said to him: Good master what good shall I do, that I may have life everlasting? 17. And he said to him: Why asketh thou me concerning good? One is good, God. But if thou wilt enter into life keep the commandments. 18. He saith to him: Which? And Jesus said: Thou shalt do no murder: Thou shalt not commit adultery: Thou shalt not steal: Thou shalt not bear false witness. 19. Honour thy father and thy mother: and, Thou shalt love thy neighbour as thyself. 20. The young man said to him: All these I have kept from my youth: What is yet wanting to me? 21. Jesus saith to him: If thou wilt be perfect, go, sell what thou hast, and give to the poor; and thou shalt have a treasure in heaven: and come follow me.—*Matthew* xix.

10. His disciples say to him: If the case of a man with his wife be so, it is not good to marry. 11. He said: All receive not this word, but they to whom it is given.—*Ibid.*

38. Therefore he that giveth his virgin in marriage doeth well: And he that giveth her not doeth better.—*1 Corinthians* vii.

[39] Matt. xxxiii. 4.   [40] Matt. xi. 28, 29, 30.

[41] 32. Wine taken with sobriety is equal life to men: If thou drink it moderately, thou shalt be sober. . . . 35. Wine was created from the beginning to make men joyful and not to make them drunk. 36. Wine drunken with moderation is joy of the soul and heart. 37. Sober drinking is health to soul and body.—*Ecc.* xxxi.

33. For John the Baptist came, neither eating bread nor drinking wine, and you say: He hath a devil. 34. The Son of man is come, eating and drinking, and you say: Behold a man that is a glutton and a drinker of wine, a friend of publicans and sinners.—*Luke* vii.

23. Do not still drink water, but use a little wine for the stomach's sake and thy frequent infirmities.—*1 Timothy* v.

example and influence, the eradication of vice, and having no need of their use, abstain altogether from ardent spirits.

We are taught by the Saviour, that without him we can do nothing.[42] We must be aided by his grace, if we would effectually overcome vice and practice virtue. They who would subdue drunkenness, who would restrain intemperance, should be sustained by him from whom is all our strength. "Unless the Lord build the house, they labour in vain that build it."[43] Much as we may esteem the motives and the object of those, who by mere human means, endeavour to produce this salutary reform, and greatly as we may prize the moral improvement in which they have aided, we are fully convinced that no lasting amendment will be insured, save by the grace of God through our Lord Jesus Christ. Hence we would desire to see established amongst us, those pious confraternities, which at all times have done so much good to true religion and to pure morals, by mutual encouragement to partake of the Sacraments, which are the channels of grace established by our blessed Saviour, to convey to our souls this precious treasure, by which we may be enriched and strengthened to every good work, to sobriety, to temperance, to justice, to benevolence, to charity, to patience, to chastity, to the fulfilment of the law, to the observance of the counsels, to the adornment of the doctrine of God our Saviour in all things.

The seductions of the world are many, and its spirit is powerful, but with the aid of the Lord, by the practice of prayer, by the habit of meditation on the law of the Lord, by mutual kind advice and friendly monition, by edifying their brethren and strangers, by their good order, and the respectability of their demeanour, and above all by the aid derived from frequently receiving the Sacraments of Penance and the Holy Eucharist, these confraternities would overcome the world, they would win upon the negligent and the criminal, they would secure respect for religion and would extend peace and good will upon earth, and contribute to the glory given to the most high God of heaven.

42 John xx. 5.   43 Psalm cxxvi.

We have to request that in your prayers you will be mindful of our benefactors. You are aware that in Europe there are two great societies, that by constant and very moderate individual contributions, have for some years back accumulated large alms for the aid of struggling missions, and their alms are   **The Societies** enriched by their daily prayers, that the   **of Lyons and** Lord would vouchsafe to bless the labours   **of Vienna.** of those who are sent forth to combat against error and vice. One of these societies extends through the Austrian dominions, and its executive council is at Vienna; the other had its origin in France, but now extends through several other nations of Europe: its labours and its funds are divided; the executive council for the Eastern hemisphere holds its sessions in Paris, that for the Western at Lyons. We have been generously aided both from Vienna and Lyons. To the benefactions of our brethren in the faith, we owe much of the progress that we have made, to these you owe many of your churches, to them you are indebted for the services of many valuable missionaries, the support of some of our seminaries, and God alone can estimate the mighty value of their pious supplications. Whilst they possess our confidence and receive our gratitude, let them not be forgotten at the holy altar, let them be remembered in our chambers, let them have a place in our hearts, so that when we lift those hearts in aspirations to heaven, the affection that we bear them may waft their deeds of charity before our Father, and he may requite their mercy with a rich reward.[44]

Let us then, beloved brethren, animated by the glorious example which they have given, and encouraged by their generous aid, exert ourselves to co-operate in the holy effort, by giving more abundantly of the means which God has placed at our disposal. Let the spirit of cordial affection for each other predominate in our churches, that we may labour

---

[44] 40. He that receiveth you, receiveth me: and he that receiveth me, receiveth him that sent me. 41. He that receiveth a prophet in the name of a prophet, shall receive the reward of a prophet: and he that receiveth a just man in the name of a just man shall receive the reward of a just man. 42. And whosoever shall give to drink to one of these little ones a cup of cold water only in the name of a disciple, Amen, I say to you, he shall not lose his reward.— *Matthew* x.

together for the great cause of our common Redeemer. Let the weak be sustained by the strong, and let the wants of the several struggling churches be considered the charge of the body, for Christ is not divided.

Amongst our various missions, one of the most interesting is that amongst our aboriginal tribes in the west. Thousands of those children of the forest, are pious members in our communion, and thousands more are desirous of instruction.

Indian Missions.

Their case has been represented to us from a most respectable quarter, as one deserving of your special attention. We therefore recommend it to you in the Lord, advising you that whatsoever you may feel disposed to contribute should be sent through your immediate pastors to your bishop, who will carefully secure its application to this most charitable object.

And now brethren, we commend you to the Lord for his holy protection, beseeching you to walk worthy of your vocation. "Let us therefore cast off the works of darkness and put on the armour of light, let us walk honestly as in the day, not in rioting and drunknness, not in chambering and impurities, not in contention and envy, but put ye on the Lord Jesus Christ:"[45] "Loving one another with brotherly love; in honour preventing one another; in solicitude not slothful; in spirit fervent; serving the Lord; rejoicing in hope; patient in tribulation; instant in prayer; communicating to the necessities of the saints; pursuing hospitality; bless them that persecute you; bless and curse not; rejoice with them that rejoice; weep with them that weep; being of one mind to one another; not high minded but condescending to the humble; be not wise in your own conceits: render to no man evil for evil; provide things good not only in the sight of God, but also in the sight of all men; if it be possible, as much as is in you have peace with all men."[46] "And the peace of God which surpasseth all understanding keep your hearts and minds in Christ Jesus."[47]—*Amen.*

Conclusion.

45 Rom. xiii. 12, 13, 14.
46 Rom. xii. 10, 11, 12, 13, 14, 15, 16, 17, 18.   47 Philip. iv. 7.

Given in Provincial Council, in Baltimore, this 23d day of May, in the year of our Lord, 1840.

✠SAMUEL, *Archbishop of Baltimore.*

✠BENEDICT JOSEPH, *Bishop of Bardstown.*

✠JOHN, *Bishop of Charleston.*

✠JOSEPH, *Bishop of St. Louis.*

✠BENEDICT, *Bishop of Boston.*

✠MICHAEL, *Bishop of Mobile.*

✠FRANCIS PATRICK, *Bishop of Arath; Coadjutor of Philadelphia.*

✠JOHN BAPTIST, *Bishop of Cincinnati.*

✠ANTHONY, *Bishop of New Orleans.*

✠MATTHIAS, *Bishop of Dubuque.*

✠RICHARD PIUS, *Bishop of Nashville.*

✠CELESTIN, *Bishop of Vincennes.*

CHAPTER VII

THE PASTORAL LETTER OF 1843

EACH Provincial Council witnessed an increasing number of prelates from the newly created dioceses, and also chronicled the passing of one or more of the great bishops who had guided previous assemblies of the hierarchy. One figure was missing from among the sixteen prelates who met at Baltimore on May 13, 1843, for the Fifth Provincial Council. Upon no prelate in the score of years that had passed since his consecration in 1820, did the American hierarchy depend so much in its deliberations as upon John England, Bishop of Charleston, who died on April 11, 1842. His was the dominating influence and the guiding spirit of the first four Provincial Councils, and his death left a vacancy in the ranks which was never filled. While no mention is made regarding the authorship of the Pastorals of 1833, 1837, and 1840, they are so similar to his nervous and manly style that we may not be wrong in attributing them to his pen. The short Pastoral of 1843, which follows, is different in tone and in the range of its subjects. There is absent from its pages any forewarning of the terrible outbreak against the Catholic faith which was to occur the following spring. Rather do the prelates appear to ignore the signs of the coming storm, and to confine themselves to the questions of education, temperance and divorce, with a passing reference to the Oxford Movement.

THE PASTORAL LETTER OF 1843

(Fifth Provincial Council of Baltimore)

Venerable Brethren of the Clergy and Beloved Brethren of the Laity: Grace to you, and peace from God our Father, and from the Lord Jesus Christ.

ENCOURAGED by the assurance of our Divine Redeemer: "Where there are two or three gathered together in my name, there am I in the midst of them;" we have assembled in council, according to the most ancient practice of the

Church, and having humbly invoked the Holy Ghost, we have deliberated on various matters appertaining to the good order of ecclesiastical affairs, and the advancement of piety. Before separating we feel impelled to address you, with a view to impart to you some spiritual grace to strengthen you, and stir you up by admonition to labour the more, that by good works you may make sure your vocation and election. We can add nothing to the divine deposit of revelation committed to the special guardianship of Peter and the other apostles, and preserved in the Church of God, which is the pillar and ground of the truth; nor dare we take away an iota from it; but it is our duty to exhort you to stand fast in faith, and to beware, lest, being led away from the error of the unwise, you fall from your own steadfastness. God requires you to captivate every understanding in obedience to Christ, and not to be more wise than it behoveth to be wise; but to be wise to sobriety. The pride of man is always ready to revolt against the truth of God. Confidence in the strength of our intellectual faculties, leads us to scan the depths of heavenly mysteries, and investigate the works of God; but he that is a searcher of majesty, shall be overwhelmed with glory. The homage of humble faith is required of us, when evidence is presented of the fact of divine revelation, and we must adore all that God reveals, however it surpass our comprehension. Of all the errors that assail divine truth, the most dangerous, because the most insidious, is that which appears to respect it, while it holds it in question, as if it were impossible to ascertain it with certainty. It were unworthy of God to have made a revelation, and left it without such marks of its origin as would satisfy the sincere enquirer, acting under divine influence; and it is absurd to suppose that we can with impunity reject any thing of which we have evidence that God is its author. There is one Lord, one faith, one baptism. Without faith it is impossible to please God. Beware then, brethren, of preferring in the least point the dictates of your erring reason to the truth, wisdom, and authority of the Most High.

It is your duty to make public profession of the faith whenever the divine honor, or the edification of your

neighbor is in question, for "with the heart we believe unto justice, but with the mouth confession is made unto salvation." Public worship and private de-
Profession of the Faith. votion must be regulated by the revealed law of God, as declared by his Church; for God must be worshipped in spirit and in truth. You should, therefore, never make acts of religion mere matters of courtesy, wherein the good pleasure of your fellow-men might be regarded rather than the sovereign will of God. It is on this account, and to avoid all participation in error, that the Church commands her children not to communicate in spiritual things with those who are out of her fold. It has nevertheless come to our knowledge, that the consciences of many in dependent situations are aggrieved by vexatious measures adopted to coerce them into conformity, under the penalty of wanting bread, and that in various public institutions attendance at Protestant worship is in many instances exacted of Catholics, notwithstanding the liberty of conscience which is guaranteed by the constitution to all citizens. We are aware that mere considerations of order have induced this custom, but as it is repugnant to the genius of our institutions, as well as to the spirit of our religion, we trust that the proper authorities, on respectful remonstrance, will afford relief to afflicted consciences.

The transmission of faith to their children was a special object of the solicitude of our fathers: for which they thought no sacrifice too great. It must be
Instruction of the Young. your care, brethren, to let the precious inheritance descend without diminution. You must, therefore, use all diligence that your children be instructed at an early age in the saving truths of religion, and be preserved from the contagion of error. We have seen with serious alarm, efforts made to poison the fountains of public education, by giving it a sectarian hue, and accustoming children to the use of a version of the Bible made under sectarian bias, and placing in their hands books of various kinds replete with offensive and dangerous matter. This is plainly opposed to the free genius of our civil institutions. We admonish parents of

the awful account they must give at the divine tribunal, should their children, by their neglect or connivance, be imbued with false principles, and led away from the path of salvation. Parents are strictly bound, like faithful Abraham, to teach their children the truths which God has revealed; and if they suffer them to be led astray, the souls of the children will be required at their hands. Let them, therefore, avail themselves of their natural rights, guaranteed by the laws, and see that no interference with the faith of their children be used in the public schools, and no attempt made to induce conformity in any thing contrary to the laws of the Catholic Church.

We would have you, brethren, most condescending in every thing that principle and duty will allow, in order the more effectually to cement together, and unite all classes of citizens in mutual affection. Yet we cannot dissemble that faith and morals are exposed and endangered by objectionable associations. All societies are to be shunned by whatsoever name they may be called, the objects whereof are not distinctly declared, and wherein the solemnity of an oath, or any corresponding engagement, is employed to veil the ends of the association, or its proceedings, from the public eye. It is plainly a rash use of the name of God, where the object for which it is employed is not distinctly understood: and since all just objects may be openly avowed and pursued, the mantle of secrecy is needlessly thrown around them. We would not judge unkindly of any body of men, or of any individuals, professing to have in view objects of philanthropy and mutual aid; but we cannot conceal our apprehensions that by assuming mere natural principles as their guide, they insensibly prepare themselves for discarding revealed religion, so that some find themselves divested of faith, before they are conscious of the tendency and influence of the society with which they have connected themselves. We, therefore, feel ourselves bound to renew thus solemnly our admonitions to all who claim to be members of the Church, and to remind them of the several decrees of the sovereign pontiffs in regard to secret societies, and to declare anew that sacra-

Secret Societies.

mental absolution cannot be lawfully or validly imparted
to persons continuing to profess themselves members of
such societies. We conjure all our children in Christ by his
tender mercies, to shun all such associations, and through
no consideration of interest or fear, to continue in a connexion so opposed to the positive laws of the Church, and
so dangerous to the integrity of faith. The privileges of
membership in the great society of the faithful are granted
on condition of obedience to the laws of the Church; and
are forfeited when acts are done to which the penalty of
privation is attached.

In calling on you brethren, to avoid these dangerous associations, we mean not to weaken, but rather to strengthen
your social relations to your fellow-citizens
generally. No difference of religious sentiment varies the eternal rules of justice:
no errors, or even crimes, deprive any one
of his claims on your charity, in virtue of the law of Him
who said: "love your enemies; do good to them that hate
you; bless them that curse you, and pray for them that persecute and calumniate you." "If it be possible," says the
apostle, "as much as in you lies, have peace with all men."
"Do good to all men," and if especially to those who are of
the household of the faith, yet to others likewise, with sincere, effectual beneficence. To you we trust for the practical refutation of all those atrocious calumnies which deluded men, severally or in odious combinations, constantly
circulate by every possible means against our holy religion.
Your strict integrity in the daily concerns of life, your
fidelity in the fulfilment of all engagements, your peaceful
demeanour, your obedience to the laws, your respect for the
public functionaries, your unaffected exercise of charity
in the many occasions which the miseries and sufferings
of our fellow-men present; in fine, your sincere virtue will
confound those vain men whose ingenuity and industry are
exerted to cast suspicion on our principles, and evoke
against us all the worst passions of human nature. Let
then, your entire deportment be good, "that whereas they
speak against you as evil doers, considering you by your
good works, they may glorify God in the day of visitation.

The Claims
of Charity.

For so is the will of God, that by doing well you may put to silence the ignorance of foolish men." Whilst you justly prize the civil rights which you enjoy in common with your fellow-citizens, be mindful of the allegiance which you owe to the King of kings and the Lord of lords. Give to God what belongs to God, the homage of enlightened faith and the cheerful obedience of your wills. "As free, and not as making liberty a cloak of malice, but as the servants of God."[1]

The enormous evils of intemperance, which no tongue can portray, have given occasion to the adoption of a remedy apparently extreme. Millions in Ireland, and many thousands in this country have publicly pledged themselves to abstain from the use of all intoxicating liquors.

The Evils of Intemperance.

We cannot but approve the determination thus taken by such as have had the misfortune to contract this dreadful vice; for we have rarely seen the drunkard reclaimed, except by the total abandonment of the occasion of his sin: we also highly applaud the generous charity and zeal of such, as through compassion for the unfortunate have stept forward to share with them the privation, but we deem it right to guard against the possible abuse of so excellent an institution. It must be distinctly understood and avowed that the moderate use of wine, or any other liquor is of itself perfectly lawful, since "every creature of God is good, and nothing is to be rejected which is received with thanksgiving, for it is sanctified by the word of God and prayer."[2] It would not be advisable to impose or to assume generally the obligation of total abstinence, since, considering human frailty, it might become a snare of souls, and change a lawful act into sin, and add to the sting of conscience the terror of despair. We will, therefore, that the pledge usually made be regarded as a resolution, which whilst it affords to those who take it the advantages of mutual examples and prayers, imposes no new moral obligation, so that the person who should fail in its observance, sins only by excess, or by exposing himself to danger in consequence of his peculiar frailty. Let each one at the

[1] 1 Peter ii. 16.   [2] 1 Tim. iv. 4.

same time remember that it is only through the grace of
Jesus Christ that we can effectually overcome temptation
and practice virtue unto salvation. "Unless the Lord build
the house they labor in vain that build it: unless the Lord
keep the city he watcheth in vain that keepeth it."[3] Let no
man presume on the strength of his determination, or on the
restraining influence of public opinion. The torrent of passion easily sweeps away these human barriers. Prayer, vigilance, the reception of the sacraments, the flight from the
occasions of sin are necessary in order to give effect to our
good purposes, which themselves must proceed from the
inspiration of divine grace, for "we are not sufficient to
think any thing of ourselves, as of ourselves, but our sufficiency is from God."[4] It is on this account we warn you
against uniting in societies not based on religious principles,
nor directed by the ecclesiastical authority, or otherwise
organised in such a way as may suppose mere human influences and means.

These things, beloved brethren, we have thought necessary to place before you that you may proceed in all things
with enlightened faith, and trusting in God who strengthens
the humble, resist with untiring efforts every temptation.
"And that knowing the time: that is now the hour for us to
rise from sleep; for now our salvation is nearer than we believed. The night is passed, and the day is at hand. Let
us, therefore, cast off the works of darkness, and put on
the armor of light. Let us walk honestly as in the day; not
in rioting and drunkenness, not in chambering and impurities, not in contention and envy. But put ye on the Lord
Jesus Christ, and make not provision for the flesh in its
concupiscences."[5]

We deplore the enormous scandal of some who, having
already contracted marriage, enter into new engagements
during the life time of their lawful con-
Divorce.   sorts. Others, though few in number, have
sought from the civil authority a divorce
from the bond of matrimony, and have ventured to pass
to a second marriage, notwithstanding the indissoluble
character of the marriage-tie,—God having prohibited the

[3] Psalm cxxvi.   [4] 2 Cor. iii. 5.   [5] Rom. xiii. 11.

separation of those whom he has united. We are determined to employ the severest authority of the Church
against persons guilty of so heinous a crime, and to cut
them off from her communion, delivering them over to
Satan, that by humiliation in time, their spirit may be saved
in the day of Christ.

   We give thanks to God for the wonderful blessing which
he has vouchsafed to his Church in these United States,
where within half a century the number of
bishops has increased from one to seven-   Obedience
teen, and the faithful are daily seen to ad-   to Church
vance in piety as well as numbers. One or   Authority.
two painful instances of insubordination
to ecclesiastical authority, which have recently occurred,
are exceptions to the general docility and obedience of our
flock; and we trust that the parties concerned will use all
their efforts, by affectionate submission, to cause the scandal of resistance to be forgotten. Our power is given us
by the Lord for edification, not for destruction; we lord it
not over you, by reason of your faith; we seek your salvation, not the display of authority. The deluded men who
occasionally resist the divine ordinance, and violate the
order which God has established, disturb the peace of the
faithful, and spread scandal and disorder, under the pretext of defending popular rights, whilst in reality they deprive the faithful of those spiritual privileges which are
their most precious inheritance. It has been already declared and defined, in the first provincial council, that
the appointment and removal of pastors are the rightful
prerogative of the bishop, and that it is the duty of the congregation to make a reasonable and just provision for the
support of the pastor so appointed; the resistance to which
right would force the bishop to a severe exercise of the
ecclesiastical authority.

   We cannot withhold the expression of our consolation
at the success which has crowned the apostolic labors of
missionaries of the Society of Jesus in the vast regions occupied by Indian tribes, especially in the Oregon territory
west of the Rocky Mountains. With zeal worthy of the
brightest ages of the Church, they have gone to those chil-

dren of nature to civilize them, and impart to them the knowledge of salvation, and God has confirmed their word, and made it fruitful. "How beautiful upon

Indian and
Liberian
Missions.

the mountains are the feet of him that bringeth good tidings and that preacheth peace: of him that showeth forth good, that preacheth salvation, that saith to Sion: Thy God shall reign. The voice of thy watchmen: they have lifted up their voice, they shall praise together: for they shall see eye to eye when the Lord shall convert Sion. Rejoice and give praise together, O ye deserts of Jerusalem: for the Lord hath comforted his people: he hath redeemed Jerusalem. The Lord hath prepared his holy arm in the sight of all the Gentiles: and all the ends of the earth shall see the salvation of our God."[6] Whilst the sons of Ignatius emulate the apostolic labors of Xavier, two devoted ecclesiastics from two of our dioceses, have generously consecrated themselves to the salvation of the colored emigrants from the United States in Africa and the natives of Western Africa. Foregoing all the comforts of civilized life, they have resolutely encountered all the difficulties of an undertaking that presents no flattering prospects of success. Pressed forward by the charity of Christ, they only considered the degraded condition of man in the country marked out for their labors, and they hasten to afford him the succors of religion, content with whatever measure of success it may please God to grant to their efforts. Let us pray, beloved brethren, that a blessing may be given to the apostolic prelate now charged with this mission, and the faithful band associated with him in the arduous undertaking. Your prayers should ascend to God for this end, and your alms cannot be better applied, than in enabling ministers of religion to meet the heavy expenses of their journeys and missionary establishments among the Indians and Africans. We recommend both missions to your generous charity and zeal.

Whilst we exhort you to extend your charity to the distant children of our common Father, we would not have you neglect more immediate objects. It is by placing the

6 Isa. lii. 7.

ecclesiastical institutions in the respective diocesses on solid foundations, that you will secure for yourselves and your children the perpetuity of the blessings wherewith it has pleased God to enrich   Supporting you in Christ Jesus. Those to whom the   Catholic wealth of this world has been given, can-   Institutions. not better employ a portion of it than in providing for the education of ministers of the altar. We are far, however, from meaning to undervalue the offerings which faith may inspire for the erection of temples to the glory of God, or charity may present for the clothing and maintenance of the orphan. We exhort you, brethren, to follow the impulse of the Holy Ghost in the various good works for which your charitable co-operation is solicited, and to remember in the day of your abundance, that whatever you set apart to the glory of God, in the exercise of charity, is so much secured against the caprice of fortune. Be not then high-minded, nor hope in uncertain riches, but in the living God (who giveth us abundantly all things to enjoy;) do good; be rich in good works; distribute readily; communicate; lay up in store for yourselves a good foundation against the time to come, that you may obtain true life.

We cannot conclude without expressing our gratitude to God for the admirable change which his grace has wrought in the minds of many in England, and the effects whereof are seen even in   The Oxford this country. We are not disposed to ex-   Movement. aggerate this moral revolution, or to form sanguine calculations as to its immediate results. It is not for us to know the times or the moments which the Father has placed in his own power, but we love to hope that the days of perfect unity may not be far distant, when the nations whom the violent passions of men have torn from the bosom of the Church, will return repentant, saying to each other: "Come and let us go up to the mountain of the Lord, and to the house of the God of Jacob, and he will teach us his ways, and we will walk in his paths."[7] At all events it is our duty to pray for so desirable an object, conformably

7 Isaiah ii. 3.

to the example of our divine Redeemer, who at his last supper prayed that all who believe in him might be one, even as He and the Father are one. Brethren, if you ask the Father anything in his name, he will give it you. "If two or three of you agree together on earth concerning anything whatsoever, it shall be granted you." How much more, then, if from the two hemispheres the supplications of fervent faith and charity ascend from innumerable multitudes, to obtain light for those who wander amidst errors, that they may see the whole truth, and courage that they may confess it, that with one mind and with one mouth they may with us glorify God and the Father of our Lord Jesus Christ.

"We beseech you, brethren, rebuke the unquiet; comfort the feeble-minded; support the weak; be patient towards all men. See that none render evil for evil to any one; but always follow that which is good towards each other, and towards all men." "The grace of our Lord Jesus Christ be with you. Amen."

Given at Baltimore, in the fifth Provincial Council, on the fifth Sunday after Easter, in the year of our Lord, MDCCCXLIII.

✝SAMUEL, *Archbishop of Baltimore.*
✝BENEDICT JOSEPH, *Bishop of Boston.*
✝MICHAEL, *Bishop of Mobile.*
✝FRANCIS PATRICK, *Bishop of Philadelphia.*
✝JOHN BAPTIST, *Bishop of Cincinnati.*
✝GUY IGNATIUS, *Bishop of Bolena, and Coadjutor of the Bishop of Louisville.*
✝ANTHONY, *Bishop of New Orleans.*
✝MATHIAS, *Bishop of Dubuque.*
✝JOHN, *Bishop of New York.*
✝RICHARD PIUS, *Bishop of Nashville.*
✝CELESTIN, *Bishop of Vincennes.*
✝JOHN JOSEPH, *Bishop of Natchez.*
✝RICHARD VINCENT, *Bishop of Richmond.*
✝PETER PAUL, *Bishop of Zela, and Administrator of the Diocess of Detroit.*

✝PETER RICHARD, *Bishop of Drasis, and Coadjutor of the Bishop of St. Louis.*

✝JOHN M., *Bishop of Claudiopolis, and Vicar Apostolic of Texas.*

RICHARD S. BAKER, *Administrator of the Diocese of Charleston.*

The year after the Council of 1843 "is written black in the history of Philadelphia, because of the un-American and un-Christian scenes of violence that disgraced the traditions of the City of Brotherly Love." Though forgotten now, the *Pastoral Letter to the Clergy and the members of the Protestant Episcopal Church in the United States of America* (Phila., Oct., 1844), not only failed to deplore the terrible outrages which took place in May and July, 1844, but apparently justified them. Only the courage of the man and the prelate who, from this time on to the Civil War, became the most potent force in the American Church, John Hughes, Archbishop of New York, saved the honour of the nation from similar outbreaks in other cities. The unspeakable calumnies of Bishop Breckinridge, of Maryland, in his *Papism in the Nineteenth Century in the United States*, were penned for one purpose—the destruction of the Catholic Church in the nation. In all Christian charity, however, the Fathers of the next Council, which met at Baltimore on May 9, 1846, deemed it best to pass over the Native Americanism of the period in silence.

CHAPTER VIII

THE PASTORAL LETTER OF 1846

THE war with Mexico was beginning while the Fathers penned this short Pastoral (May, 1846). The Sixth Provincial Council was an important assembly of the American hierarchy, not only on account of the number and prestige of the bishops who were in attendance, but for the fact that among its enactments was one decreeing that the Blessed Virgin Mary, under the title of the Immaculate Conception, was henceforth the Patroness of the Church in the United States.

THE PASTORAL LETTER OF 1846

(Sixth Provincial Council of Baltimore)

The Archbishop and Bishops of the United States to the Clergy and Faithful of their charge: Grace to you, and Peace from God our Father, and from the Lord Jesus Christ.

ASSEMBLED together in Council, by the merciful permission of God, we have endeavored, by united prayer and mutual consultation, to obtain the necessary light for the promotion of the important interests confided to our care. From the harmony which prevailed in our deliberations, we have reason to believe that Christ, according to his promise, was in the midst of us, directing us by his truth, and animating us by his Spirit. After consultation with our brethren of the second order of the clergy, we have adopted some regulations for your spiritual advantage which, when approved of by our venerable Chief, the successor of Peter, to whose examination and correction, according to ancient custom, we have submitted them, we shall make known to you, fully confident that you will embrace them with docility, and, emulating the example of the first believers, receive our decrees with the reverence with which they regarded the precepts of the apostles and ancients, delivered in the council of Jerusalem. We bear willing testimony to your faith and piety, and we feel confident that you will testify that the exercise of our authority over you has not been in a spirit of domination, as if we lorded it over you, on account of your faith; but that we have had solely in view the salvation of your souls. To aid in the accomplishment of this end, we will willingly spend, and be ourselves spent over and above; and, carefully avoiding whatever might prove a hindrance to the progress of the gospel, we will endeavor to be your pattern from the heart, that we may please the Prince of Pastors, and obtain from his hands a glorious and unfading crown.

We have abundant motives for devout thanksgiving in the steady progress of our holy religion, which daily gains the homage of the intelligent and learned, as well as of the lowly and poor, whom God **Progress of** has specially chosen, rich in faith. The **the Faith.** return of so many distinguished individuals in England to the Catholic communion, from which that illustrious nation was torn by the strong arm of the civil power, has filled us with joy, since all the portions of the church must rejoice in her triumphs, as they sympathize in her afflictions. Their example should have considerable influence on all who feel themselves inclined to re-examine the cause of separation and to embrace unity, whose importance and value become daily more obvious even to those who are withheld. Conflicts in doctrine among the professors of Christianity are calculated to afford a triumph to the unbeliever, who sets no value on a revelation which appears to him uncertain and contradictory whilst they scandalize and confound the unlearned, who abandon the inquiry after truth, in despair of ascertaining it with certainty. Hence the claims of the church to our assent are strengthened in the minds of serious and reflecting men, who are struck with the unchangeable character of her teaching, the same always, every where, and by all. One Lord, one faith, one baptism, is inscribed on her standard by an inspired apostle. As faith is the homage of the human understanding to divine revelation, it can admit of no doctrinal diversity, since God has not revealed contradictions, and his wisdom must have devised a sure means for ascertaining the truths which he has revealed.

After three centuries of contention the human mind, weary of doubt and unbelief, seems eager to repose on that authority whose support it once proudly rejected, in the confidence of its own strength. The great Augustin, whose sublime genius, great learning, and exalted piety, have gained the admiration of the Christian world, commended authority as the compendious and easy way to truth;[1] and after wandering through the mazes of error, under the delusive hope of discovering the reason and evidence of all things, he found himself obliged to rest his belief in the revealed truths on the authority of the Catholic church. Many persons, highly distinguished for talent and learning, have recently followed his example. The process to which the doctrines of religion have been subjected by the skeptical spirit of the sixteenth century, has resulted in the successive abandonment of one doctrine after another by professed believers in the Gospel, until scarcely any thing of the deposit of revelation remains uncontroverted. In the name of the divine Scriptures, every mystery has been assailed, as if it were allowable to deny all they contain, provided respect be professed for the sacred oracles themselves. But the Providence of God has at length brought about another result from the bold scrutiny into things divine, which the pride of man thus attempted. Many sincere inquirers have acknowledged the Catholic doctrines, of which they found evidence in the Scriptures, as well as in the writings of the ancient fathers. Some have embraced the whole body of Catholic truth, as propounded and defined in the holy Council of Trent, who nevertheless remain outside the church, fondly clinging to local institutions, or cherishing the fallacious hope that they may, without peril to their souls, remain in a position which was not originally of their own choosing. The profession of Catholic doctrine can not, it is obvious, avail them whilst they remain separated from the church of Christ, and from the pastor to

The Oxford Movement.

---

1 De quantit. animæ, c. vii. n. 12.

whom he entrusted his lambs and sheep, that is, his whole flock, that there might be one fold and one shepherd.

Brethren, we would wish to excite your charity for those who, whilst struggling forward towards truth and unity, are drawn back by the interests of this world, and love the glory of men, rather than the glory of God. It is no easy matter to be disabused of all the prejudices of education; but it is still more difficult to go forth from one's kindred to the mountain to which the Lord points, there to glorify him by obedience and sacrifice. You should pray that light and grace may be given them, that others, encouraged by their example, may follow into the temple of the heavenly King, to give him the homage which he demands. To the prayers offered up in the various places for those separated from the unity of the church, we may principally ascribe the extraordinary change effected in so many learned professors, who from teachers of error have become disciples of truth; in so many ministers, who have left the place of honor in which they stood, to mingle with the undistinguished crowd of devout worshippers. All things are promised to prayer. If the petition of two or three, who agree on any thing, finds acceptance with the Father, when offered in the name of his beloved Son, what may we not hope for when thousands and millions unite in supplication for that which was the object of the prayer of Christ on the night before the consummation of his sacrifice for the sins of men? Be instant, brethren, in prayer. We desire most especially that supplications, prayers, intercessions, and thanksgivings be made for all men. For this is good and acceptable in the sight of God our Saviour, who will have all men to be saved, and to come to the knowledge of the truth.

The paternal authority of the chief Bishop is constantly misrepresented and assailed by the adversaries of our holy religion, especially in this country, and is viewed with suspicion even by some who   The Papacy. acknowledge its powerful influence in preserving faith and unity. It is unnecessary for us to tell you, brethren, that the kingdom of Christ of which the Bishop of Rome, as successor of Peter, has received the keys, is not of this world;—and that the obedience due to the Vicar of the Saviour is in no way inconsistent with your civil allegiance, your social duties as citizens, or your rights as men. We can confidently appeal to the whole tenor of our instructions, not only in our public addresses, but in our most confidential communications; and you can bear witness that we have always taught you to render to Cæsar the things that are Cæsar's, to God the things that are God's. Be not, then, heedful of the misrepresentations of foolish men, who, unable to combat the evidences of our faith, seek to excite unjust prejudice against that authority which has always proved its firmest support. Continue to practise justice and charity towards all your fellow citizens; respect the magistrates, observe the laws, shun tumult and disorder: as free, and not as having liberty as a cloak for malice, but as the servants of God. Thus you will put to shame the calumniators of our faith, and vindicate it more effectually than by any abstract profession or disclaimer. You, brethren, have been called unto liberty: only make not liberty an occasion to the flesh, but, by charity of spirit, serve one another. For all the law is fulfilled in one word: Thou shalt love thy neighbor as thyself.

We shall not attempt distinctly to notice the various artifices employed to impede the progress of our holy religion by designing and interested men: but we rejoice that its truth and beauty are daily more manifest to sincere inquirers. By the example of a holy life and by prayer, you, brethren, can effectually promote its interests.

The zeal of our brethren in Europe has given rise to an Association for the propagation of the faith, which, originating in Lyons, has spread throughout many nations of Europe, and even numbers among its contributors many in America and remote Asia. The small donation of a cent a week, offered by many millions of persons, creates a fund which supports missionaries in various parts of the world, and from which we ourselves have received, from time to time, generous succors for various wants of our dioceses. Although the adversaries of the faith have given most exaggerated views

The Society of the Propagation of the Faith.

of the amount of this aid, yet we cheerfully avow our indebtedness to the generous charity of this Association; and we hope that the time is not distant when branches of it may be established extensively in these United States to aid our struggling brethren in heathen lands, and thus afford the zeal and piety of our people an opportunity of entering into this holy communion of oblations and prayers, which has been sanctioned and encouraged by the grant of indulgences from the Sovereign Pontiffs. Whilst we gratefully acknowledge the aid bestowed on us, we are anxious to share in the merits of the donors, since it is more blessed to give than to receive. France, from which the infidels of the last century sought to root out Christianity, has become the fountain head of an institution which spreads its beneficent streams throughout the world to impart fertility to distant lands and to refresh the pilgrim missionary on his way. The blessings which have descended in return on that kingdom are known only to Him who suffers not a cup of cold water, given in his name, to pass without reward. We exhort you, brethren, to continue to emulate the zeal and generous charity of the members of this association, by contributing, according to the means which God has given you, to support the religious institutions existing amongst you, and by responding generously to the just calls of your prelates and pastors for their necessary support, and for the various undertakings which their enlightened zeal may propose for the diffusion of religion. The aid which has been hitherto afforded from abroad may be at any time withdrawn. It is, moreover, altogether inadequate to our most pressing wants. On you it depends to give, especially to those who labor in word and doctrine, that support which will leave them without solicitude for the things of this world, that they may wholly apply themselves to the exercise of the holy ministry. We beseech you, brethren, to know them who labor among you; and are over you in the Lord and admonish you: that you esteem them more abundantly in charity for their work's sake. To you we look for means to educate youth for the ecclesiastical state, that, when fully instructed in the duties of their holy vocation, and trained in discipline, they may become fit ministers of the church, and adorn it by their piety and zeal, as well as by their talents. You should aid in the erection of the temples in which you and your children are to worship, and see that the house of God be not unworthy of the sublime functions which are to be performed in it. Of the worldly goods which God has bestowed on you, you should set apart a reasonable portion to be devoted specially to his glory: and you should rejoice at the opportunity thus afforded you to manifest your gratitude for his benefits.

Whilst we thus exhort you to the exercise of Christian generosity, we are still more solicitous that you should attend to your personal sanctification, for this is the will of God. Follow then, beloved brethren, holiness, without which no man shall see God. Be not deceived; God is not mocked. For what things a man shall sow, those also shall he reap. For he that soweth in his flesh, of the flesh also shall reap corruption. But he that soweth in the spirit, of the spirit shall reap life everlasting. Dearly beloved, we beseech you as strangers and pilgrims, to refrain yourselves from carnal desires which war against the soul. We caution you especially against the degrading excesses of intemperance, and against every indulgence which might lead to them. The frail man must abstain not only from unlawful gratification, but from that moderate use of drink which to him may be an immediate occasion of sin, since he that loveth danger shall perish in it. You, then, employing all care, minister in your faith, virtue: and in virtue, knowledge: and in knowledge, abstinence: and in abstinence, patience: and in patience, godliness: and in godliness, love of brotherhood: and in love of brotherhood, charity.

We take this occasion, brethren, to communicate to you the determination, unanimously adopted by us, to place ourselves, and all entrusted to our charge throughout the United States, under the special patronage of the holy Mother of God, whose immaculate conception is venerated by the piety of the faithful throughout the Catholic church. By the aid of her prayers, we entertain the confident hope

that we will be strengthened to perform the arduous duties
of our ministry, and that you will be enabled to practise the
sublime virtues, of which her life presents
a most perfect example. The Holy Ghost, *The Mother of*
by her own lips, has foretold that all gen- *God, Patroness*
erations shall call her blessed; and we can *of the*
not doubt that a blessing is attached to *American*
those who take care to fulfil this prediction. *Church.*
To her, then, we commend you, in the confidence that, through the one Mediator of God and men, the
man Christ Jesus, who gave himself a redemption for all,
she will obtain for us grace and salvation.

The grace of our Lord Jesus Christ be with you all.
Amen.

*Given at Baltimore, in the sixth Provincial Council, on
the fifth Sunday after Easter, in the year of our Lord*
MDCCCXLVI.

✠SAMUEL, *Archbishop of Baltimore.*
✠MICHAEL, *Bishop of Mobile.*
✠FRANCIS PATRICK, *Bishop of Philadelphia.*
✠JOHN BAPTIST, *Bishop of Cincinnati.*
✠GUY IGNATIUS, *Bishop of Bolena, and Coadjutor of
    Louisville.*
✠ANTHONY, *Bishop of New Orleans.*
✠MATHIAS, *Bishop of Dubuque.*
✠JOHN, *Bishop of New York.*
✠RICHARD PIUS, *Bishop of Nashville.*
✠CELESTINE, *Bishop of Vincennes.*
✠JOHN JOSEPH, *Bishop of Natchez.*
✠RICHARD VINCENT, *Bishop of Richmond.*
✠PETER PAUL, *Bishop of Zela and Administrator of
    Detroit.*
✠PETER RICHARD, *Bishop of St. Louis.*
✠JOHN MARY, *Bishop of Claudiopolis and V. Apostolic
    of Texas.*
✠MICHAEL, *Bishop of Pittsburg.*
✠ANDREW, *Bishop of Little Rock.*
✠WILLIAM, *Bishop of Chicago.*

✠JOHN, *Bishop of Axiern and Coadjutor of New York.*
✠WILLIAM, *Bishop of Hartford.*
✠IGNATIUS ALOYSIUS, *Bishop of Charleston.*
✠JOHN MARTIN, *Bishop of Milwaukie.*
✠JOHN BERNARD, *Bishop of Callipolis.*

CHAPTER IX

THE PASTORAL LETTER OF 1849

THE last of the Provincial Councils of Baltimore to legislate for the Church in the entire country, was held in May, 1849. At the close of the Sixth Provincial Council, the Archbishop of Baltimore was the sole metropolitan in the United States. A second archiepiscopal See was erected in Oregon City, on July 24, 1846. This caused confusion for a time, since the Bishop of St. Louis, who apparently held jurisdiction over the Far West, saw a whole ecclesiastical province set down within the borders of his diocese. The boundaries of the Oregon Territory, moreover, had been in dispute between the United States and England, and there was question whether the new See would not conflict with the jurisdiction of the Canadian Church. In June, 1846, a treaty was ratified between England and the United States fixing the boundary of Oregon at the forty-ninth parallel. In 1848, the region was organized as a regular territory. The treaty of Guadaloupe Hidalgo of February 2, 1848, which the Senate accepted on March 10, 1848, brought additional territory into the United States. The Vicariate of New Mexico was postulated by the Seventh Provincial Council, and erected the following year (1850). Texas had been erected into a Vicariate on July 16, 1841; and after the Mexican War, the erection of the See of Monterey (1850) completed the plan of placing the faithful of all the acquired territory within the jurisdiction of the American hierarchy. The promotion of St. Louis to an archiepiscopal See on July 20, 1847, resulted in the division of the United States into three ecclesiastical provinces—Baltimore, Oregon, and St. Louis, with twenty-three suffragan Sees, over one thousand priests, and about nine hundred and sixty churches with resident pastors. It was the intention of Archbishop Eccleston of Baltimore to hold the first Plenary Council in 1849, but the Archbishop of Oregon and his suffragans found it impossible to attend the meeting owing to the great distance which separated them from the East. In consequence, although attended by Archbishop Peter Richard Kenrick, of St. Louis, the Council was considered a provincial one. Among its principal decrees was the

petition of the American bishops for the promulgation of the
dogma of the Immaculate Conception. The decision also was
reached to hold a Plenary Council the following year. In their
Pastoral Letter the Fathers of the Council devote practically
the whole of the document to the practice and belief of the
Church regarding the Immaculate Conception of the Blessed
Mother of God.

THE PASTORAL LETTER OF 1849

(Seventh Provincial Council of Baltimore)

*The Archbishops and Bishops of the United States as-
sembled in the Seventh Provincial Council of Baltimore, to the Clergy and Faithful of their charge.
Venerable brethren of the clergy, and beloved brethren
of the laity:*

IN compliance with the Sacred Canons we have again assembled to deliberate on the general interests of religion
in these United States, under the invocation of the Divine
Spirit, whose guidance is specially promised to the pastors
of the church. The known wishes of our Holy Father Pius
IX. directed our attention in the first place to the more complete organization of our Hierarchy, which, when it shall
have received his necessary sanction, will be made known
to you. The temporary absence of the Pontiff from his See
is not likely to occasion any extraordinary delay in the confirmation of our acts, since his personal energy, and the
vigor of the Apostolic office have been strikingly manifested
in the place of his exile.

And here, brethren, we cannot withhold the expression
of our sentiments in regard to the events which have
marked the brief period which has elapsed
Pius IX.   since he was raised to the pontificate. Although the kingdom of Christ is not of this
world, and the successor of Peter has of divine right no
temporal dominion, yet through the munificence of Christian princes, and the spontaneous acts of a people redeemed
from bondage by the paternal influence of the Bishop of
Rome, a small principality has been attached, during more
than a thousand years, to the Holy See under the name of the

patrimony of St. Peter. Finding himself charged with the duties of temporal governor in consequence of his election to the office of Chief Bishop of the Catholic Church, his Holiness commenced his civil administration by acts of clemency, and by measures of a liberal policy, directed to improve the social condition of his subjects. These concessions elicited, as might have been expected, unbounded expressions of gratitude from the people of the Roman States, and won the admiration and applause of the whole civilized world. We need not say what a return has been made for this enlightened and spontaneous policy. Willingly would we persuade ourselves that the outrages committed against his authority are to be ascribed to the desperate machinations of a small number of abandoned men. As we are not subject to him as a temporal ruler, and as we are devotedly attached to the republican institutions under which we live, we feel ourselves to be impartial judges of the events which have resulted in his flight from his capital, and of the subsequent attempts to strip him of all civil power: yet as friends of order and liberty, we cannot but lament that his enlightened policy has not been suffered to develop itself, and that violence and outrage have disgraced the proceedings of those who proclaim themselves the friends of social progress. We must at the same time avow our conviction, that the temporal principality of the Roman States has served, in the order of Divine Providence, for the free and unsuspicious exercise of the spiritual functions of the Pontificate, and for the advancement of the interests of religion, by fostering institutions of charity and of learning. Were the Bishop of Rome the subject of a civil ruler, or the citizen of a republic, it might be feared that he would not always enjoy that freedom of action which is necessary, that his decrees and measures be respected by the faithful throughout the world. We know, indeed, that if at any time it please God to suffer him to be permanently deprived of all civil power, He will divinely guard the free exercise of his spiritual authority, as was the case during the first three ages, under the reign of the Pagan emperors, when the Bishops of Rome displayed an apostolic energy, which was every where felt and respected. On account of the more excellent principality attached to the Church of Rome from the beginning, as founded by the glorious apostles Peter and Paul, every local church, that is, all Christians in every part of the world, felt bound to harmonize in the faith with that most ancient and illustrious Church, and to cherish inviolably her communion. The Successor of Peter, even under circumstances so unfavorable, watched over the general interests of religion in Asia and Africa, as well as in Europe, and authoritatively proscribed every error opposed to divine revelation, and every usage pregnant with danger to its integrity.

The pontifical office is of divine institution, and totally independent of all the vicissitudes to which the temporal principality is subject. When Christ our Lord promised to Peter that He would build His Church on him as on a rock, He gave him the assurance that the gates of hell, that is, the powers of darkness, should not prevail against it; which necessarily implies that his office is fundamental and essential to the Church, and must continue to the end of time. Peter was constituted pastor of the lambs and sheep, namely, of the whole flock of Christ, which through him is one fold under one shepherd. Our Lord at His last supper prayed that His disciples, and those who through their ministry should believe in Him, might be one, even as He and the Father are one: and as He is always heard, we cannot doubt that this unity is an inseparable characteristic of the Church: whence the office of Chief Pastor, by which unity is maintained, can never cease. We exhort you, brethren, to continue steadfast in your attachment to the Chair of Peter, on which you know that the Church was built. Since it has pleased Divine Providence to establish that chair in the City of Rome—the capital of the Pagan world—in order to show forth, in the most striking manner, the power of Christ, he is a schismatic and prevaricator who attempts to establish any other Chair in opposition to the Roman See, or independent of it. That Church was consecrated by the martyrdom of the apostles Peter and Paul, who bequeathed to her their whole doctrine with their blood. Christ our Lord has placed the doctrine of truth in the Chair of unity,

The Papacy.

and has charged Peter and his successors to confirm their brethren, having prayed specially that the faith of Peter may not fail. By means of the uninterrupted tradition of that Church, coming down through the succession of bishops from the apostles, we confound those who through pride, self-complacency, or any other perverse influence, teach otherwise than divine revelation warrants, and attempt to adulterate the doctrine, which, as pure streams from an unpolluted fountain, flows thence throughout the whole world.

Under the circumstances of peculiar difficulty in which the Chief Bishop is placed by the temporary privation of his temporal dominions and of the reve- nues annexed to them, it becomes all the   **Collection for** children of the Church to give evidence of   **the Pope.** sincere sympathy, by contributing of their worldly substance to enable him to meet the extraordinary expenses which the government of the Church imposes on him. Since the Holy See has watched over the churches of these States with maternal solicitude, and has fed us with the milk of pure doctrine as new-born infants, giving us gratuitously all that was necessary to lead us to the maturity of Christian virtue, it becomes us who have received spiritual things from her disinterested charity, to furnish the exiled Pontiff with temporal things in the time of his distress and affliction. At the instance of the Most Reverend Archbishop of Baltimore, we have unanimously and, with acclamation, resolved to invite you to present your free offerings towards his relief, and have for this purpose appointed the first Sunday of July, being within the octave of the feast of Saints Peter and Paul, for a general collection in all the churches of the United States. Let every one of you, brethren, put apart with himself, laying up what it may well please him, that he may present his gift as a token of his attachment to the Chief Pastor. Let the collections made on the day already mentioned be transmitted without delay to the respective Bishops of each diocess, who will forward the same to the Metropolitan of Baltimore, for the purpose of being placed at the disposal of the Holy Father, in testimony of the sympathy of all his spiritual children in these States, and as a contribution to his support.

The repeated solicitations of Bishops from various parts of the Church, presented to the Apostolic See, have moved his Holiness to address all his colleagues, for counsel in regard to the definition of the doctrine, that the Mother of our Lord was preserved by divine grace from all stain of original sin. This has hitherto been considered as a pious belief, which derived strength and sanction from the solemnity in honor of her Conception, celebrated during several ages throughout the whole Church. In the East it was observed as early as the fifth century, under the title of the Conception of Saint Anne, the mother of the holy Virgin, although it is not known to have been introduced into the West before the ninth century. Every where throughout the whole Church from the earliest period Mary was styled holy and immaculate, as is evident from the liturgical books and from the writings of the Fathers. Saint Ephrem of Syria, in the fourth century, proclaimed her purity and sanctity to be far greater than that of the most sublime spirits that surround the throne of God, since it is her singular privilege to be the Mother of the Word Incarnate. "She is," he says, "an immaculate and undefiled Virgin, incorrupt and chaste, and altogether free from all defilement and stain of sin, the Spouse of God—the Virgin Mother of God, inviolate, holy, and entirely pure and chaste: holier than the Seraphs, and incomparably more glorious than all the celestial hosts."[1] Although the attention of the Church in the early ages was specially fixed on the mystery of the Incarnation, and her authority was employed chiefly against the destructive heresies that directly assailed it, yet the honor of the Virgin Mother was vindicated whenever it came in question. When Nestorius endeavored to divide Christ, ascribing to His human nature a distinct personality, the great Council of Ephesus, in proscribing the novelty, proclaimed Mary the Mother of God, in conformity with the constant doctrine of all antiquity. Her perpetual virginity was subsequently declared, when denied by inno-

The
Immaculate
Conception.

[1] Orat. in Ss. Dei Genitricem.

vators. Her exemption from actual sin was stated by the
Holy Council of Trent, in a definition of faith; and the same
venerable authority designated her "immaculate" in a declaration annexed to the canons, regarding original sin.
These fathers declare that it is not their intention to include
the Blessed and Immaculate Virgin Mary in these decrees,
but that the constitutions of Pope Xystus IV. on this point
are to be observed. This Pontiff, in consequence of disputes
raised concerning her Conception, had found it necessary
to forbid under heavy penalties, the branding as heresy
either the pious sentiment, or the contradictory opinion. It
happened in regard to this point, as on many others, that
in the progress of time doubts were excited as to the tradition and faith of the Church. The disputes which arose on
this subject were tolerated by her with that consideration
and patience with which the conflict of sentiment in regard
to the necessity of the ceremonial observances was suffered in the first Council of Jerusalem, until the voice of
Peter terminated the discussion. She abstained from pro-
nouncing judgment whilst the excitement prevailed, content with the protestations of the contending parties of un-
reserved submission to her authority, and leaving every
proof and every difficulty to be maturely canvassed, and to
be weighed in the scales of the sanctuary. Whilst the Pontiffs allowed to theologians the right of private investigation, they were careful to maintain the usage of celebrating
the festival, and forbade, under heavy penalties, any public expression of sentiment derogatory to the belief which
the faithful piously cherished.

Since the divine Scriptures teach that all men sinned
in Adam, and that we are by nature children of wrath, the
Virgin Mary, as his natural descendant, would have incurred the common penalty, had not she been preserved
from it by divine grace. The Angel Gabriel assured her
that she had found grace with God, and saluted her as full
of grace. She was declared blessed among women, both
by the heavenly messenger, and by her cousin Elizabeth,
speaking under the inspiration of the Holy Ghost. St. Iren-
æus represents her as repairing by her obedience the evils
brought on mankind by the disobedience of the mother of

the human family. Her exemption from the general malediction may be inferred from the fact, that she was chosen
to be Mother of our Redeemer, whose body was formed of
her substance. St. Augustin speaking of actual sin, which,
in the strongest terms, he ascribed to every child of Adam,
observed that he must not be understood to include the
Virgin Mother, concerning whom he would suffer no thought
to be entertained when sin was in question, for the honor
of our Lord; "for we know," he says, "that grace was bestowed on her to overcome sin in every respect, since she
was chosen to conceive and bring forth Him who was utterly
free from sin."[2] Guided by this most just principle we can
interpret the general assertions of the fathers without prejudice to the Blessed One whose womb, as a most hallowed
shrine, bore our Redeemer; whose breasts gave him suck.

The living faith and oral tradition of the Church must
be deemed the echo of ancient apostolic tradition, and the
genuine expression of revealed truth. The Holy Ghost is
always with the successors of the apostles, to guide them
into all truth, and to impress on their minds those doctrines
which were originally delivered by Christ, and which must
always remain, although heaven and earth should pass
away. He watches over them, that the revealed doctrine
may be preserved free from all admixture of error.

We do not mean to anticipate the solemn judgment of
the Chief Bishop; but in the mean time we exhort you
brethren, to continue to cherish a tender devotion to the
Mother of our Lord, since the honor given to her is founded
on the relation which she bears to Him, and is a homage
rendered to the mystery of His incarnation. The more highly
you venerate her, as the purest and holiest of creatures,
the deeper sense you manifest of His divinity: wherefore
her devout clients in ancient and later times have always
been distinguished by zeal to maintain the great mysteries
of faith. From St. Ephrem of Syria to St. Bernard of Clair-
vaux, and St. Thomas of Aquin, or even to St. Alphonsus
de Liguori, all have glowed with the love of Jesus Christ,
and have been distinguished by the purity of their lives,
and by their zeal for the attainment of Christian perfec-

[2] L. de Natura et Gratia.

tion. On the contrary those who have assailed the veneration of the Virgin have easily fallen into the denial of the divinity of her Son. Devotion to her is as an outwork of the Church protecting the belief of the divine mystery.

We doubt not, brethren, that the powerful intercession of Mary will obtain, through the merits of Jesus Christ our Lord and Redeemer, from the Father of lights, and the Giver of all good gifts, the necessary light and aid for the Chief Pastor of the Church, and graces and blessings for the Christian people. When we survey the Christian world, and see thrones overturned, monarchs fleeing in fear, society convulsed, destructive errors spread abroad by the untiring efforts of impious men, and confusion and disorder widely prevailing, we are afflicted almost to despondency: but when we raise our thoughts on high to the kingdom of light and love, where Mary stands near the throne of her Divine Son, we are inspired with confidence, that she, who, at the foot of the cross, received us all as her children in the person of the Beloved Disciple, will effectually plead our cause. Through her we have received all grace, since she brought forth Him who has redeemed us by His blood, and through Him she has crushed the head of the infernal serpent. Let us then go with confidence to the throne of mercy, relying on the infinite merits of Jesus Christ, our only Saviour, and commending ourselves to the prayers of His holy Mother, who is always heard on account of her intimate relation to Him, and her tender love for Him. Let us ask that the hydra-head of heresy may be crushed for ever, and that revealed truth in all its fulness may be acknowledged by all mankind; so that the prayer of the Psalmist may be accomplished: "Let people praise Thee, O God: let all people give praise to Thee." Let us pray that all division and strife may be brought to an end, and that all the professors of the Christian name may be united in religious communion, earnestly cherishing the unity of the spirit in a bond of peace. At the same time we must with increased fervor ask that scandals may be rooted out from the fold of Christ, and that the purity of morals and beauty of holiness may everywhere flourish.

Take unto you, brethren, the helmet of salvation, and

the sword of the spirit, (which is the word of God). By all prayer and supplication praying at all times in the spirit; and in the same watching with all instance and supplication for all the saints; and for us that speech may be given us, that we may open our mouths with confidence, to make known the mystery of the Gospel. Peace be to you brethren, and charity with faith from God the Father, and the Lord Jesus Christ.

Given under our hands, in Provincial Council at Baltimore on the fifth Sunday after Easter in the year of our Lord MDCCCXLIX.

✝SAMUEL, *Archbishop of Baltimore.*
✝PETER RICHARD, *Archbishop of St. Paul.*
✝MICHAEL, *Bishop of Mobile.*
✝FRANCIS PATRICK, *Bishop of Philadelphia.*
✝JOHN BAPTIST, *Bishop of Cincinnati.*
✝ANTHONY, *Bishop of New Orleans.*
✝MATHIAS, *Bishop of Dubuque.*
✝JOHN, *Bishop of New York.*
✝RICHARD PIUS, *Bishop of Nashville.*
✝JOHN JOSEPH, *Bishop of Natchez.*
✝RICHARD VINCENT, *Bishop of Richmond.*
✝PETER PAUL, *Bishop of Zela, in partibus, and Administrator of the Diocess of Detroit.*
✝JOHN MARY, *Bishop of Galveston.*
✝MICHAEL, *Bishop of Pittsburg.*
✝ANDREW, *Bishop of Little Rock.*
✝JOHN, *Bishop of Albany.*
✝WILLIAM, *Bishop of Hartford.*
✝IGNATIUS ALOYSIUS, *Bishop of Charleston.*
✝JOHN MARTIN, *Bishop of Milwaukie.*
✝JOHN BERNARD, *Bishop of Boston.*
✝AMEDEUS, *Bishop of Cleveland.*
✝JOHN, *Bishop of Buffalo.*
✝MARTIN JOHN, *Bishop of Lengo, in partibus, and Coadjutor of the Bishop of Louisville.*
✝MAURICE, *Bishop of Vincennes.*
✝JAMES OLIVER, *Bishop of Chicago.*

CHAPTER X

The Pastoral Letter of 1852

OWING to the illness of Archbishop Eccleston, who had presided over five of the Provincial Councils, the convocation of the First Plenary Council was not made in 1850. After his death (April 22, 1851), Francis Patrick Kenrick, Bishop of Philadelphia, was promoted to the archiepiscopal See of Baltimore (August 3, 1851). On August 19, Pius IX. appointed him Apostolic Delegate for the Council, and on November 21, Archbishop Kenrick called the Council—the First Plenary Council of the Church in the United States—for the following May. Before the opening of its sessions on May 9, 1852, the Holy See had erected three more ecclesiastical provinces in the United States—New Orleans, Cincinnati and New York. The Council was attended by six Archbishops and by thirty-five suffragan bishops. Twenty-five decrees were enacted by the Fathers of the Council. Archbishop Kenrick viewed the purpose of the Council as follows: "The object for which this Council is summoned, is by wise enactments and measures to promote discipline, and enforce the sacred Canons, or to submit such modifications of them as local circumstances may require, to the mature and enlightened judgment of the chief bishop, who is divinely charged with the solicitude of all the churches. We come together, brethren, not for idle display of ceremonial pomp, but to take mutual counsel after imploring divine guidance, for we watch, 'as being to render an account of your souls.' The power committed to us by our Lord is to be exercised for edification, for the building up of the body of Christ, whose members should be closely joined together in religious communion."

One source of confusion in the discipline of the Church came from the varied customs which had been brought from Europe by the immigration of the period previous to the Council. The Fathers assembled in 1852, had the delicate task of unifying the ecclesiastical discipline of the country in such a way that national and racial divergencies should not be offended. The work of the Council was divided among six different committees and then discussed in general sessions.

The Fathers decreed that the legislation of the Seven Provincial Councils of Baltimore should extend to all parts of the United States. The old trustee evil was nearly extinct, but the decrees against it in previous Councils were reënacted. The bishops were exhorted to build parochial schools in all their parishes, and the present system of supporting the schools was inaugurated. The special topics of the Pastoral Letter of 1852, which was written by Archbishop Kenrick, of St. Louis, are those of ecclesiastical authority and Catholic education.

THE PASTORAL LETTER OF 1852

(First Plenary Council of Baltimore)

The Archbishops and Bishops of the United States in National Council assembled at Baltimore, to the Clergy and Laity of their charge, health and benediction! Venerable Brethren of the Clergy, and Beloved Children of the Laity:

ASSEMBLED in National Council, under the sanction of Our Most Holy Father, Pius IX, we find no duty more imperative, and, at the same time, more agreeable to our feelings, than to address the flock committed to our care. The attachment to the doctrines and practices of Our Holy Religion which characterizes the Catholics of the United States; the docility and obedience which they have uniformly manifested; the cordial union which, notwithstanding the diversity of origin, customs and language, reigns throughout the whole Catholic Body in this vast country; their general fervour and devotedness in the exercise of the virtues of the Gospel, fill our hearts with joy, and more than compensate us for the cares and solicitudes of the pastoral office. We are able to adopt the words of the apostle: "Our mouth is open to you,—our heart is enlarged."[1] "Great is *our* confidence for you; great is *our* glorying for you. We are filled with comfort: We exceedingly abound with joy in all our tribulation."[2]

The authority we exercise has been given us by Christ. We are His Ministers; ambassadors for Him. We claim no

[1] 2 Cor. vi. 11.   [2] 2 Cor. vii. 4.

power, and seek no influence which He has not willed us to have. It is our duty to guard the sacred deposit of the faith; for to us has it been committed, and from us will it be one day demanded by   **Episcopal** our Heavenly Master. Having vouchsafed   **Authority.** to speak, at sundry times, and in divers manners, in times past to the fathers by the prophets, last of all hath God spoken to us by His Son; and this Divine Son, —the brightness of His Father's glory, the figure of His substance,—has made us the depositaries of His doctrine, and "has given to us the ministry of reconciliation."[3] Man having had need that God should teach him, ever requires to receive this divine teaching through a channel in which it shall be preserved from whatever might taint its purity, and thus destroy its authority. Not only must we know that God has spoken; we must also be assured that His voice is heard throughout all time. Although no longer visible to men, Christ, our God, has not left us orphans. He has sent the Holy Spirit, the Paraclete whom He promised; He has infused into the earthly elements which He selected for the formation of His Church, the breath of undying life; and that Holy Spirit ever abides in the Church, teaches her all truth, preserves her from every error, and renders her a sure guide to the pastures of salvation, to the fountain whence springs up water to eternal life. Thus is fulfilled the word: "He that heareth you, heareth me:"[4] thus is the Church, "the House of the Living God, the Pillar and the ground of truth;"[5] and on this is grounded the obligation which we urge with no less confidence than did the Apostles of Christ: "Obey your prelates, and be subject to them. For they watch as being to render an account of your souls, that they may do this with joy, and not with grief."[6]

The source of this authority is Christ. The channel through which it is communicated to the other members of the church is the Bishop   **The Source** of Rome. The successor of St. Peter, is   **of Episcopal** the heir of the privileges conferred on the   **Authority.** Prince of the Apostles; on him as on the solid foundation which the wise architect has chosen, is

---

3 2 Cor. v. 18.   4 Luke x. 16.   5 1 Tim. iii. 15.   6 Heb. xiii. 17.

the Church built; to him, in the person of Peter, for whom Christ specially prayed, has it been given to confirm his brethren. As in the case of every other country where the Church has been established, our hierarchy has grown up under his fostering care; has developed itself, with his sanction and approval, in dignity and number; and its members, although spread over the wide extent which separates ocean from ocean, have, on the present occasion, joyfully obeyed his summons to assemble in National Council, under the presidency of a special representative of the Holy See in the person of the Most Rev. Archbishop of Baltimore. We rejoice at the occasion of proclaiming our attachment to the centre of Catholic unity; and we exhort you, brethren, to cherish a love for the Holy See, in which is preserved an unbroken succession of Pastors from the time of Christ to the present day; which has condemned all the errors that men have sought to combine with the doctrines of revelation; and which ever watches over the integrity of faith and ever guards the purity of ecclesiastical discipline. Let us hope that the erroneous ideas entertained by so many of our fellow-citizens, of the nature of the power which we recognise in the Bishop of Rome, as successor of St. Peter, will be removed, and that this chief See, whence sacerdotal unity has derived its origin, may be acknowledged as the centre of ecclesiastical authority, the source of all that is grand and imposing in the extent, union and permanence of the Church. Let us pray that all who are separated from the Church may be brought to the knowledge of the truth; that the appalling extremes to which error is hurrying those who have cast off the authority appointed by Christ, may cause men to recognise a principle which alone can unite them in the one fold of the one shepherd. Let your united prayers ascend to the Father of mercies, who wishes all men to be saved, and to come to the knowledge of the truth, that this most desirable end be attained, remembering that what is impossible to man may be rendered possible by the influence of Divine grace.

Among the causes which, in a few instances, and, principally in days now happily past, led to the forgetfulness of the extent which belongs to the authority that we exercise,

must be reckoned the attempt to apply to the Catholic
Church, in the administration of the temporalities belong-
ing to her, principles and rules foreign to
her spirit and irreconciliable with the   Administration
authority of her Pastors. The result was   of Church
such as might have been expected. Peace   Property.
and harmony were disturbed, the progress
of religion checked or entirely impeded, and the Church
reproached with the misconduct of her unworthy children.
For the purpose of guarding against the recurrence of such
evils, we deem it necessary to make a public and authentic
declaration of Catholic principles on this important subject. Whatever is offered to God, and solemnly consecrated
to His service, whether it be the material temple in which
His worshippers assemble; or the ground set apart for the
interment of those who repose in God's field awaiting the
promised resurrection, or property, real or personal, intended for the purposes of Divine service, or for the education, support and maintenance of the clergy,—every such
thing is sacred and belongs to the Church, and cannot be
withdrawn from the service of God without the guilt of
sacrilege. The donor or donors of such gifts can exercise
no right of ownership over them. With these temporal
things, thus separated from common purposes and set apart
for the service of the sanctuary, the Church cannot allow
any interference that is not subordinate to her authority.
The Bishop of each diocess is the representative and organ
of that authority, and, without his sanction, no arrange-
ment, howsoever in itself of a purely temporal nature, that
has reference to religious worship, has, or can have, force
or validity. Whenever the Bishop deems it advisable to
acquiesce in arrangements for the administration of Church
temporalities which have not originated with the ecclesiastical authority, or which may have arisen from ignorance
of its rights, or from a spirit of opposition to them, we declare that such arrangements have force and effect in the
Catholic Church, in consequence of such acquiescence, and
not from any other cause or principle whatever. And we
furthermore declare, that whenever the Bishop of a diocess
recognises such arrangements, or acquiesces in them, those

charged with the care of Church temporalities, whether laymen or clergymen, are bound to render an annual account
of their administration to the Bishop, agreeably to the rule
prescribed in such cases by the Holy Council of Trent.[7]

We exhort you, brethren, to sustain your prelates in
their efforts to maintain the discipline of the Church in this
no less than in other matters. It is from them, and not from
the stranger, and still less from the disobedient brethren,—
that you are to learn her principles, and those rules of conduct which the experience of centuries has taught her to
regard as conducive to your real interests. In this no less
than in matters of faith and practice, you have to attend to
the Apostle's admonition: "Obey your prelates and be subject to them."[8]

The Church claims obedience not only when she teaches
you the truths of faith, but also when she prescribes rules
of conduct. We have the consolation to
know that her claims are recognised, to
their full extent, by the vast majority of
her children; but we know also, that some
who profess to look upon her as the Mother who has brought
them forth in Christ,—who alone has the words of eternal
life;—have, in disregard of her authority,—attached themselves to certain societies, which she either entirely condemns, or views with well founded apprehension. What
want, either of body or of mind, is left unprovided for
in the principles she teaches and in the holy associations
which she has sanctioned? Because men, having rejected
the principle of Christian charity, feel the void which they
themselves have created, they endeavor to substitute human virtues as the remedy for the evils which nothing less
than a divine grace can heal. There can, then, be no necessity for the children of the Church to seek out of her what
they can find in her alone; nor any excuse for the insubordination which would regard the exercise of her authority
in this matter as uncalled for or injudicious. We exhort
our venerable Brethren the clergy to urge the faithful to
observe all the regulations on this subject that have emanated from the Holy See, as also those contained in the de-

_Church
Discipline._

---

[7] Sess. xxii. De reformatione, cap. 9.   [8] Heb. xii. 17.

crees of the Councils of Baltimore, which have received the
sanction of the Supreme Pastor of the Church.

The wants of the Church in this vast country, so rapidly
advancing in population and prosperity, impose on us, your
pastors, and on you, our children in Christ,
peculiar and very arduous duties. We not   The Needs of
only have to build up the Church, by the   the Church
preaching of the Gospel, and the inculca-   in America.
tion of all the virtues it teaches, but also
to supply the material wants of religious worship in proportion to the unexampled rapidity with which our flocks
increase. We have to establish missions in places where,
but a few years since, none, or but few, Catholics were to
be found, and where now the children of the Church cry
with clamorous importunity for the bread of life. We have
to build the Church, where before God's name was not publicly worshipped; and to multiply his temples where they
no longer suffice for the constantly increasing wants of the
faithful. We have to provide a ministry for the present
and future wants of the country, and, in this matter, have
to contend with difficulties which are unknown in countries
where Religion has been long established, and where the
piety and zeal of past generations have furnished ample
means for this most important object. We have to provide
for the Catholic education of our youth. Not only have we
to erect and maintain the Church, the Seminary and the
School-house, but we have to found Hospitals, establish orphanages, and provide for every want of suffering humanity, which Religion forbids us to neglect. We thank the
Giver of all good gifts for the extraordinary benediction
which He has hitherto bestowed upon our efforts, and those
of the venerable men whose places we fill. We rejoice at
having the opportunity of bearing public testimony to the
generous assistance which we have received from our flocks
in our respective dioceses. Much, however, as has been
done, much still remains to be accomplished. Our churches
are nowhere equal to the wants of the Catholic population,
and in many places are far from being sufficiently spacious
to afford one-half of our people the opportunity of attending Divine worship. We, therefore, exhort you, Brethren,

to co-operate generously and cheerfully with your pastors, when they appeal to you in behalf of works of charity and religious zeal. In contributing to Divine worship, you make an offering to God of the gifts He has bestowed on you, and a portion of which He requires should be consecrated to His service, as a testimony of your continued dependence on His Sovereign Mercy. We hope that the examples of your Catholic forefathers, and even of some among yourselves, will be generally felt and not unfrequently imitated; and that here, as well as elsewhere, the Church will be able to show the proofs of her children's faith in the numerous temples raised to the honor of God's name, in the beauty of His Sanctuary which the true Christian will ever love, and in the ample and permanent provision made for the maintenance of public worship.

The education of candidates for the ministry is one of our most urgent wants. Notwithstanding the multiplied privations, difficulties and embarrassments which our predecessors experienced, and which have not yet entirely disappeared, they spared no sacrifice in order to rear up successors to the ministry who should be equal to the wants, and worthy of the piety, of their people. These wants increase with the increase of the population; and we have no hesitation in avowing that the efforts hitherto made to supply our churches with priests are far from being adequate. To attain this—the most important of all means to be employed for the maintenance and diffusion of Religion,—we need your co-operation, which we are confident will not be refused. We ask not for ourselves, but for you, and for your children. We seek to avert the evil of hearing the cries of the little ones in Christ for the bread of life, without being able to afford them one to break it to them. We seek to avert the evils resulting from the want of a regular and permanent source for the perpetuation of the ministry, which we have so often experienced, and which, if left without a remedy, must continue to produce most disastrous results.

Without priests educated in the science of the sanctuary and trained up to the practice of its virtues, under our own

Education of Priests.

eyes, or under the care of those to whom we may commit this important trust, we cannot hope to behold the ministry adapted to the wants of the country, or equal to the work which the providence of God has assigned to us. Co-operate, then, generously and perseveringly, with your respective prelates in their efforts to provide a suitable ministry for our infant churches; cultivate the virtuous dispositions of those among your children, who, attracted by the beauty of holiness, manifest in an early age of desire—most frequently the inspiration of divine grace—to consecrate themselves to the service of the altar. Let it be for you a matter of devout thanksgiving and holy exultation, that your offspring prefer the service of God's altar, to all the attractions of worldly ambition and cupidity. Invoke by fervent prayer the mercy of God, that he may send laborers into His vineyard, that he may raise up ministers of His sanctuary, powerful in word and work, and who, while they possess that knowledge which the lips of the priest are commanded to keep, may exhibit all the virtues of the apostolate which they are called to exercise.

No portion of our charge fills us with greater solicitude than that which our Divine Master, by word and example, has taught us to regard with more than ordinary sentiments of affection—the **Catholic** younger members of our flock. If our **Schools.** youth grow up in ignorance of their religious duties or unpractised in their consoling fulfilment; if, instead of the words of eternal life, which find so full and sweet an echo in the heart of innocence, the principles of error, unbelief or indifferentism, are imparted to them; if the natural repugnance, even in the happiest period of life, to bend under the yoke of discipline, be increased by the example of those whose relation to them gives them influence or authority,—what are we to expect but the disappointment of all hopes which cause the Church to rejoice in the multiplication of her children! We therefore address you brethren, in the language of affectionate warning and solemn exhortation. Guard carefully those little ones of Christ; "suffer them to approach Him, and prevent them not, for of such is the kingdom of heaven."[9] To you, Christian parents, God has committed these His children, whom He permits you to regard as yours; and your natural affection towards whom must ever be subordinate to the will of Him "from whom all paternity in heaven and on earth is named."[10] Remember that if for them you are the representatives of God, the source of their existence, you are to be for them depositaries of His authority, teachers of His law, and models by imitating which they may be perfect, even as their Father in heaven is perfect. You are to watch over the purity of their faith and morals with jealous vigilance, and to instil into their young hearts principles of virtue and perfection. What shall be the anguish of the parent's heart,—what terrible expectation of judgment that will fill his soul, should his children perish through his criminal neglect, or his obstinate refusal to be guided in the discharge of his paternal duties, by the authority of God's Church.[11] To avert this evil give your children a Christian education, that is an education based on religious principles, accompanied by religious practices and always subordinate to religious influence. Be not led astray by the false and delusive theories whch are so prevalent, and which leave youth without religion, and, consequently, without anything to control the passions, promote the real happiness of the individual, and make society find in the increase of its members, a source of security and prosperity. Listen not to those who would persuade you that religion can be separated from secular instruction. If your children, while they advance in human sciences, are not taught the science of the saints, their minds will be filled with every error, their hearts will be receptacles of every vice, and that very learning which they have acquired, in itself so good and so necessary, deprived of all that could shed on it the light of heaven, will be an additional means of destroying the happiness of the child, embittering still more the chalice of parental disappointment, and weakening the foundations of social order. Listen to our voice, which tells you to walk in the ancient paths; to bring up your children as you yourselves were brought up by your pious parents; to make re-

9 Mark x. 14.   10 Eph. iii. 16.   11 John xvii. 12.

ligion the foundation of the happiness you wish to secure
for those whom you love so tenderly, and the promotion
of whose interests is the motive of all your efforts, the solace
which sustains you in all your fatigues and privations. Encourage the establishment and support of Catholic schools;
make every sacrifice which may be necessary for this object: spare our hearts the pain of beholding the youth
whom, after the example of our Master, we so much love,
involved in all the evils of an uncatholic education, evils
too multiplied and too obvious to require that we should do
more than raise our voices in solemn protest against the
system from which they spring. In urging on you the discharge of this duty, we are acting on the suggestion of the
Sovereign Pontiff, who in an encyclical letter, dated 21
November, 1851, calls on all the Bishops of the Catholic
world, to provide for the religious education of youth. We
are following the example of the Irish Hierarchy, who
are courageously opposing the introduction of a system
based on the principle which we condemn, and who
are now endeavoring to unite religious with secular
instruction of the highest order, by the institution
of a Catholic University,—an undertaking in the success
of which we necessarily feel a deep interest, and which,
as having been suggested by the Sovereign Pontiff, powerfully appeals to the sympathies of the whole Catholic world.

Our Holy Father Pius IX has recommended to our notice,
as well as to that of all the Bishops of the Church, the Society established at Lyons in France, for
the purpose of aiding apostolic mission-   The Society
aries in the Propagation of the Faith. In-   of the
dependently of the authority which has   Propagation
thus spoken, our own feelings would   of the Faith.
prompt us to address you on the subject.
From the time of its first establishment, almost thirty years
ago, up to the present time, this association has contributed,
generously and uninterruptedly, to the support of our missions. If our churches have so rapidly multiplied; if our
religious and educational establishments are now comparatively numerous; if new missions and new dioceses have,
amidst most appalling discouragements, still continued to

be founded,—we must, in truth and justice, acknowledge, that in all this the Association for the Propagation of the Faith has afforded us the most generous and most enlightened co-operation. We feel the obligations which we have to an Association which is identified with the progress of religion in every part of the world; and we, therefore, exhort you Brethren to encourage its establishment in your respective districts, agreeably to the wishes of the Sovereign Pontiff, who desires to see the whole Catholic world united in an effort to diffuse the Gospel of Christ throughout all nations. The small annual contribution made to this Association will not interfere with any other effort of Christian zeal or charity; and we cherish the conviction, that its establishment will draw down from God the choicest blessings on all who unite in this truly good work.

Attachment to the civil institutions under which you live, has always marked our conduct: and if we address you on this subject, it is not from any apprehension that you are likely to vary from the course which you have hitherto pursued.

Civil Allegiance.

After the example of the apostle, St. Paul, we cannot, however, deem it altogether unnecessary to exhort you ever to discharge your civil duties from the higher motives which religion suggests. Obey the public authorities, not only for wrath but also for conscience sake. Show your attachment to the institutions of our beloved country by prompt compliance with all their requirements, and by the cautious jealousy with which you guard against the least deviation from the rules which they prescribe for the maintenance of public order and private rights. Thus will you refute the idle babbling of foolish men, and will best approve yourselves worthy of the privileges which you enjoy, and overcome, by the sure test of practical patriotism, all the prejudices which a misapprehension of your principles but too often produces.

We now address, in a particular manner, our venerable Brethren of the clergy, our fellow-laborers in the vineyard, the praise of whose labors is not with men but with God, and who await the coming of the Master of the vineyard, when the Shepherd and Bishop of souls shall bestow an eternal recompense on zeal and perseverance. Agreeably to the direction of the Holy Council at Trent, we have to exhort them, to endeavor, by the whole tenor of their lives, no less than by the exercise of   Exhortation the apostolic ministry, to guide the flock of   to the Clergy. Christ to safe and salutary pastures. To the ministers of the New Law the words spoken by God to the Levitical priesthood are more imperatively addressed: "Be ye holy; for I, the Lord, your God, am holy."[12] Great as is the dignity of the priesthood, holy as are its functions, we must ever remember that we carry about this precious treasure in frail vessels; that we are surrounded with infirmity; and that to us especially is addressed the admonition: "Watch and pray, that ye enter not into temptation."[13] We are the light of the world; and to our actions, even more than to our words, do the faithful look up for the rule they are to follow, the example they are to imitate. We are the salt of the earth; and by the wholesome severity of Christian discipline, we are to preserve from the all pervading corruption of the age those whom the Providence of God has committed to our guardianship. Not only have we to consider the faithful of our charge; we have also to remember those other sheep which are not yet of the fold of Christ, and whom the Shepherd of souls designs to bring within its sacred pale. Let us be mindful of the apostolic admonition, and "give offence to no one, that our ministry may not be reviled;"[14] that the prejudices of education may not be strengthened; or the persevering misrepresentation by which we are assailed receive apparent confirmation from the faults or imperfections that may be discovered in us. Let us be the example of the faithful in word, in conversation, in charity, in faith, in chastity; let us attend to reading, to exhortation and to doctrine, and thus we shall save ourselves and those that hear us.

Nor can we close this Letter without addressing the consecrated Virgins, who, in the admirable variety of occupations, suggested by zeal and charity, are now, as in the days of St. Cyprian, the more illustrious portion of the flock of Christ, the flower and ornament of the Church.

12 Lev. xi. 44.   13 Matt. xxvi. 41.   14 2 Cor. vi. 3.

Them we address, after the example of the same holy martyr, in language of affectionate reverence rather than in the words of authority. Them also we The Catholic must exhort to keep their lamps filled with Sisterhoods. the oil of good works; to labor assiduously to render themselves still more and more worthy of their Heavenly Spouse, by going from virtue to virtue; and them also we must admonish, that in proportion to the sublime course of religious perfection on which they have entered, is the solicitude we feel that they should secure the crown which is to be their exceeding great reward. To each of them, the Spouse of their souls says: "Behold I come quickly: hold fast that which thou hast, that no man take thy crown."[15]

And to you, beloved children of the Laity,—our joy and our crown,—we desire, in concluding, to address a few words of affectionate admonition. We Exhortation know your faith and the fervor which so to the Laity. many of you exhibit: but our office is one of solicitude and concern. Until the victory is achieved we cannot be without apprehension; and our cares will only cease when we shall have given an account of the stewardship which we have received. Although of the household of God, and children of the faith, you have, by good works, to make your calling and election sure. You are to co-operate with us in preaching the Gospel of Christ by the care of your own households, and by the good example you give to all who come within the sphere of your influence. Walk worthy of your calling; refute the calumnies which are so frequently uttered against the Mother who has brought you forth in Christ, by having your conversation good among those who are estranged from her influence; "that whereas they speak against you as evil doers, they may, by the good works which they shall behold in you, glorify God in the day of visitation."[16] "For the rest, brethren, whatsoever things are true, whatsoever modest, whatsoever just, whatsoever holy, whatsoever lovely, whatsoever of good fame, if there be any virtue, any praise of discipline, think on these things. The things which you

15 Apoc. iii. 2.   16 1 Peter ii. 12.

have both learned and received, and heard and seen—
these do ye, and the God of peace shall be with you."—"The
grace of our Lord Jesus Christ be with your spirit." [17]

We direct this our Pastoral Letter to be read publicly in
all the churches subject to our jurisdiction.

*Given at Baltimore, in National Council, on the Feast of
the Ascension, in the year of our Lord 1852.*

✠FRANCIS PATRICK, *Archbishop of Baltimore, and Delegate of the Apostolic See.*

✠FRANCIS NORBERT, *Archbishop of Oregon.*

✠PETER RICHARD, *Archbishop of St. Louis.*

✠ANTHONY, *Archbishop of New Orleans.*

✠JOHN, *Archbishop of New York.*

✠JOHN BAPTIST, *Archbishop of Cincinnati.*

✠MICHAEL, *Bishop of Mobile.*

✠MATTHIAS, *Bishop of Dubuque.*

✠RICHARD PIUS, *Bishop of Nashville.*

✠JOHN JOSEPH, *Bishop of Natchez.*

✠RICHARD VINCENT, *Bishop of Wheeling.*

✠PETER PAUL, *Bishop of Zela and Administrator of
Detroit.*

✠JOHN MARY, *Bishop of Galveston.*

✠MICHAEL, *Bishop of Pittsburg.*

✠ANDREW, *Bishop of Little Rock.*

✠JOHN, *Bishop of Albany.*

✠IGNATIUS ALOYSIUS, *Bishop of Charleston.*

✠JOHN MARTIN, *Bishop of Milwaukie.*

✠JOHN BERNARD, *Bishop of Boston.*

✠AMEDEUS, *Bishop of Cleveland.*

✠JOHN, *Bishop of Buffalo.*

✠MARTIN JOHN, *Bishop of Louisville.*

✠JAMES OLIVER, *Bishop of Chicago.*

✠AUGUSTIN, M. M., *Bishop of Nesqualy.*

✠JOSEPH SADOC, *Bishop of Monterey.*

✠BERNARD, *Bishop of Hartford.*

✠FRANCIS XAVIER, *Bishop of Savannah.*

17 Philip. iv. 8, 9.

✠JOHN, *Bishop of Richmond.*

✠JOHN, *Bishop of Agathon, Vicar Apostolic of New Mexico.*

✠JOSEPH, *Bishop of St. Paul.*

✠JOHN BAPTIST, *Bishop of Messena, Vicar Apostolic of the Indian Territory East of Rocky Mountains.*

✠JOHN NEPOMUCEN, *Bishop of Philadelphia.*

CHAPTER XI

THE PASTORAL LETTER OF 1866

BETWEEN the First and Second Plenary Councils of Baltimore there lies shrouded in sorrow the saddest of all historical periods in American history. The Second Plenary Council was to be held in 1862, but when that year came, the North and the South were in deadly conflict; and the nation beheld the singular spectacle of Catholics in the front ranks of Federal and Confederate armies, with their respective spiritual leaders, priests and bishops, encouraging them in what all believed to be their duty. Among the churches, only the Catholic faith preserved its unity and survived the shock of that cleavage. In November, 1861, Archbishop John Hughes of New York was entrusted by Secretary Seward with the important mission of enlisting the sympathies of France for the Union, and his interviews with the leading French statesmen, and particularly with Napoleon III and the Empress, will always be a vital part of the history of the Civil War. The revival of bigotry through the reorganization of Native-Americanism in 1852 caused considerable uneasiness in the country. Outbreaks by the "Know-nothings" as the new party was called, had occurred in Providence, R. I., in 1851; and in 1854-55, there were numerous outrages committed upon Catholic Church property and upon the homes of Irish Catholics in various cities. One peak of violence was reached during Archbishop Bedini's visit to the United States (1853). It was in October, 1854, that the unspeakable outrage upon Father John Bapst, S. J., took place in a northern city. The following year, on August 5, rioting and bloodshed occurred in Louisville, and gave the day the unsavory name of "Bloody Monday." Massachusetts passed (1854) a bill for the inspection of the convents of nuns, and the law was carried out in a very offensive manner. The effort to create a national society for the purpose of driving all Catholics from public office was unsuccessful. These un-American tendencies were incidently subdued by the Civil War.

Shortly after the close of the War, Archbishop Martin John Spalding, of Baltimore, as Apostolic Delegate, issued a call (March 19, 1866) for the Second Plenary Council. The principal motive for holding the Council was "that at the close of the national crisis, which had acted as a dissolvent upon all sectarian ecclesiastical institutions, the Catholic Church might present to the country and the world a striking proof of the strong bond of unity with which her members are knit together." The decrees of the Second Plenary Council are divided into titles and chapters. The result of the deliberations was a complete recasting of all the older legislation. The Pastoral Letter treats in a particular way the bearing of this legislation upon the clergy and people. The Second Plenary Council is treated in the last pages of Shea's great work, the *History of the Catholic Church in the United States*. He was on his death-bed when these pages were written, and it is to be regretted that he did not live to give us the benefit of his wide knowledge of the prelates and of the legislation of the Council. The *Acta et Decreta* of the Council were published in Baltimore (1868). Smith, the canonist of the last generation of the clergy, published in New York (1874), his *Notes on the Second Plenary Council*. Perrine published (Baltimore, 1914) a translation of a very interesting commentary on the Council printed in Frankfort, Germany, in 1867. The *Sermons of the Council* were published in Baltimore in 1866. It is from this last volume that the Pastoral Letter is taken.

THE PASTORAL LETTER OF 1866

(Second Plenary Council of Baltimore)

The Archbishops and Bishops of the United States, in Plenary Council assembled, to the Clergy and Laity of their charge. Venerable Brethren of the Clergy: Beloved Children of the Laity:

AFTER the lapse of more than fourteen years it has again been permitted us to assemble in Plenary Council, for the purpose of more effectually uniting our efforts for the promotion of the great object of our ministry—the advancement of the interests of the Church of God. God, indeed, needs not human agency, although He vouchsafes to employ it. As in assuming our nature our Divine Redeemer subjected Himself to its conditions, and was made like unto us, sin only excepted;[1] so he has willed that in the establishment and maintenance of His Church, human agency should be

1 Heb. iv. 15.

employed, and the means best adapted for the attainment of its great end should be selected.

Among these means the assembling in council of the Bishops placed over the different portions of Christ's flock, in union with, and in obedience to, the Chief Bishop, to whom he has committed the care of the whole—lambs and sheep, people and pastors—has always been reckoned as among the most efficacious. Hence the reverence with which the Christian World has ever regarded the Councils of the Church. Of these some are called General, because representing the universal Church—the body of Pastors in union with its Head—and are therefore the highest expression of the authority which Christ has given to His Church. Local Councils, being but partial representations of the Church,— because composed of the Bishops of one or more Provinces, —are of inferior weight, but still are embodiments of the same principle. Among these Local Councils those called Plenary, because representing several Ecclesiastical Provinces—ordinarily under one civil government, and therefore sometimes called National—hold the highest place. They are assembled by express direction of the Sovereign Pontiff; who appoints a representative of his authority in the Apostolic Delegate he commissions to preside over them. Such Councils have not ordinarily to define the doctrines of the Church, although they furnish suitable occasions for making authoritative statements of them. Their principal object, however, is to regulate discipline, whether by the correction of abuses, or the establishment of such rules of conduct as circumstances may require.

I. AUTHORITY OF PLENARY COUNCILS.

The authority exercised in these councils is original, not delegated; and hence their decrees have, from the time of their promulgation, the character of ecclesiastical law for the faithful in the district or region subject to the jurisdiction of the Bishops by whom they have been enacted. By a wise regulation, however, which combines the benefit of central authority with the advantages of local legislation, the decrees of such councils are not promulgated or published until they have been submitted to the Holy See. This

is not only for the purpose of imparting to them a still higher
authority, but also to guard against any inaccuracy in doctrinal statements, or any enactment not in conformity with
the general discipline of the Church, or that might be contrary to the spirit of Ecclesiastical legislation.

II. ECCLESIASTICAL AUTHORITY.

The authority thus exercised is divine in its origin, the
Holy Ghost having "placed Bishops to rule the Church of
God."[2] Obedience to it—whether there be question of "the
faith once delivered to the saints," or of rules of conduct—
is not submission to man but to God; and consequently
imposes on the Faithful no obligation incompatible with the
true dignity of man. It would be a gross error to confound
the liberty "wherewith Christ has made us free,"[3] with the
license which would reject the authority He has established:
As obedience to law is the basis on which society rests, and
the only condition on which civil liberty can be enjoyed; so
in Religion, respect for the authority established by God,
obedience to its commands, and reverence for those in whom
it is vested, are not incompatible with Christian Freedom,
but form, in fact, the condition of its existence. In neither
order, is liberty freedom from all restraint, but only from
unjust and unauthorized control. In the temporal order,
the limits of lawful power vary with the constitution of society in each particular nation, but in the Church, the universal society—divine in its origin and constitution no less
than in its object, and bounded by no local limit—it is determined by the will of God, made known to men by that Revelation of which it forms a part, and of which the tribunal by
whose authority it is exercised is the witness, the guardian,
and the interpreter. To the Apostles, as a Ministerial Body
which was to have perpetual existence by the perpetual succession of its members, Christ gave the powers He himself
had received from the Father: "As the Father hath sent me,
I also send you."[4] "He who hears you, hears Me."[5] Hence
St. Paul identifies the ministry established by Christ, with
Christ Himself, and accounts its acts as the acts of the Redeemer: "But all things are of God, who hath reconciled

2 Acts xx.   3 St. John viii.   4 John xx. 21.   5 Luke x. 16.

us to Himself in Christ, and has given us the ministry of reconciliation. For God was in Christ, reconciling the world to Himself, not imputing to them their sins; and he hath placed in us the word of reconciliation. For Christ we are ambassadors; God as it were exhorting by us." [6]

We have deemed it not unnecessary to recall these truths to your minds, from our knowledge of the false light in which the nature of ecclesiastical authority is so often presented to view. Civil society requires a supreme tribunal for the adjudication of controversies in the temporal order; and without such a tribunal no society could exist. Much more does the Society, which Christ established, require that all controversies regarding the doctrines He taught and the duties He imposed, should be determined by an authority, whose decision should be final, and which, as all are bound to obey it, must be an infallible oracle of truth.

Nor is this principle less conformable to the dictates of reason than to the inspired language to which we have referred. Religion, considered as a Revelation, or extraordinary manifestation of supernatural truths, originally made to man by the ministry of men, necessarily implies the agency of men in its continued promulgation. When the Eternal Word assumed the nature of man, He made an outward manifestation of those truths which men never could have known but from his testimony. "No man at any time hath seen God: the only begotten Son, who is in the bosom of the Father, he hath declared Him." [7] What Christ made known to the Apostles, He commanded them to make known to men: "teaching them to observe all things whatsoever I have commanded you." [8] He gave their teaching the sanction of His personal authority, and placed no limit to the continuance of the commission thus imparted: "Behold I am with you all days, even to the consummation of the world" [9]—a phrase once before used by Our Lord, and once by the same Evangelist, St. Matthew, to designate the "end of the world." [10] To suppose that this commission was fulfilled by the preaching or writing of the Apostles, so that after them, men were not to have living teachers, who no less than

6 2 Cor. v. 18, 19, 20.　　　　　　　7 John i. 18.
8 Matt. xxviii. 20.　　　9 Ibid.　　10 Matt. xiii. 30; xxiv. 3.

they should speak with the authority of Christ, is to suppose that Christ departed from the plan he originally traced out, and adopted another plan of which he made no mention. But such a supposition is irreconcilable with the plain and authoritative language He used, and incompatible with His divine character.

The Apostles certainly did not so understand the words of their Divine Master. They "appointed priests in every city:"[11] to these they gave the power of associating others with themselves in the office of teaching: as they themselves had been associated with the Apostles: and as the Apostles had been associated with Christ. Hence the charge which St. Paul gave to Timothy, was, no doubt, given to all who, like Timothy, had received the imposition of hands for the work of the ministry. "Thou, therefore, my son, be strong in the grace which is in Christ Jesus; and the things which thou hast heard from me before many witnesses, the same commend to faithful men, who shall be fit to teach others also." [12] Hence the principle, elsewhere enunciated by the same Apostle, that "faith comes by hearing," [13] is that by which the knowledge of Christ's religion was to be continued, as it was that by which it was first made known. The announcement of divine truth by preachers, who have a divine commission to preach, is clearly expressed by the same Apostle in the series of questions which precede the words above quoted, and from which these words are a consequence. Having stated that all who call on the name of the Lord, whether Jew or Greek, shall be saved, he asks himself, for the purpose of answering a possible objection, the following questions: "How shall they then call on Him in whom they have not believed? Or how shall they believe in Him of whom they have not heard? And how shall they hear without a preacher? And how can they preach unless they be sent; as it is written: 'How beautiful are the feet of them that preach the gospel of peace, of them that bring glad tidings of good things!' "[14]

Those who refuse to obey this authority, and who condemn it as an unwarranted assumption of power on the part of the Church, deprive themselves of the only means by

11 Tit. i. 5.   12 2 Tim. ii. 2.   13 Rom. x. 17.   14 *Ibid.*, 14, 15.

which they can learn with entire certainty the truths God requires them to believe and the duties He imposes, in order to be saved. With such persons opinion is necessarily substituted for faith, which is firm and unwavering belief, on authority external to the believer. Nor can it be said, that those who reject the authority of the Church believe, on the authority of God, what they find Him to have revealed in His written Word. The meaning of that Word—whether it be supposed attainable by the exercise of the judgment aided by prayer for divine Light, or by a supposed immediate inspiration by the Holy Ghost,—in every such case, is ascertained by the individual whose judgment may err, and whose belief of a divine Inspiration may therefore be an illusion. Experience shows, that this must be the case in most instances; and reason suggests that it may be the case in all. The most contradictory conclusions are arrived at by men of great talent, vast learning, and undoubted sincerity of purpose. The most absurd and blasphemous ideas have been regarded by many as the teachings of the Holy Spirit, under the influence of the illusion, that what was the suggestion of their own imagination—if not the promptings of Satan, who sometimes "transforms himself into an angel of light,"—was indeed the voice of God. The tradition of the Church—that is the handing down from pastor to pastor, under the divine protection and guarantee, the doctrines originally received—is the only rational ground we can have for our belief, that God has revealed the truths which we believe. "Although I," says St. Paul, "or an angel from heaven, preach to you a gospel other than you have received, let him be anathema."[15] The same tradition, joined with the authority of the pastors of the Church, is the criterion by which St. John teaches us to try the spirits: "We are of God. He that knoweth God heareth us. He that is not of God, heareth us not. By this we know the spirit of truth and the spirit of error."[16]

What the plain words of Christ and reason itself establish, experience confirms. The authority recognized in the Catholic Church "preserves the unity of the spirit in the bond of peace," and exhibits to the world One Body and One

[15] Gal. i. 8.   [16] 1 John iv. 6.

Spirit, because there is One Faith, as there is but One Lord whose revelation it is.[17]   Outside of this One Fold of the One Shepherd, divisions arise and are perpetuated, because there is no supreme tribunal by which they might be extinguished; sects are multiplied, and religious indifference or unbelief is sought as a refuge from the contradiction of tongues. Hence the principles of morality, which derive the only efficacious motives for their practice from the Revelation of which they form a part, are weakened, if not entirely undermined; the believer is embarrassed and perplexed, and the unbeliever, who cannot always distinguish between the Church and the sects, finds a plausible excuse for incredulity in the diversities of religious systems and the divisions of professing Christians.

This authority is exercised not only in defining the truths of Faith, and in determining whatever controversies may arise in relation to them, but also in warning the Flock of Christ by seasonable admonitions, against whatever might interfere with the purity of Christian Morals, and by rebuke and reprehension, when they are found necessary for the correction of abuses. "Obey your Prelates," says St. Paul, "and be subject to them; for they watch, as having to render an account for your souls, that they may do this with joy, and not with grief. For this is not expedient for you."[18] We cheerfully acknowledge, Venerable and Beloved Brethren, the general and willing acceptance by you of this important principle of a living, guiding authority, which distinguishes the Church as a divine Institution, from the various sects that surround her. We wish, however, to impress upon the minds of all our spiritual children the obligation imposed on them of obeying their respective Prelates—each in his own Diocese—by receiving their directions as the expression of the Authority which Christ has established in His Church. So long as such directions are not set aside by superior authority, they are to be received as a rule of conduct; nor can they be evaded without transgressing the Apostolic precept, "Obey your Prelates." No motive derived from the possible misconception of the nature of that which is forbidden, or from the real or supposed difference

17 Ephes. iv. 5.   18 Heb. xiii. 17.

of opinion—the action or inaction of other Prelates—will excuse the Catholic from the crime of disobedience towards his own Bishop, if he refuse to be guided by him, and presume to dictate when it is his duty to obey. Hence when we warn you, either collectively, as in the present instance, or singly in our respective Dioceses, to avoid secret societies and all associations which we deem unlawful, you cannot, on the peril of your souls, disregard our admonitions: because the authority we exercise in such cases is that of Him who has said: "He who hears you hears Me, and he who despises you despises Me; and he that despises Me despises Him that sent Me."[19]

III. RELATIONS OF THE CHURCH TO THE STATE.

The enemies of the Church fail not to represent her claims as incompatible with the independence of the Civil Power, and her action as impeding the exertions of the State to promote the well-being of society. So far from these charges being founded in fact, the authority and influence of the Church will be found to be the most efficacious support of the temporal authority by which society is governed. The Church, indeed, does not proclaim the absolute and entire independence of the Civil Power, because it teaches with the Apostle, that "all Power is of God;" that the temporal magistrate is His minister, and that the power of the sword he wields is a delegated exercise of authority committed to him from on high.[20] For the children of the Church obedience to the Civil Power is not a submission to force which may not be resisted; nor merely the compliance with a condition for peace and security; but a religious duty founded on obedience to God, by whose authority the Civil Magistrate exercises his power. This power, however, as subordinate and delegated, must always be exercised agreeably to God's Law. In prescribing anything contrary to that Law the Civil Power transcends its authority, and has no claim on the obedience of the citizen. Never can it be lawful to disobey God, as the Apostles, Peter and John, so explicitly declared before the tribunal which sat in judgment on them:

[19] Luke x. 1.   [20] Rom. xiii. 1-5.

"If it be just in sight of God to hear you rather than God, judge ye."[21] This undeniable principle does not, however, entail the same consequences in the Catholic system as in those of the sects. In these, the individual is the ultimate judge of what the law of God commands or forbids, and is consequently liable to claim the sanction of the higher law, for what after all may be, and often is, but the suggestions of an undisciplined mind, or an over-heated imagination. Nor can the Civil Government be expected to recognize an authority which has no warrant for its character as divine, and no limits in its application, without exposing the State to disorder and anarchy. The Catholic has a guide in the Church, as a divine Institution, which enables him to discriminate between what the Law of God forbids or allows; and this authority the State is bound to recognize as supreme in its sphere—of moral, no less than dogmatic teaching. There may, indeed, be instances in which individual Catholics will make a misapplication of the principle; or in which, while the principle of obedience to Civil Authority is recognized as of divine obligation, the seat of that authority may be a matter of doubt, by reason of the clashing opinions that prevail in regard to this important fact. The Church does not assume to decide such matters in a temporal order, as she is not the judge of civil controversies, although she always, when invited to do so, has endeavored to remove the misconceptions from which disputes so often arise, and to consult for every interest while maintaining the peace of society and the rights of justice.

While cheerfully recognizing the fact, that hitherto the General and State Governments of our country, except in some brief intervals of excitement and delusion, have not interfered with our ecclesiastical organization or civil rights, we still have to lament that in many of the States we are not as yet permitted legally, to make those arrangements for the security of Church Property, which are in accordance with the canons and discipline of the Catholic Church. In some of the States we gratefully acknowledge that all is granted in this regard that we could reasonably ask for. The right of the Church to possess property, whether churches, resi-

21 Acts iv. 19.

dences for the clergy, cemeteries, or school-houses, asylums, etc., cannot be denied without depriving her of a necessary means of promoting the end for which she has been established. We are aware of the alleged grounds for this refusal to recognize the Church in her corporate capacity, unless on the condition, that, in the matter of the tenure of ecclesiastical property, she conform to the general laws providing for this object. These laws, however, are for the most part based on principles which she cannot accept, without departing from her practice from the beginning, as soon as she was permitted to enjoy liberty of worship. They are the expression of a distrust of ecclesiastical power, as such; and are the fruit of the misrepresentations which have been made of the action of the Church in past ages. As well might the civil power prescribe to her the doctrines she is to teach and the worship with which she is to honor God, as to impose on her a system of holding her temporalities, which is alien to her principles, and which is borrowed from those who have rejected her authority. Instead of seeking to disprove the various reasons alleged for this denial of the Church's rights in some of the States, we content ourselves with the formal protest we hereby enter against it; and briefly remark, that even in the supposition, which we by no means admit, that such denial was the result of legitimate motives, the denial itself is incompatible with the full measure of Ecclesiastical or Religious Liberty, which we are supposed to enjoy.

Nor is this an unimportant matter, or one which has not practical results of a most embarrassing character. Not only are we obliged to place church property in conditions of extreme hazard, because not permitted to manage our Church temporalities on Catholic principles; but in at least one of these United States—Missouri—laws have been passed by which all Church property, not held by corporations, is subjected to taxation; and the avowed object of this discriminating legislation, is hostility to the Catholic Church. In concluding these remarks, we merely refer to the attempt made in that State to make the exercise of ecclesiastical ministry depend on a condition laid down by the civil power.

IV. AID FOR THE POPE.

When last assembled in Plenary Council, we called on you to aid the Holy Father, by your contributions, and you generously responded to our appeal. Since then the richest and most fertile portions of the States of the Church have been wrested from him by the hands of violence, and his position has become still more critical and embarrassed. In order to enable him to assist those who are dependent on him, and to carry on the affairs of the Universal Church, it is absolutely necessary that the children of the Church in all parts of the world should come to his help. We have therefore felt it to be our duty to direct that an annual collection be henceforth taken up in all the Dioceses in the country, on the Sunday within the Octave of the Feast of SS. Peter and Paul, or such other Sunday as the Ordinary may direct, to be devoted to this purpose.

We need not remind you that the obligation of supplying the temporal wants of those who minister to your spiritual necessities applies in a special manner to the Sovereign Pontiff, who necessarily incurs great expenses in discharging the duties of his high office. We abstain from more than an allusion to the trials and humiliations to which the political changes in Italy, which have since occurred, have exposed him. However much the prevalence of false ideas, and an erroneous estimate of the real character of the charges referred to may mislead the judgment, all must admire the noble courage which the Holy Father has maintained, in the midst of these outrages; as all must be struck by that visible protection which Providence appears to have afforded him, so that he alone of all the princes of Italy yet retains his sovereignty and his independence. The imminent dangers, to which he has been exposed in his long and eventful Pontificate, have been hailed by the enemies of the Church as a triumph, and they have awakened in the latter the liveliest exultation and the most extravagant anticipations. You know, Brethren, how fallacious are such expectations, how delusive such hopes. You need not to be told, that the condition of the Church of Christ on earth is one of trial and endurance; that the Spouse of Christ is never more worthy of His love than when assimilated to Him by walking in His footsteps:[22] that the temporary triumph of her enemies is the forerunner of their ultimate defeat; and that every trial to which she is subjected is the preparation for her final victory. The more violent the storm, the more firmly, when it shall have spent its fury, will this tree of life be found to have struck its roots into the soil, in which the right hand of the Father hath planted it. A holy Pope, who filled the chair of Peter in the year 494, wrote thus to the Greek Emperor Anastasius: "What is of divine institution may be attacked by human presumption, but it cannot be overcome, no matter how great the power employed against it. Would that the impiety which impels them were as innoxious to its assailants, as that which God has established is superior to all violence. 'The sure foundation of God standeth firm.'[23] Does not experience shew that the Church, when attacked, instead of being overcome, is rendered the more invincible by that which appeared to ensure its destruction?"[24] Or, as St. Augustine forcibly expresses the same idea; the greater the violence with which earthly vessels strike against this rock the greater the destruction in which they are involved.

How consoling and encouraging the fact, that we can adopt this language, and may learn from the eighteen centuries of her eventful existence, that every successive trial of the Church proves the truth of the prophet's promise: "When thou shalt pass through the waters, I will be with thee; and the rivers shall not cover thee: when thou shalt walk through the fire, thou shalt not be burnt, and the flames shall not burn in thee." [25] "O poor little one, tossed with tempest without all comfort; behold I will lay thy stones in order, and will lay thy foundations with sapphires. And I will make thy bulwarks of jasper, and thy gates of graven stones, and all thy borders of desirable stones. All thy children shall be taught of the Lord, and great shall be the peace

22 Peter ii. 21.   23 2 Tim. ii. 19.

24 Impeti possunt humanis præsumptionibus quæ divino sunt judicio constituta: vinci autem quorumlibet potestate non possunt. Atque utinam sic contra nitentibus perniciosa non sit audacia, quemadmodum quod ab ipso sacræ Religionis Auctore præfixum est, non potest ulla virtute convelli. *Firmamentum enim Dei stat.* Num quidnam cum aliquibus infesta Religio est, quantacunque potuit novitate superari, et non magis hæc invicta permansit quo æstimata est posse succumbere?—*Gelasius ad Anastasium.*   25 Isaias xliii. 2.

of thy children. And thou shalt be founded in justice; depart far from oppression, for thou shalt not fear: and from terror, for it shall not come near thee. No weapon that is formed against thee shall prosper, and every tongue that resists thee in judgment, thou shalt condemn." [26]

V. THE SACRAMENT OF MATRIMONY.

To that sacrament of the Church which is highest in its typical signification—the sacrament of matrimony—we feel it our duty to direct in a particular manner your attention. From the beginning, as we learn from St. Paul, the union of man and woman was a great mystery or sacrament; because, from the beginning, it prefigured the union of Christ with His Church.[27]   In nothing perhaps is the influence of the Spirit of Truth more evident in the teaching of the Church, than in the care with which she has protected this "great sacrament," which, by so many, agreeably to what St. Paul had foretold,[28] was stigmatized as unlawful, while by others it was unduly exalted above sacred virginity, contrary to the express teaching of Christ [29] and his inspired Apostle.[30] The holiness of Christian matrimony is connected with our most sacred associations and duties; and it cannot be lost sight of in however small degree, without entailing the most serious consequences. The Church has shown in reference to this subject, a spirit of watchfulness and solicitude, which alone would entitle her to the gratitude of man, and cause her to be regarded as the most faithful guardian of public and private morality. Many of the innumerable contests in which she was compelled to engage with the depositaries of the Civil Power, during the middle ages, were in defence of the stability and sanctity of the marriage-tie; and, at a later period, she preferred to see England torn from her side, rather than yield compliance with the will of a monarch, who sacrificed his country's faith to his unbridled passions. In this matter she knew no distinction between the private man and the monarch; contrary to what an apologist for the worst passions and most cruel deeds of this unhappy Ruler insists should have been her

26 Isaias liv. 11, 12, 13, 14, 17.
27 Eph. v. 32.   28 1 Tim. iv. 3.   29 Matt. xix. 11, 12.   30 1 Cor. vii. 29-40.

line of conduct.[31] Even in our own days, her conservative authority has been exerted in the same cause; and the anger of the first Napoleon was incurred by the refusal of Pius VII., of holy memory, to declare invalid a marriage contracted between that Ruler's brother and a Protestant lady of the city in which we are now assembled. When this same monarch sought to break his first faith, he was obliged to have recourse to an extinct tribunal of the diocese of Paris —resuscitated for that special purpose,—which presumed to decide a question which the wisdom of the Holy See has reserved for its own exclusive jurisdiction.

We recall these facts, because they most strongly express the principle of the Church in regard to matrimony, and must be regarded by every well regulated mind as among the brightest jewels of her crown. We recall them, also, in order to enforce our solemn admonition to our flocks, to give no ear to the false and degrading theories on the subject of matrimony, which are boldly put forward by the enemies of the Church. According to these theories, marriage is a mere civil contract, which the Civil Power is to regulate, and from which an injured or dissatisfied party may release himself or herself by the remedy of divorce, so as to be able lawfully to contract new engagements. This is in evident contradiction to the words of Christ: "What God has joined together, let no man put asunder." [32] As the guardian of God's holy Law, the Church condemns this false theory, from which would follow a successive polygamy, no less opposed to the unity and stability of Christian marriage than that simultaneous polygamy, which, to the scandal of Christendom, is found within our borders. No State law can authorize divorce, so as to permit the parties divorced to contract new engagements; and every such new engagement, contracted during the joint lives of the parties so divorced, involves the crime of adultery. We refer with pain to the scandalous multiplication of these unlawful separations, which, more than any other cause, are sapping the foundations of morality and preparing society for an entire dissolution of the basis on which it rests.

If so many marriages become unhappy, and the bond

[31] Froude, 1 vol., chap. 2, p. 132, American edition.   [32] Matt. xix. 6.

which unites the married couple prove so often a galling yoke, this is to be attributed, in most instances, to the neglect and disregard of the Church's laws in reference to this subject. These, as you know, forbid marriage between persons related to each other in certain degrees of consanguinity and affinity, as also between Catholics and non-Catholics. Whatever exceptions may be found to the general observation as to the result of such unions, they are in principle condemned by the Church; and that from the most serious motives; which in the case of consanguinity, are founded in well ascertained physiological principles; in the case of affinity, in the danger to which possible unions may place parties who are necessarily brought into fraternal relations; and in the case of mixed marriages, to the danger of perversion, to which the Catholic party and the offspring of such marriages are exposed.

But something more than the observance of these laws of the Church in relation to marriage is required in order that Christians should discharge their entire duty, when about to enter the conjugal state. Its sacred character, and the obligations towards God's society which it imposes, should always be kept in mind. Purity of life, and affection that has better and more lasting grounds than the impulse of passion, are the only proper dispositions for entering upon a state of life which death alone can change, and which involves so many important consequences from time and eternity.

"Who (asks Tertullian) can express the happiness of that marriage which the Church approves, which sacrifice (the Mass) confirms, and which blessing seals—angels announce it, and the Father ratifies?" [33]

Bearing in mind the sanctity of Marriage, and the time-honored usages of the Church in the administration of the Sacrament, we cannot too strongly urge upon you the importance of contracting it before the Altar of God, and with the Marriage Mass, so as to receive that especial blessing which carries with it so many graces, to enable those who enter upon this holy state to fulfil its most important duties.

[33] Tert. ad uxorem, lib. II., cap. ult.

VI.   ON BOOKS AND NEWSPAPERS—THE PRESS.

The Council of Trent [34] requires, that all books which treat of Religion should be submitted before publication to the Ordinary of the Diocese in which they are to be published, for the purpose of obtaining his sanction, so as to assure the faithful that they contain nothing contrary to faith or morals. This law is still of force; and in the former Plenary Council its observance was urged, and the Bishops were exhorted to approve of no book which had not been previously examined by themselves, or by clergymen appointed by them for that purpose, and to confine such approbation to works published in their respective dioceses. The faithful should be aware that such approbation is rather of a negative than of a positive character; that it by no means imparts to the statements or sentiments such works may contain any episcopal sanction; but merely guarantees them as free from errors in faith or morals.

In many also of our dioceses there are published Catholic Papers, mostly of a religious character; and many of such papers bear upon them the statement that they are the "organs" of the Bishop of the diocese in which they are published, and sometimes of other Bishops in whose dioceses they circulate. We cheerfully acknowledge the services the Catholic Press has rendered to Religion, as also the disinterestedness with which, in most instances, it has been conducted, although yielding to publishers and editors a very insufficient return for their labors. We exhort the Catholic community to extend to these publications a more liberal support, in order that they may be enabled to become more worthy the great cause they advocate.

We remind them, that the power of the press is one of the most striking features of modern society; and that it is our duty to avail ourselves of this mode of making known the truths of our Religion, and removing the misapprehensions which so generally prevail in regard to them. If many of these papers are not all that we would wish them to be, it will be frequently found, that the real cause of their shortcomings is the insufficient support they receive from the Catholic Public. Supply and demand act and react on each

[34] Sess. IV. Dec. de editione et usu sacrorum librorum.

other; and if in many instances the former produces the latter, in regard at least to Catholic publications, demand must precede supply. We also wish to guard against the misapprehension, which frequently arises from the Bishop's name being connected with such papers, in so far as they are recognized as "organs," that is, as mediums through which the Ordinary communicates with his diocesans. This circumstance gives no sanction to the articles which appear in such papers, other than they may derive from the name of the writer when given: still less does it identify the Bishop with the paper, so as to justify the conclusion that whatever appears in it has his sanction and authority. It merely designates the paper as one in which the Bishop will cause to be inserted such official documents as he, from time to time, may have to publish, and in regard to which it is obviously desirable that there should be some regular mode of communication.

In connection with this matter we earnestly recommend to the Faithful of our charge the CATHOLIC PUBLICATION SOCIETY, lately established in the City of New York by a zealous and devoted clergyman. Besides the issuing of short tracts, with which this Society has begun, and which may be so usefully employed to arrest the attention of many whom neither inclination nor leisure will allow to read larger works, this Society contemplates the publication of Catholic Books, according as circumstances may permit, and the interests of Religion appear to require. From the judgment and good taste evinced in the composition and selection of such tracts and books as have already been issued by this Society, we are encouraged to hope that it will be eminently effective in making known the truths of our Holy Religion, and dispelling the prejudices which are mainly owing to want of information on the part of so many of our fellow-citizens. For this, it is necessary that a generous co-operation be given, both by clergy and laity, to the undertaking, which is second to none in importance, among the subsidiary aids which the inventions of modern times supply to our Ministry for the diffusion of Catholic Truth.

VII. Education of Youth.

We recur to the subject of the education of youth, to which, in the former Plenary Council, we already directed your attention, for the purpose of reiterating the admonition we then gave, in regard to the establishment and support of Parochial Schools; and of renewing the expression of our conviction, that religious teaching and religious training should form part of every system of school education. Every day's experience renders it evident, that to develop the intellect and store it with knowledge, while the heart and its affections are left without the control of religious principle, sustained by religious practices, is to mistake the nature and object of education; as well as to prepare for parent and child the most bitter disappointment in the future, and for society the most disastrous results. We wish also to call attention to a prevalent error on the subject of the education of youth, from which parents of the best principles are not always exempt. Naturally desiring the advancement of their children, in determining the education they will give them, they not unfrequently consult their wishes, rather than their means, and the probable position of their children in mature age. Education, to be good, need not necessarily be either high or ornamental, in the studies or accomplishments it embraces. These things are in themselves unobjectionable; and they may be suitable and advantageous or otherwise, according to circumstances. Prepare your children for the duties of the state or condition of life they are likely to be engaged in: do not exhaust your means in bestowing on them an education that may unfit them for these duties. This would be a sure source of disappointment and dissatisfaction, both for yourselves and for them. Accustom them from their earliest years to habits of obedience, industry, and thrift: and deeply impress on their minds the great principle, that happiness and success in life, as well as acceptance with God, do not so much depend on the station we fill, as on the fidelity with which we discharge its duties. Teach them, that the groundwork of true happiness must be placed in habitual and cheerful submission of our wills to the dispensations of

Providence, who has wisely consulted for the happiness of all, without, however, bestowing on all an equal share of the goods of fortune.

VIII.   CATHOLIC PROTECTORIES AND INDUSTRIAL SCHOOLS.

Connected with this subject of education, is the establishment of Protectories and Industrial Schools for the correction or proper training of youth, which has of late years attracted universal attention. It is a melancholy fact, and a very humiliating avowal for us to make, that a very large proportion of the idle and vicious youth of our principal cities are the children of Catholic parents. Whether from poverty or neglect, the ignorance in which so many parents are involved as to the true nature of education, and of their duties as Christian parents, or the associations which our youth so easily form with those who encourage them to disregard parental admonition; certain it is, that a large number of Catholic parents either appear to have no idea of the sanctity of the Christian family, and of the responsibility imposed on them of providing for the moral training of their offspring, or fulfil this duty in a very imperfect manner. Day after day, these unhappy children are caught in the commission of petty crimes, which render them amenable to the public authorities; and, day after day, are they transferred by hundreds from the sectarian reformatories in which they have been placed by the courts, to distant localities, where they are brought up in ignorance of, and most commonly in hostility to, the Religion in which they had been baptized. The only remedy for this great and daily augmenting evil is, to provide Catholic Protectories or Industrial Schools, to which such children may be sent; and where, under the only influence that is known to have really reached the roots of vice, the youthful culprit may cease to do evil and learn to do good. We rejoice that in some of our dioceses—would that we could say in all!— a beginning has been made in this good work; and we cannot too earnestly exhort our Venerable Brethren of the Clergy to bring this matter before their respective flocks, to endeavor to impress on Christian parents the duty of guarding their children from the evils above referred to, and to invite them to make persevering and effectual efforts for the establishment of Institutions, wherein, under the influence of religious teachers, the waywardness of youth may be corrected, and good seed planted in the soil in which, while men slept, the enemy had sowed tares.

IX. Vocations to the Priesthood.

We continue to feel the want of zealous priests, in sufficient number to supply the daily increasing necessities of our dioceses. While we are gratified to know, that in some parts of our country the number of youths who offer themselves for the Ecclesiastical state is rapidly increasing, we are obliged to remark, that in the other parts, notwithstanding all the efforts and sacrifices which have been made for this object, and the extraordinary encouragements which have been held out to youthful aspirants to the ministry, in our Preparatory and Theological Seminaries, the number of such as have presented themselves and persevered in their vocations has hitherto been lamentaßly small. Whatever may be the cause of this unwillingness to enter the sacred ministry on the part of our youth, it cannot be attributed to any deficiency of ours in such efforts as circumstances have enabled us to make. We fear that the fault lies, in great part, with many parents, who, instead of fostering the desire, so natural to the youthful heart, of dedicating itself to the service of God's sanctuary, but too often impart to their children their own worldly-mindedness, and seek to influence their choice of a state in life, by unduly exaggerating the difficulties and dangers of the priestly calling, and painting in too glowing colors the advantages of a secular life. To such parents we would most earnestly appeal; imploring them not to interfere with the designs of God on their children, when they perceive in them a growing disposition to attach themselves to the service of the Altar. If God rewards the youthful piety of your sons by calling them to minister in His sanctuary, the highest privilege He confers on man, do not endeavor to give their thoughts another direction. Do not present to your children the priesthood in any other light than as a sublime and holy state, having, indeed, most sacred duties and most serious obligations, but having also the promise of God's grace to strengthen and sustain human weakness in their fulfilment, and the divine blessing, here and hereafter, as their reward. To those whom God invites to co-operate with Him, in the most divine of all works, the salvation of souls, the words of Christ to His Apostles are applicable: "Amen, I say to you, that you who have followed me, in the regeneration, when the Son of Man shall sit in the seat of His majesty, you also shall sit on twelve seats, judging the twelve tribes of Israel; and every one that hath left house, or brother or sisters, or father or mother, or wife or children, or lands, for My name's sake, shall receive a hundredfold, and shall possess life everlasting." [35]

And whilst speaking to you upon this subject, we would renew our exhortations to the Faithful, to contribute to the extent of their means to the Diocesan fund for the support of Ecclesiastical students. Situated as the Church is in this country, with a Catholic population so rapidly increasing from emigration, there is no work of charity that can take precedence of it, and none which will bring so rich a reward.

X. THE LAITY.

We continue to have great consolation in witnessing the advance of Religion throughout the various Dioceses, as shewn in the multiplication and improved architectual character of our churches, the increase of piety in the various congregations, and the numerous conversions of so many who have sacrificed early prejudices and every consideration of their temporal interests and human feelings at the shrine of Catholic Truth. We must, however, in all candor say, that we cannot include all, or indeed the greater part of those who compose our flocks, in this testimony to fidelity and zeal. Too many of them, including not unfrequently men otherwise of blameless lives, remain for years estranged from the sacraments of the Church, although they attend the celebration of the divine Mysteries, and listen to the preaching of God's word with an earnestness

[35] Matt. xix. 27, 28.

and attention in themselves deserving of all praise. There
are, indeed, others who, carried away by the impulse of
passion, and but too easily influenced by evil examples,
oblige us to rank them, as we do, weeping, after the example
of the Apostle, among "the enemies of the Cross of Christ,
whose end is destruction; whose God is their belly; and
whose glory is in their shame; who mind earthly things." [36]
It is impossible to estimate the injury these unworthy Catholics, and especially those who are the slaves of intemperance and its consequent vices, inflict on the Church.
In the minds of but too many uninformed and unreflecting
persons, these evils are taken as the confirmation of early
prejudices; and the name of God is blasphemed among the
nations by reason of the evil acts of those who, whilst they
bear the name of Catholics, bring disgrace on their religion
by their evil lives. Willingly would we have avoided reference to this painful subject; but we are not without hope,
that is our solemn protest against the evils we deplore may
diminish, if not entirely remove, the scandal which they
occasion; and that our united remonstrance may not be
unheeded by those for whom "we watch, having to render
an account of their souls:" [37] that they may be roused from
the fatal lethargy in which they live, and, by sincere repentance and the practice of every good work compatible
with their condition, repair, in some measure, the scandals
they have given and the injury they have inflicted on the
Church, by the irregularity of their past lives.

In this connection, we consider it to be our duty to warn
our people against those amusements which may easily become to them an occasion of sin, and especially against
those fashionable dances, which, as at present carried on,
are revolting to every feeling of delicacy and propriety, and
are fraught with the greatest danger to morals. We would
also warn them most solemnly against the great abuses
which have sprung up in the matter of Fairs, Excursions,
and Picnics, in which, as too often conducted, the name of
Charity is made to cover up a multitude of sins. We forbid
all Catholics from having anything to do with them, except
when managed in accordance with the regulations of the

36 Philipp. iii. 18, 19.   37 Heb. xiii. 17.

Ordinary, and under the immediate supervision of their respective Pastors.

We have noticed, with the most sincere satisfaction and gratitude to God, the great increase among us of Societies and Associations, especially of those composed of young and middle-aged men, conducted in strict accordance with the principles of the Catholic Religion, and with an immediate view to their own sanctification. We cannot but anticipate the most beneficial results to the cause of morality and religion from the conduct and example of those who thus combine together, to encourage one another in the frequentation of the sacraments, and in works of Christian charity. We urge their extension, and especially of the Society of St. Vincent of Paul and of Young Men's Catholic Associations, in all the dioceses and parishes of the country, not only as useful auxiliaries to the Parochial clergy, in the care of the poor, and of destitute and vagrant children, but also as one of the most important means of diminishing the vices and scandals of which we have spoken.

XI.   THE CLERGY.

We exhort our venerable Brethren of the Clergy, who share our cares and responsibilities, to unremitting zeal in the great work to which they have been called. Let them honor their ministry, having ever before their eyes "the High-Priest, holy, innocent, undefiled, separated from sinners," [38] whose representatives they are. By purity of life, exemplariness and devotedness, let them be "a pattern of the flock from the heart," [39]—"the example of the faithful in word, in conversation, in charity, in faith, in chastity" [40] —"giving no offence to any man, that our ministry be not blamed, but in all things exhibiting ourselves as the ministers of God;" [41] so that "when the Prince of Pastors shall appear, they may receive a neverfading crown of glory." [42]

XII.   THE EMANCIPATED SLAVES.

We must all feel, beloved Brethren, that in some manner a new and most extensive field of charity and devotedness

[38] Heb. vii. 26.   [39] 1 Peter v. 3.   [40] 1 Tim. iv. 12.
[41] 1 Cor. vi. 3, 4.   [42] 1 Pet. v. 4.

has been opened to us, by the emancipation of the immense slave population of the South. We could have wished, that in accordance with the action of the Catholic Church in past ages, in regard to the serfs of Europe, a more gradual system of emancipation could have been adopted, so that they might have been in some measure prepared to make a better use of their freedom, than they are likely to do now. Still the evils which must necessarily attend upon the sudden liberation of so large a multitude, with their peculiar dispositions and habits, only make the appeal to our Christian charity and zeal, presented by their forlorn condition, the more forcible and imperative.

We urge upon the Clergy and people of our charge the most generous co-operation with the plans which may be adopted by the Bishops of the Dioceses in which they are, to extend to them that Christian education and moral restraint which they so much stand in need of. Our only regret in regard to this matter is, that our means and opportunity of spreading over them the protecting and salutary influences of our Holy Religion, are so restricted.

XIII. Religious Communities.

We are filled with sentiments of the deepest reverence for those holy Virgins, who, in our various religious communities, having taken counsel of St. Paul, have chosen the better part, that they may be holy "in body and in spirit." [43] These serve God with undivided heart; and, like Mary, sit at the feet of Jesus in devout contemplation; or, like Martha, devote themselves to the service of their neighbor, instructing youth or tending old age, ministering to the sick, or calming the remorses and encouraging the hopes of the penitent. To such the prophet's words are applicable: "I will give to them in my house and within my walls a place and a name better than sons and daughters." [44] Their state on earth is likened by Christ Himself to that "of the angels in heaven;" [45] and to those who embrace it is promised a special reward hereafter. Of these virgins it is written: "These follow the Lamb whithersoever He

[43] 1 Cor. vii. 34.   [44] Isaias lvi. 5.   [45] Matt. xx. 30.

goeth;"[46] and of these it is said: "No man could say the canticle, but those hundred and forty-four thousand;—for they are virgins."[47] "How great, think you," asks a devout writer of the middle ages, commenting on these tests, "will be the glory that environs the Virgins that follow Christ by purity of heart and mind. Alone they follow the Lamb whithersoever He goeth, reflecting this glory of the Sun of Justice, as does the Moon that of the Orb of day. As the moon outshines the stars, so, in that heavenly kingdom, they will shine more brightly than those who have not emulated their purity."[48] Great, indeed, are the privileges and great the rewards promised to these chaste spouses of Christ; and corresponding is the reverence with which they have ever been regarded in the Church. "The glorious fruitfulness of our Mother, the Church," observes St. Cyprian, "rejoices and exults in them; and the more she entwines of these lilies in her crown, the deeper her joy, the more intense her exultation. These we address," continues the Saint, "these we exhort; using rather the language of affection than of authority: not that we, the humblest, the most deeply conscious of our own infirmity, have any rebuke to make, any reprehension to utter: but because of our obligation to be watchful, we are the more solicitous to guard against the enemy of the devil."[49]

We adopt this language of the great Bishop and Martyr of the third century. We discharge a grateful duty, in rendering a public testimony to the virtue and heroism of these Christian Virgins; whose lives shed the good odor of Christ in every place, and whose devotedness and spirit of

---

[46] Apoc. xiv. 4.   [47] Apoc. xiv. 2, 3.

[48] Quanta putas ibi gloria fulgebunt Virgines Christi, cordis simul et mentis puritate Christum sequentes! Quis sanctorum chorus melius lunæ comparatur quam Virgines? Solæ sequuntur Solem justitiæ, Christum, ut Agnum Patris, quocunque ierit. Unde et solæ illi similes sunt atque simillimæ. Honorabuntur ergo præ cæteris in eodem regno existentibus splendore quidem excellentiori, sicut lunam videmus præ cæteris sideribus præ-eminere, possidebuntque in domo Domini locum meliorem multo quam cæterorum filiorum qui virginitatis merito non sunt insignes. *Vitis Mystica*, Capt. xxxi., inter Opera S. Bernardi, t. v., p. 125.

[49] Gaudet per illas atque in illis floret Ecclesiæ matris gloriosa fæcunditas, quantoque plus copiosa Virginitas numero suo addit, tanto plus gaudium matris augescit. Ad has loquimur; has adhortamur affectione potiusquam potestate; non quod extremi et minimi, et humilitatis nostræ admodum conscii, aliquod ad licentiam censuræ vindicemus: sed quod ad solicitudinem magis cauti, plus de diaboli infestatione timeamus. S. Cyprianus, *De Disciplina et Habitu Virginum*.

self-sacrifice have, more perhaps than any other cause, contributed to effect a favorable change in the minds of thousands estranged from our faith. To each of them, however, we feel impelled to address the words spoken to the angel of the Church of Philadelphia: "Hold fast that which thou hast, that no one take thy crown." [50]

CONCLUSION.

We have every confidence, Venerable and dearly Beloved Brethren, that the Council which is this day brought to a close, will exert a most beneficial influence in the cause of our Holy Religion.

We have taken advantage of the opportunity of the assembling of so large a number of Bishops from every part of our vast country, to enact such decrees as will tend to promote uniformity of discipline and practice amongst us, and to do away with such imperfect observance of the rites and approved ceremonies of the Church, as may have been made necessary by the circumstances of past times, but which no length of prescription can ever consecrate, and thus to give the services of our Religion that beauty, and dignity, which belongs to them, and for which we should be all so zealous.

For the furtherance of these important objects, we have caused to be drawn up a clear and compendious series of Statements upon the most essential points of Faith and Morals, with which we have embodied the decrees of the Seven Provincial Councils of Baltimore, and of the First Plenary Council, together with the Decrees enacted by us in the present Council, which, when they have been examined and approved of by the Holy See, will form a compendium of Ecclesiastical Law, for the guidance of our Clergy in the exercise of their Holy Ministry.

The result of our labors when thus returned to us, will be promulgated more fully in our Provincial Councils and Diocesan Synods, and we will then take advantage of the opportunity to bring more fully under the notice of the Clergy, and the people committed to our pastoral charge, the details of what we have done, and the exact nature of

50 Apoc. iii. 2.

the means by which we hope to give increased efficiency to the whole practical system of the Church in this country.

We have also recommended to the Holy See, the erection of several additional Episcopal Sees, and Vicariates Apostolic, which are made necessary by our rapidly increasing Catholic population, and the great territorial extent of many of our present Dioceses.

You will all rejoice, Venerable and Beloved Brethren, in these evidences of the vitality and diffusion of our Holy Faith, in the midst of the difficulties and evils that surround us. We depend on your fidelity to its sacred teachings, and your zealous co-operation, to give effect to our labors in your behalf, that so, all that has been planned and done by us, may be to the Glory of God, the Exaltation of His Holy Church, and the Salvation of Souls for which Christ died.

"For the rest, Brethren, whatsoever things are true, whatsoever modest, whatsoever just, whatsoever holy, whatsoever lovely, whatsoever of good fame; if there be any virtue, if any praise of discipline, think on these things. The things which you have both learned and received, and heard and seen,—these do ye, and the God of Peace shall be with you." [51]

Given at Baltimore, in Plenary Council, on the Feast of the Maternity of our Lady, October the 21st, in the year of our Lord 1866.

✝M. J. SPALDING, D.D., *Archbishop of Baltimore, Delegate Apostolic, President of the Council.*

✝F. N. BLANCHET, D.D., *Archbishop of Oregon City.*

✝P. R. KENRICK, D.D., *Archbishop of St. Louis.*

✝J. S. ALEMANY, D.D., *Archbishop of San Francisco.*

✝J. B. PURCELL, D.D., *Archbishop of Cincinnati.*

✝J. M. ODIN, D.D., *Archbishop of New Orleans.*

✝JOHN MCCLOSKEY, D.D., *Archbishop of New York.*

✝RICHARD V. WHELAN, D.D., *Bishop of Wheeling.*

✝P. P. LEFEVRE, D.D., *Bishop of Zela, and Administrator of Detroit.*

✝J. M. HENNI, D.D., *Bishop of Milwaukee.*

✝A. M. A. BLANCHET, D.D., *Bishop of Nesqualy.*

51 Philipp. iv. 8, 9.

✠A. RAPPE, D.D., *Bishop of Cleveland.*

✠JOHN TIMON, D.D., *Bishop of Buffalo.*

✠M. DEMERS, D.D., *Bishop of Vancouver's Island.*

✠M. DE ST. PALAIS, D.D., *Bishop of Vincennes.*

✠J. B. LAMY, D.D., *Bishop of Santa Fé.*

✠JOHN McGILL, D.D., *Bishop of Richmond.*

✠JOHN LOUGHLIN, D.D., *Bishop of Brooklyn.*

✠J. R. BAYLEY, D.D., *Bishop of Newark.*

✠L. DE GOESBRIAND, D.D., *Bishop of Burlington.*

✠G. A. CARRELL, D.D., *Bishop of Covington.*

✠T. AMAT, D.D., *Bishop of Monterey and Los Angeles.*

✠A. MARTIN, D.D., *Bishop of Nachitoches.*

✠D. W. BACON, D.D., *Bishop of Portland.*

✠F. BARAGA, D.D., *Bishop of Marquette.*

✠H. D. JUNCKER, D.D., *Bishop of Alton.*

✠JAMES DUGGAN, D.D., *Bishop of Chicago.*

✠WILLIAM H. ELDER, D.D., *Bishop of Natchez.*

✠J. H. LUERS, D.D., *Bishop of Fort Wayne.*

✠P. N. LYNCH, D.D., *Bishop of Charleston.*

✠F. P. McFARLAND, D.D., *Bishop of Hartford.*

✠J. M. O'GORMAN, D.D., *Vicar Apostolic of Nebraska.*

✠T. L. GRACE, D.D., *Bishop of St. Paul.*

✠JOHN QUINLAN, D.D., *Bishop of Mobile.*

✠J. F. WOOD, D.D., *Bishop of Philadelphia.*

✠M. DOMENEC, D.D., *Bishop of Pittsburg.*

✠E. O'CONNELL, D.D., *Vicar Apostolic of Marysville, California.*

✠AUG. VEROT, D.D., *Bishop of Savannah.*

✠C. M. DUBUIS, D.D., *Bishop of Galveston.*

✠P. J. LAVIALLE, D.D., *Bishop of Louisville.*

✠J. J. CONROY, D.D., *Bishop of Albany.*

✠P. A. FEEHAN, D.D., *Bishop of Nashville.*

✠J. J. WILLIAMS, D.D., *Bishop of Boston.*

✠J. HENNESSY, D.D., *Bishop of Dubuque.*

✠S. H. ROSECRANS, D.D., *Auxiliary Bishop of Cincinnati.*

JOHN D. CODY, *Administrator of Erie, sede vacante.*

FERD. COOSMANS, S.J., *Procurator of the Vicar Apostolic of Kansas.*

CHAPTER XII

The Pastoral Letter of 1884

NEARLY twenty years were to pass before the Third Plenary Council formally opened its sessions at Baltimore (November 9, 1884). Archbishop Gibbons was appointed Apostolic Delegate for the Council by Leo XIII (January 4, 1884); on March 19, letters of convocation were sent to the American hierarchy. The number of prelates present at the Council was nearly double that of the assembly of 1866. Fourteen archbishops, sixty American bishops and five visiting bishops from Canada and Japan, and ninety theologians participated in the proceedings of the Council. A recent biographer of Cardinal Gibbons has summed up the assembly as follows: "Many subjects were considered in the Council, including changes in the discipline and administration of the Church in this country. The country was making such tremendous strides forward, and Catholicity was keeping pace with it, that such changes were demanded. The debates at the sessions covered all phases of the various questions discussed. Every member of the Council was given opportunity to state his views freely without fear or embarrassment. The debates at times became vigorous, but always the spirit of Christian charity prevailed. There was an Ireland in that Council, a Ryan, a Keane, a Spalding, men whose oratorical ability held the delegates bound by virtue of their eloquence and whose arguments provoked deep thought. With the greatest minds of the United States there, all conscious of their responsibility before Almighty God, all loving the Church with a loyalty and devotion intense in quality,—the Council reflected in all its proceedings the real spirit of the Church, and its work redounded to the greater honor and glory of God. So successful was it that it was taken as a model for similar councils held in Ireland, Australia and other parts of the world." The Council legislated for the increased establishment of Catholic parochial schools and reached the decision that the time had come for the erection of the Catholic University of America, at Washington, D. C. The Pastoral Letter of 1884 surpassed all those that preceded it by its lofty eloquence and by the variety

of questions it discussed. Its broad and patriotic view of the
problems affecting American life in general and the high-
minded exposition of Christian principles in their relation to
civic affairs won for the Pastoral the praise of leaders of all
classes and a profound respect and appreciation from Americans of other creeds. The Pastoral is taken from the *Memorial
Volume: A History of the Third Plenary Council of Baltimore*
(Baltimore, 1885).

THE PASTORAL LETTER OF 1884

(Third Plenary Council of Baltimore)

*The Archbishops and Bishops of the United States to the
clergy and laity of their charge.*
*The Archbishops and Bishops of the United States, in Third
Plenary Council assembled, to their clergy and faithful people—"Grace unto you and peace from God our
Father, and from the Lord Jesus Christ." Venerable
brethren of the clergy, beloved children of the laity:*

FULL eighteen years have elapsed since our predecessors
were assembled in Plenary Council to promote uniformity of discipline, to provide for the exigencies of the
day, to devise new means for the maintenance and diffusion of our holy religion, which should be adequate to the
great increase of the Catholic population. In the interval,
the prelates, clergy and faithful have been taught by a
wholesome experience to appreciate the zeal, piety and prudence that inspired the decrees of those venerable Fathers
and to listen with cheerful submission to their authoritative
voice, whether uttered in warning, in exhortation or positive enactment. And the whole American Church deeply
feels and cordially proclaims her gratitude for the treasure
bequeathed to us by their wise and timely legislation. Its
framers, in great part, have gone before us with the sign
of Faith and now sleep the sleep of peace. But their work,
after following them to the dread tribunal of the great
Judge to plead in their behalf and insure their reward,
has remained upon earth a safe guide and rich blessing for
the clergy and people of their generation.

Since that time, however, the body of our clergy and

religious has grown to wonderful dimensions, our Catholic institutions have been multiplied tenfold, with a corresponding increase in the number of our faithful laity. The territory, likewise, over which they are spread, has been greatly enlarged. The land of the far West, that was once desolate and impassable, through God's providential mercy, now rejoices and flourishes like the lily. Under His guiding hand, it has been taught to bud forth and blossom and rejoice with joy and praise. The wilderness has exchanged its soltitude for the hum of busy life and industry; and the steps of our missionaries and Catholic settlers have invariably either preceded or accompanied the westward progress of civilization. Forests have given away to cities, where Catholic temples re-echo the praises of the Most High, where the priceless perfume of the "Clean Oblation," foretold by Malachi, daily ascends to heaven, and where the life-giving sacraments of Holy Church are dispensed by a devoted clergy. In view of this great progress of our holy religion, this marvellous widening of the tabernacles of Jacob, it has been judged wise and expedient, if not absolutely necessary, to examine anew the legislation of our predecessors, not with any purpose of radical change, much less of abrogation, but to preserve and perfect its spirit by adapting it to our altered circumstances. And as every day gives birth to new errors, and lapse of time or distance of place allows abuses to gradually creep into regular discipline, we have judged it the duty of our pastoral office to check the latter by recalling and enforcing established law, and to guard our flock against the former by timely words of paternal admonition.

Such, too, has been the expressed wish and injunction of our Holy Father Leo XIII, happily reigning, to whom, as Supreme Pontiff and successor of the Prince of the Apostles, by inherent right belongs the power of convoking this our Third National or Plenary Council, and of appointing (as he has graciously done) an Apostolic Delegate to preside over its deliberations.

One of the most important events that our age has witnessed was the assembling by Pius IX, of happy memory, of the General Council of the Vatican. It was held three years

after the close of our Second Plenary Council, and all, or
nearly all, of its members, and many besides of the prelates
now assembled in this Third Plenary Council, enjoyed the
rare privilege of sitting with the other Princes of the Church
in the only Ecumenical Synod vouchsafed these latter ages.
Its appointed task was to condemn the most influential and
insidious errors of the day, and to complete the legislation
on weighty matters of discipline that had been contem-
plated and discussed, but left undecided, by the Council of
Trent. Like its predecessor, the Council of the Vatican was
interrupted by the disturbed condition of Europe; and the
Fathers, leaving the work of their deliberations unfinished,
returned to their homes, some to this Western continent,
others to remote regions of the East. But we would fain
cherish the hope, and lift up to heaven our earnest prayer,
that the Father of mercies and God of all consolation, who
is ever ready to comfort His Church in all her tribulations,
who holds in His hand the counsels of princes and the devices of peoples, may deign, in His own good time, to re-
unite the prelates, or their successors, over the tomb of St.
Peter or elsewhere, as may seem best to His infinite wisdom.
The Vatican Council, however, during its short session of
seven months, gave solemn authoritative utterance to some
great truths which the Church had unvaryingly held
from the days of Christ and His Apostles; but which she
found it once more necessary to recall and inculcate against
the widespread skepticism and unbelief of our day. Besides condemning the philosophy, no less wicked than false
and teeming with contradictions, of the last two centuries,
and especially of our own times, she had to uphold (such
is the lamentable downward course of those who rebelled
against her divine commission to teach all nations!) the
truth and divinity of the Sacred Books against the very
children of those who once appealed to Scripture to disprove her teachings, and to maintain the dignity and
value of human reason against the lineal descendants of
those who once claimed reason as the supreme and only
guide in picking out from her creed what mysteries they
would retain, what mysteries they would reject. Nobly did
she perform her duty and assert in the face of a forgetful

or unbelieving world that reason is God's highest and best gift to man in the natural order, and that this most salutary aid of his weakness is not only not impaired, but strengthened, supplemented and ennobled by the supernatural gift of Divine revelation.

We have no reason to fear that you, beloved brethren, are likely to be carried away by these or other false doctrines condemned by the Vatican Council, such as materialism or the denial of God's power to create, to reveal to mankind His hidden truths, to display by miracles His almighty power in this world which is the work of His hands. But neither can we close our eyes to the fact that teachers of skepticism and irreligion are at work in our country. They have crept into the leading educational institutions of our non-Catholic fellow-citizens, they have (though rarely) made their appearance in the public press and even in the pulpit. Could we rely fully on the innate good sense of the American people and on that habitual reverence for God and religion which has so far been their just pride and glory, there might seem comparatively little danger of the general diffusion of those wild theories which reject or ignore Revelation, undermine morality, and end not unfrequently by banishing God from His own creation. But when we take into account the daily signs of growing unbelief, and see how its heralds not only seek to mould the youthful mind in our colleges and seats of learning, but are also actively working amongst the masses, we cannot but shudder at the dangers that threaten us in the future. When to this we add the rapid growth of that false civilization which hides its foulness under the name of enlightenment—involving, as it does, the undisguised worship of mammon, the anxious search after every ease, comfort and luxury for man's physical well-being, the all-absorbing desire to promote his material interests, the unconcern or rather contempt for those of his higher and better nature— we cannot but feel that out of all this must grow a heartless materialism, which is the best soil to receive the seeds of unbelief and irreligion, which threaten to desolate the country at no distant day. The first thing to perish will be our liberties. For men, who know not God or religion, can never respect the inalienable rights which man has received from His Creator. The State in such case must become a despotism, whether its power be lodged in the hands of one or many.

To you, beloved brethren, who possess the treasure of Catholic faith, we may safely address the reiterated injunctions of the Lord to the chosen leader of His people.

"Take courage and be strong . . . take courage and be very valiant. . . . Behold I command thee, take courage and be strong. Fear not and be not dismayed, because the Lord thy God is with thee." [1] The latter clause gives the reason why we should take courage and be strong. An intermediate verse gives the means of securing God's assistance: "Let not the book of this law depart from thy mouth, but thou shalt meditate on it day and night, that thou mayest observe and do the things that are written in it." Keep, then, day and night, before your eyes the Law of God and His teachings through that Holy Church that He has appointed mother and mistress of all men. Fly the reading of all infidel books, and keep them from your children, as you would the poison of asp or basilisk. Teach them that you and they, in listening to Holy Church, have the guidance of Him who said, "I am the way, the truth and the life." Let others doubt or deny, but with the Apostle, you know whom you have believed, and you are certain that He will make good the trust you have reposed in Him. [2]

Christ our Lord commissioned His Apostles to teach mankind the truths they had been taught by Him. They received no commandment to write on any doctrine, much less to draw up a body of articles of faith such as our children now learn from the catechism. They preached and taught by word of mouth; or, when occasion offered itself, they wrote as the Divine Spirit prompted them. What they wrote and what they delivered by oral instruction are equally God's Word. And this two-fold Word, written and unwritten, is the Deposit of divine truth, committed to the keeping of the Catholic Church, and chiefly to him on whom the Church was built—the only Apostle who, in the full sense of the words, yet lives and rules in the person of his

[1] Josue 1. 6, 7, 8, 9.   [2] 2 Tim. 1. 12.

successors, and from his unfailing chair imparts to all who seek it the truth of Christian faith.[3] It is his office to confirm his brethren, and the history of the Church exhibits him, from the beginning and through all ages, as faithfully fulfilling the charge entrusted to him by his Master.[4] From the earliest ages down to our own, the voice of Peter has been foremost in condemning all deviations from apostolic doctrine. No threats of worldly power could subdue or silence that voice. To such threats Peter, through his successors, has ever given the same answer that he gave at Jerusalem to the assembled priests and ancients.[5] No pleading of princes and potentates could ever win Rome's sympathy for error; no heresy under false semblance of Catholic truth ever yet eluded her vigilant eye.[6] As soon as any novelty appeared, all hearts and eyes were turned towards the Chair of Peter, and when that Chair gave its decision, the Christian people yielded obedience. Those who would not were cut off from the communion of the Church, and became thenceforth as the heathen and the publican.

This doctrine, therefore, which had so thoroughly wrought itself into the life and action of the Church, the Vatican Council deemed proper to consecrate by a solemn definition. Hence, that no one in future may craftily pretend not to know how and whence to ascertain what the Church officially teaches; above all, that no one may henceforth scatter the baneful seeds of false doctrine with impunity, under the mask of an appeal from the judgment of the Holy See (whether it be to learned universities, or State tribunals, or future councils, particular or general, as was done by Luther and the Jansenists), the Church of the living God, through the Fathers of the Vatican Council, has unequivocally declared that her authentic spokesman is the successor of St. Peter in the Apostolic See of Rome, and that what he, as Head of the Church, officially decides is part of the Deposit of Faith intrusted to her keeping by Christ Our Lord, and hence subject to neither denial, doubt nor revision, but to be implicitly received and believed by all.

In this authoritative declaration there is nothing new,

---

3 See Epist. S. Petri Chrysologi inter Epp. S. Leonis M.
4 Luke xii. 32.   5 Acts iv. 19-20.   6 Cf. Cyprian. Ep. lix.

nothing to give cause for wonder. It is only setting the solemn seal of definition upon what has always been the belief and practice of the Church. Yet "the gates of Hell," the powers of darkness that forever assail the Church built on Peter—though knowing (for the very devils believe and tremble in believing) [7] that they cannot prevail against it nor make void God's promise [8]—seem to have been stirred to their very depths by the proclamation of this great truth. And their impotent rage has found its echo upon earth. The definition evoked a storm of fierce obloquy and reckless vituperation, such as has been seldom witnessed amongst our opponents. And a wretched handful of apostate Catholics "went out from us, but they were not of us." [9]

But, what was far more serious, the kings of the earth stood up and the princes assembled together against the Lord [10] and against His anointed Vicar, because of the definition. They revived the old war-cry raised by the Jews against our Saviour [11] and so often renewed by the persecutors of the Church. They pretended that by defining the infallibility of St. Peter's successor, she had made herself the enemy of Cæsar. Herein we see plainly verified the strong language of Scripture: "Iniquity hath lied to itself." [12] The Pope, even after the proclamation of his infallibility, is no more the enemy of Cæsar and of human governments, than was the infallible Peter the enemy of Nero, or Christ our Lord, who is infallible truth itself, the enemy of Augustus and Tiberius under whom He was born into the world, taught and suffered. The governments by which, three centuries ago, the new tenets of Luther, Zwingli and Calvin had been imposed on reluctant people by the sword, were the first, indeed the only ones, to again unsheathe it against Catholic believers, and especially against the bishops and clergy. It was their purpose to exterminate by degrees the Catholic hierarchy, and replace it by a servile priesthood that would subordinate its preaching and ministry to the will of the State. To do this they had to trample on solemn treaties and organic laws. But the Catholics of Prussia, clergy and people, while proving

---

[7] Credunt et contremiscunt, James ii. 19.   [8] Matt. xvi. 18.
[9] John ii. 19.   [10] Acts iv. 26.   [11] John xix. 12, 15.   [12] Ps. xxvi. 19.

themselves most devoted and faithful to their country's laws, stood up like a wall of adamant against the tyranny of its rulers. With generous vigor and admirable constancy, they availed themselves of every legal and constitutional means to check the advances of despotism and save their own freedom and that of their country. They have given to the world a glorious example, which it is to be hoped the victims of tyrannous Liberalism in Catholic countries may some day have the wisdom or the courage to imitate. The struggle has now lasted fourteen years; but the very friends of this persecuting legislation have been driven at last to acknowledge that it has proved to be a miserable failure; and no better proof of it could be found than the fact, that the rulers of Prussia have had to fall back on the patriotism of the Catholic body to stay the threatening march of socialism and revolution. In Switzerland, too, the persecution has yielded to the policy of mildness and conciliation adopted by Our Holy Father, Leo XIII.

Beloved brethren, we have no need to encourage you to hold steadfastly to this doctrine of the Vatican Council; for you were trained from infancy to believe it, as were your fathers before you, while it was not yet invested with the formalities of a definition, just as the early Christians held firmly to the divinity of the Son and of the Holy Ghost three hundred years before the Church found it necessary to define them in the Councils of Nice and Byzantium.

And in our own country, writers and speakers who know the Church only by the caricatures drawn by prejudice, have occasionally re-echoed the same charge; but despite local and temporary excitements, the good sense of the American people has always prevailed against the calumny. We think we can claim to be acquainted both with the laws, institutions and spirit of the Catholic Church, and with the laws, institutions and spirit of our country; and we emphatically declare that there is no antagonism between them. A Catholic finds himself at home in the United States; for the influence of his Church has constantly been exercised in behalf of individual rights and popular liberties. And the right-minded American nowhere finds himself more at home than in the Catholic Church, for nowhere else can he breathe more freely that atmosphere of Divine truth, which alone can make him free.[13]

We repudiate with equal earnestness the assertion that we need to lay aside any of our devotedness to our Church, to be true Americans; the insinuation that we need to abate any of our love for our country's principles and institutions, to be faithful Catholics. To argue that the Catholic Church is hostile to our great Republic, because she teaches that "there is no power but from God;"[14] because, therefore, back of the events which led to the formation of the Republic, she sees the Providence of God leading to that issue, and back of our country's laws the authority of God as their sanction,—this is evidently so illogical and contradictory an accusation, that we are astonished to hear it advanced by persons of ordinary intelligence. We believe that our country's heroes were the instruments of the God of Nations in establishing this home of freedom; to both the Almighty and to His instruments in the work, we look with grateful reverence; and to maintain the inheritance of freedom which they have left us, should it ever—which God forbid—be imperilled, our Catholic citizens will be found to stand forward, as one man ready to pledge anew "their lives, their fortunes, and their sacred honor."

No less illogical would be the notion, that there is aught in the free spirit of our American institutions, incompatible with perfect docility to the Church of Christ. The spirit of American freedom is not one of anarchy or license. It essentially involves love of order, respect for rightful authority, and obedience to just laws. There is nothing in the character of the most liberty-loving American, which could hinder his reverential submission to the Divine authority of Our Lord, or to the like authority delegated by Him to His Apostles and His Church. Nor are there in the world more devoted adherents of the Catholic Church, the See of Peter, and the Vicar of Christ, than the Catholics of the United States. Narrow, insular, national views and jealousies concerning ecclesiastical authority and Church organization, may have sprung naturally enough from the

13 John viii. 32.   14 Rom. xiii. 1.

selfish policy of certain rulers and nations in by-gone times; but they find no sympathy in the spirit of the true American Catholic. His natural instincts, no less than his religious training, would forbid him to submit in matters of faith to the dictation of the State or to any merely human authority whatsoever. He accepts the religion and the Church that are from God, and he knows well that these are universal, not national or local,—for all the children of men, not for any special tribe or tongue. We glory that we are, and, with God's blessing, shall continue to be, not the American Church, nor the Church of the United States, nor a Church in any other sense exclusive or limited, but an integral part of the one, holy, Catholic and Apostolic Church of Jesus Christ, which is the Body of Christ, in which there is no distinction of classes and nationalities,— in which all are one in Christ Jesus.[15]

While the assaults of calumny and persecution directed against the Church since the Vatican Council have abundantly shown how angry the powers of evil have been at the Council's luminous utterances of Divine truth, our Holy Father the Pope has been, naturally enough, the main object of attack. And Divine Providence has been pleased to leave him, for a while at the mercy of his enemies, in order that their impious violence might work out the demonstration of its own injustice; that the true character and the indestructibility of the office of St. Peter might be made manifest to the world; that the wisdom of the Providence which has guarded the independence of that office in the past, might be vindicated and reaffirmed for the future. The great and beloved Pius IX died the "Prisoner of the Vatican," and Leo XIII has inherited his Apostolic trials, together with his Apostolic office. Day after day he has seen the consecrated patrimony of religion and charity swept into Cæsar's coffers by the ruthless hand of spoliation and confiscation. At this moment, he sees that same grasp laid upon the property of the Propaganda, piously set apart for spreading the Gospel of Jesus Christ throughout the missionary countries of the world. So utterly unjustifiable an act has called forth a cry of indignant protest from the

15 Gal. iii. 28.

Catholics of all countries, and from no country has the cry gone forth clearer and louder than from our own. We thank our government for the action that saved the American College from confiscation; and we hope that the protest and appeal of all governments and people that "love justice and hate iniquity" may yet shame the spoiler into honesty. Meanwhile the hearts of all Catholics go out all the more lovingly towards their persecuted Chief Pastor; and from their worldly means, be they abundant or scanty, they gladly supply him with the means necessary for carrying on the administration of his high office. Such has been your liberality in the past, beloved brethren, that we hardly need exhort you to generosity in the collection for the Holy Father, which will continue to be made annually throughout all the dioceses of the country. Let your devoted affection be shown by your deeds, and the persistency of injustice be more than matched by the constancy of your faithful and generous love.

While enduring with the heroism of a martyr the trials which beset him, and trustfully awaiting the Almighty's day of deliverance, the energy and wisdom of Leo XIII are felt to the ends of the earth. He is carrying on with the governments of Europe the negotiations which promise soon to bring peace to the Church. In the East he is preparing the way for the return to Catholic unity of the millions whom the Greek schism has so long deprived of communion with the See of Peter, and is following the progress of exploration in lands hitherto unknown or inaccessible with corresponding advances of Catholic missions. To the whole world his voice has again and again gone forth in counsels of eloquence and wisdom, pointing out the path to the acquisition of truth in the important domain of philosophy and history—the best means for the improvement of human life in all its phases, individual, domestic and social—the ways in which the children of God should walk—"that all flesh may see the salvation of God."

But in all the wide circle of his great responsibility, the progress of the Church in these United States forms, in a special manner, both a source of joy and an object of solicitude to the Holy Father. With loving care his predecessors watched and encouraged her first feeble beginnings. They cheered and fostered her development in the pure atmosphere of freedom, when the name of Carroll shone with equal lustre at the head of her newborn Hierarchy, and on the roll of our country's patriots. Step by step they directed her progress, as with marvellous rapidity, the clergy and the dioceses have multiplied; the hundreds of the faithful have increased to thousands and to millions; her churches, schools, asylums, hospitals, academies and colleges, have covered the land with homes of divine truth and Christian charity. Not yet a century has elapsed since the work was inaugurated by the appointment of the first Bishop of Baltimore, in 1789; and as we gaze upon the results already reached we must exclaim: "By the Lord hath this been done, and it is wonderful in our eyes." [16]

In all this astonishing development, from the rude beginning of pioneer missionary toil, along the nearer and nearer approaches to the beauteous symmetry of the Church's perfect organization, the advance so gradual yet so rapid has been safely guided in the lines of Catholic and Apostolic tradition, by the combined efforts and wisdom of our local Hierarchy and of the successors of St. Peter. It was in order to take counsel with the representatives of the American Hierarchy concerning the important interests of religion in this country, that the Holy Father, last year, invited the Archbishops of the United States to Rome. And the object of the present council is to put into practical shape the means of religious improvement then resolved upon or suggested.

One of our first cares has been to provide for the more perfect education of aspirants to the holy Priesthood. It has always been the Church's endeavor that her clergy should be eminent in learning. For she has always considered that nothing less than this is required by their sacred office of guarding and dispensing Divine truth. "The lips of the priest shall keep knowledge," says the Most High, "and the people shall seek the law at his mouth." This is

Education of the Clergy.

[16] Matt. xxi. 42; Ps. cxvii. 22.

true in all times; for no advance in secular knowledge, no
diffusion of popular education, can do away with the office
of the teaching ministry, which Our Lord has declared shall
last forever. In every age it is and shall be the duty of
God's priests to proclaim the salutary truths which our
Heavenly Father has given to the world through His Divine
Son; to present them to each generation in the way that will
move their minds and hearts to embrace and love them;
to defend them, when necessary, against every attack of
error. From this it is obvious that the priest should have a
wide acquaintance with every department of learning that
has a bearing on religious truth. Hence in our age, when
so many misleading theories are put forth on every side,
when every department of natural truth and fact is actively
explored for objections against revealed religion, it is
evident how extensive and thorough should be the knowledge of the minister of the Divine Word, that he may be able
to show forth worthily the beauty, the superiority, the necessity of the Christian religion, and to prove that there is
nothing in all that God has made to contradict anything that
God has taught.

Hence the priest who has the noble ambition of attaining to the high level of his holy office, may well consider
himself a student all his life; and of the leisure hours which
he can find amid the duties of his ministry, he will have
very few that he can spare for miscellaneous reading, and
none at all to waste. And hence, too, the evident duty
devolving on us, to see that the course of education in our
ecclesiastical colleges and seminaries be as perfect as it can
be made. During the century of extraordinary growth now
closing, the care of the Church in this country has been to
send forth as rapidly as possible holy, zealous, hard-work-
ing priests, to supply the needs of the multitudes calling
for the ministrations of religion. She has not on that
account neglected to prepare them for their divine work by
a suitable education, as her numerous and admirable seminaries testify; but the course of study was often more rapid
and restricted than she desired. At present our improved
circumstances make it practicable both to lengthen and

widen the course, and for this the Council has duly provided.

We are confident, beloved brethren, that you feel as deeply interested as ourselves in the accomplishment of these great results. This you have hitherto manifested by the zealous liberality by which you have enabled us to build and support our seminaries; and we are well assured that you will not be found wanting, should even greater efforts be necessary, to enable us to make the education and usefulness of the clergy as perfect as we desire. In the future, as in the past, look upon your annual contribution to the Seminary fund as one of your most important duties as Catholics, and let your generosity be proportioned to the dignity and sacredness of the object for which you offer it.

And here we remind those among our Catholic people to whom God has been pleased to give wealth, that it is their duty and their privilege to consider themselves the Lord's stewards, in the use of what His Providence has placed in their hands; that they should be foremost in helping on the work of the Church of Christ during life, and make sure to have God among their heirs when they die; and we recommend to them as specially useful the founding of scholarships, either in their diocesan or provincial Seminaries, or in the American College in Rome, or elsewhere, as circumstances may suggest.

No small portion of our attention has been bestowed on the framing of such legislation as will best secure the rights and interests of your pastors, and of all ranks of the clergy in this country. It is but natural, beloved brethren, that the first and dearest object of our solicitude should be our venerable clergy. They are our dearest brethren, bound to us by ties more sacred than those of flesh and blood. Our elevation to a higher office only draws them to us more closely, since their happiness and welfare are thereby made the first object of our responsibility, and since upon their devoted labors must mainly depend the welfare of the souls entrusted to our charge. We need not tell you, beloved brethren, how admirably they fulfil their sacred trust. You are witnesses to their lives of toil and

Pastoral Rights.

sacrifice. And to them we can truly say in the words of St. Paul, "You are our glory and our joy." [17]

The rights of the clergy have reference chiefly to their exercising the sacred ministry in their missions, to the fixity of their tenure of office and to the inviolableness of their pastoral authority within proper limits. It is the spirit of the Church that the various grades of authority in her organization should in no wise be in rivalry or conflict, but orderly and harmonious. This she has secured by her wise laws, based upon the experience of centuries, and representing the perfection of Church organization. It is obvious that in countries like our own, where from rudimentary beginnings our organization is only gradually advancing towards perfection, the full application of these laws is impracticable; but in proportion as they become practicable, it is our desire, not less than that of the Holy See, that they should go into effect. For we have the fullest confidence in the wisdom with which the Church devised these laws, and we heartily rejoice at every approach towards perfect organization in the portion of the vineyard over which we have jurisdiction. This has been to some degree accomplished by regulations enacted during recent years, and still more by the decrees of the present Council.

But while it is our desire to do all on our part that both justice and affection can prompt, for fully securing all proper rights and privileges to our priests, let us remind you, beloved brethren, that on your conduct must their happiness chiefly depend. A grateful and pious flock is sure to make a happy pastor. But if the people do not respond to their pastor's zeal, if they are cold and ungrateful or disedifying, then indeed is his lot sad and pitiable. Since, therefore, the Priests of God leave all things to devote themselves to your spiritual welfare, show by your affection, by your co-operation with their efforts for your spiritual improvement, and even by your care for their physical comfort, that you appreciate their devotedness and the reciprocal obligation which it imposes. Look upon your priests as your best friends, your trustiest advisors, your surest guides. If duty sometimes calls upon them to admonish

17 Thes. ii. 20.

or rebuke you, remember that the reproof is meant for your good, and take it in the spirit in which it is given. And if perchance they have to speak to you oftener than is pleasant about church finances and the demands of charity, understand that it must be at least as disagreeable to them as it is to you; that it is not for themslves, but for the needs of the parish church or school, which are intended for your benefit, or of the parish poor, who are your charge, that they have to plead; and that, while they are to bear in mind the advisability of speaking of money as seldom as possible, you must be mindful to make your generosity equal to the need, and thereby save both your pastors and yourselves the painful necessity of frequent appeals.

And here we deem it proper to say a few words concerning church properties and church debts. The manner of holding the legal title to these properties is different in different places, according to the requirements of local civil laws; but whether the title be held by the bishop, or by boards of diocesan or parish trustees, it always remains true that the properties are held in trust for the Church for the benefit of the people. One generation buys or builds, another generation improves and adorns, and each generation uses and transmits for the use of others yet to come, —bishops and priests having the burden of the administration and being sacredly responsible for its faithful performance.

In the discharge of this duty it often becomes necessary to contract church debts. Where the multiplication of the Catholic population has been so rapid, rapid work had to be done in erecting churches and schools. And if, under such circumstances, pastors had to wait till all the funds were in hand before beginning the work, a generation would be left without necessary spiritual aids, and might be lost to the Church and to God. We fully recognize, beloved brethren, how strictly we are bound to prevent the contraction of debts without real necessity; and this we have endeavored to secure by careful legislation. Still, despite all our efforts, it must inevitably happen that the burden imposed on us by our gigantic task of providing for the spiritual wants of the present and the rising generation

will always be heavy, and will weigh upon us all. But the
special Providence of God towards our country, which has
made the work and the need so great, has never failed
hitherto to inspire our people with a zeal equal to the demand. You have rivaled your pastors in the ardor of their
desire for the building up of the Church of Christ and the
extension of His Kingdom; and we are confident that you
will preserve your zeal unto the end, and transmit it un-
diminished to your descendants. It is our earnest wish that
existing debts should be liquidated as soon as possible, in
order that the money now consumed in paying interest may
be employed in the great improvements still to be made,
and especially in helping on the glorious work of Christian
education.

Scarcely, if at all, secondary to the Church's desire for
the education of the clergy, is her solicitude for the education of the laity. It is not for themselves,
but for the people, that the Church wishes   **Christian
her clergy to be learned, as it is not for   Education.**
themselves only, but for the people that
they are priests. Popular education has always been a
chief object of the Church's care; in fact, it is not too much
to say that the history of civilization and education is the
history of the Church's work. In the rude ages, when semi-
barbarous chieftains boasted of their illiteracy, she succeeded in diffusing that love of learning which covered
Europe with schools and universities; and thus from the
barbarous tribes of the early middle ages, she built up the
civilized nations of modern times. Even subsequent to the
religious dissensions of the sixteenth century, whatever
progress has been made in education is mainly due to the
impetus which she had previously given. In our own country notwithstanding the many difficulties attendant on first
beginnings and unexampled growth, we already find her
schools, academies and colleges everywhere, built and sustained by voluntary contributions, even at the cost of great
sacrifices, and comparing favorably with the best educational institutions in the land.

These facts abundantly attest the Church's desire for
popular instruction. The beauty of truth, the refining and

elevating influences of knowledge, are meant for all, and she wishes them to be brought within the reach of all. Knowledge enlarges our capacity both for self-improvement and for promoting the welfare of our fellow-men; and in so noble a work the Church wishes every hand to be busy. Knowledge, too, is the best weapon against pernicious errors. It is only " a little learning" that is "a dangerous thing." In days like ours, when error is so pretentious and aggressive, every one needs to be as completely armed as possible with sound knowledge,—not only the clergy, but the people also that they may be able to withstand the noxious influences of popularized irreligion. In the great coming combat between truth and error, between Faith and Agnosticism, an important part of the fray must be borne by the laity, and woe to them if they are not well prepared. And if, in the olden days of vassalage and serfdom, the Church honored every individual, no matter how humble his position, and labored to give him the enlightenment that would qualify him for future responsibilities, much more now, in the era of popular rights and liberties, when every individual is an active and influential factor in the body politic, does she desire that all should be fitted by suitable training for an intelligent and conscientious discharge of the important duties that will devolve upon them.

Few, if any, will deny that a sound civilization must depend upon sound popular education. But education, in order to be sound and to produce beneficial results, must develop what is best in man, and make him not only clever but good. A one-sided education will develop a one-sided life; and such a life will surely topple over, and so will every social system that is built up of such lives. True civilization requires that not only the physical and intellectual, but also the moral and religious, well-being of the people should be promoted, and at least with equal care. Take away religion from a people, and morality would soon follow; morality gone, even their physical condition will ere long degenerate into corruption which breeds decrepitude, while their intellectual attainments would only serve as a light to guide them to deeper depths of vice and ruin. This has been so often demonstrated in the history of the

past, and is, in fact, so self-evident, that one is amazed to
find any difference of opinion about it. A civilization without religion, would be a civilization of "the struggle for
existence, and the survival of the fittest," in which cunning
and strength would become the substitutes for principle,
virtue, conscience and duty. As a matter of fact, there
never has been a civilization worthy of the name without
religion; and from the facts of history the laws of human
nature can easily be inferred.

Hence education, in order to foster civilization, must
foster religion. Now the three great educational agencies
are the home, the Church, and the school. These mould
men and shape society. Therefore each of them, to do its
part well, must foster religion. But many, unfortunately,
while avowing that religion should be the light and the
atmosphere of the home and of the Church, are content to
see it excluded from the school, and even advocate as the
best school system that which necessarily excludes religion.
Few surely will deny that childhood and youth are the
periods of life when the character ought especially to be
subjected to religious influences. Nor can we ignore the
palpable fact that the school is an important factor in the
forming of childhood and youth,—so important that its
influence often outweighs that of home and Church. It
cannot, therefore, be desirable or advantageous that religion should be excluded from the school. On the contrary,
it ought there to be one of the chief agencies for moulding
the young life to all that is true and virtuous, and holy. To
shut religion out of the school, and keep it for home and the
Church, is, logically, to train up a generation that will consider religion good for home and the Church, but not for
the practical business of real life. But a more false and
pernicious notion could not be imagined. Religion, in order
to elevate a people, should inspire their whole life and rule
their relations with one another. A life is not dwarfed, but
ennobled by being lived in the presence of God. Therefore
the school, which principally gives the knowledge fitting
for practical life, ought to be pre-eminently under the holy
influence of religion. From the shelter of home and school,
the youth must soon go out into the busy ways of trade or

traffic or professional practice. In all these, the principles of religion should animate and direct him. But he cannot expect to learn these principles in the work-shop or the office or the counting-room. Therefore let him be well and thoroughly imbued with them by the joint influences of home and school, before he is launched out on the dangerous sea of life.

All denominations of Christians are now awaking to this great truth, which the Catholic Church has never ceased to maintain. Reason and experience are forcing them to recognize that the only practical way to secure a Christian people, is to give the youth a Christian education. The avowed enemies of Christianity in some European countries are banishing religion from the schools, in order gradually to eliminate it from among the people. In this they are logical, and we may well profit by the lesson. Hence the cry for Christian education is going up from all religious bodies throughout the land. And this is no narrowness and "sectarianism" on their part; it is an honest and logical endeavor to preserve Christian truth and morality among the people by fostering religion in the young. Nor is it any antagonism to the State; on the contrary, it is an honest endeavor to give to the State better citizens, by making them better Christians. The friends of Christian education do not condemn the State for not imparting religious instruction in the public schools as they are now organized; because they well know it does not lie within the province of the State to teach religion. They simply follow their conscience by sending their children to denominational schools, where religion can have its rightful place and influence.

Two objects therefore, dear brethren, we have in view, to multiply our schools, and to perfect them. We must multiply them, till every Catholic child in the land shall have within its reach the means of education. There is still much to do ere this be attained. There are still thousands of Catholic children in the United States deprived of the benefit of a Catholic school. Pastors and parents should not rest till this defect be remedied. No parish is complete till it has schools adequate to the needs of its children, and the pastor and people of such a parish should feel that they have not accomplished their entire duty until the want is supplied.

But then, we must also perfect our schools. We repudiate the idea that the Catholic school need be in any respect inferior to any other school whatsoever. And if hitherto, in some places, our people have acted on the principle that it is better to have an imperfect Catholic school than to have none, let them now push their praiseworthy ambition still further, and not relax their efforts till their schools be elevated to the highest educational excellence. And we implore parents not to hasten to take their children from school, but to give them all the time and all the advantages that they have the capacity to profit by, so that, in after life, their children may "rise up and call them blessed."

We need hardly remind you, beloved brethren, that while home life would not, as a rule, be sufficient to supply the absence of good or counteract the evil of dangerous influences in the school, it is **The Christian** equally true, that all that the Christian **Home.** school could accomplish would be inadequate without the co-operation of the Christian home. Christian schools sow the seed, but Christian homes must first prepare the soil, and afterwards foster the seed and bring it to maturity.

1. *Christian Marriage.*—The basis of the Christian home is Christian marriage; that is, marriage entered into according to religion, and cemented by God's blessing. So great is the importance of marriage to the temporal and eternal welfare of mankind, that, as it had God for its Founder in the Old Law, so, in the New Law, it was raised by Our Divine Lord to the dignity of a sacrament of the Christian religion. Natural likings and instincts have their own value and weight; but they ought not by themselves be a decisive motive in so important a step as Christian marriage; nor are they a safe guarantee for the proper fulfillment of the high ends for which marriage was ordained. That Christian hearts and lives may be wisely and rightly joined, God must join them, and religion sanctify the union; and though the Church sometimes permits the contraction

of mixed marriages, she never does so without regret and without a feeling of anxiety for the future happiness of that union and for the eternal salvation of its offspring.

2. *The Indissolubility of Marriage.*—The security of the Christian home is in the indissolubility of the marriage tie. Christian marriage, once consummated, can never be dissolved save by death. Let it be well understood that even adultery, though it may justify "separation from bed and board," cannot loose the marriage tie, so that either of the parties may marry again during the life of the other. Nor has "legal divorce" the slightest power, before God, to loose the bond of marriage and to make a subsequent marriage valid. "Whom God hath joined together, let not man put asunder."[18] In common with all Christian believers and friends of civilization, we deplore the havoc wrought by the divorce-laws of our country. These laws are fast loosening the foundations of society. Let Catholics, at least remember that such divorces are powerless in conscience. Let them enter into marriage only through worthy and holy motives, and with the blessings of religion, especially with the blessing of the Nuptial Mass. And then, far from wishing for means of escape from their union, they will rejoice that it cannot be divided but by death.

3. *Home Virtues.*—The pervading atmosphere of the Christian home should be Christian charity—the love of God and of the neighbor. It should be the ambition and study of Christian parents to make their home a sanctuary, in which no harsh or angry, no indelicate or profane word, should be uttered,—in which truth, unselfishness, self-control, should be carefully cultivated, in which the thought of God, the desire to please God, should be, sweetly and naturally, held before the children as their habitual motives. From the home sanctuary, the incense of prayer should ascend as a most sweet morning and evening sacrifice to the Lord. How beautiful and rich in blessing is the assembling of parents and children for morning and evening prayer! Our hearts are filled with consolation when, in the course of our pastoral visits, we meet families in which this holy practice is faithfully observed. In such families, we are

18 Matt. xix, 6.

sure to find proofs of the special benedictions of heaven. Faith, religion and virtue are there fostered to luxuriant growth, and final perseverance almost assured. We earnestly exhort all parents to this salutary custom. And if it be not always feasible in the morning, at least every evening, at a fixed hour, let the entire family be assembled for night prayers, followed by a short reading from the Holy Scriptures, the Following of Christ, or some other pious book.

4. *Good Reading.*—Let the adornments of the home be chaste and holy pictures, and, still more, sound, interesting, and profitable books. No indelicate representation should ever be tolerated in a Christian home. Artistic merit in the work is no excuse for the danger thus presented. No child ought to be subjected to temptation by its own parents and in its own home. But let the walls be beautified with what will keep the inmates in mind of our Divine Lord, and of his saints, and with such other pictures of the great and the good as will be incentives to civic and religious virtue.

The same remark applies equally to books and periodicals. Not only should the immoral, the vulgar, the sensational novel, the indecently illustrated newspaper, and publications tending to weaken faith in the religion and the Church of Jesus Christ, be absolutely excluded from every Christian home, but the dangerously exciting and morbidly emotional, whatever, in a word, is calculated to impair or lower the tone of faith or morals in the youthful mind and heart, should be carefully banished. Parents would be sure to warn and withhold their children from anything that would poison or sicken their bodies; let them be at least as watchful against intellectual and moral poison. But let the family book-shelves be well supplied with what is both pleasant and wholesome. Happily, the store of Catholic literature, as well as works which, though not written by Catholics nor treating of religion, are pure, instructive and elevating, is now so large that there can be no excuse for running risk of wasting one's time with what is inferior, tainted, or suspicious. Remember, Christian parents, that the development of the youthful character is intimately connected with the development of the taste for reading. To books as well as to associations may be applied the wise saying: "Show me your company and I will tell you what you are." See, then, that none but good books and newspapers, as well as none but good companions, be admitted to your homes. Train your children to a love of history and biography. Inspire them with the ambition to become so well acquainted with the history and doctrines of the Church as to be able to give an intelligent answer to any honest inquiry. Should their surroundings call for it, encourage them, as they grow older, to acquire such knowledge of popularly mooted questions of a scientific or philosophical character as will suffice to make them firm in their faith and proof against sophistry. We should be glad to see thoroughly solid and popular works on these important subjects, from able Catholic writers, become more numerous. Teach your children to take a special interest in the history of our country. We consider the establishment of our country's independence, the shaping of its liberties and laws as a work of special Providence, its framers "building wiser than they knew," the Almighty's hand guiding them. And if ever the glorious fabric is subverted or impaired it will be by men forgetful of the sacrifices of the heroes that reared it, the virtues that cemented it, and the principles on which it rests, or ready to sacrifice principle and virtue to the interests of self or party. As we desire therefore that the history of the United States should be carefully taught in all our Catholic schools, and have directed that it be specially dwelt upon in the education of the young ecclesiastical students in our preparatory seminaries; so also we desire that it form a favorite part of the home library and home reading. We must keep firm and solid the liberties of our country by keeping fresh the noble memories of the past and thus sending forth from our Catholic homes into the arena of public life not partisans but patriots.

5. *The Holy Scriptures.*—But it can hardly be necessary for us to remind you, beloved brethren, that the most highly valued treasure of every family library, and the most frequently and lovingly made use of, should be the Holy Scriptures. Doubtless you have often read A'Kempis's

burning thanksgiving to our Lord for having bestowed on us not only the adorable treasure of His Body in the Holy Eucharist, but also that of the Holy Scriptures, "the Holy Books, for the comfort and direction of our life." [19]   And you have before your eyes, prefixed to the Douay version of the Holy Bible, the exhortation of Pope Pius the Sixth in his letter to the Archbishop of Florence, that "the faithful should be moved to the reading of the Holy Scriptures; for these," he says, "are most abundant sources which ought to be left open to every one to draw from them purity of morals and of doctrine, to eradicate the errors which are so widely disseminated in these corrupt times."   And St. Paul declares that "what things soever were written, were written for our learning; that through patience and the comfort of the Scriptures we might have hope." [20]   We hope that no family can be found amongst us without a correct version of the Holy Scriptures.   Among other versions, we recommend the Douay, which is venerable as used by our forefathers for three centuries, which comes down to us sanctioned by innumerable authorizations, and which was suitably annotated by the learned Bishop Challoner, by Canon Haydock, and especially by the late Archbishop Kenrick.

But in your reading remember the admonition of A'Kempis: "The Holy Scriptures must be read in the same spirit in which they were written; if thou wilt derive profit, read with humility, simplicity and faith." [21]   And keep ever before your mind the principle laid down by St. Peter in the first chapter of his second Epistle: "Understanding this first, that no prophecy of Scripture is made by private interpretation, for prophecy came not by the will of man at any time, but the holy men of God spoke, inspired by the Holy Ghost."   And this other given by St. John, in the fourth chapter of his first Epistle, in the name of the Apostolic teaching Church: "Dearly beloved, believe not every spirit, but try the spirits if they be of God.   We are of God; he that knoweth God heareth us; he that is not of God heareth us not; by this we know the spirit of truth and the

[19] Fol. of Christ, B. 4. c. ii.   [20] Rom. xv.   [21] B. 1, c. v.

spirit of error." In these two divinely inspired rules you have always a sure safe-guard against the danger of error.

6. *The Catholic Press.*—Finally, Christian parents, let us beg your earnest consideration of this important truth, that upon you, singly and individually, must practically depend the solution of the question, whether or not the Catholic press is to accomplish the great work which Providence and the Church expect of it at this time. So frequently and so forcibly has the providential mission of the press been dwelt upon by Popes and prelates and distinguished Catholic writers, and so assiduously have their utterances been quoted and requoted everywhere, that no one certainly stands in need of arguments to be convinced of this truth. But all this will be only words in the air, unless it can be brought home to each parent and made practical in each household. If the head of each Catholic family will recognize it as his privilege and his duty to contribute towards supporting the Catholic press, by subscribing for one or more Catholic periodicals, and keeping himself well acquainted with the information they impart, then the Catholic press will be sure to attain to its rightful development and to accomplish its destined mission. But choose a journal that is thoroughly Catholic, instructive and edifying; not one that would be, while Catholic in name or pretense, uncatholic in tone and spirit, disrespectful to constituted authority, or biting and uncharitable to Catholic brethren.

Beloved brethren, a great social revolution is sweeping over the world. Its purpose, hidden or avowed, is to dethrone Christ and religion. The ripples of the movement have been observed in our country; God grant that its tidal wave may not break over us. Upon you, Christian parents, it mainly depends whether it shall or not; for, such as our homes are, such shall our people be. We beseech you, therefore, to ponder carefully all that we have said concerning the various constitutents of a true Christian home, and, to the utmost of your ability, to carry them into effect. And we entreat all pastors of souls to bear unceasingly in mind, that upon the Christian school and the Christian homes in their parishes must mainly depend the fruit of their priestly labors. Let them concentrate their

efforts on these two points,—to make the schools and the
homes what they ought to be;—then indeed will they carry
to the Lord of the harvest full and ripe sheaves, and the
future generation will bless them for transmitting unimpaired the priceless gifts of faith and religion.

There are many sad facts in the experience of nations,
which we may well store up as lessons of practical wisdom.
Not the least important of these is the fact
that one of the surest marks and measures   **The**
of the decay of religion in a people, is   **Lord's Day.**
their non-observance of the Lord's Day.
In traveling through some European countries, a Christian's
heart is pained by the almost unabated rush of toil and
traffic on Sunday. First, grasping avarice thought it could
not afford to spare the day to God; then unwise governments, yielding to the pressure of mammon, relaxed the laws
which for many centuries had guarded the day's sacredness
—forgetting that there are certain fundamental principles,
which ought not to be sacrificed to popular caprice or greed.
And when, as usually happens, neglect of religion had
passed, by lapse of time, into hostility to religion, this growing neglect of the Lord's Day was easily made use of as a
means to bring religion itself into contempt. The Church
mourned, protested, struggled, but was almost powerless to
resist the combined forces of popular avarice and Cæsar's
influence, arrayed on the side of irreligion. The result is
the lamentable desecration which all Christians must deplore.

And the consequences of this desecration are as manifest
as the desecration itself. The Lord's Day is the poor man's
day of rest; it has been taken from him,—and the laboring
classes are a seething volcano of social discontent. The
Lord's Day is the home day, drawing closer the sweet domestic ties, by giving the toiler a day with wife and children; but it has been turned into a day of labor,—and home
ties are fast losing their sweetness and their hold. The
Lord's Day is the church-day, strengthening and consecrating the bond of brotherhood among all men, by their kneel-
ing together around the altars of the one Father in heaven;
but men are drawn away from this blessed communion of

Saints,—and as a natural consequence they are lured into
the counterfeit communion of Socialism, and other wild
and destructive systems. The Lord's Day is God's Day,
rendering ever nearer and more intimate the union between
the creature and his Creator, and thus ennobling human
life in all its relations; and where this bond is weakened, an
effort is made to cut man loose from God entirely, and to
leave him, according to the expression of St. Paul, "without God in this world." [22] The profanation of the Lord's
Day, whatever be its pretext, is a defrauding both of God
and His creatures, and retribution is not slow.

In this country, there are tendencies and influences at
work to bring about a similar result; and it behooves all
who love God and care for society, to see that they be
checked. As usual, greed for gain lies at the bottom of
the movement. Even when the pretence put forward is
popular convenience or popular amusement, the clamor
for larger liberty does not come so much from those who
desire the convenience or the amusement, as from those
who hope to enrich themselves by supplying it. Now far be
it from us to advocate such Sunday-laws as would hinder
necessary work, or prohibit such popular enjoyments as
are consistent with the sacredness of the day. It is well
known, however, that the tendency is to rush far beyond
the bounds of necessity and propriety, and to allege these
reasons only as an excuse for virtually ignoring the sacredness of the day altogether. But no community can afford
to have either gain or amusement at such a cost. To turn
the Lord's Day into a day of toil, is a blighting curse to a
country; to turn it into a day of dissipation would be worse.
We earnestly appeal, therefore, to all Catholics without distinction, not only to take no part in any movement tending
toward a relaxation of the observance of Sunday, but to
use their influence and power as citizens to resist in the
opposite direction.

There is one way of profaning the Lord's Day which is
so prolific of evil results, that we consider it our duty to
utter against it a special condemnation. This is the practice
of selling beer or other liquors on Sunday, or of frequent-

22 Ephes. ii. 12.

ing places where they are sold. This practice tends more than any other to turn the Day of the Lord into a day of dissipation, to use it as an occasion for breeding intemperance. While we hope that Sunday-laws on this point will not be relaxed, but even more rigidly enforced, we implore all Catholics, for the love of God and of country, never to take part in such Sunday traffic, nor to patronize or countenance it. And we not only direct the attention of all pastors to the repression of this abuse, but we also call upon them to induce all of their flocks that may be engaged in the sale of liquors to abandon as soon as they can the dangerous traffic, and to embrace a more becoming way of making a living.

And here it behooves us to remind our workingmen, the bone and sinew of the people and the specially beloved children of the Church, that if they wish to observe Sundays as they ought, they must keep away from drinking places on Saturday night. Carry your wages home to your families, where they rightfully belong. Turn a deaf ear, therefore, to every temptation; and then Sunday will be a bright day for all the family. How much better this than to make it a day of sin for yourselves, and of gloom and wretchedness for your home, by a Saturday night's folly or debauch. No wonder that the Prelates of the Second Plenary Council declared that "the most shocking scandals which we have to deplore spring from intemperance." No wonder that they gave a special approval to the zeal of those who, the better to avoid excess, or in order to give bright example, pledge themselves to total abstinence. Like them we invoke a blessing on the cause of temperance, and on all who are laboring for its advancement in a true Christian spirit. Let the exertions of our Catholic Temperance Societies meet with the hearty co-operation of pastors and people; and not only will they go far towards strangling the monstrous evil of intemperance, but they will also put a powerful check on the desecration of the Lord's Day, and on the evil influences now striving for its total profanation.

Let all our people "remember to keep holy the Lord's Day." Let them make it not only a day of rest, but also a

day of prayer. Let then sanctify it by assisting at the adorable Sacrifice of the Mass. Besides the privilege of the
morning Mass, let them also give their souls the sweet enjoyment of the Vesper service and the Benediction of the
Blessed Sacrament. See that the children not only hear
Mass, but also attend the Sunday-school. It will help them
to grow up more practical Catholics. In country places,
and especially in those which the priest cannot visit every
Sunday, the Sunday-school ought to be the favorite place
of reunion for young and old. It will keep them from going
astray, and will strengthen them in the faith. How many
children have been lost to the Church in country districts,
because parents neglected to see that they obeserved the
Sunday properly at home and at Sunday-school, and
allowed them to fall under dangerous influences!

One of the most striking characteristics of our times is
the universal tendency to band together in societies for the
promotion of all sorts of purposes. This
Forbidden   tendency is the natural outgrowth of an
Societies.   age of popular rights and representative
institutions. It is also in accordance with
the spirit of the Church, whose aim, as indicated by her
name Catholic, is to unite all mankind in brotherhood. It
is consonant also with the spirit of Christ, who came to
break down all walls of division, and to gather all in the
one family of the one heavenly Father.

But there are few good things which have not their
counterfeits, and few tendencies which have not their dangers. It is obvious to any reflecting mind that men form
bad and rash as well as good and wise designs; and that
they may band together for carrying out evil or dangerous
as well as laudable and useful purposes. And this does not
necessarily imply deliberate malice, because, while it is
unquestionably true that there are powers at work in the
world which deliberately antagonize the cause of Christian
truth and virtue, still the evil or the danger of purposes
and associations need not always spring from so bad a
root. Honest but weak and erring human nature is apt to
be so taken up with one side of a question as to do injustice
to the other; to be so enamored of favorite principles as to

carry them to unjustifiable extremes; to be so intent upon
securing some laudable end as to ignore the rules of prudence, and bring about ruin instead of restoration. But no
intention, no matter how honest, can make lawful what is
unlawful. For it is a fundamental rule of Christian morals
that "evil must not be done that good may come of it,"
and "the end can never justify the means," if the means
are evil. Hence it is the evident duty of every reasonable
man, before allowing himself to be drawn into any society,
to make sure that both its ends and its means are consistent
with truth, justice and conscience.

In making such a decision, every Catholic ought to be
convinced that his surest guide is the Church of Christ.
She has in her custody the sacred deposit of Christian truth
and morals; she has the experience of all ages and all nations; she has at heart the true welfare of mankind; she
has the perpetual guidance of the Holy Ghost in her authoritative decisions. In her teaching and her warnings therefore, we are sure to hear the voice of wisdom, prudence,
justice and charity. From the hill-top of her Divine mission and her world-wide experience, she sees events and
their consequences far more clearly than they who are
down in the tangled plain of daily life. She has seen associations that were once praiseworthy, become pernicious
by change of circumstances. She has seen others, which
won the admiration of the world by their early achievements, corrupted by power or passion or evil guidance, and
she has been forced to condemn them. She has beheld
associations which had their origin in the spirit of the
Ages of Faith, transformed by lapse of time, and loss of
faith, and the manipulation of designing leaders, into the
open or hidden enemies of religion and human weal. Thus
our Holy Father Leo XIII has lately shown that the Masonic
and kindred societies,—although the offspring of the ancient Guilds, which aimed at sanctifying trades and trades-
men with the blessings of religion; and although retaining,
perhaps, in their "ritual," much that tells of the religious-
ness of their origin; and although in some countries still
professing entire friendliness toward the Christian religion,—have nevertheless already gone so far, in many coun-

tries, as to array themselves in avowed hostility against Christianity, and against the Catholic Church as its embodiment; that they virtually aim at substituting a worldwide fraternity of their own, for the universal brotherhood of Jesus Christ, and at disseminating mere Naturalism for the supernatural revealed religion bestowed upon mankind by the Saviour of the world. He has shown, too, that, even in countries where they are as yet far from acknowledging such purposes, they nevertheless have in them the germs, which under favorable circumstances, would inevitably blossom forth in similar results. The Church, consequently, forbids her children to have any connection with such societies, because they are either an open evil to be shunned or a hidden danger to be avoided. She would fail in her duty if she did not speak the word of warning, and her children would equally fail in theirs, if they did not heed it.

Whenever, therefore, the Church has spoken authoritatively with regard to any society, her decision ought to be final for every Catholic. He ought to know that the Church has not acted hastily or unwisely, or mistakenly; he should be convinced that any worldly advantages which he might derive from his membership of such society, would be a poor substitute for the membership, the sacraments, and the blessings of the Church of Christ; he should have the courage of his religious convictions, and stand firm to faith and conscience. But if he be inclined or asked to join a society on which the Church has passed no sentence, then let him, as a reasonable and Christian man, examine into it carefully, and not join the society until he is satisfied as to its lawful character.

There is one characteristic which is always a strong presumption against a society, and that is secrecy. Our Divine Lord Himself has laid down the rule: "Every one that doth evil, hateth the light and cometh not to the light, that his works may not be reproved. But he that doth truth cometh to the light that his works may be made manifest, because they are done in God." [23] When, therefore associations veil themselves in secrecy and darkness, the presump-

23 John iii. 20, 21.

tion is against them, and it rests with them to prove that there is nothing evil in them.

But if any society's obligation be such as to bind its members to secrecy, even when rightly questioned by competent authority, then such a society puts itself outside the limits of approval; and no one can be a member of it and at the same time be admitted to the sacraments of the Catholic Church. The same is true of any organization that binds its members to a promise of blind obedience—to accept in advance and to obey whatsoever orders, lawful or unlawful, that may emanate from its chief authorities; because such a promise is contrary both to reason and conscience. And if a society works or plots, either openly on in secret, against the Church, or against lawful authorities, then to be a member of it is to be excluded from the membership of the Catholic Church.

These authoritative rules, therefore, ought to be the guide of all Catholics in their relations with societies. No Catholic can conscientiously join, or continue in, a body in which he knows that any of these condemned features exist. If he has joined it in good faith and the objectionable features become known to him afterwards, or if any of these evil elements creep into a society which was originally good, it becomes his duty to leave it at once. And even if he were to suffer loss or run the risk by leaving such a society or refusing to join it, he should do his duty and brave the consequences regardless of human consideration.

To these laws of the Church, the justice of which must be manifest to all impartial minds, we deem it necessary to add the following admonition of the Second Plenary Council:[24] "Care must be taken lest workingmen's societies, under the pretext of mutual assistance and protection, should commit any of the evils of condemned societies; and lest the members should be induced by the artifices of designing men to break the laws of justice, by withholding labor to which they are rightfully bound, or by otherwise unlawfully violating the rights of their employers."

But while the Church is thus careful to guard her children against whatever is contrary to Christian duty, she is

24 No. 519.

no less careful that no injustice should be done to any association, however unintentionally. While therefore the Church, before prohibiting any society, will take every precaution to ascertain its true nature, we positively forbid any pastor, or other ecclesiastic, to pass sentence on any association or to impose ecclesiastical penalties or disabilities on its members without the previous explicit authorization of the rightful authorities.

It is not enough for Catholics to shun bad or dangerous societies, they ought to take part in good and useful ones. If there ever was a time when merely neg-

Catholic ative goodness would not suffice, such Societies. assuredly is the age in which we live. This is pre-eminently an age of action, and what we need to-day is active virtue and energetic piety. Again and again has the voice of the Vicar of Christ been heard, giving approval and encouragement to many kinds of Catholic associations, not only as a safeguard against the allurements of dangerous societies, but also as a powerful means of accomplishing much of the good that our times stand in need of. Not only should the pastors of the Church be hard at work in building up "the spiritual house,"[25] "the tabernacle of God with men,"[26] but every hand among the people of God should share in the labor.

In the first place, we hope that in every parish in the land there is some sodality or confraternity to foster piety among the people. We therefore heartily endorse anew all approbations previously given to our many time-honored and cherished confraternities, such as those of the Sacred Heart of Jesus, of the Blessed Sacrament, and of the Blessed Virgin.

Next come the various associations for works of Christian zeal and charity: the Society for the Propagation of the Faith, and the Holy Childhood, than which there are none more deserving; societies for the support of Catholic education; Christian doctrine societies for the work of Sunday-schools; societies for improving the condition of the poor, among which stands pre-eminent the Society of St. Vincent de Paul; church-debt societies; societies for sup-

25 Pet. ii. 5.   26 Apoc. xxi, 3.

plying poor churches with vestments and other altar requirements; local sanctuary societies; and other methods of uniting the efforts of the people of the parish for useful and holy purposes. It ought to be the comfort and the honest pride of every Catholic to take an active part in these good works; and if any are hindered from contributing a portion of their time and labor, they should contribute as liberally as they can out of their pecuniary resources.

Then there are associations for the checking of immorality, prominent among which are our Catholic Temperance Societies. These should be encouraged and aided by all who deplore the scandal given and the spiritual ruin wrought by intemperance. It is a mistake to imagine that such societies are made up of the reformed victims of intemperance. They should be, and we trust that they everywhere are largely composed of zealous Catholics who never were tainted by that vice, but who mourn over the great evil and are energetically endeavoring to correct it.

We likewise consider as worthy of particular encouragement associations for the promotion of healthful social union among Catholics,—and especially those, whose aim is to guard our Catholic young men against dangerous influences, and supply them with the means of innocent amusement and mental culture. It is obvious that our young men are exposed to the greatest dangers, and therefore need the most abundant helps. Hence, in the spirit of our Holy Father Leo XIII, we desire to see the number of thoroughly Catholic and well organized associations for their benefit greatly increased, especially in our large cities; we exhort pastors to consider the formation and careful direction of such societies as one of their most important duties; and we appeal to our young men to put to good profit, the best years of their lives, by banding together, under the direction of their pastors, for mutual improvement and encouragement in the paths of faith and virtue.

And in order to acknowledge the great amount of good that the "Catholic Young Men's National Union" has already accomplished, to promote the growth of the Union and to stimulate its members to greater efforts in the future, we cordially bless their aims and endeavors and recommend the Union to all our Catholic young men.

We also esteem as a very important element in practical Catholicity, the various forms of Catholic beneficial societies and kindred association of Catholic workingmen. It ought to be, and we trust is everywhere their aim to encourage habits of industry, thrift, and sobriety; to guard the members against the dangerous attractions of condemned or suspicious organizations; and to secure the faithful practice of their religious duties, on which their temporal as well as their eternal welfare so largely depends.

With paternal affection we bestow our blessing upon all those various forms of combined Catholic action for useful and holy purposes. We desire to see their number multiplied and their organization perfected. We beseech them to remember that their success and usefulness must rest in a great measure, upon their fidelity to the spirit of the Church, and on their guarding carefully against influences that might make them disloyal. The more closely pastors and people are united in good works, the more abundantly will those associations be blessed and their ends accomplished, the more perfectly will all Christians be united in fraternal charity, and the more widely and firmly will the Kingdom of Christ on the earth be established.

The duties of a Christian begin with his own household and his own parish; but they do not end there. The charity and zeal in his heart must be like that in the heart of the Church, whose very name is Catholic,—like that in the heart of Christ, who "died for all men, and gave Himself a redemption for all." [27] The Divine commission to the Church stands forever: "Go, teach all nations; preach the Gospel to every creature;" [28] and every one who desires the salvation of souls, should yearn for its fulfillment, and consider it a privilege to take part in its realization. The more we appreciate the gift of faith, the more must we long to have it imparted to others. The heart of every true Catholic must glow as he reads of the heroic labors of our missionaries among the heathen nations

Home and
Foreign
Missions.

[27] 2 Cor. v. 15; 1 Tim. ii. 6.   [28] Matt. xxviii. 19; Mark xvi. 15.

in every part of the world, and especially among the Indian tribes of our country. The missionary spirit is one of the glories of the Church and one of the chief characteristics of Christian zeal.

In nearly all European countries there are Foreign Mission Colleges, and also associations of the faithful for the support of the missions by their contributions. Hitherto we have had to strain every nerve in order to carry on the missions of our own country, and we were unable to take any important part in aiding the missions abroad. But we must beware lest our local burdens should make our zeal narrow and uncatholic. There are hundreds of millions of souls in heathen lands to whom the light of the Gospel has not yet been carried, and their condition appeals to the charity of every Christian heart. Among our own Indian tribes, for whom we have a special responsibility, there are still many thousands in the same darkness of heathenism, and the missions among our thousands of Catholic Indians must equally look to our charity for support. Moreover, out of the six millions of our colored population there is a very large multitude, who stand sorely in need of Christian instruction and missionary labor; and it is evident that in the poor dioceses in which they are mostly found, it is most difficult to bestow on them the care they need, without the generous co-operation of our Catholic people in more prosperous localities. We have therefore urged the establishment of the Society for the Propagation of the Faith in every parish in which it is not yet erected, and also ordered a collection to be made yearly in all the dioceses, for the foreign missions and the missions among our Indians and Negroes. We have done this through a deep sense of duty, and we trust that our noble-hearted people will not regard it as a burden imposed on them, but as an opportunity presented to them of co-operating in a work which must be specially dear to the Heart of our Divine Saviour.

These are the leading matters, venerable and beloved brethren, which have engaged our attention during this Council. The objects of our deliberations have been the same that have occupied the energies of the Church and her pastors ever since the days of the Apostles,—namely, the extension of the kingdom of God, the building up the Body of Christ, the giving greater "glory to God in the highest, and peace on earth to men of good will," by shedding abroad more abundantly the blessings of religion, and the graces of redemption. Our legislation is not intended to impose burdens or limitations upon you, but, on the contrary, to enlarge and secure to you "the liberty of the children of God." The path of duty and virtue is clearly marked and pointed out, not to restrain your freedom, but that you may journey safely, that you may live wisely and virtuously, that you may have happiness temporal and eternal.

And now we write you these things, that you may be partners in our solicitude, that every heart may cry out "Thy Kingdom come," that every hand may be active in establishing and extending it. Accept with willing and loving minds these lessons which spring from hearts full of love for you, and entirely consecrated to your service. Give joy to us and to our Divine Lord by putting them faithfully in practice. And may the blessing of Almighty God, the Father, the Son, and the Holy Ghost, descend upon you abundantly, and abide with you forever.

Given at Baltimore, in the Plenary Council, on the 7th day of December, in the year of our Lord 1884.

In his own name and in the name of all the Fathers,

✠JAMES GIBBONS,

Archbishop of Baltimore and Apostolic Delegate.

CHAPTER XIII

THE PASTORAL LETTER OF 1919

DURING the next thirty-five years (1884-1919) the legislation of the Third Plenary Council of Baltimore was found sufficient for the guidance and direction of priests and people of the Catholic Church in the United States. More than once, however, in that period the peace and unity of the Church were threatened by divergent views on important matters of ecclesiastical polity and of discipline. The School Controversy in the early 'nineties found some of our prelates with serious misgivings on the problem of freedom in education. The papal rescript of January 22, 1899, on "Americanism" was the last word in a controversy which had become international. The creation of the Apostolic Delegation at Washington in 1892 brought the American hierarchy into closer relations with the Holy See. The dominant personality of Cardinal Gibbons, as a great churchman and a great citizen of the Republic, helped powerfully to bridge over the seriousness of the crisis in 1893, when another anti-Catholic movement was begun, the American Protective Association. The entrance of the United States into the World War in April, 1917, found the archbishops of the country assembled in their Annual Meeting at the Catholic University of America. Headed by His Eminence of Baltimore, they addressed a letter to President Wilson, reaffirming in that hour of stress and trial their most sacred and sincere loyalty and patriotism towards our country, our government and our flag. "Our peoples," they wrote, "now as ever, will rise as one man to serve the nation. Our priests and consecrated women will once again, as in every former trial of our country, win by their bravery, their heroism and their service new admiration and approval." An annual meeting of the entire hierarchy of the United States was decided upon, and in September, 1919, the first notable gathering of the archbishops and bishops was held at the Catholic University of America. We have the result of this meeting in the Pastoral Letter of September 26, 1919.

The Pastoral Letter of 1919 bears on its pages the unmistakable signs of the best Catholic scholarship of our times. It

is divided into fourteen sections, which treat in order: the
progress of the Church during the years which had intervened
since 1884; secular conditions surrounding Catholic life in the
Republic; Catholic war activities and the lessons of the war;
the post-war situation with its alarming need of re-construc-
tion according to the principles of Christianity; the obligation
of justice and of charity; the social relations arising from the
sacredness of the marriage tie; the evils of divorce; the influence
of women; industrial relations between capital and labour; the
right of labour to a living wage and the problem of labour
unions; national conditions requiring prudent adjustment, and
the value of the press for the removal of evil in political affairs;
our international relations; education in general and the principles of a sound educational system; with a closing appeal in
the Name of Christ, the Master, to all citizens of the Republic,
Catholic and non-Catholic, to look beyond the horizons of life
to the higher destiny God has prepared for them that love Him.

PASTORAL LETTER OF THE ARCHBISHOPS AND BISHOPS
OF THE UNITED STATES

*The Archbishops and Bishops of the United States in Con-
ference assembled, to their Clergy and faithful people—
Grace unto you and peace from God our Father, and
from the Lord Jesus Christ. Venerable Brethren of the
Clergy, Beloved Children of the Laity:*

THIRTY-FIVE years have elapsed since the Fathers of
the Third Plenary Council of Baltimore addressed their
Pastoral Letter to the faithful of their charge. In it they
expressed their deliberate thought upon the state of religion
at the time, upon its needs and its abundant resources. Surveying the growth of the Church during a century, they saw
with thankfulness the evident design of God in behalf of
our country; and turning to the future, they beheld the
promise of a still more fruitful development. With wise
enactment and admonition they imparted new vigor to our
Catholic life. With a foresight which we can now appreciate, they prepared the Church in America to meet,
on the solid ground of faith and discipline, the changing
conditions of our earthly existence. As Pope Leo XIII of

happy memory declared: "the event has proven, and still does prove, that the decrees of Baltimore were wholesome and timely. Experience has demonstrated their value for the maintenance of discipline, for stimulating the intelligence and zeal of the clergy, for protecting and developing the Catholic education of youth." [1]

The framers of that legislation were men of power, shewing forth in their wisdom the dignity of prophets and instructing the people with holy words. They are gone, nearly all, to their rest and reward; but their godly deeds have not failed. They have left us a sacred inheritance; their labors are held in remembrance and their names in benediction forever.

Following the example of our predecessors, and like them trusting in the guidance of the Holy Spirit, we lately took counsel together for the welfare of the Church and of our country. The whole Hierarchy of the United States assembled in Washington, to consider the problems, the needs and the possibilities for good which invite us to new undertakings. In the record of the last three decades, we found much to console and inspire us. We also knew well that you with whom and for whom we have labored, would rejoice in considering how abundantly God has blessed our endeavors. And we therefore determined, for His glory and for your comfort, to point out the significant phases in our progress, and to set forth the truths which contain the solution of the world's great problems.

This course we adopted the more hopefully because of the approval and encouragement given us by our Holy Father, Pope Benedict XV, in the Letter which he sent us last April. Knowing how deeply the Sovereign Pontiff is concerned for the restoration of all things in Christ, and how confidently he looks at this time to the Church in America, we felt that by uniting our thought and our effort we should cooperate, in the measure of our opportunity, toward his beneficent purpose. In his name, and in our own, we greet you, dear brethren, as children of the Holy Catholic Church and as citizens of the Republic on whose preservation the future of humanity so largely depends.

[1] Encyc. *Longinqua oceani spatia*, Jan. 6, 1895.

We exhort you, as of one mind and heart, to ponder well the significance of recent events, so that each of you, as circumstance requires, may rightly fulfil his share of our common obligation.

First of all, it is our bounden duty to offer up praise and thanksgiving to Almighty God who in His gracious Providence, has restored the nations to peace. He has shown us His mercy, and the light of His countenance is shining upon us, that we may know His way upon earth, which is the way of salvation for all the peoples. Now that the storm is subsiding, we can see the true meaning of its causes. We can review more calmly the changes and movement which brought it about; and we can discern more surely their import for our various human interests.

I. PROGRESS OF THE CHURCH

In the spiritual order, there has been a steady advance. The issue between truth and error with regard to all that religion implies, is now quite clearly drawn. As human devices, intended to replace the Gospel, have gradually broken down, Christianity, by contrast, appears distinct and firm in its true position. The Church indeed has suffered because it would not sanction the vagaries of thought and policy which were leading the world to disaster. And yet the very opposition which it encountered, an opposition which would have destroyed the work of man, has given the Church occasion for new manifestations of life. With larger freedom from external interference, it has developed more fully the power from on high with which the Holy Spirit endued it. Far from being weakened by the failure of outward support, its activity is seen as the expression of its inner vitality. Its vigor is shown in its ready adaptation to the varying conditions of the world, an adaptation which means no supine yielding and no surrender of principle, but rather the exertion of power in supplying as they arise, the needs of humanity. Because it maintains inviolate the deposit of Christian faith and the law of Christian morality, the Church can profit by every item of truth and every means for the betterment of man

which genuine progress affords. It thrives wherever freedom really lives, and it furnishes the only basis on which
freedom can be secure.

The inner vitality of the Church has been shown and
enhanced by the action of the Holy See in giving fresh
impetus to the minds and hearts of the
faithful; in stimulating philosophical,   **Action of**
historical and biblical studies; in creating **the Holy See.**
institutions of learning; in revising the
forms of liturgical prayer; in quickening devotion, and in
reducing to a compact body of law the manifold enactments
of canonical legislation. At the same time, the Sovereign
Pontiffs have promoted the welfare of all mankind by insisting on the principles which should govern our social,
industrial and political relations; by deepening respect for
civil authority; by enjoining upon Catholics everywhere
the duty of allegiance to the State and the discharge of
patriotic obligation. They have condemned the errors
which planned to betray humanity and to undermine our
civilization. Again and again, the charity of Christ con-
straining them, they have sought out the peoples which sat
in darkness and the shadow of death; and they have urged
all Christians who are yet "as children tossed to and fro
and carried about with every wind of doctrine," to enter
the haven of the Church and anchor upon the confession
of "one Lord, one faith, one baptism." [2]

From these salutary measures the Church in America
has derived in full its share of benefit. But it has also received, to its great advantage, especial
marks of pontifical favor. To Pope Leo   **The Holy See**
XIII we are indebted for the establishment   **and the**
of the Apostolic Delegation, whereby we   **Church**
are brought into closer union with the   **in America.**
Holy See. The presence in our midst of
the representative of the Holy Father has invigorated our
ecclesiastical life, and facilitated to a marked degree the
administration of our spiritual affairs, in keeping with our
rapid development.

Though its organization had extended to every part of

[2] Eph. iv. 14, 5.

the United States, the Church, until 1908, was still on a missionary basis, as it had been from the beginning. By the action of Pope Pius X, it was advanced to full canonical status and ranked with the older Churches of Europe. It now observes the same laws and enjoys the same relations with the Apostolic See.

From the beginning of his pontificate, Pope Benedict XV, though burdened with sorrow and trial, has given his children in America continual proof of his fatherly care. He has guided us with his counsel, encouraged us with his approbation, and rejoiced in our prosperity. Recognizing the importance of America for the world's restoration, he sees from his exalted position the broader range of opportunity which now is given the Church in our country. By word, and yet more by example, he shows how effectually the Catholic spirit can renew the face of the earth.

It is a source of happiness for us that the Catholics of America have appreciated the evidences of paternal affection bestowed on them by the Vicar of Christ. For we can truly say that no people **Needs of** is more loyal to the Holy See, none more **the Holy See.** diligent in providing for its needs. Our assistance at the present time will give the Holy Father special consolation, owing to the fact that the faithful in so many countries are no longer able to share with him their scanty means. It is to the Pope, on the contrary, that they in their destitution, are looking for aid. And it is in their behalf that he has more than once appealed. Touching, indeed, are the words with which he implores all Christians throughout the world, and "all who have a sense of humanity," for the love of the Infant Saviour, to help him in rescuing from hunger and death the children of Europe. In the same Encyclical Letter,[3] he commends most highly the Bishops and the faithful of the United States for their prompt and generous response of his earlier appeal, and he offers their action as an example to all other Catholics. Let us continue to deserve his approval. It is sufficient for us to know that the Holy Father, with numberless demands upon him, is in need.

3 *Paterno iam diu,* Nov. 24, 1919.

The growth of the Church in America was fittingly brought to view at the celebration, in 1889, of the first centenary of the Hierarchy. Within a hundred years, the number of dioceses **The Church** had risen from one to seventy-five. Dur- **in Our** ing the last three decades, the same rate of **Country.** progress has been maintained, with the result that at present one-sixth of the citizens of the United States are members of the Catholic Church, in a hundred flourishing dioceses.

But what we regard as far more important is the growth and manifestation of an active religious spirit in every diocese and parish. "We are bound to give thanks always to God for you, brethren, as it is fitting, because your faith groweth exceedingly, and the charity of every one of you toward each other aboundeth." [4] You have not contented yourselves with bearing the Catholic name or professing your faith in words: you have shown your faith by your works: by the performance of your religious duties, by obedience to the laws of the Church and by cooperation in furthering the kingdom of God. For thus "the whole body, being compacted and fitly joined together, by what every joint supplieth, according to the operation in the measure of every part, maketh increase of the body unto the edifying of itself in charity." [5]

With you, dear brethren of the clergy, we rejoice in the fruits of your zeal, your loyalty and your concern for the welfare of the souls entrusted to your care. You have learned by a happy experience how much can be accomplished through your daily ministration, your immediate contact with the people, your words of advice and instruction, above all, through your priestly example. To you we gladly attribute the provision of the material means which are needed for the worship of God and for the countless forms of charity. You "have loved the beauty of His house and the place where His glory dwelleth." [6] What is yet more essential, you have builded in the souls of your people, and especially in the little ones of Christ, the temple of the living God. In the work of our Catholic schools, you have

4 Thess. i. 3.   5 Eph. iv. 16.   6 Ps. xxv. 8.

both the honor and the responsibility of laying the first foundation. We know that you have laid it with care, and that the whole structure of Catholic education is securely based upon Jesus Christ, the chief corner-stone: "in whom all the building being fitted together, groweth up into an holy temple in the Lord. . . . an habitation of God in the Spirit." [7]

You, likewise, beloved children of the laity, we heartily commend for your willingness, your correspondence with the intent of your pastors, your support so cheerfully given to the cause of religion. When we consider that every church and school, every convent, asylum and hospital represents the voluntary offering brought by you, out of your plenty and more often out of your want, we cannot but marvel and glorify God who has made you "worthy of His vocation and fulfilled in you all the good pleasure of His goodness and the work of faith in power." [8] For as faith is expressed in deeds; so, conversely, is it strengthened by doing: "by works faith is made perfect." [9] And since the bond of perfection is charity, we look upon your generosity both as an evidence of your good will toward the whole of God's Church and as a token of His heavenly favor. "Wherefore, brethren, labor the more that by good works you may make sure your calling and election." [10]

We would have you bear always in mind that your faith is your most precious possession and the foundation of your

Faith.

spiritual life, since "without faith, it is impossible to please God." [11] Without faith, the outward forms of worship avail us nothing, the sacraments are beyond our reach, the whole plan and effect of redemption is made void. It behooves us, then, to guard with jealous care the treasure of faith by thankfulness to God for so great a gift and by loyalty to "the Church of the living God, the pillar and ground of the truth." [12] The fact that unbelief is so common, that firm and definite teaching of Christian truth is so often replaced by vague uncertain statements, and that even these are left to individual preference for acceptance

7 Eph. ii. 21, 22.   8 2 Thess. i. 11.   9 James ii. 22.
10 2 Peter i. 10.   11 Heb. xi. 6.   12 1 Tim. iii. 15.

or rejection—the fact, in a word, that by many faith is no
longer regarded as of vital consequence in religion, should
the more determine us to "watch, stand fast in the faith, do
manfully and be strengthened." [13] While we must needs
look with sorrow upon the decay of positive belief, let us
recognize, with gratitude, the wisdom of Him who, being
the "author and finisher of our faith," established in His
Church a living authority to "teach all nations, teaching
them to observe all things whatsoever I have commanded
you." [14] Let us also consider the splendid courage with
which that mission has been accomplished through the
centuries, by the witness of martyrs, the constancy of faithful peoples, the zeal of preachers and pastors, the firmness
of Pontiffs who, amid the storms of error and the assaults
of worldly power, stood fast in the faith upon the assurance
given them by Christ: "the gates of hell shall not prevail." [15]

The Catholic who appreciates the blessing of faith and
the sacrifices which generous men and women in all ages
have made to preserve it, will take heed to himself and beware of the things whereby some "have made shipwreck
concerning the faith." [16] For this disaster is usually the end
and culmination of other evils, of sinful habits, of neglect of
prayer and the sacraments, of cowardice in the face of
hostility to one's belief, of weakness in yielding to the
wishes of kindred or friends, of social ambition and the
hope of advantage in busines or public career. More subtle
are the dangers arising from an atmosphere in which unbelief is mingled with culture and gentle refinement, or in
which the fallacy spreads that faith is hopelessly at variance
with scientific truth. To counteract these influences, it is
necessary that they who love the truth of Christ, should
"the more and more abound in knowledge and in all understanding." [17] As they advance in years, they should lay
firmer hold upon the teachings of religion and be prepared
to explain and defend it. They will thus "continue in faith,
grounded and settled and immovable from the hope of the
Gospel," [18] ready always to give "a reason of that hope that

[13] 1 Cor. xvi. 13.   [14] Matt. xxviii. 20.   [15] Matt. xvi. 18.
[16] 1 Tim. i. 19.   [17] Phil. i. 9.   [18] Coloss. i. 23.

is in them," [19] and, if needs be, to "contend earnestly for the faith once delivered to the saints." [20]

To the Church which is taught all truth by the Holy Spirit, Christ entrusted the whole deposit of divine revelation. To the watchful care of the Church we owe the preservation of that Book from which Christians in every age have derived instruction and strength. How needful was the warning of the Apostle that "no prophecy of Scripture is made by private interpretation," [21] appears in the history of those movements which began by leaving each individual to take his own meaning from the sacred text, and now, after four centuries, have ended in rejecting its divine authority. The Church, on the contrary, with true reverence for the Bible and solicitude for the spiritual welfare of its readers, has guarded both it and them against the dangers of false interpretation. In the same spirit, dear brethren, we exhort you to acquire a loving familiarity with the written word: "for what things soever were written, were written for our learning; that through patience and the comfort of the Scriptures we might have hope." [22] This intimate knowledge of Holy Writ will bring you close to the person and life of our Saviour and to the labors of His Apostles. It will renew in your hearts the joy with which the first Christians received the tidings of salvation. And it will deepen in you the conviction that the Scriptures are indeed the word of God, "which can instruct you unto salvation by the faith which is in Christ Jesus" [23]—a conviction which cannot be shaken either by the disputations of the learned who "stumble at the word," or by the errors of the unlearned and unstable who wrest the Scriptures "to their own destruction." [24]

The knowledge of our holy religion will enkindle in you a love of the Church, which Christ so loved that He gave Himself for it, purchasing it with His blood. It is the Church not of one race or of one nation, but of all those who truly believe in His name. The more you dwell upon its teaching, its practice and its history, the stronger will be your sense of unity with the multitude of believers throughout the world. You will clearly understand that the true interests of each part, of each diocese and parish, are the interests of the Church Universal. "You are the body of Christ and members of member. And if one member suffer anything, all the members suffer with it; or, if one member glory, all the members rejoice with it." [25] This is the practical meaning of Catholicity and its saving strength as opposed to the weakness of localism. The really Catholic mind is careful not only for the needs which affect its immediate surroundings, but for those also which press upon the Church in less prosperous sections, or which, in far countries, hinder the spread of religion. Such was the mind of those Christians to whom St. Paul appealed in behalf of their distant brethren: "In this present time, let your abundance supply their want; that their abundance also may supply your want, that there may be an equality." [26]

The Catholic Spirit.

Your Catholic sense will also enable you to see how tireless the Church has been in providing both for the souls of men and for their temporal needs: how much of what is best in modern civilization, how much that we value in the way of liberty and law, of art and industry, of science, education and charity, is due to the Catholic spirit. Like its Founder, the Church has gone about the world doing good to all men; and with Him the Church can say: "the works that I do in the name of my Father, they give testimony of me. . . . though you will not believe me, believe the works." [27] And this ministry of love the Church will continue. It will adopt all agencies and means that may render its service of better effect; it will quicken them all with the fervor of charity lest they harden to mechanical form; and it will take utmost care that they be employed to draw men nearer to Christ.

The spirit that made Vincent de Paul a Saint and a hero of charity, lives on in his followers. According to the pattern which he gave, they minister to those who are in any distress, quietly and effectually. Of late they have notably increased their power for good. Through the Conference

25 1 Cor. xii. 26-27.   26 2 Cor. viii. 14.   27 John x. 25, 38.

of Catholic Charities a "great door and evident" is opened upon a wider range of usefulness. To all who are joined together in this holy undertaking we say with the Apostle: "May the Lord multiply you and make you abound in charity one toward another and toward all men; as we do toward you." [28]

Be instant, therefore, dear brethren, in helping those who suffer or want; but take heed also to your own spiritual life, that in thought and purpose and motive, as well as in outward deed, you may be acceptable in the sight of God. From the teaching of the Church and from your own experience, you know that without the divine assistance you cannot walk in the footsteps of Christ. And you need not be reminded that the principal means of grace are prayer and the sacraments.

Prayer.

Through prayer we lift up our hearts to God, and He in turn enlightens our minds, kindles our affections, gives power to our wills. For whether we adore His majesty or praise Him for His wonderful works, whether we render Him thanks for His goodness, or beseech Him for pardon, or beg Him to help and defend us, our prayer is pleasing to Him: it goes up as incense before Him, as the voice of His children to the Father who loves them, who pursues them with mercy and offers them speedy forgiveness. Wherefore, in joy and in sorrow, in adversity and in prosperity, "in everything, by prayer and supplication with thanksgiving, let your petitions be made known to God." [29]

We are certain that amid the trials of the last few years, you have prayed without ceasing—for those who had gone from you to the post of duty and danger, for your country, for the untold millions who fell in the struggle. Many of you surely have found that it is "a holy and wholesome thought to pray for the dead that they may be loosed from sins." [30] This doctrine and practice, so fully according with the impulse of human affection, appeals to us now with singular force. For those who mourn, it is a source of comfort; for all, it is the exercise of purest charity. And no petition could be more pleasing to the Father of mercies

[28] 1 Thess. iii. 42.   [29] Phil. iv. 6.   [30] 2 Mach. xii. 46.

than that which implores Him to grant to our departed
brethren everlasting rest in a place of refreshment, light and
peace. The remembrance of those who are gone before
us with the token of faith, will raise up our hearts above
worldly desires; and whereas we are saddened by the certain prospect of death, yet shall we be comforted with the
promise of immortal life, knowing that "if our earthly
house of this habitation be dissolved, we have a building
of God, a house not made with hands, eternal in heaven." [81]

We heartily commend the beautiful practice of family
prayer. "Where there are two or three gathered in My
name, there am I in the midst of them." [32] If this is
true of the faithful in general, it applies with particular
meaning to those who are members of the same household.
The presence of Jesus will surely be a source of blessing to
the home where parents and children unite to offer up
prayer in common. The spirit of piety which this custom
develops, will sanctify the bonds of family love and ward
off the dangers which so often bring sorrow and shame.
We appeal in this matter with special earnestness to young
fathers and mothers, who have it in their power to mould
the hearts of their children and train them betimes in the
habit of prayer.

This will also inspire them with love for the public
services of the Church and, above all, for the central act of
Catholic worship, the Holy Sacrifice of the
Mass. For the truly Catholic heart, there   The Sacrifice
should be no need of insisting on the duty   and the
which the Church enjoins of hearing Mass   Sacraments.
on Sundays and festivals of obligation.
We have only to stir up the faith that is in us and consider that on the altar is offered the same clean oblation
whereby the world was redeemed on the Cross; and as
today no Christian can stand unmoved on Calvary, or pass
with indifference along the road which Jesus trod, so is it
inconceivable that any who believe in the word of Christ
and His Church, should allow household cares, or business
pursuits, or the love of pleasure and ease to keep them

81 2 Cor. v. 1.   82 Matt. xviii. 20.

away from Mass. Negligence in respect to this duty may
often result from lack of proper instruction; and we therefore desire to impress upon parents, teachers and pastors
the importance and the necessity of explaining to those in
their charge, the origin, nature and the value of the Holy
Sacrifice, the meaning of the sacred rites with which it is
offered, and the order of the liturgy as it advances from
season to season. There is so much beauty in the worship
of the Church, so much power to fill the mind with great
thoughts and lift up the heart to heavenly things, that
one who hears Mass with intelligent devotion cannot but
feel in his soul an impulse to holier living. Such is the
experience of those especially who begin each day by attending at Mass, and we rejoice to know that their number
is increasing. They will grow in faith and fervor, and their
piety will be for all a source of edification.

It is likewise consoling to see in our time a revival of
the spirit which, in primitive ages, led the Christian to
receive each day "the Bread that came down from heaven."
In the Holy Eucharist, the love of Jesus Christ for men
passes all understanding. "He that eateth My flesh and
drinketh My blood, abideth in Me and I in him." [33] A worthy
communion unites us with our Saviour, and even transforms our spiritual being, so that we may say with the
Apostle: "I live, now not I; but Christ liveth in me." [34] As
by His continual abiding within it, the Church is holy and
without blemish, so does the presence of Christ in each
soul purify it even as He is pure, and give it power to do
all things in Him who strengthens it.

The sense of our unworthiness may incline us to draw
back from the Holy Table; but, as St. Paul tells us: "Let a
man prove himself and so let him eat of that bread and
drink of the chalice." [35] Only sin can separate us from the
love of God which is in Christ Jesus our Lord, and for sin
He has provided a remedy in the sacrament of His mercy.
"If we confess our sins, He is faithful and just to forgive us
our sins and cleanse us from all iniquity." [36] Through these
two sacraments, the one given for the healing of our souls,

33 John vi. 57.   34 Gal. ii. 20.   35 1 Cor. xi. 28.   36 1 John i. 9.

the other for their nourishment, we are established in the life of grace and are "filled unto all the fullness of God." [37]

What grace can accomplish in His creatures, God has shown in the person of her whom He chose to be His mother, preserving her from all stain and endowing her with such pureness of heart **Mary** that she is truly "full of grace" and **the Mother** "blessed among women." The unique **of Christ.** privilege of Mary as cooperating in the Incarnation, entitles her to reverence and honor; but in the Catholic mind it is love that prompts veneration for the Mother of Christ. It is indeed beyond comprehension that any who sincerely love Jesus, should be cold or indifferent in regard to His mother. No honor that we may pay her can ever equal that which God himself has conferred, and much less can it detract from the honor that is due to Him.

In keeping with her singular dignity is the power of Mary's intercession. If the prayers of holy men avail to obtain the divine assistance, the petitions of Mary in our behalf must be far more efficacious. With good reason, then, does the Church encourage the faithful to cultivate a tender devotion for the Blessed Virgin. But if all generations should call her blessed, and if the peoples of earth should glory in her protection, we in the United States have a particular duty to honor Mary Immaculate as the heavenly Patroness of our country. Let her blessed influence preserve our Catholic homes from all contagion of evil, and keep our children in pureness of heart. Let us also pay her the tribute of public honor in a way that will lead all our people to a fuller appreciation of Mary, the perfect woman and the surpassing model of motherhood. As Pope Benedict has declared, it is eminently fitting that the devotion of American Catholics to the Mother of God should find expression in a temple worthy of our Celestial Patroness. May the day soon dawn when we shall rejoice at the completion of so grand an undertaking; for, as the Holy Father says in commending the project of the National Shrine of the Immaculate Conception, "our human society has reached that stage in which it stands in most urgent

[37] Eph. iii. 19.

need of the aid of Mary Immaculate, no less than of the joint endeavors of all mankind." [38]

The nursery of Christian life is the Catholic home; its stronghold, the Catholic school. "In the great coming com-

Catholic Education.

bat between truth and error, between Faith and Agnosticism, an important part of the fray must be borne by the laity. . . . And if, in the olden days of vassalage and serfdom, the Church honored every individual, no matter how humble his position, and labored to give him the enlightenment that would qualify him for higher responsiblities, much more now, in the era of popular rights and liberties, when every individual is an active and influential factor in the body politic, does she desire that all should be fitted by suitable training for an intelligent and conscientious discharge of the important duties that may devolve upon them."

The timely warning contained in these words from the Pastoral Letter of 1884, shows how clearly our predecessors discerned the need, both present and future, of Christian education. Their forecast has been verified. The combat which they predicted has swept around all the sources of thought, and has centered upon the school. There, especially, the interests of morality and religion are at stake; and there, more than anywhere else, the future of the nation is determined. For that reason, we give most hearty thanks to the Father of Lights who has blessed our Catholic schools and made them to prosper. We invoke His benediction upon the men and women who have consecrated their lives to the service of Christian education. They are wholesome examples of the self-forgetfulness which is necessary in time of peace no less than in crisis and danger. Through their singleness of purpose and their sacrifice, the Church expresses the truth that education is indeed a holy work, not merely a service to the individual and society, but a furtherance of God's design for man's salvation. With them we realize more fully than ever before, the necessity of adhering to the principles on which our schools are established. If our present situation is beset

[38] Letter to the Hierarchy, April 10, 1919.

with new problems, it is also rich in opportunity; and we
are confident that our teachers will exert themselves to the
utmost in perfecting their work. Their united counsel in
the Catholic Educational Association has already produced
many excellent results, and it justifies the hope that our
schools may be organized into a system that will combine
the utilities of free initiative with the power of unified
action. With a common purpose so great and so holy to
guide them, and with a growing sense of solidarity, our
educators will recognize the advantage which concerted
effort implies both for the Catholic system as a whole and
for each of the allied institutions.

We deem it necessary at this time to emphasize the
value for our people of higher education, and the importance of providing and receiving it under Catholic auspices.
"Would that even now, as we trust will surely come to pass
in the future, the work of education were so ordered and
established that Catholic youth might proceed from our
Catholic elementary schools to Catholic schools of higher
grade and in these attain the object of their desires." [39]
This wish and ideal of our predecessors, in a gratifying
measure, has been realized through the establishment of
Catholic high schools and the development of our Catholic
colleges. These have more than doubled in number; they
have enlarged their facilities and adjusted their courses to
modern requirements. We congratulate their directors and
teachers, and with them we see in the present condition of
their institutions, the possibility and the promise of further
achievement in accordance with their own aspirations.

In educational progress, the teacher's qualification is
the vital element. This is manifestly true of the Catholic
school, in which the teacher's personality contributes so
much toward the building of character and the preservation
of faith along with the pupil's instruction in knowledge. If,
therefore, the aim of our system is to have Catholic youth
receive their education in its completeness from Catholic
sources, it is equally important, and even more urgently
necessary, that our teachers should be trained under those
influences and by those agencies which place the Catholic

[39] Third Plenary Council: Acts and Decrees, 208.

religion at the heart of instruction, as the vitalizing principle of all knowledge and, in particular, of educational theory and practice. We note with satisfaction that our teachers are eager for such training, and that measures have been taken to provide it through institutes, summer schools and collegiate courses under university direction. We are convinced that this movement will invigorate our education and encourage our people, since the work of teachers who are thoroughly prepared is the best recommendation of the school.

We cannot too highly approve the zeal and liberality of those who, with large amount or small, have aided us in building up our schools. For what we value as significant in their action is not alone the material help which it renders, essential as this has become; but rather and chiefly the evidence which it affords of their spiritual sense and perception. It shows that they appreciate both the necessity of Catholic education and the unselfish devotion of our teachers. At a time, especially, when vast fortunes are so freely lavished upon education in other lines, it is edifying to see our people either dedicating their individual wealth to the cause of religious instruction or, as members of Catholic associations, combining their means for the same noble purpose. They, assuredly, have given an object lesson, teaching all by their example, "to do good, to be rich in good works, to give easily, to communicate to others, to lay up in store for themselves a good foundation against the time to come, that they may lay hold on the true life." [40]

It was the progress of our academies, colleges and seminaries, from colonial days onward, that made the University possible; and it was the demand,
The Catholic   created by them, for larger opportunities
University.   that made it a necessity. Established, at
the instance of the Bishops, by Pope Leo XIII, it represents the joint action of the Holy See and of the American Hierarchy in behalf of higher education. Like the first universities of Europe, it was designed to be the home of all the sciences and the common base of all our educational forces. This twofold purpose has guided its

40 1 Tim. vi. 18-19.

development. As in the Ages of Faith and Enlightenment, the various Religious Orders gathered at the centers of learning which the Holy See had established, so in our own day, the Orders have grouped their houses of study about the University, in accordance with the express desire of its Founders. "We exhort you all," said the Pontiff, "to affiliate your seminaries, colleges and other Catholic institutions of learning with your University on the terms which its statutes suggest." [41] As the process of affiliation is extended to our high schools, it benefits them and also provides a better class of students for our colleges. In keeping, then, with the aims of its Founders, the University exists for the good and the service of all our schools. Through them and through their teachers, it returns with interest the generous support of our clergy and laity.

"By no means surprising or unexpected," said Pope Pius X, "is the steady and vigorous growth of the Catholic University which, located at Washington, the Capital City of the American Republic, built up by the offerings of the Catholic people and invested by the Apostolic See with full academic authority, is now become the fruitful parent of knowledge in all the sciences both human and divine. . . . We are fully determined on developing the Catholic University. For we clearly understand how much a Catholic university of high repute and influence can do toward spreading and upholding Catholic doctrine and furthering the cause of civilization. To protect it, therefore, and to quicken its growth, is, in Our judgment, equivalent to rendering most valuable service to religion and to country alike." [42]

To the same intent, Pope Benedict XV writes: "We have followed with joy its marvellous progress so closely related to the highest hope of your Churches . . . well knowing that you have all hitherto contributed in no small measure to the development of this seat of higher studies, both ecclesiastical and secular. Nor have we any doubt but that henceforth you will continue even more actively to support

[41] Apostolic Letter, *Magni Nobis gaudii*, March 7, 1889.
[42] Letter to the Cardinal Chancellor, Jan. 5, 1912.

an institution of such great usefulness and promise as is the University." [43]

It is our earnest desire that the University should attain fully the scope of its Founders, and thereby become an educational center worthy of the Church in America, worthy also of the zeal which our clergy and laity have shown in behalf of education. Its progress and prosperity will make it, as the Holy Father trusts, "the attractive center about which all will gather who love the teachings of our Catholic Faith."

Considering the great good accomplished by our Catholic societies, the Fathers of the Third Plenary Council expressed the desire "to see their number multiplied and their organization perfected." That desire has been fulfilled. The rapid development of our country provides ample occasion, even under normal conditions, for those activities which attain success through organization. Continually, new problems appear and opportunities arise to spread the Faith, to foster piety, to counteract tendencies which bode evil, either openly or under attractive disguise. In response to these demands, our Catholic associations have increased their usefulness by selecting special lines of activity, and by following these out wherever the cause of religion was in need or in peril. Through the hearty cooperation of clergy and laity, these agencies have wrought "good to all men, especially to those who are of the household of the faith." [44] They have enlisted our Catholic youth in the interests of faith and charity, provided in numberless ways for the helpless and poor, shielded the weak against temptation, spread sound ideas of social and industrial reform and furthered the public welfare by their patriotic spirit and action. We rejoice in the fruits of their fellowship, and we desire of them that they strive together for the highest and best, "considering one another to provoke unto charity and to good works." [45]

The tendency on the part of our societies to coalesce in larger organizations, is encouraging. It arises from their consciousness of the Catholic purpose for which each and

Catholic Societies.

[43] Letter to the Hierarchy, April 10, 1919. [44] Gal. vi. 10. [45] Heb. x. 24.

all are striving; and it holds out the promise of better results, both for the attainment of their several objects and for the promotion of their common cause, the welfare of the Church. The aim which inspired the Federation of our Catholic Societies, and which more recently has led to the Federation of Catholic Alumnae, is worthy of the highest commendation. It manifests a truly Catholic spirit, and it suggests wider possibilities for good which a more thorough organization will enable us to realize.

We regard as specially useful the work of associations like the Church Extension Society and the Missionary Unions, in securing the blessings of religion and the means of worship for those who suffer from poverty or isolation. The sections of our country in which Catholics are few, offer, no less than the populous centers, a field for zealous activity; and we heartily encourage all projects for assisting those who, in spite of adverse circumstances, have preserved the faith, for reclaiming many others who have lost it, and for bringing to our non-Catholic brethren the knowledge of our holy religion.

As we thus survey the progress of the Church in our country and throughout the world, we cannot but think of the greater good which might result if men of worthy disposition were all united   **Home** in faith. For we gladly recognize the up-   **Missions.** right will and generosity of many who are not yet "come to the city of the living God" and "to the Church of the first-born." [46] We know that among them are men of judgment, who with spiritual insight are looking to the Catholic Church for the sure way of salvation; and that not a few, with exceptional talent for historical research, have set forth in their scholarly writings the unbroken succession of the Church of Rome from the Apostles, the integrity of its doctrine and the steadfast power of its discipline. To all such earnest inquirers we repeat the invitation given them by Pope Leo XIII: "Let our fervent desire toward you, even more than our words, prevail. To you we appeal, our brethren who for over three centuries have differed from us regarding our Christian faith; and

[46] Heb. xii. 22.

to all of you likewise who in later times, for any reason whatsoever, have turned away from us. Let us all 'meet together in the unity of faith and of the knowledge of the Son of God.'[47] Suffer that we invite you to the unity which always has existed in the Catholic Church and which never can fail. Lovingly we stretch forth our hands to you; the Church, our mother and yours, calls upon you to return; the Catholics of the whole world await you with brotherly longing, that you together with us may worship God in holiness, with hearts united in perfect charity by the profession of one Gospel, one faith and one hope."[48]

We give thanks to our Lord Jesus Christ, for His mercy upon so many who were scattered abroad and in distress even as sheep that have no shepherd. Year by year, "the multitude of men and women who believe in the Lord is more increased."[49] But though conversions are numerous, much remains to be done. "Other sheep I have that are not of this fold: them also I must bring, and they shall hear my voice, and there shall be one fold and one shepherd."[50]

Pray fervently, therefore, that light may be given to those who yet are seeking the way, that they may understand the nature of that union and concord so clearly set forth by Christ himself, when He prayed to the Father, not only for His Apostles, "but for them also who through their word shall believe in me: that they all may be one, as thou, Father, in me and I in thee; that they also may be one in us, that the world may believe that thou hast sent me."[51] Now Christ and the Father are one, not by any outward bond of the least possible agreement but by perfect identity in all things.

In our own country there are fields of missionary labor that call in a special manner for assiduous cultivation. There are races less fortunate in a worldly

Negro and Indian Missions.
sense and, for that very reason, more fully dependent on Christian zeal. The lot of the Negro and Indian, though latterly much improved, is far from being what the Church would desire. Both have been hampered by ad-

47 Eph. iv. 13.   48 Apostolic Letter, *Præclara gratulationis*, June 20, 1894.
49 Acts v. 14.   50 John x. 16.   51 John xvii. 20, 21.

verse conditions, yet both are responsive to religious ministration. In the eyes of the Church there is no distinction
of race or of nation; there are human souls, and these have
all alike been purchased at the same great price, the blood
of Jesus Christ.

This is the truth that inspires our Catholic missionaries
and enables them to make such constant efforts in behalf
of those needy races. We commend their work to the faithful in every part of our country. In the name of justice
and charity, we deprecate most earnestly all attempts at
stirring up racial hatred; for this, while it hinders the progress of all our people, and especially of the Negro, in the
sphere of temporal welfare, places serious obstacles to the
advance of religion among them. We concur in the belief
that education is the practical means of bettering their condition; and we emphasize the need of combining moral and
religious training with the instruction that is given them in
other branches of knowledge. Let them learn from the
example and word of their teachers the lesson of Christian
virtue: it will help them more effectually than any skill
in the arts of industry, to solve their problems and to take
their part in furthering the general good.

"The mission which our Lord Jesus Christ, on the eve
of His return to the Father, entrusted to His disciples, bid-
ding them 'go into the whole world and
preach the Gospel to every creature'[52]—
that office most high and most holy—was
certainly not to end with the life of the
Apostles: it was to be continued by their successors even
to the consummation of the world, as long, namely, as there
should live upon earth men to be freed by the truth."[53]

These words of the Holy Father, addressed, with his
characteristic love of souls, to all the Bishops of the Church,
have for us in America a peculiar force and significance.
The care of our Catholic population, which is constantly
increased by the influx of immigrants from other countries,
hitherto has fully occupied the energies of our clergy and of
our missionary organizations. Until quite recently, the
Church in the United States was regarded as a missionary

Foreign Missions.

---

[52] Mark xvi. 15.   [53] Apostolic Letter, *Maximum illud*, Nov. 30, 1919.

field. As such it has drawn upon Europe for recruits to the priesthood and the religious Orders, and for financial assistance, which it owes so largely to the Society for the Propagation of the Faith.

The time now has come to show our grateful appreciation: "freely have you received, freely give." [54] Wherever we turn in this whole land, the memory of the pioneers of our Faith confronts us. Let it not appeal in vain. Let it not be said, to our reproach, that American commerce has outstripped American Catholic zeal, or that others have entered in to reap where Catholic hands had planted, perchance where Catholic blood had watered the soil.

"Lift up your eyes, and see the countries, for they are white already to harvest." [55] Consider the nations that lie to the south of our own, and in them the manifold needs of religion. Look to the farther East where of old a Francis Xavier spread the light of the Gospel. Think of the peoples in Asia, so long estranged from the Faith which their forefathers received from the Apostles. In some of these lands, entire populations grow up and pass away without hearing the name of Christ. In others, the seed of God's word has been planted and there is promise of vigorous growth; but there is none to gather the fruit. "The harvest indeed is great, but the laborers are few." [56]

"Pray ye therefore the Lord of the harvest that He send forth laborers into his harvest." [57] This, as the Holy Father reminds us, is our first obligation in regard to the missions. However eager the missionaries, they will labor in vain, unless God give the increase. This is also the appropriate object of the Apostleship of Prayer, whose members, to our great joy, are steadily becoming more numerous. Let all the faithful associate themselves with it and thus contribute, by their prayers at least, to the success of the missions.

In the next place, measures must be taken to increase the supply of laborers. They were few before the war; and now they are fewer. Unite with us, therefore, in praying that the special grace and vocation which this holy enterprise demands, may be granted more abundantly. We gladly encourage young men who feel in their souls the

[54] Matt. x. 8.   [55] John iv. 35.   [56] Matt. ix. 37.   [57] Ibid. 38.

prompting and desire for the missionary career. And we bless with cordial approval the efforts of those who, in our colleges and seminaries, develop this apostolic spirit and train up workers for the distant parts of the vineyard.

We appeal, finally, to the generosity of the faithful in behalf of the devoted men who already are bearing the heat of the day and the burden. They have given all. Let us help them at least to overcome the difficulties which the War has occasioned, and to develop the work which they are doing, with inadequate means, in their schools, orphanages and other institutions. So shall we have some part in their labors, and likewise in their reward. For "he that reapeth received wages, and gathereth fruit unto life everlasting; that both he that soweth and he that reapeth, may rejoice together." [58]

As the departments of Catholic activity multiply, and as each expands to meet an urgent need, the problem of securing competent leaders and workers becomes day by day more serious. The   Vocations. success of a religious enterprise depends to some extent upon the natural ability and character of those who have it in charge. But if it be truly the work of God, it must be carried on by those whom He selects. To His Apostles the Master said: "You have not chosen me: but I have chosen you, and have appointed you, that you should go and should bring forth fruit; and your fruit should remain." [59] Of the priesthood St. Paul declares: "Neither doth any man take the honor to himself, but he that is called of God." [60] The same applies, in due proportion, to all who would enter the Master's service in any form of the religious state. And since our educational, charitable and missionary undertakings are for the most part conducted by the Priest, the Brother and the Sister, the number of vocations must increase to supply the larger demand.

God, assuredly, in His unfailing providence, has marked for the grace of vocation those who are to serve Him as His chosen instruments. It lies with us to recognize these vessels of election and to set them apart, that they may be duly

[58] John iv. 36.   [59] John xv. 16.   [60] Heb. v. 4.

fashioned and tempered for the uses of their calling. To this end, we charge all those who have the care of souls to note the signs of vocation, to encourage young men and women who manifest the requisite dispositions, and to guide them with prudent advice. Let parents esteem it a privilege surpassing all worldly advantage, that God should call their sons or daughters to His service. Let teachers also remember that, after the home, the school is the garden in which vocations are fostered. To discern them in time, to hedge them about with careful direction, to strengthen and protect them against worldly allurement, should be our constant aim.

In our concern and desire for the increase of vocations, we are greatly encouraged as we reflect upon the blessings which the Church has enjoyed in this respect. The generosity of so many parents, the sacrifices which they willingly make that their children may follow the calling of God, and the support so freely given to institutions for the training of priests and religious, are edifying and consoling. For such proofs of zeal, we return most hearty thanks to Him who is pleased to accept from His faithful servants the offering of the gifts which He bestows.

The training of those who are called to the priesthood, is at once a privilege and a grave responsibility. This holiest of all educational duties we entrust to the directors and teachers of our seminaries. Because they perform it faithfully, we look with confidence to the future, in the assurance that our clergy will be fully prepared for the tasks which await them. "That the man of God may be perfect, furnished to every good work"[61] is the end for which the seminary exists. The model which it holds up is no other than Jesus Christ. Its course of instruction begins with St. Paul's exhortation: "holy brethren, partakers of the heavenly vocation, consider the apostle and high priest of our confession, Jesus;"[62] and it ends with the promise: "thou shalt be a good minister of Christ Jesus, nourished up in the words of faith and of the good doctrine which thou hast attained unto."[63]

The functions of the Catholic Press are of special value

[61] 2 Tim. iii. 17.   [62] Heb. iii. 1.   [63] 1 Tim. iv. 6.

to the Church in our country. To widen the interest of our
people by acquainting them with the prog-
ress of religion throughout the world, to   The Catholic
correct false or misleading statements re-   Press.
garding our belief and practice, and, as
occasion offers, to present our doctrine in popular form—
these are among the excellent aims of Catholic journalism.
As a means of forming sound public opinion it is indispensable. The vital issues affecting the nation's welfare usually
turn upon moral principles. Sooner or later, discussion
brings forward the question of right and wrong. The
treatment of such subjects from the Catholic point of view,
is helpful to all our people. It enables them to look at
current events and problems in the light of the experience
which the Church has gathered through centuries, and it
points the surest way to a solution that will advance our
common interests.

The unselfish zeal displayed by Catholic journalists entitles them to a more active support than hitherto has been
given. By its very nature the scope of their work is spe-
cialized; and, within the limitations thus imposed, they are
doing what no other agency could accomplish or attempt,
in behalf of our homes, societies and schools.

In order to obtain the larger results and the wider appreciation which their efforts deserve and which we most
earnestly desire, steps must be taken to coordinate the various lines of publicity and secure for each a higher degree of usefulness. Each will then offer to those who are
properly trained, a better opportunity for service in this
important field.

At all times helpful to the cause of religion, a distinc-
tively Catholic literature is the more urgently needed now
that, owing to the development of scholarship in our country and the progress of education, there has grown up a
taste for reading and, among many of our people, a desire
for accurate knowledge of the Church. In recent times, and
notably during the past three decades, there has been a
gratifying increase in the number of Catholic authors,
and their activity has been prolific of good results. By the
simple process of telling the truth about our faith and its

practice, they have removed, to a considerable extent, those prejudices and erroneous views which so often hinder even fairminded thinkers from understanding our position. As so much had been accomplished by individual writers in this and other countries, it was wisely thought that even greater benefit would accrue from their cooperation. The realization of this idea in the Catholic Encyclopedia has given us a monumental work, and opened to all inquirers a storehouse of information regarding the Church, its history, constitution and doctrine. It has furthermore shown the value and power for good of united effort in behalf of a high common purpose; and we therefore trust that while serving as a means of instruction to our clergy and people, it will give inspiration to other endeavors with similar aim and effect, in every field of Catholic action.

The progress of the Church which we have reviewed, has been no easy achievement. There have The Obvious been trials and difficulties; and as Christ Outcome. predicted, there have been frequent at-tempts to hamper the Church just where and when it was doing the greatest good for our common humanity.

In the net result, however, the Church has been strengthened, to its own profit and to that of the world at large. In an age that is given to material pursuits, it upholds the ideals of the spiritual life. To minds that see only intellectual values, it teaches the lesson of moral obligation. Amid widespread social confusion, it presents in concrete form the principle of authority as the basis of social order. And it appears as the visible embodiment of faith and hope and charity, at the very time when the need of these is intensified by conditions in the temporal order.

II. SECULAR CONDITIONS

The temporal order, in the last thirty-five years, has undergone radical changes. It has been affected by movements which, though checked for a time or reversed, have steadily gathered momentum. Their direction and goal are no longer matters of surmise or suspicion. Their outcome is plainly before us.

During the first three decades of this period, the advance of civilization was more rapid and more general than in any earlier period of equal length. The sound of progress, echoing beyond its traditional limits, aroused all the nations to a sense of their possibilities, and stirred each with an ambition to win its share in the forward movement of the world. At the same time, the idea of a human weal for whose promotion all should strive and by whose attainment all should profit, seemed to be gaining universal acceptance. If rivalry here and there gave occasion for friction or conflict, it was treated as incidental; the general desire for harmony, apparently, was nearing fulfilment.

Toward this end the highest tendencies in the secular order were steadily converging. A wider diffusion of knowledge provided the basis for a mutual understanding of rights and obligations. Science, while attaining more completely to the mastery of nature, placed itself more effectually at the service of man. Through its practical applications, it hastened material progress, facilitated the intercourse of nation with nation, and thus lowered the natural barriers of distance and time. But it also made possible a fuller exchange of ideas, and thereby revealed to the various peoples of earth that in respect of need, aspiration and purpose, they had more in common than generally was supposed. It helped them to see that however they differed in race, tradition and language, in national temper and political organization, they were humanly one in the demand for freedom with equal right and opportunity.

As this consciousness developed in mankind at large, the example of our own country grew in meaning and influence. For a century and more, it had taught the world that men could live and prosper under free institutions. During the period in question, it has continued to receive the multitudes who came not, as in the early days, from a few countries only, but from every foreign land, to enjoy the blessings of liberty and to better their worldly condition. In making them its own, America has shown a power of assimilation that is without precedent in the temporal order. With their aid it has undertaken and achieved industrial tasks on a scale unknown to former generations.

The wealth thus produced has been used in generous measure to build up institutions of public utility. Education, in particular, has flourished; its importance has been more fully recognized, its problems more widely discussed, the means of giving and obtaining it more freely supplied. While its aim has been to raise the intellectual level and thereby enhance the worth of the individual, experience has shown the advantage of organized effort for the accomplishment of any purpose in which the people as a whole, or any considerable portion, has an interest. Hence the remarkable development of associations which, though invested with no authority, have become powerful enough to shape public opinion and even to affect the making of laws. If, in some instances, the power of association has been directed toward ends that were at variance with the general good and by methods which created disturbance, there has been, on the whole, a willingness to respect authority and to abide by its decisions.

Thus, as it appeared, the whole trend of human affairs was securing the world in peace. The idea of war was farthest from the minds of the peoples. The possibility of war had ceased to be a subject for serious discussion. To adjust their disputes, the nations had set up a tribunal. The volume of seeming prosperity swelled.

III. CATHOLIC WAR ACTIVITIES

Once it had been decided that our country should enter the War, no words of exhortation were needed to arouse the Catholic spirit. This had been shown in every national crisis. It had stirred to eloquent expression the Fathers of the Third Plenary Council.

"We consider the establishment of our country's independence, the shaping of its liberties and laws, as a work of special Providence, its framers 'building better than they knew,' the Almighty's hand guiding them. . . . We believe that our country's heroes were the instruments of the God of nations in establishing this home of freedom; to both the Almighty and to His instruments in the work we look with grateful reverence; and to maintain the inheritance of freedom which they have left us, should it ever—which God forbid—be imperilled, our Catholic citizens will be found to stand forward as one man, ready to pledge anew 'their lives, their fortunes and their sacred honor.' "

The prediction · has been fulfilled. The traditional patriotism of our Catholic people has been amply demonstrated in the day of their country's trial. And we look with pride upon the record which proves, as no mere protestation could prove, the devotion of American Catholics to the cause of American freedom.

To safeguard the moral and physical welfare of our Catholic soldiers and sailors, organized action was needed. The excellent work already accomplished by the Knights of Columbus, pointed the way to further undertaking. The unselfish patriotism with which our various societies combined their forces in the Catholic Young Men's Association, the enthusiasm manifested by the organizations of Catholic women, and the eagerness of our clergy to support the cause of the nation, made it imperative to unify the energies of the whole Catholic body and direct them toward the American purpose. With this end in view, the National Catholic War Council was formed by the Hierarchy. Through the Committee on Special War Activities and the Knights of Columbus Committee on War Activities, the efforts of our people in various lines were coordinated and rendered more effective, both in providing for the spiritual needs of all Catholics under arms and in winning our country's success. This unified action was worthy of the Catholic name. It was in keeping with the pledge which the Hierarchy had given our Government: "Our people, now as ever, will rise as one man to serve the nation. Our priests and consecrated women will once again, as in every former trial of our country, win by their bravery, their heroism and their service new admiration and approval." [64]

To our Chaplains especially we give the credit that is their due for the faithful performance of their obligations. In the midst of danger and difficulty, under the new and trying circumstances which war inevitably brings, they acted as priests.

The account of our men in the Service adds a new page

[64] Letter to the President, April 18, 1917,

to the record of Catholic loyalty. It is what we expected and what they took for granted. But it has a significance that will be fairly appreciated when normal conditions return. To many assertions it answers with one plain fact.

IV. THE NATIONAL CATHOLIC WELFARE COUNCIL

In view of the results obtained through the merging of our activities for the time and purpose of war, we determined to maintain, for the ends of peace, the spirit of union and the coordination of our forces. We have accordingly grouped together, under the National Catholic Welfare Council, the various agencies by which the cause of religion is furthered. Each of these, continuing its own special work in its chosen field, will now derive additional support through general cooperation. And all will be brought into closer contact with the Hierarchy, which bears the burden alike of authority and of responsibility for the interests of the Catholic Church.

Under the direction of the Council and, immediately, of the Administrative Committee, several Departments have been established, each with a specific function, as follows:

The Department of Education, to study the problems and conditions which affect the work and development of our Catholic schools;

The Department of Social Welfare, to coordinate those activities which aim at improving social conditions in accordance with the spirit of the Church;

The Department of Press and Literature, to systematize the work of publication;

The Department of Societies and Lay Activities, to secure a more thoroughly unified action among our Catholic organizations.

For the development and guidance of missionary activity, provision has been made through The American Board of Catholic Missions, which will have in charge both the Home and the Foreign Missions.

The organization of these Departments is now in progress. To complete it, time and earnest cooperation will be required. The task assigned to each is so laborious and yet

so promising of results, that we may surely expect, with
the Divine assistance and the loyal support of our clergy
and people, to promite more effectually the glory of God,
the interests of His Church, and the welfare of our country.

V. LESSONS OF THE WAR

In order that our undertakings may be wisely selected
and prudently carried on, we should consider seriously the
lessons of the War, the nature of our present situation and
the principles which must guide the adjustment of all our
relations.

Our estimate of the War begins, naturally, with the
obvious facts: with the number of peoples involved, the
vastness and effectiveness of their armaments, the outlay in
treasure and toil, the destruction of life and the consequent
desolation which still lies heavy on the nations of Europe.
Besides these visible aspects, we know somewhat of the
spiritual suffering—of the sorrow and hopelessness which
have stricken the souls of men. And deeper than these,
beyond our power of estimation, is the moral evil, the
wrong whose magnitude only the Searcher of hearts can
determine.

For we may not forget that in all this strife of the peoples, in the loosening of passion and the seeking of hate,
sin abounded. Not the rights of man alone but the law of
God was openly disregarded. And if we come before Him
now in thankfulness, we must come with contrite hearts, in
all humility beseeching Him that He continue His mercies
toward us, and enable us so to order our human relations
that we may atone for our past transgressions and
strengthen the bond of peace with a deeper charity for our
fellowmen and purer devotion to His service.

We owe it to His goodness that our country has been
spared the suffering and desolation which war has spread
so widely. Our homes, our natural resources, our means of
intercourse and the institutions which uphold the life of
our nation, have all been preserved. We are free, without
let or hindrance, to go forward in the paths of industry,
of culture, of social improvement and moral reform. The

sense of opportunity has quickened us, and we turn with eagerness to a future that offers us boundless advantage.

Let us not turn hastily. Our recent experience has taught us innumerable lessons, too full and profund to be mastered at once. Their ultimate meaning a later generation will ponder and comprehend. But even now we can recognize the import of this conspicuous fact: a great nation conscious of power yet wholly given to peace and unskilled in the making of war, gathered its might and put forth its strength in behalf of freedom and right as the inalienable endowment of all mankind. When its aims were accomplished, it laid down its arms, without gain or acquisition, save in the clearer understanding of its own ideals and the fuller appreciation of the blessings which freedom alone can bestow.

The achievement was costly. It meant interruption of peaceful pursuits, hardship at home and danger abroad. Not one class or state or section, but the people as a whole had to take up the burden. This spirit of union and sacrifice for the common weal, found its highest expression in the men and women who went to do service in distant lands. To them, and especially to those who died that America might live, we are forever indebted. Their triumph over self is the real victory, their loyalty the real honor of our nation, their fidelity to duty the bulwark of our freedom.

To such men and their memory, eulogy is at best a poor tribute. We shall not render them their due nor show ourselves worthy to name them as our own, unless we inherit their spirit and make it the soul of our national life. The very monuments we raise in their honor will become a reproach to us, if we fail in those things of which they have left us such splendid example.

VI. THE PRESENT SITUATION

We entered the War with the highest of objects, proclaiming at every step that we battled for the right and pointing to our country as a model for the world's imitation. We accepted therewith the responsibility of leadership in accomplishing the task that lies before mankind. The world awaits our fulfilment. Pope Benedict himself has declared that our people, "retaining a most firm hold on the principles of reasonable liberty and of Christian civilization, are destined to have the chief rôle in the restoration of peace and order on the basis of those same principles, when the violence of these tempestuous days shall have passed." [65]

This beyond doubt is a glorious destiny, far more in keeping with the aims of our people than the triumph of armies or the conquest of wider domain. Nor is it an impossible destiny, provided we exemplify in our own national life "the principles of reasonable liberty and of Christian civilization."

At present, however, we are confronted with problems at home that give us the gravest concern. Intent as we were on restoring the order of Europe, we did not sufficiently heed the symptoms of unrest in our own country, nor did we reckon with movements which, in their final result, would undo both our recent achievement and all that America has so far accomplished.

These are due, partly, to the disturbance which war invariably causes, by turning men away from their usual occupations, by reducing production, increasing taxation and adding to the number of those who are dependent and helpless. The majority of the people do not realize to what an extent the necessities of war diverted industrial and other activities from their ordinary course. There naturally results irritation and impatience at the slowness with which reconstruction proceeds.

Deeper and more ominous is the ferment in the souls of men, that issues in agitation not simply against defects in the operation of the existing order, but also against that order itself, its framework and very foundation. In such a temper men see only the facts—the unequal distribution of wealth, power and worldly advantage—and against the facts they rebel. But they do not discern the real causes that produce those effects, and much less the adequate means by which both causes and effects can be removed. Hence, in the attempt at remedy, methods are employed which result in failure, and beget a more hopeless confusion.

[65] Letter to the Hierarchy, April 10, 1919.

To men of clearer vision and calmer judgment, there comes the realization that the things on which they relied for the world's security, have broken under the strain. The advance of civilization, the diffusion of knowledge, the un-limited freedom of thought, the growing relaxation of moral restraint—all these, it was believed, had given such ample scope to individual aims and desires that conflict, if it arose at all, could be readily and thoroughly adjusted.

The assumption is not borne out by the facts. On the contrary, as in the War destruction was swifter and wider because of the progress of science, so our present situation is complicated by increased ability to plan, to organize and to execute in any direction that may lead to any success. Education provided at the public expense can now be used as the strongest means of attacking the public weal; and to this end it will surely be used unless thinking and doing be guided by upright motives. The consciousness of power, quickened by our achievement in war but no longer checked by discipline nor directed to one common purpose, has aroused parties, organizations and even individuals to a boldness of undertaking hitherto unknown. The result is an effort to press onward in the pursuit of self-appointed ends, with little regard for principles and still less for the altruism which we professed on entering the War.

On the other hand, it is true, intelligence, initiative and energy have been exerted to accomplish higher and worth-ier aims. It was thought that the enthusiasm and eager-ness for service which war had called forth, might easily be directed toward useful and needed reforms. With this persuasion for their impulse and guidance, various move-ments have been inaugurated either to uproot some evil or to further some promising cause.

Now it is obvious that neither the pursuit of lofty ideals nor earnest devotion to the general welfare, can do away with the fact that we are facing grave peril. Much less can we hide that fact from view by increasing the means and following the inclination to pleasure. No sadder contrast indeed can be found than that which appears between careless enjoyment in countless forms, and the grim strug-gle that is shaking the foundations of social existence.

Craving for excitement and its reckless gratification may blind us to danger; but the danger is none the less real.

The practical conclusion which the present situation forces upon us, is this: to bring order out of confusion, we must first secure a sound basis and then build up consistently. Mere expedients no longer suffice. To cover up evil with a varnish of respectability or to rear a grand structure on the quicksand of error, is downright folly. In spite of great earnestness on the part of their leaders, reforms without number have failed, because they moved along the surface of life, smoothing indeed its outward defects, yet leaving the source of corruption within.

One true reform the world has known. It was effected, not by force, agitation or theory, but by a Life in which the perfect ideal was visibly realized, becoming the "light of men." That light has not   Christ and
grown dim with the passing of time. Men   the Church.
have turned their eyes away from it; even
His followers have strayed from its pathway; but the truth and the life of Jesus Christ are real and clear today—for all who are willing to see. There is no other name under heaven whereby the world can be saved.

Through the Gospel of Jesus and His living example, mankind learned the meaning, and received the blessing, of liberty. In His person was shown the excellence and true dignity of human nature, wherein human rights have their center. In His dealings with men, justice and mercy, sympathy and courage, pity for weakness and rebuke for hollow pretence, were perfectly blended. Having fulfilled the law, He gave to His followers a new commandment. Having loved His own who were in the world, He loved them to the end. And since He came that they might have life and have it more abundantly, He gave it to them through His death.

The Church which Christ established has continued His work, upholding the dignity of man, defending the rights of the people, relieving distress, consecrating sacrifice and binding all classes together in the love of their Saviour. The combination of authority and reasonable freedom which is the principal element in the organization of the

Church, is also indispensable in our social relations. Without it, there can be neither order nor law nor genuine freedom.

But the Church itself would have been powerless save for the abiding presence of Christ and his Spirit. "Without me, you can do nothing;" but again, "Behold I am with you all days." Both these sayings are as true today as when they were spoken by the Master. There may be philosophies and ideals and schemes of reform; the wise may deliberate and the powerful exert their might; but when the souls of men have to be reached and transformed to a better sense, that justice may reign and charity abound, then more than ever is it true that without Christ our efforts are vain.

Instructed by His example, the Church deals with men as they really are, recognizing both the capacities for good and the inclinations to evil that are in every human being. Exaggeration in either direction is an error. That the world has progressed in many respects, is obviously true; but it is equally plain that the nature of man is what it was twenty centuries ago. Those who overlooked this fact, were amazed at the outbreak of war among nations that were foremost in progress. But now it is evident that beneath the surface of civilization lay smoldering the passions and jealousies that in all time past had driven nations to conflict. Pope Benedict expressed this truth when he pointed to the causes of war: lack of mutual good will, contempt for authority, conflict of class with class, and absorption in the pursuit of the perishable goods of this world, with utter disregard of things that are nobler and worthier of human endeavor.[66]

The Sources of Evil.

These are the seed and prolific sources of evil. As tendencies perhaps, they cannot be wholly extirpated; but to justify them as principles of action, to train them into systems of philosophy and let them, through education, become the thought of the people, would be fatal to all our true interests. As long as the teaching of false theory continues, we cannot expect that men will act in accordance

[66] Encyc. *Ad beatissimi* Nov. 1, 1914.

with truth. It is a mistake to suppose that philosophy has a meaning for only the chosen few who enjoy the advantage of higher education and leisurely thinking; and it is worse than a mistake to punish men for acting out pernicious ideas, while the development and diffusion of those same ideas is rewarded as advancement of knowledge. We surely need no further proof of the dangers of materialism, of atheism and of other doctrines that banish God from His world, degrade man to the level of the brute and reduce the moral order to a struggle for existence. Argument against such doctrines, or theoretical testing of their value, is superfluous, now that we see the result of their practical application. And while, with every legitimate means we strive, as we must, to uphold the rights of the public by the maintenance of order, let us be fully convinced that we are dealing with the final and logical outcome of false doctrine. Here again the source lies farther back. If we find that the fruit is evil, we should know what to do with the root.

It cannot be denied that the growth of knowledge and its application to practical needs have made the earth a better habitation for man; many appear to consider it as his first and only abode. As **The** the means of enjoyment are multiplied, **Fundamental** there is an increasing tendency to become **Error.** absorbed in worldly pursuits and to neglect those which belong to our eternal welfare. The trend of speculative thought is in the same direction; for while the development of science continually affords us evidence of law and order and purpose in the world about us, many refuse to acknowledge in creation the work of an intelligent author. They profess to see in the universe only the manifestation of a Power, whose effects are absolutely determined through the operation of mechanical forces; and they extend this conception to life and all its relations. But once this view is accepted, it is easy to draw the conclusion that the really decisive factor in human affairs is force. Whether by cunning or by violence, the stronger is sure to prevail. It is a law unto itself and it is accountable to none other, since the idea of a Supreme Lawgiver has vanished.

This indeed is the root-evil whence spring the immediate causes of our present condition. God, from whom all things are and on whom all things depend, the Creator and Ruler of men, the source and sanction of righteousness, the only Judge who with perfect justice can weigh the deeds and read the hearts of men, has, practically at least, disappeared from the whole conception of life so far as this is dominated by a certain type of modern thought. Wherever this sort of thinking is taken as truth, there is set up a scheme of life, individual, social and political, which seeks, not in the eternal but in the human and transitory, its ultimate foundation. The law of morals is regarded as a mere convention arranged by men to secure and enjoy the goods of this present time; and conscience itself as simply a higher form of the instinct whereby the animal is guided. And yet withal it lies in the very nature of man that something must be supreme, something must take the place of the divine when this has been excluded; and this substitute for God, according to a predominant philosophy, is the State.   Possessed of unlimited power to establish rights and impose obligations, the State becomes the sovereign ruler in human affairs; its will is the last word of justice, its welfare the determinant of moral values, its service the final aim of man's existence and action.

When such an estimate of life and its purpose is accepted, it is idle to speak of the supreme value of righteousness, the sacredness of justice or the
God sanctity of conscience. Nevertheless, these
the Supreme are things that must be retained, in name
Ruler. and in reality: the only alternative is that
supremacy of force against which humanity protests. To make the protest effectual, it is imperative that we recognize in God the source of justice and right; in His law, the sovereign rule of life; in the destiny which He has appointed for us, the ultimate standard by which all values are fixed and determined. Reverent acknowledgment of our dependence on Him and our responsibility to Him, acknowledgment not in word alone but in the conduct of our lives, is at once our highest duty and our strongest title to the enjoyment of our rights. This acknowledg-

ment we express in part by our service of prayer and worship. But prayer and worship will not avail, unless we also render the broader service of good will which, in conformity with His will, follows the path of duty in every sphere of life.

As we are not the authors of our own being, so we are not, in an absolute sense, masters of ourselves and of our powers. We may not determine for ourselves the ultimate aim of our existence or the means of its attainment. God has established, by the very constitution of our nature, the end for which He created us, giving us life as a sacred trust to be administered in accordance with His design. Thereby He has also established the norm of our individual worth, and the basis of our real independence. Obedience to His law, making our wills identical with His, invests us with a personal dignity which neither self-assertion nor the approval of others can ever bestow. The man who bows in obedience to the law of his Maker, rises above himself and above the world to an independence that has no bounds save the Infinite. To do as God commands, whatever the world may think or say, is to be free, not by human allowance but under the approval of Him whose service is perfect freedom.

In the light of this central truth, we can understand and appreciate the principle on which our American liberties are founded—"that all men are endowed by their Creator with certain inalienable rights." These are conferred by God with equal bounty upon every human being, and therefore, in respect of life, liberty and the pursuit of happiness, the same rights belong to all men and for the same reason. Not by mutual concession or covenant, not by warrant or grant from the State, are these rights established; they are the gift and bestowal of God. In consequence of this endowment, and therefore in obedience to the Creator's will, each of us is bound to respect the rights of his fellowmen. This is the essential meaning of justice, the great law antecedent to all human enactment and contrivance, the only foundation on which may rest securely the fabric of society and the structure of our political, legal and economic systems.

VII. JUSTICE

The obligation to give every man his due, is binding at all times and under all conditions. It permits no man to say, I will be just only when justice falls in with my aims, or furthers my interests; and I will refrain from injustice when this would expose me to failure, to loss of reputation or to penalty enacted by law. The obligation is binding in conscience, that representative of God which He has established in our innermost selves, which requires our obedience not merely out of self-respect or as a matter of our preference, but as speaking in His name and expressing His mandate.

Let this spirit of justice and conscientious observance prevail in the dealings of man with man: it will soon determine what practices are honest, what methods are justified by the necessities of competition, by economic law, by opportunity of profit, by the silence of the civil law or the laxity of its administration. It will weigh in the same even balance the deeds of every man, whatever his station or power; and it will appraise at their true moral value all schemes and transactions, whether large or small, whether conducted by individuals or groups or complex organizations.

The same spirit of justice that condemns dishonesty in private dealings, must condemn even more emphatically any and every attempt on the part of individuals to further their interests at the expense of the public welfare. The upright citizen refuses as a matter of conscience to defraud his neighbor, to violate his pledges or to take unfair advantage. Likewise, in his business relations with the community as a whole, whatever the character of his service, he is careful to observe the prescriptions of justice. He feels that if it is wrong to overreach or circumvent his brother in any matter, the wrong is not less but far more grevious when inflicted on the commonwealth.

The true remedy for many of the disorders with which we are troubled, is to be found in a clearer understanding of civil authority. Rulers and people alike must be guided by the truth that the State is not merely an invention of human forethought, that its power is not created by human agree-

ment or even by nature's device. Destined as we are by our
Maker to live together in social intercourse and mutual co-
operation for the fulfilment of our duties,
the proper development of our faculties   Origin of
and the adequate satisfaction of our wants,   Authority.
our association can be orderly and pros-
perous only when the wills of the many are directed by
that moral power which we call authority. This is the
unifying and coordinating principle of the social structure. It has its origin in God alone. In whom it shall
be vested and by whom exercised, is determined in various
ways, sometimes by the outcome of circumstances and providential events, sometimes by the express will of the people. But the right which it possesses to legislate, to execute
and administer, is derived from God himself. "There is
no power but from God; and those that are, are ordained of
God." [67] Consequently, "he that resisteth the power, resisteth the ordinance of God." [68]

The State, then, has a sacred claim upon our respect and
loyalty. It may justly impose obligations and demand
sacrifices, for the sake of the common welfare which it is established to promote.   Powers
It is the means to an end, not an end in   of the State.
itself; and because it receives its power
from God, it cannot rightfully exert that power through any
act or measure that would be at variance with the divine
law, or with the divine economy for man's salvation.
As long as the State remains within its proper limits and
really furthers the common good, it has a right to our obedience. And this obedience we are bound to render, not
merely on grounds of expediency but as a conscientious
duty. "Be subject of necessity, not only for wrath but also
for conscience sake." [69]

The end for which the State exists and for which authority is given it, determines the limit of its powers. It must
respect and protect the divinely established rights of the
individual and of the family. It must safeguard the liberty
of all, so that none shall encroach upon the rights of others.
But it may not rightfully hinder the citizen in the discharge

[67] Romans xiii. 1.   [68] *Ibid.* 2.   [69] *Ibid.* 5.

of his conscientious obligation, and much less in the performance of duties which he owes to God. To all commands that would prevent him from worshipping the Creator in spirit and truth, the citizen will uphold his right by saying with the Apostles: "We ought to obey God rather than men." [70]

Where the State protects all in the reasonable exercise of their rights, there liberty exists. "The nature of human liberty," says Leo XIII, "however it be considered, whether in the individual or in society, whether in those who are governed or in those who govern, supposes the necessity of obedience to a supreme and eternal law, which is no other than the authority of God, commanding good and forbidding evil; and so far from destroying or even diminishing their liberty, the just authority of God over men protects it and makes it perfect." [71]

The State itself should be the first to appreciate the importance of religion for the preservation of the common weal. It can ill afford at any time, and least of all in the present condition of the world, to reject the assistance which Christianity offers for the maintenance of peace and order. "Let princes and rulers of the people," says Pope Benedict XV, "bear this in mind and bethink themselves whether it be wise and salutary, either for public authority or for the nations themselves, to set aside the holy religion of Jesus Christ, in which that very authority may find such powerful support and defense. Let them seriously consider whether it be the part of political wisdom to exclude from the ordinance of the State and from public instruction, the teaching of the Gospel and of the Church. Only too well does experience show that when religion is banished, human authority totters to its fall. That which happened to the first of our race when he failed in his duty to God, usually happens to nations as well. Scarcely had the will in him rebelled against God when the passions arose in rebellion against the will; and likewise, when the rulers of the people disdain the authority of God, the people in turn despise the authority of men. There remains, it is true, the usual expedient of suppressing rebellion by force; but to

---

70 Acts v. 29.   71 Encyc. *Libertas præstantissimum*, June 20, 1888.

what effect? Force subdues the bodies of men, not their souls." [72]

VIII. CHARITY

The spiritual endowment of man, his rights and his liberties have their source in the goodness of God. Infinitely just as Ruler of the world, He is infinitely good as Father of mankind. He uses His supreme authority to lay upon men the commandment of love. "Thou shalt love the Lord thy God with thy whole heart, and with thy whole soul, and with thy whole mind. This is the greatest and the first commandment. And the second is like to this: thou shalt love thy neighbor as thyself." [73]

Let us not persuade ourselves that we have fully complied with the divine law in regard to our relations with our fellowmen, when we have carefully discharged all the obligations of justice. For its safeguard and completion, the stern law of justice looks to the gentler but none the less obligatory law of charity. Justice presents our fellowman as an exacting creditor, who rightly demands the satisfaction of his rightful claims. Charity calls on us as children of the one universal family whose Father is God, to cherish for one another active brotherly love second only to the love which we owe to Him. "It is not enough," says St. Thomas, "that peace and concord reign among the citizens: love also must prevail. Justice prevents them from injuring one another; it does not require them to help one another. Yet it often happens that some need aid which falls under no obligation of justice. Here charity steps in and summons us to further service in the name of the love we owe to God." [74] Though different in kind from justice, the precept of charity imposes duties which we may not disregard. To love the neighbor is not simply a matter of option or a counsel which they may follow who aim at moral perfection: it is a divine command that is equally binding on all. It extends beyond kindred and friends to include all men, and it obligates us in thought and will no less than in outward action.

As commonly understood, charity is manifested in deeds

---

[72] Encyc. *Ad beatissimi,* November 1, 1914.
[73] Matt. xxii. 37-39.   [74] Contra Gentes. iii. 129.

that tend to the relief of suffering in any of its various forms, or that provide opportunities of advancement for those who have none, or that add somewhat to the scant pleasure of many laborious lives. And these beyond question are deeds that deserve all praise. But it is in the source whence they come, in the good will which prompts them, that the essence of charity consists. We may love others from a sense of our common humanity, from sympathy, from natural pity for pain and distress. Yet this benevolence is securely based and immeasurably ennobled, when it is quickened with the higher motive of love for God, the heavenly Father. Then the pale form of altruism or humanitarianism is replaced by the divine presence of charity.

By its very nature, charity is a social virtue. Wherever a social group is formed—in the home, the community, the civic association—good will is a necessity. It is charity rather than justice that overcomes selfishness, casts out rancour, forbids hatred, clears away misunderstanding, leads to reconciliation. After justice has rendered impartial decision, it is charity that brings men back to fellowship. And if at times it be fitting that mercy should season justice, the quality of mercy itself is but charity touched to compassion.

The law of charity is essentially the law of the Gospel, the "new commandment" which Jesus gave His disciples.

The Law of the Gospel. It is the distinctive badge of the Christian: "By this shall all men know that you are my disciples, if you have love one for another." [75] And more than this: the Incarnation itself was evidence of the divine goodwill toward men: "By this hath the charity of God appeared toward us, because God hath sent his only begotten Son into the world that we may live by Him." [76]

It is therefore significant that, as the world moves farther away from Christ and loses the spirit of His teaching, there should be less and less of the charity which He would have His disciples to practice. On the other hand, we, as Christians, must ask ourselves whether we have so fully observed the "new commandment" of love as to leave the

[75] John xiii. 35.   [76] 1 John iv. 9.

world without excuse for its unbelief. There are countless forms of charity which seek no publicity and ask no earthly reward: these the world could hardly be expected to know. But it cannot help seeing such evidences of love as appear in the ordinary conduct of genuine Christians, in their daily intercourse, their speech and habits of thought. That men in exceptional conditions should rise to great heights of self-sacrifice, is proof indeed of a natural disposition, which may remain latent until it is stirred into action by sudden disaster or national peril: then it becomes heroic. Charity, however, does not wait for such occasions; it finds its opportunity in season and out of season, and it makes heroes of men in peace no less than in war. This, then, should be our concern, this constant exercise of good will toward all men, that they may see in us the disciples of Christ and be led to Him through the power of love.

IX. SOCIAL RELATIONS

The security of the nation and the efficiency of government for the general weal depend largely upon the standards which are adopted, and the practices which are admitted, in social relations. This is characteristic of a democracy, where the makers of law are commissioned to do the will of the people. In matters pertaining to morality, legislation will not rise above the level established by the general tone and tenor of society. It is necessary, then, for the preservation of national life, that social morality, in its usage and sanction, be sound and steadfast and pure.

This aim can be accomplished only by reaching the sources in which life has its origin, and from which the individual character receives its initial direction. As the family is the first social **Marriage.** group, it is also the center whose influence permeates the entire social body. And since family life takes its rise from the union of husband and wife, the sanctity of marriage and of marital relations is of prime importance for the purity of social relations.

The esteem in which marriage is held, furnishes an index of a people's morality. If honor and respect be due an institution in proportion to its sacredness, its signifi-

cance for human happiness and the measure of responsibility which it implies, marriage must claim the reverence
of every mind that is capable of paying tribute to anything
good. A lowering of the general estimate is a symptom of
moral decline.

That such a lowering has taken place is due, in part, to
the disregard of those requirements which even the prospect of marriage imposes. While emphasis is laid, and
rightly, upon physical qualifications, not sufficient importance is attached to moral fitness, the real basis of marital
happiness.

It is essential, in the first place, that clean living before
marriage be equally obligatory on men and women. The
toleration of vicious courses in one party while the other is
strictly held to the practice of virtue, may rest on convention or custom; but it is ethically false, and it is plainly at
variance with the law of God, which enjoins personal purity upon each and all.

Those who contemplate marriage should further make
sure that their motives are upright. Where the dominant
aim is selfish, where choice is controlled by ambition or
greed, and where superficial qualities are preferred to character, genuine love is out of the question: such marriages
are bargains rather than unions, and their only result is
discord.

The same consequence may be expected from one-sided
views of the marital relation. It is a vain idealism that
anticipates joy in perfection, but takes no thought of the
mutual forbearance which is constantly needed, or of the
courage which trial demands, or of the serious obligations
which family life implies. Illusion in such matters is the
worst kind of ignorance.

On the other hand, it is idealism of the truest and most
practical sort that sees in marriage the divinely appointed
plan for cooperating with the Creator in perpetuating the
race, and that accepts the responsibility of bringing children into the world, who may prove either a blessing or a
curse to society at large.

Where such ideals prevail, the fulfilment of marital
duties occasions no hardship. Neither is there any con-

sideration for the fraudulent prudence that would improve upon nature by defeating its obvious purpose, and would purify life by defiling its source. The selfishness which leads to race suicide with or without the pretext of bettering the species, is, in God's sight, "a detestable thing." [77] It is the crime of individuals for which, eventually, the nation must suffer. The harm which it does cannot be repaired by social service, nor offset by pretending economic or domestic advantage. On the contrary, there is joy in the hope of offspring, for "the inheritance of the Lord are children; and His reward, the fruit of the womb." [78] The bond of love is strengthened, fresh stimulus is given to thrift and industrious effort, and the very sacrifices which are called for become sources of blessing.

For the Christian the performance of these duties is lightened by the fact that marriage is not a mere contract: it is a sacrament and therefore, in the truest sense, a holy estate. It sanctifies the union of husband and wife, and supplies them with graces that enable them to fulfil their obligations. Hence it is that the Church invests the celebration of marriage with a solemnity becoming its sacramental importance, performs the sacred rite at the foot of the Altar, and unites it in the Nuptial Mass with the sublimest of religious functions.

Originating in such solemn circumstances, the family life receives, at its very inception, a blessing and a consecration. The "sacredness of home" has a definite meaning deeper than its natural privacy, its intimacy and inviolability: the home is sacred because it is established with God's benediction to carry out His purpose in regard to mankind.

Public authority and social sanction unite to safeguard the home, to protect its rights and condemn their violation. But its strongest defense is in the keeping of those who make it, in their mutual fidelity and careful observance of their respective duties. These alone can ward off temptation and forestall the intrusion from without of influences which, through treachery, bring about ruin.

There is need of greater vigilance in protecting the home

[77] Gen. xxxviii. 10.　　　　　　　　　　[78] Ps. cxxvi.

at this time, owing to conditions which tend to weaken its influence. The demands of industry, of business and of social intercourse subject the family tie to a strain that becomes more severe as civilization advances. Parents who are sensible of their obligations, will exert themselves to meet external pressure by making the home more attractive. They will set their children the example of giving home their first consideration. And while they contribute their share of service and enjoyment as their social position requires, they will not neglect their children for the sake of amusement or pleasure.

In this matter we appeal with special earnestness to Catholic mothers, whose position in the home gives them constant opportunity to realize its needs and provide for its safety. Let them take to heart the words of Holy Scripture in praise of the virtuous woman: "Strength and beauty are her clothing. . . . She hath opened her mouth in wisdom and the law of clemency is on her tongue. She hath looked well to the paths of her house and hath not eaten her bread in idleness. Her children rose up and called her blessed; her husband, and he praised her." [79] The home that is ruled by such a woman has nothing to fear in the way of domestic trouble.

Of itself and under normal conditions, marital love endures through life, growing in strength as time passes and renewing itself in tenderness in the children that are its pledges. The thought of separation even by death is repugnant, and nothing less than death can weaken the bond. No sane man or woman regards divorce as a good thing; the most that can be said in its favor is that, under given circumstances, it affords relief from intolerable evil.

Divorce.

Reluctantly, the Church permits limited divorce: the parties are allowed for certain cause to separate, though the bond continues in force and neither may contract a new marriage while the other is living. But absolute divorce which severs the bond, the Church does not and will not permit.

We consider the growth of the divorce evil an evidence

[79] Proverbs xxxi. 25-28.

of moral decay and a present danger to the best elements
in our American life. In its causes and their revelation by
process of law, in its results for those who are immediately
concerned and its suggestion to the minds of the entire community, divorce is our national scandal. It not only dis-
rupts the home of the separated parties, but it also leads
others who are not yet married, to look upon the bond as
a trivial circumstance. Thus, through the ease and fre-
quency with which it is granted, divorce increases with an
evil momentum until it passes the limits of decency and
reduces the sexual relation to the level of animal instinct.

This degradation of marriage, once considered the holiest of human relations, naturally tends to the injury of
other things whose efficacy ought to be secured, not by co-
ercion but by the freely given respect of a free people.
Public authority, individual rights and even the institutions
on which liberty depends, must inevitably weaken. Hence
the importance of measures and movements which aim at
checking the spread of divorce. It is to be hoped that they
succeed; but an effectual remedy cannot be found or applied, unless we aim at purity in all matters of sex, restore
the dignity of marriage and emphasize its obligations.

By divine ordinance, each human being becomes a member of the larger social group, and in due course enters
into social relations. These are, and
should be, a means of promoting good will   Social
and an occasion for the practice of many   Intercourse.
virtues, notably of justice and charity.

That social enjoyment is quite compatible with serious
occupation and with devotion to the public good, is evident
from the services rendered during the War by all classes
of people, and especially by those who gave up their comfort and ease in obedience to the call of their country. Let
this same spirit prevail in time of peace and set reasonable
limits to the pursuit of pleasure. With the tendency to
excess and the craving for excitement, there comes a willingness to encourage in social intercourse abuses that would
not be tolerated in the privacy of home. For the sake of
notoriety, the prescriptions of plain decency are often set
aside, and even the slight restraints of convention are dis-

regarded. Fondness for display leads to lavish expenditure, which arouses the envy of the less fortunate classes, spurs them to a foolish imitation, and eventually brings about conflict between the rich and the poor.

Though many of these abuses are of short duration, their effect is none the less harmful: they impair the moral fiber of our people and render them unfit for liberty. The plainest lessons of history show that absorption in pleasure is fatal to free institutions. Nations which had conquered the world were unable to prevent their own ruin, once corruption had sapped their vitality. Our country has triumphed in its struggle beyond the sea; let it beware of the enemy lurking within.

There should be no need of legal enactments to improve our social relations, and there will be none, if only we act on the principle that each of us is in duty bound to set good example. Society no less than its individual members, is subject to God's law. Neither convention nor fashion can justify sin. And if we are prompt to remove the causes of bodily disease, we must be just as energetic in banishing moral contagion.

"Ye are the salt of the earth: but if the salt lose its savour, wherewith shall it be salted?" [80] Let Catholics in particular reflect on this saying, and keep it before their minds under all circumstances, whether at home or abroad. Each in his own social sphere has a mission to perform, sometimes by explaining or defending the faith, sometimes by condemning what is wrong, but always by doing what is right. It is the eloquence of deeds that convinces where words are of no avail. The light is silent. "So let your light shine before men, that they may see your good works and glorify your Father who is in heaven." [81]

In society as in the home, the influence of woman is potent. She rules with the power of gentleness, and, where men are chivalrous, her will is the social **Woman's** law. To use this power and fashion this **Influence.** law in such wise that the world may be better because of her presence, is a worthy ambition. But it will not be achieved by devices that arouse

[80] Matt. v. 13.   [81] Matt. v. 16.

the coarser instincts and gratify vanity at the expense of decency. There will be less ground to complain of the wrong inflicted on women, when women themselves maintain their true dignity. "Favor is deceitful and beauty is vain; the woman that feareth the Lord, she shall be praised." [82]

The present tendency in all civilized countries is to give woman a larger share in pursuits and occupations that formerly were reserved to men. The sphere of her activity is no longer confined to the home or to her social environment; it includes the learned professions, the field of industry and the forum of political life. Her ability to meet the hardest of human conditions has been tested by the experience of war; and the world pays tribute, rightfully, to her patriotic spirit, her courage and her power of restoring what the havoc of war had well-nigh destroyed.

Those same qualities are now to undergo a different sort of trial; for woman by engaging in public affairs, accepts, with equal rights, an equal responsibility. So far as she may purify and elevate our political life, her use of the franchise will prove an advantage; and this will be greater if it involve no loss of the qualities in which woman excels. Such a loss would deprive her of the influence which she wields in the home, and eventually defeat the very purpose for which she has entered the public arena. The evils that result from wrong political practice must surely arouse apprehension, but what we have chiefly to fear is the growth of division that tends to breed hatred. The remedy for this lies not in the struggle of parties, but in the diffusion of good will. To reach the hearts of men and take away their bitterness, that they may live henceforth in fellowship one with another—this is woman's vocation in respect of public affairs, and the service which she by nature is best fitted to render.

X. INDUSTRIAL RELATIONS

In 1891, Pope Leo XIII published his Encyclical *Rerum Novarum,* a document which shows the insight of that great Pontiff into the industrial conditions of the time, and his wisdom in pointing out the principles needed for the solv-

[82] Proverbs xxxi. 30.

ing of economic problems. "That the spirit of revolutionary
change which has long been disturbing the nations of the
world, should have passed beyond the sphere of politics
and made its influence felt in the cognate sphere of practical economics, is not surprising. The elements of the conflict now raging are unmistakable, in the vast expansion of
industrial pursuits and the marvelous discoveries of
science; in the changed relations between masters and workmen; in the enormous fortunes of some few individuals,
and the utter poverty of the masses; in the increased self-
reliance and closer mutual combination of the working
classes; as also, finally, in the prevailing moral degeneracy.
The momentous gravity of the state of things now obtaining
fills every mind with painful apprehension; wise men are
discussing it; practical men are proposing schemes; popular meetings, legislatures and rulers of nations are all
busied with it—and actually there is no question that has
taken a deeper hold on the public mind."

How fully these statements apply to our present situation, must be clear to all who have noted the course of events
during the year just elapsed. The War indeed has sharp-
ened the issues and intensified the conflict that rages in the
world of industry; but the elements, the parties and their
respective attitudes are practically unchanged. Unchanged
also are the principles which must be applied, if order is to
be restored and placed on such a permanent basis that our
people may continue their peaceful pursuits without dread
of further disturbance. So far as men are willing to accept
those principles as the common ground on which all parties
may meet and adjust their several claims, there is hope of
a settlement without the more radical measures which the
situation seemed but lately to be forcing on public authority. But in any event, the agitation of the last few months
should convince us that something more is needed than
temporary arrangements or local readjustments. The atmosphere must be cleared so that, however great the difficulties which presently block the way, men of good will
may not, through erroneous preconceptions, go stumbling
on from one detail to another, thus adding confusion to
darkness of counsel.

"It is the opinion of some," says Pope Leo XIII, "and the error is already very common, that the social question is merely an economic one, whereas in point of fact, it is first of all a moral and religious   Nature of matter, and for that reason its settlement is   the Question. to be sought mainly in the moral law and the pronouncements of religion." [83] These words are as pertinent and their teaching as necessary today as they were nineteen years ago. Their meaning, substantially, has been reaffirmed by Pope Benedict XV in his recent statement that "without justice and charity there will be no social progress." The fact that men are striving for what they consider to be their rights, puts their dispute on a moral basis; and wherever justice may lie, whichever of the opposing claims may have the better foundation, it is justice that all demand.

In the prosecution of their respective claims, the parties have, apparently, disregarded the fact that the people as a whole have a prior claim. The great number of unnecessary strikes which have occurred within the last few months, is evidence that justice has been widely violated as regards the rights and needs of the public. To assume that the only rights involved in an industrial dispute are those of capital and labor, is a radical error. It leads, practically, to the conclusion that at any time and for an indefinite period, even the most necessary products can be withheld from general use until the controversy is settled. In fact, while it lasts, millions of persons are compelled to suffer hardship for want of goods and services which they require for reasonable living. The first step, therefore, toward correcting the evil is to insist that the rights of the community shall prevail, and that no individual claim conflicting with those rights shall be valid.

Among those rights is that which entitles the people to order and tranquillity as the necessary conditions for social existence. Industrial disturbance invariably spreads beyond the sphere in which it originates, and interferes, more or less seriously, with other occupations. The whole economic system is so compacted together and its parts are

[83] Apostolic Letter, *Graves de communi*, January 18, 1901.

so dependent one upon the other, that the failure of a single element, especially if this be of vital importance, must affect all the rest. The disorder which ensues is an injustice inflicted upon the community; and the wrong is the greater because, usually, there is no redress. Those who are responsible for it pursue their own ends without regard for moral consequences and, in some cases, with no concern for the provisions of law. When such a temper asserts itself, indigation is aroused throughout the country and the authorities are urged to take action. This, under given circumstances, may be the only possible course; but, as experience shows, it does not eradicate the evil. A further diagnosis is needed. The causes of industrial trouble are generally known, as are also the various phases through which it develops and the positions which the several parties assume. The more serious problem is to ascertain why, in such conditions, men fail to see their obligations to one another and to the public, or seeing them, refuse to fulfil them except under threat and compulsion.

"The great mistake in regard to the matter now under consideration is to take up with the notion that class is naturally hostile to class, and that the **Mutual** wealthy and the workingmen are intended **Obligations.** by nature to live in mutual conflict." [84] On the contrary, as Pope Leo adds, "each needs the other: Capital cannot do without Labor, nor Labor without Capital. Religion is a powerful agency in drawing the rich and the bread-winner together, by reminding each class of its duties to the other and especially of the obligation of justice. Religion teaches the laboring man and the artisan to carry out honestly and fairly all equitable agreements freely arranged, to refrain from injuring person or property, from using violence and creating disorder. It teaches the owner and employer that the laborer is not their bondsman, that in every man they must respect his dignity and worth as a man and as a Christian; that labor is not a thing to be ashamed of, if we listen to right reason and to Christian philosophy; but is an honorable calling, enabling a man to sustain his life in a way upright and cred-

84 *Rerum Novarum.*

itable; and that it is shameful and inhuman to treat men like
chattels, as means for making money, or as machines for
grinding out work." The moral value of man and the dignity of human labor are cardinal points in this whole question. Let them be the directive principles in industry, and
they will go far toward preventing disputes. By treating
the laborer first of all as a man, the employer will make him
a better workingman; by respecting his own moral dignity
as a man, the laborer will compel the respect of his employer
and of the community.

The settlement of our industrial problems would offer
less difficulty if, while upholding its rights, each party were
disposed to meet the other in a friendly spirit. The strict
requirements of justice can be fulfilled without creating
animosity; in fact, where this arises, it is apt to obscure the
whole issue. On the contrary, a manifest desire to win over,
rather than drive, the opponent to the acceptance of equitable terms, would facilitate the recognition of claims which
are founded in justice. The evidence of such a disposition
would break down the barriers of mistrust and set up in
their stead the bond of good will. Not an armistice but a
conciliation would result; and this would establish all parties in the exercise of their rights and the cheerful performance of their duties.

The right of labor to organize, and the great benefit to be
derived from workingmen's associations, were plainly set
forth by Pope Leo XIII. In this connection,
we would call attention to two rights, one   Respective
of employes and the other of employers,   Rights.
the violation of which contributes largely
to the existing unrest and suffering. The first is the right of
the workers to form and maintain the kind of organization
that is necessary and that will be most effectual in securing
their welfare. The second is the right of employers to the
faithful observance by the labor unions of all contracts and
agreements. The unreasonableness of denying either of
these rights is too obvious to require proof or explanation.

A dispute that cannot be adjusted by direct negotiation
between the parties concerned should always be submitted
to arbitration. Neither employer nor employe may reason-

ably reject this method on the ground that it does not bring about perfect justice. No human institution is perfect or infallible; even our courts of law are sometimes in error. Like the law court, the tribunal of industrial arbitration provides the nearest approach to justice that is practically attainable; for the only alternative is economic force, and its decisions have no necessary relation to the decrees of justice. They show which party is economically stronger, not which is in the right.

The right of labor to a living wage, authoritatively and eloquently reasserted more than a quarter of a century ago by Pope Leo XIII, is happily no longer denied by any considerable number of persons. What is principally needed now is that its content should be adequately defined, and that it should be made universal in practice, through whatever means will be at once legitimate and effective. In particular, it is to be kept in mind that a living wage includes not merely decent maintenance for the present, but also a reasonable provision for such future needs as sickness, invalidity and old age. Capital likewise has its rights. Among them is the right to "a fair day's work for a fair day's pay," and the right to returns which will be sufficient to stimulate thrift, saving, initiative, enterprise, and all those directive and productive energies which promote social welfare.

In his pronouncement on Labor,[85] Pope Leo XIII describes the advantages to be derived by both employer and employe from "associations and organizations which draw the two classes more closely together." Such associations are especially needed at the present time. While the labor union or trade union has been, and still is, necessary in the struggle of the workers for fair wages and fair conditions of employment, we have to recognize that its history, methods and objects have made it essentially a militant organization. The time seems now to have arrived when it should be, not supplanted, but supplemented by associations or conferences, composed jointly of employers and employes, which will place emphasis upon

Benefits of Association.

[85] *Rerum Novarum.*

the common interests rather than the divergent aims of the two parties, upon cooperation rather than conflict. Through such arrangements, all classes would be greatly benefited. The worker would participate in those matters of industrial management which directly concern him and about which he possesses helpful knowledge; he would acquire an increased sense of personal dignity and personal responsibility, take greater interest and pride in his work, and become more efficient and more contented. The employer would have the benefit of willing cooperation from, and harmonious relations with, his employes. The consumer, in common with employer and employe, would share in the advantages of larger and steadier production. In a word, industry would be carried on as a cooperative enterprise for the common good, and not as a contest between two parties for a restricted product.

Deploring the social changes which have divided "society into two widely different castes," of which one "holds power because it holds wealth," while the other is "the needy and powerless multitude," Pope Leo XIII declared that the remedy is "to induce as many as possible of the humbler classes to become owners." [86] This recommendation is in exact accord with the traditional teaching and practice of the Church. When her social influence was greatest, in the later Middle Ages, the prevailing economic system was such that the workers were gradually obtaining a larger share in the ownership of the lands upon which, and the tools with which, they labored. Though the economic arrangements of that time cannot be restored, the underlying principle is of permanent application, and is the only one that will give stability to industrial society. It should be applied to our present system as rapidly as conditions will permit.

Whatever may be the industrial and social remedies which will approve themselves to the American people, there is one that, we feel confident, they will never adopt. That is the method of revolution. For it there is neither justification nor excuse under our form of government. Through the ordinary and orderly processes of education,

[86] *Rerum Novarum.*

organization and legislation, all social wrongs can be righted. While these processes may at times seem distressingly slow, they will achieve more in the final result than violence or revolution. The radicalism, and worse than radicalism, of the labor movement in some of the countries of Europe, has no lesson for the workers of the United States, except as an example of methods to be detested and avoided.

Pope Benedict has recently expressed a desire that the people should study the great encyclicals on the social question of his predecessor, Leo XIII. We heartily commend this advice to the faithful and, indeed, to all the people of the United States. They will find in these documents the practical wisdom which the experience of centuries has stored up in the Holy See and, moreover, that solicitude for the welfare of mankind which fitly characterizes the Head of the Catholic Church.

XI. NATIONAL CONDITIONS

Our country had its origin in a struggle for liberty. Once established as an independent Republic, it became the refuge of those who preferred freedom in America to the conditions prevailing in their native lands. Differing widely in culture, belief and capacity for self-government, they had as their common characteristics the desire for liberty and the pursuit of happiness. Within a century, those diverse elements had been formed together into a nation, powerful, prosperous and contented. As they advanced in fortune, they broadened in generosity; and today, the children of those early refugees are restoring the breath of life to the peoples of Europe.

These facts naturally inspire us with an honest pride in our country, with loyalty to our free institutions and confidence in our future. They should also inspire us with gratitude to the Giver of all good gifts who has dealt so favorably with our nation: "He hath not done in like manner to every nation." [87] Our forefathers realized this, and accordingly there is evident in the foundation of the Republic and its first institutions, a deep religious spirit.

87 Ps. cxlvii.

It pervades the home, establishes seats of learning, guides the deliberation of law-making bodies. Its beneficent results are our inheritance; but to enjoy this and transmit it in its fulness to posterity, we must preserve in the hearts of the people the spirit of reverence for God and His law, which animated the founders of our nation. Without that spirit, there is no true patriotism; for whoever sincerely loves his country, must love it for the things that make it worthy of the blessings it has received and of those for which it may hope through God's dispensation.

We are convinced that our Catholic people and all our citizens will display an equally patriotic spirit in approaching the tasks which now confront us. The tasks of peace, though less spectacular in their accomplishment than those of war, are not less important and surely not less difficult. They call for wise deliberation, for self-restraint, for promptness in emergency and energy in action. They demand, especially, that our people should rise above all minor considerations and unite their endeavors for the good of the country. At no period in our history, not even at the outbreak of the war, has the need of unity been more imperative. There should be neither time nor place for sectional division, for racial hatred, for strife among classes, for purely partisan conflict imperilling the country's welfare. There should be no toleration for movements, agencies or schemes that aim at fomenting discord on the ground of religious belief. All such attempts, whatever their disguise or pretext, are inimical to the life of our nation. Their ultimate purpose is to bring discredit upon religion, and to eliminate its influence as a factor in shaping the thought or the conduct of our people. We believe that intelligent Americans will understand how foreign to our ideas of freedom and how dangerous to freedom itself, are those designs which would not only invade the rights of conscience but would make the breeding of hatred a conscientious duty.

Such movements are the more deplorable because they divert attention from matters of public import that really call for improvement, and from problems whose solution requires the earnest cooperation of all our citizens. There is much to be done in behalf of those who, like our forefathers, come from other countries to find a home in America.

Care for Immigrants.

They need an education that will enable them to understand our system of government and will prepare them for the duties of citizenship. They need warning against the contagion of influences whose evil results are giving us grave concern. But what they chiefly need is that Christian sympathy which considers in them the possibilities for good rather than the present defects, and instead of looking upon them with distrust, extends them the hand of charity. Since many of their failings are the consequence of treatment from which they suffered in their homelands, our attitude and action toward them should, for that reason, be all the more sympathetic and helpful.

The constant addition of new elements to our population obliges us to greater vigilance with regard to our internal affairs.

Clean Politics.

The power of assimilation is proportioned to the soundness of the organism; and as the most wholesome nutriment may prove injurious in case of functional disorder, so will the influx from other countries be harmful to our national life, unless this be maintained in full vigor. While, then, we are solicitous that those who seek American citizenship should possess or speedily attain the necessary qualifications, it behooves us to see that our political system is healthy. In its primary meaning, politics has for its aim the administration of government in accordance with the express will of the people and for their best interests. This can be accomplished by the adoption of right principles, the choice of worthy candidates for office, the direction of partisan effort toward the nation's true welfare and the purity of election; but not by dishonesty. The idea that politics is exempt from the requirements of morality, is both false and pernicious: it is practically equivalent to the notion that in government there is neither right nor wrong, and that the will of the people is simply an instrument to be used for private advantage.

The expression or application of such views accounts for the tendency, on the part of many of our citizens, to hold

aloof from politics. But their abstention will not effect the
needed reform, nor will it arouse from their apathy the
still larger number who are so intent upon their own pursuits that they have no inclination for political duties. Each
citizen should devote a reasonable amount of time and
energy to the maintenance of right government by the exercise of his political rights and privileges. He should
understand the issues that are brought before the people,
and cooperate with his fellow-citizens in securing, by all
legitimate means, the wisest possible solution.

In a special degree, the sense and performance of duty
is required of those who are entrusted with public office.
They are at once the servants of the people
and the bearers of an authority whose   **Public Office**
original source is none other than God.   **and**
Integrity on their part, shown by their im-   **Legislation.**
partial treatment of all persons and ques-
tions, by their righteous administration of public funds and
by their strict observance of law, is a vital element in the
life of the nation. It is the first and most effectual remedy
for the countless ills which invade the body politic and,
slowly festering, end in sudden collapse. But to apply the
remedy with hope of success, those who are charged with
the care of public affairs, should think less of the honor
conferred upon them than of the great responsibility. For
the public official above all others, there is need to remember the day of accounting, here, perhaps, at the bar of human opinion, but surely hereafter at the judgment seat of
Him whose sentence is absolute: "Give an account of thy
stewardship." [88]

The conduct of one's own life is a serious and often a
difficult task. But to establish, by the use of authority, the
order of living for the whole people, is a function that demands the clearest perception of right and the utmost fidelity to the principles of justice. If the good of the country
is the one true object of all political power, this is pre-
eminently true of the legislative power. Since law, as the
means of protecting right and preserving order, is essential
to the life of the State, justice must inspire legislation, and

[88] Luke xvi. 2.

concern for the public weal must furnish the single motive
for enactment. The passing of an unjust law is the suicide
of authority.

The efficacy of legislation depends on the wisdom of
laws, not on their number. Fewer enactments, with more
prudent consideration of each and more vigorous execu-
tion of all, would go far towards bettering our national
conditions. But when justice itself is buried under a multi-
plicity of statutes, it is not surprising that the people grow
slack in observance and eventually cease to respect the
authority back of the laws. Their tendency then is to
assume the function which rightly belongs to public executive power, and this they are more likely to do when aroused
by the commission of crimes which, in their opinion, demand swift retribution instead of the slow and uncertain
results of legal procedure. The summary punishment
visited on certain offenses by those who take the law into
their own hands, may seem to be what the criminal deserves; in reality, it is a usurpation of power and therefore
an attack upon the vital principle of public order. The
tardiness of justice is surely an evil, but it will not be removed by added violations of justice, in which passion too
often prevails and leads to practices unworthy of a civilized nation.

For the removal of evil and the furtherance of good in
the social and political spheres, an enlightened public opinion is requisite. The verdict rendered by
The Press.   the people must express their own judgment, but this cannot be safely formed
without a knowledge of facts and an appreciation of the
questions on which they have to decide. As the needed information ordinarily is supplied by the Press, it is at once
obvious that the publicist has a large measure both of influence and of responsibility. He speaks to the whole public, and often with an authority that carries conviction.
In a very real sense he is a teacher, with the largest opportunity to instruct, to criticize, to fashion opinions and to
direct movements. When the use of this great power is
guided by loyalty to truth, to moral principle and patriotic
duty, the Press is an agency for good second only to public

authority. When through its influence and example, the people are led to respect law, to observe the precept of charity, to detest scandal and condemn wrong-doing, they may well regard the Press as a safeguard of their homes and a source of purity in their social and political relations. From it they will learn whatsoever things are just and pure, whatsoever are lovely and of good report. But no man has a right to scatter germs of moral corruption any more than he has to pollute the water supply of a city. The Press which condemns the one as a criminal deed, cannot lend countenance, much less cooperation, to the other.

XII. INTERNATIONAL RELATIONS

Though men are divided into various nationalities by reason of geographical position or historical vicissitude, the progress of civilization facilitates intercourse and, normally, brings about the exchange of good offices between people and people. War, for a time, suspends these friendly relations; but eventually it serves to focus attention upon them and to emphasize the need of readjustment. Having shared in the recent conflict, our country is now engaged with international problems and with the solution of these on a sound and permanent basis. Such a solution, however, can be reached only through the acceptance and application of moral principles. Without these, no form of agreement will avail to establish and maintain the order of the world.

Since God is the Ruler of nations no less than of individuals, His law is supreme over the external relations of states as well as in the internal affairs of each. The sovereignty that makes a nation independent of other nations, does not exempt it from its obligations toward God; nor can any covenant, however shrewdly arranged, guarantee peace and security, if it disregard the divine commands. These require that in their dealings with one another, nations shall observe both justice and charity. By the former, each nation is bound to respect the existence, integrity and rights of all other nations; by the latter, it is obliged to assist other nations with those acts of beneficence and good will which can be performed without undue incon-

venience to itself. From these obligations a nation is not
dispensed by reason of its superior civilization, its industrial activity or its commercial enterprise; least of all, by
its military power. On the contrary, a state which possesses these advantages, is under a greater responsibility to
exert its influence for the maintenance of justice and the
diffusion of goodwill among all peoples. So far as it ful-
fils its obligation in this respect, a state contributes its share
to the peace of the world: it disarms jealousy, removes all
ground for suspicion and replaces intrigue with frank co-
operation for the general welfare.

The growth of democracy implies that the people shall
have a larger share in determining the form, attributions
and policies of the government to which they look for the
preservation of order. It should also imply that the calm
deliberate judgment of the people, rather than the aims of
the ambitious few, shall decide whether, in case of international disagreement, war be the only solution. Knowing that the burdens of war will fall most heavily on them,
the people will be slower in taking aggressive measures,
and, with an adequate sense of what charity and justice require, they will refuse to be led or driven into conflict by
false report or specious argument. Reluctance of this sort
is entirely consistent with firmness for right and zeal for national honor. If it were developed in every people, it would
prove a more effectual restraint than any craft of diplo-
macy or economic prudence. The wisest economy, in fact,
would be exercised by making the principles of charity and
justice an essential part of education. Instead of planning
destruction, intelligence would then discover new methods
of binding the nations together; and the good will which
is now doing so much to relieve the distress produced by
war, would be so strengthened and directed as to prevent
the recurrence of international strife.

One of the most effectual means by which states can
assist one another, is the organization of international
peace. The need of this is more generally felt at the present
time when the meaning of war is so plainly before us. In
former ages also, the nations realized the necessity of com-
pacts and agreements whereby the peace of the world would

be secured. The success of these organized efforts was
due, in large measure, to the influence of the Church. The
position of the Holy See and the office of the Sovereign
Pontiff as Father of Christendom, were recognized by the
nations as powerful factors in any undertaking that had for
its object the welfare of all. A "Truce of God" was not to
be thought of without the Vicar of Christ; and no other
truce could be of lasting effect. The Popes have been the
chief exponents, both by word and act, of the principles
which must underlie any successful agreement of this nature. Again and again they have united the nations of Europe, and history records the great services which they
rendered in the field of international arbitration and in the
development of international law.

The unbroken tradition of the Papacy with respect to
international peace, has been worthily continued to the
present by Pope Benedict XV. He not only made all possible efforts to bring the recent war to an end, but was also
one of the first advocates of an organization for the preservation of peace. In his Letter to the American people on
the last day of the year, 1918, the Holy Father expressed
his fervent hope and desire for an international organization, "which by abolishing conscriptions will reduce armaments, by establishing international tribunals will eliminate
or settle disputes, and by placing peace on a solid foundation will guarantee to all independence and equality of
rights." These words reveal the heart of the Father whose
children are found in every nation, and who grieves at the
sight of their fratricidal struggle. That they were not then
heeded or even rightly understood, is but another evidence
of the degree to which the passions aroused by the conflict
had warped the judgment of men. But this did not prevent
the Pontiff from intervening in behalf of those who were
stricken by the fortunes of war, nor did it lessen his determination to bring about peace. To him and to his humane
endeavor, not Catholics alone, but people of all creeds
and nationalities, are indebted for the example of magna-
nimity which he gave the whole world during the most fate-
ful years of its history.

XIII. EDUCATION

The interests of order and peace require that our domestic, social and national relations be established on the solid basis of principle. For the attainment of this end, much can be done by wise legislation and by organized effort on the part of associations. We are confident that such effort and enactment will hasten the desired result. With their practical sense and their love of fairness, the American people understand that our national life cannot develop normally without adequate protection for the rights of all and faithful performance of duty by every citizen. And as they united to secure freedom for other nations, they now will strive together to realize their country's ideals.

Once more, however, we must emphasize the need of laying a sure foundation in the individual mind and conscience. Upon the integrity of each, upon his personal observance of justice and charity, depends the efficacy of legislation and of all endeavor for the common good. Our aim, therefore, should be, not to multiply laws and restrictions, but to develop such a spirit as will enable us to live in harmony under the simplest possible form, and only the necessary amount, of external regulation. Democracy, understood as self-government, implies that the people as a whole shall rule themselves. But if they are to rule wisely, each must begin by governing himself, by performing his duty no less than by maintaining his right.

Inasmuch as permanent peace on a sound basis is the desire of all our people, it is necessary to provide for the future by shaping the thought and guiding the purpose of our children and youth toward a complete understanding and discharge of their duties. Herein lies the importance of education and the responsibility of those to whom it is entrusted. Serious at all times, the educational problem is now graver and more complex by reason of the manifold demands that are made on the school, the changes in our industrial conditions, and above all, by reason of the confusion and error which obscure the purpose of life and therefore of true education.

Need of Sound Education.

Nevertheless, it is mainly through education that our

country will accomplish its task and perpetuate its free institutions. Such is the conviction that inspires much of the activity displayed in this field, whether by individuals or by organizations. Their confidence is naturally strengthened by the interest which is taken in the school, the enlarged facilities for instruction and the increased efficiency of educational work.

But these again are so many reasons for insisting that education shall move in the right direction. The more thorough it becomes, the greater is its power either for good or for evil. A trained intelligence is but a highly tempered instrument, whose use must depend on the character of its possessor. Of itself knowledge gives no guarantee that it will issue in righteous action, and much less that it will redound to the benefit of society. As experience too plainly shows, culture of the highest order, with abundance of knowledge at its command, may be employed for criminal ends and be turned to the ruin of the very institutions which gave it support and protection. While, therefore, it is useful to improve education by organizing the work of the schools, enriching the content of knowledge and refining the methods of teaching, it is still more necessary to insure that all educational activity shall be guided by sound principles toward the attainment of its true purpose.

The Church in our country is obliged, for the sake of principle, to maintain a system of education distinct and separate from other systems. It is supported by the voluntary contributions of Catholics who, at the same time, contribute as required by law to the maintenance of the public schools. It engages in the service **Principles of Catholic Education.** of education a body of teachers who consecrate their lives to this high calling; and it prepares, without expense to the State, a considerable number of Americans to live worthily as citizens of the Republic.

Our system is based on certain convictions that grow stronger as we observe the testing of all education, not simply by calm theoretic discussion, but by the crucial experience of recent events. It should not have required the pitiless searching of war to determine the value of any theory or system, but since that rude test has been so drastically applied and with such unmistakable results, we judge it opportune to restate the principles which serve as the basis of Catholic education.

First: The right of the child to receive education and the correlative duty of providing it, are established on the fact that man has a soul created by God and endowed with capacities which need to be developed for the good of the individual and the good of society. In its highest meaning therefore, education is a cooperation by human agencies with the Creator for the attainment of His purpose in regard to the individual who is to be educated, and in regard to the social order of which he is a member. Neither self-realization alone nor social service alone is the end of education, but rather these two in accordance with God's design, which gives to each of them its proportionate value. Hence it follows that education is essentially and inevitably a moral activity, in the sense that it undertakes to satisfy certain claims through the fulfilment of certain obligations. This is true independently of the manner and means which constitute the actual process; and it remains true, whether recognized or disregarded in educational practice, whether this practice include the teaching of morality, or exclude it, or try to maintain a neutral position.

Second: Since the child is endowed with physical, intellectual and moral capacities, all these must be developed harmoniously. An education that quickens the intelligence and enriches the mind with knowledge, but fails to develop the will and direct it to the practice of virtue, may produce scholars, but it cannot produce good men. The exclusion of moral training from the educative process is more dangerous in proportion to the thoroughness with which the intellectual powers are developed, because it gives the impression that morality is of little importance, and thus sends the pupil into life with a false idea which is not easily corrected.

Third: Since the duties we owe our Creator take precedence of all other duties, moral training must accord the first place to religion, that is, to the knowledge of God and His law, and must cultivate a spirit of obedience to His commands. The performance, sincere and complete, of religious duties, ensures the fulfilment of other obligations.

Fourth: Moral and religious training is most efficacious when it is joined with instruction in other kinds of knowledge. It should so permeate these that its influence will be felt in every circumstance of life, and be strengthened as the mind advances to a fuller acquaintance with nature and a riper experience with the realities of human existence.

Fifth: An education that unites intellectual, moral and religious elements, is the best training for citizenship. It inculcates a sense of responsibility, a respect for authority and a considerateness for the rights of others, which are the necessary foundations of civic virtue—more necessary where, as in a democracy, the citizen, enjoying a larger freedom, has a greater obligation to govern himself. We are convinced that, as religion and morality are essential to right living and to the public welfare, both should be included in the work of education.

There is reason to believe that this conviction is shared by a considerable number of our fellow-citizens who are not of the Catholic faith. They realize that the omission of religious instruction is a defect in education and also a detriment to religion. But in their view, the home and the church should give the needed training in morality and religion, leaving the school to provide only secular knowledge. Experience, however, confirms us in the belief that instead of dividing education among these several agencies, each of them should, in its own measure, contribute to the intellectual, moral and religious development of the child, and by this means become helpful to all the rest.

In order that the educative agencies may cooperate to the best effect, it is important to understand and safeguard their respective functions and rights. The office of the Church instituted by Christ is **The Right** to "teach all nations," teaching them to **to Educate.** observe whatsoever He commanded. This commission authorizes the Church to teach the truths of salvation to every human being, whether adult or child, rich or poor, private citizen or public official.

In the home with its limited sphere but intimate relations, the parent has both the right and the duty to educate his children; and he has both, not by any concession from an earthly power, but in virtue of a divine ordinance. Parenthood, because it means cooperation with God's design for the perpetuation of human kind, involves responsibility, and therefore implies a corresponding right to prepare for complete living those whom the parent brings into the world.

The school supplements and extends the educational function of the home. With its larger facilities and through the agency of teachers properly trained for the purpose, it accomplishes in a more effectual way the task of education, for which the parent, as a rule, has neither the time, the means nor the requisite qualifications. But the school cannot deprive the parent of his right nor absolve him from his duty, in the matter of educating his children. It may properly supply for certain deficiencies of the home in the way of physical training and cultivation of manners; and it must, by its discipline as well as by explicit instruction, imbue its pupils with habits of virtue. But it should not, through any of its administrations, lead the parent to believe that having placed his children in school, he is freed from responsibility, nor should it weaken the ties which attach the child to parent and home. On the contrary, the school should strengthen the home influence by developing in the child those traits of character which help to maintain the unity and happiness of family life. By this means it will cooperate effectually with the parent and worthily discharge its function.

Since the child is a member not only of the family but also of the larger social group, his education must prepare him to fulfil his obligations to society. The community has the right to insist that those who as members share in its benefits, shall possess the necessary qualifications. The school, therefore, whether private or public as regards maintenance and control, is an agency for social welfare, and as such it bears responsibility to the whole civic body.

While the social aspect of education is evidently important, it must be remembered that social righteousness depends upon individual morality. There are virtues, such as justice and charity, which are exercised in our relations with others; but there is no such thing as collective virtue which can be practiced by a community whose individual members do not possess it in any manner or degree. For this very reason, the attempt to develop the qualities of citizenship without regard for personal virtue, or to make civic utility the one standard of moral excellence, is doomed to failure. Integrity of life in each citizen is the only sure guarantee of worthy citizenship.

As the public welfare is largely dependent upon the intelligence of the citizen, the State has a vital concern in education. This is implied in the original purpose of our government which, as set forth in the preamble to the Constitution, is "to form a more perfect union, establish justice, ensure domestic tranquillity, provide for the common defense, promote the general welfare, and secure the blessings of liberty to ourselves and our posterity." **Function of the State.**

In accordance with these purposes, the State has a right to insist that its citizens shall be educated. It should encourage among the people such a love of learning that they will take the initiative and, without constraint, provide for the education of their children. Should they through negligence or lack of means fail to do so, the State has the right to establish schools and take every other legitimate means to safeguard its vital interests against the dangers that result from ignorance. In particular, it has both the right and the duty to exclude the teaching of doctrines which aim at the subversion of law and order and therefore at the destruction of the State itself.

The State is competent to do these things because its essential function is to promote the general welfare. But on the same principle, it is bound to respect and protect the rights of the citizen and especially of the parent. So long as these rights are properly exercised, to encroach upon them is not to further the general welfare but to put it in peril. If the function of government is to protect the liberty of the citizen, and if the aim of education is to prepare the individual for the rational use of his liberty, the State cannot rightfully or consistently make education a pretext for interfering with rights and liberties which the Creator, not the State, has conferred. Any advantage that might accrue even from a perfect system of State education, would be more than offset by the wrong which the violation of parental rights would involve.

In our country, government thus far has wisely refrained from placing any other than absolutely necessary restrictions upon private initiative. The result is seen in the development of our resources, the products of inventive genius and the magnitude of our enterprises. But our most valuable resources are the minds of our children; and for their development, at least the same scope should be allowed to individual effort as is secured to our undertakings in the material order.

The spirit of our people is in general adverse to State monopoly, and this for the obvious reason that such an absorption of control would mean the end of freedom and initiative. The same consequence is sure to follow when the State attempts to monopolize education; and the disaster will be greater inasmuch as it will affect, not simply the worldly interests of the citizen, but also his spiritual growth and salvation.

With great wisdom our American Constitution provides that every citizen shall be free to follow the dictates of his conscience in the matter of religious belief and observance. While the State gives no preference or advantage to any form of religion, its own best interests require that religion as well as education should flourish and exert its wholesome influence upon the lives of the people. And since education is so powerful an agency for the preservation of religion, equal freedom should be secured to both. This is the more needful where the State refuses religious instruction any place in its schools. To compel the attendance of all children at these schools, would be practically equivalent to an invasion of the rights of conscience, in respect of those parents who believe that religion forms a necessary part of education.

Our Catholic schools are not established and maintained with any idea of holding our children apart from the gen-

eral body and spirit of American citizenship. They are
simply the concrete form in which we exercise our rights
as free citizens, in conformity with the dictates of conscience. Their very existence is a great moral fact in American life. For while they aim, openly and avowedly, to
preserve our Catholic faith, they offer to all our people an
example of the use of freedom for the advancement of
morality and religion.

XIV. OUR HIGHER DESTINY

The adjustment of the relations which we have considered, is intended to further our welfare on earth. That
mankind through freedom and peace should advance in
prosperity, is a large and noble aim. But it is not the ultimate aim of human existence; nor is it the highest criterion
whereby the value of all other ends and the worth of our
striving for any of them can be rightly determined. "For
we have not here a lasting city, but we seek one that is to
come." [89] We look for "a City that hath foundations; whose
builder and maker is God." [90]

In the light of our higher destiny, we can judge and
surely appraise the things which men desire, which they
hate or despise or fear. We can see in their true perspec-
tive the manifold changes of the world, and in their right
proportion its losses and gains, its achievements and fail-
ures. We can understand the confusion, the dismay and
the dread of what may come, which have clouded the vision of many. For these are the final result of the vast
experiment whereby the world would have proven its self-
sufficiency. To those who imagine that humanity has out-
grown the need of religion, that result is bewildering. To
the Catholic mind it brings distress, but no perplexity. It
repeats with an emphasis proportioned to the weight of disaster, the lesson which history has written again and again
as the meaning of such upheavals.

"They shall perish, but thou shalt continue; and they
shall all grow old as a garment. And as a vesture shalt thou
change them, and they shall be changed; but thou art the
self-same, and thy years shall not fail." [91] What is declared

[89] Heb. xiii. 14.   [90] Ibid. xi. 10.   [91] Heb. i. 11, 12; Ps. ci. 27, 28.

in these words as regards the heavens and the earth, is likewise true of our human affairs. And the more fully we realize that change is the law of our existence, the more readily should we turn our thought, with humble confidence, toward our Creator and His eternal law.

As we look upon the record which the past unfolds, we cannot but note that it is filled with the struggles of mankind, with their building up and tearing down, with searchings for truth which often end in illusion, with strivings after good which lead to disappointment. The very monuments which were reared to celebrate human triumph, remain simply to tell of subsequent downfall. Not rarely, the greatness of human achievement is learned from the vast extent of its ruins.

But above it all, standing out clearly through the mists of error and the grosser darkness of evil, is One, in raiment white and glistering, who has solved the problem of life, has given to sorrow and pain a new meaning and, by dying, has overcome death: "Jesus Christ yesterday, and today; and the same forever." [92]

There are numberless paths, but the Way is one. There are many degrees of knowledge, but only one Truth. There are plans and ideals of living, but in real fulfilment there is only one Life. For none other than He could say: "I am the way and the truth and the life." [93]

Pray, therefore, dearly beloved, that the spirit of Jesus Christ may abide with us always, that we may walk on His footsteps in justice and charity, and that the blessing of God may descend abundantly upon the Church, our country and the whole American people.

Given at Washington, in Conference, on the 26th day of September, in the year of our Lord, 1919.

In his own name and in the name of the Hierarchy,

JAMES CARDINAL GIBBONS,

Archbishop of Baltimore.

---

[92] Heb. xiii. 8.   [93] John xiv. 6.

INDEX

A

Abana, 70.

Abiding spirit of Christ, 340.

Abiu, 53.

Absolute divorce, 314.

Abstinence, laws of, 75; 36; total, 135.

Academies, 282.

Acta et Decreta, of Provincial Councils of Baltimore, 60; of Second Plenary, 198.

Activities, Catholic War, 294.

Acts of religion, 7, 152.

Adam, fall of, 63.

Administration Committee (N. C. W. C.), 296.

Administration, of Sacraments, 20; of Church property, 185.

Advancement of piety, 151.

Advantages of Catholic education, 3, 125; of religious, 4.

Adversaries of the Papacy, 165.

Africa, missions in, 158; religious conditions in, 174.

Ages of Faith, 257, 283.

Agencies of education, 245.

Agnosticism, 244, 280.

Agreement (1810), of American Hierarchy, 16.

Aid, foreign, for American Church, 113; for Pope, 208; from Lyons Society, 191.

Aim, of Catholic education, 281.

A'Kempis, Thomas, 250, 251.

Alabama, Vicariate of (1829), 39.

Alemany, Bishop, 195, 224.

Allegiance, Catholic, 90-1; "double," 90; civil, 192-3; to Holy See, meaning of, 172.

"All religions are alike," 36.

Allurements of the world, 58.

Alms, 77.

Alumnae, Federation of Catholic, 285.

Amat, Bishop, 225.

Ambassadors of Christ, 40, 51-2.

Ambition, worldly, 75.

Amendment, on religious liberty, 82.

America, Mary, the Mother of God, Patroness of, 1.

America, liberty in, 82; importance of, in world reconstruction, 270; growth of Church in (1884-1919), 271; racial assimilation in, 293; ideals of, 324.

American Board of Catholic Missions, 296.

American Catholics, devotion of, to Holy See, 182; in the World War, 295.

American Church and Holy See, 18; foreign interference in, 17; needs of, (1810), 16; grievances in, 18.

American College, at Rome, 236, 240.

American Constitution, religious freedom in, 338.

American Hierarchy, agreement of (1810), 16, 184; and President Wilson, 265; and the Catholic University of America, 282.

American history, study of, 253.

American ideals, and Catholic doctrine, 235.

American liberties, 305.

American Protestant Association (A. P. A.), 265.

American Protestants, and falsehoods, 92.

"Americanism," 265.

Amusements, idle, frivolous, 52, 219.

Ananias and Saul, 96.

Annual Collection for the Pope (1866), 208.

Anti-Catholic bitterness, 80; feelings, (1833), 61; fanaticism, 80; books, 92-3; libels, 94; literature, 114, 127.

Anti-Catholicism, in American public school textbooks, 28; in United States, 27-8.

A. P. A., 265.

Apocalypse, horsemen of, 22.

Apostles, counsel of, on education of young, 3; persecution of, 95; Peter and Paul, 174; as a ministerial body, 200.

Apostolic Succession, 40; Communion, 201.

Apostolic Delegate, to Second Plenary Council, 197; over Councils, 199; (Gibbons) at Third Plenary Council, 228.

Apostolic Delegation, 269; at Washington, D. C., 265.

Apostolicity of the Church, 102, 175.

Arbitration, of labour disputes, 321.

Archdiocese of Baltimore, 16.

Archiepiscopal See, of Oregon, 171; of St. Louis, 171.

Armaments, reduction of, 331.

Asia, religious conditions of, 174; need of missions in, 288.

"Association," the Protestant, 92-3.

Association, of the Holy Childhood, 261; Catholic Educational, 281.

Assumption, national Catholic feast day, 14.

Attacks, on the Faith, 27, 61; upon the Church, 28; from Protestant pulpits, 83; good effects of, 85.

Attendance, at Holy Mass, 15, 236; at Sunday, 1, 8, 11.

Attitude, bitter, towards Church, 80.

Atonement of Christ, 76.

Austria, help for Church here, 75.

Authority, source of, in priesthood, 7; of bishops, 32; source of episcopal, 103, 183; obedience to Church, 157; ecclesiastical, 182, 200; spiritual, of